SCREEN TRAFFIC

CHARLES R. ACLAND

DUKE UNIVERSITY PRESS   DURHAM & LONDON 2003

SCREEN TRAFFIC

MOVIES, MULTIPLEXES, AND GLOBAL CULTURE

© 2003 Duke University Press   All rights reserved

Printed in the United States of America on acid-free paper ∞

Designed by Rebecca M. Giménez   Typeset in Adobe Minion by

Keystone Typesetting, Inc.   Library of Congress Cataloging-in-

Publication Data appear on the last printed page of this book.

CONTENTS

APPENDICES

TABLES

FIGURES

Growing up in a suburban community outside of Ottawa, every week I looked forward to Saturday morning when the new television guide would arrive with the newspaper. Once I had it in my adolescent hands, I would scour it to map out my movie watching for the week, taking a pencil and circling the appealing films, with only the short blurb to help me in making that assessment. Information on movies was as scarce as the films themselves, and the descriptions or a television critic's recommendations were practically all I had to go on, aside from pestering anyone who would listen. This, after all, was before the wide availability of various popular resources like the Leonard Maltin, Roger Ebert, and Video Hound guides, or the Internet Movie Database, which have done so much to change the sheer quantity of film information, as well as the kinds of ideas about film, in popular circulation.

As I understand it, the deepening of my film fandom involved an encounter with television. And a sense of scarcity sweetened the familiarity with film culture that I had begun to build. Careful attentiveness to broadcast films was the lone way I could be introduced to these works. In the years before home video, there was no archive or backlog readily available to most. There were the new films in theaters, and the closest theater to my home required a trip downtown, which meant negotiating transportation, financing, and parents. The only other influential sources were Richard J. Anobile's books of frame-by-frame reconstructions of film classics. It was in this print format that I, along with my equally enthusiastic friends, first "saw" *The Maltese Falcon, Casa-*

blanca, Frankenstein, and *Psycho.* The television broadcasts, however, drew significantly more attention, as plans had to be made to take advantage of one-time-only film events. Late-night broadcasts of *The Guns of Navarone, Where Eagles Dare,* and *The Longest Day* generated excitement of suitably epic proportions, including setting up camp in front of the television set, the selection of special snack foods, and efforts to finish the Alastair Maclean and Cornelius Ryan works before the big evening. More routine was TVO's *Magic Shadows,* which required watching twenty-odd minutes of, say, *Sabotage* in daily installments after school, or the same station's weekly double bill, *Saturday Night at the Movies,* which was my introduction to films ranging from *Accident* to *Sullivan's Travels.* CBC's evening presentations of *The Rowdyman* and *Paperback Hero* were formative, but especially memorable were afternoon showings of the wholesome Lewis and Martin, Andy Hardy, and Abbott and Costello films. More "adult" was CTV's Montreal affiliate, CFCF, which was noted for its all-night series of films and more liberal censorship policy. There, *Mean Streets* and *Perfect Friday* made vivid and lasting impressions.

This formation has meant that I have trouble understanding the so-called film purist who limits "true" film life to theaters. From my earliest incarnation as a fan, film was not about cinemagoing only. Instead, cinemagoing held a special place precisely because there were other, appended patterns of film culture. This "ordinary" experience in so many ways has driven my thinking about cinema culture. To expand, the mere existence of film texts tell us little if we do not also consider their circulation and availability. The way films move about in the world, where they are presented, for how long they might be seen, and the information obtainable about films and film events establish parameters that mark out who has access to them. This is as much the case for passionate lovers of the cinema as it is for more casual seekers of amusement. The significance is that these temporal and spatial elements of popular life play a role in determining how people encounter not just the movies but one another, that is, what they share and what manner of community they build or destroy. Any changes in the relations among media, the ruling ideas about culture, and the circulation of cultural forms produce corresponding changes in the constitution of communal existence. With this in mind, this book is an attempt to chart the parameters that have developed in response to one period of shifting intermedia relations.

Over the years of its development, I have benefited from the commentary and criticisms of a number of people. It is only through their generous advice, perceptive recommendations, and sustained argument that I have been able to complete this project. In short, they have kept me alert and have improved the work incalculably. Many thanks go to my colleagues in Communication Studies at Concordia University, as well as the staff and students, who together make for an invigorating intellectual environment. Discussions with Martin Allor, Bill Buxton, Monika Kin Gagnon, Kim Sawchuk, Rae Staseson, and Peter Van Wyck were particularly influential in the shaping of this study. No one has listened to and challenged the ideas presented here more consistently, and perceptively, than Keir Keightley, whose acumen has contributed far more than a "thank you" could possibly capture. Will Straw, Blaine Allan, and Peter Urquhart went above and beyond friendship and collegiality by reading the manuscript and offering exacting commentary. Conversations with Barri Cohen provided invaluable insight, and she continues to expand my grasp of the issues concerning film in Canadian life. A few of the others who have participated in discussion and counsel along the way are Bill Burns, Barbara Crow, Jeff Derksen, Kevin Dowler, Mark Fenster, Larry Grossberg, James Hay, Toby Miller, Holly Kruse, Julian Samuel, and Beth Seaton. My gratitude is matched only by my respect for each and every one of these individuals.

The superb research facilities at Montreal's Cinémathèque québécoise made the examination of diverse sources possible. I have been fortunate to have had several research assistants who contributed massively to the collection and organization of material. They include Garnet Butchart, Joseph Cooperman, Steve Logan, and Michael Schulz. JoAnne Stober and Nicole Porter deserve special recognition and gratitude for their extended involvement. I don't know what I would have done without the hard work and commitment of all these students.

A number of people at theater chains and other organizations agreed to share their resources and knowledge with me. Among them are Olga Budimirovic, Laura Patel, Andrew Sherbin, and Barry Patterson. I thank them all. Ken

Wissoker, Fiona Morgan, Pam Morrison, and the entire production staff at Duke University Press were outstanding in their professionalism and overall commitment to scholarship.

Most importantly, Haidee Wasson helped in innumerable ways, applying her keen mind to problems of argument and sharing her profound understanding of the labor of writing and research. I thank her for making joy a prevailing aspect of work and life.

SUPPORT CAME FROM the Social Science and Humanities Research Council of Canada Standard Research Grants, University of Calgary, and Concordia University. Selections of this work were presented at University of Western Ontario, McGill University, Concordia University, Carleton University, the Film Studies Association of Canada conference (St. John's and Sherbrooke), the Canadian Communications Association conference (Ottawa), "Screen" conference (Glasgow), Society for Cinema Studies (Denver), International Critical Geographers conference (Vancouver), and the Conjunctures Working Group (Atlanta). Portions of a couple of chapters appeared in an earlier stage of development as "Cinemagoing and the Rise of the Megaplex," *Television and New Media* 1, no. 4, 2000: 375–402, and "From Absent Audience to Expo-Mentality," in *A Passion for Identity: Canadian Studies for the 21st Century,* 4th edition, ed. David Taras and Beverly Rasporich (Toronto: Nelson, 2001), 275–291.

PART ONE

Theorizing Contemporary Cinemagoing

CHAPTER ONE

Global Audiences and the Current Cinema

At the ceremony for the 1996 Academy Awards, on Monday, March 24, 1997, Canadian comic Jim Carrey took the stage to present the Oscar for Special Effects. When he reached the podium, he stopped, gave a broad smarmy grin, and shouted, "And how was *your* weekend? Mine was *good!*" He then stood back from the microphone with his arms outstretched triumphantly while the crowd erupted with laughter. As oblique as the comment may now appear, the background information necessary to the humor was readily available. Carrey was referring to the opening of his new movie, *Liar Liar* (Tom Shadyac 1997), the highest-grossing domestic release that past weekend, March 21–23. The film opened wide, which means prints were sent out to thousands of cinemas so they could premiere on the same day across the United States and Canada. Over its first weekend, it took in $31,423,025 at 2,845 theaters. *Liar Liar* received middling reviews in weekend papers, so no stunning cinematic achievement explains this resounding success. Instead, audience expectations based on the film's ample marketing, the genre of American humanist comedy, and Carrey's own star persona provide reasonable explanations for a box office smash hit like this one. On the evidence of box office revenue alone one can conclude that in early spring of that year audiences took *Liar Liar* as an appropriate weekend leisure option, and that its availability not only in large urban centers but in multiplexes throughout the United States and Canada meant that this assumption could be acted on. And with equal certainty, these box office receipts tell us nothing of how the film was enjoyed, ridiculed, or made sense of in any manner.

What was striking about the "How was *your* weekend?" comic bit was Carrey's confidence that it would work, not only for the industry audience present at the Shrine Auditorium in Los Angeles but for a wider viewing audience. One can only speculate on reception, here. It is not as though some laugh meter might have measured what instance of levity ran through the millions of homes watching the event, as the absurd dreams of some quantitative researchers would have it. I am willing to trust Carrey's instincts as a popular comic whose work does not rest on the intellectual alienation of his fans, to put it mildly. In fact, Carrey's star persona has been in equal parts about his exaggeratedly lowbrow antics *and* his career, his rise to fame, and his increasing paycheck. In a sense, between his wild-eyed craziness and his puppy dog sentimentality, Carrey has been letting people in on the joke of the entertainment racket. Carrey is a self-reflexive star performer in that he announces the machinations that have produced him, as in the outtakes accompanying the end credits of *Liar Liar* in which he quips that overacting has been the secret to his success. Displaying points of continuity between his television work on *In Living Color,* his talk show appearances, and his popular films, Carrey has been able to meld facial contortions with an exposé of the workings of the film industry.

Regardless of the number of those left out of the joke—and I'm sure there were many, for the film would only open in subsequent weeks elsewhere in the world—Carrey's bit that evening presumed familiarity with an important industrial measure, one that has become a solid component of cinema culture. For movie fans, awareness of box office winners has now joined star biographies and genre identification as a fundamental component of film knowledge. The ability to roughly estimate film budgets is a corollary of the ability to name a director's oeuvre. The publication in Monday's newspapers of the weekend's top-grossing films is likewise a corollary of the reviews clustered in the Thursday, Friday, and Saturday papers.

This expanded circulation and salience of industry information has been matched by a newly invigorated industry of film-consumption statistics, whose dramatically expanded professionalization and standardization are a product of the 1980s.[1] At that time, National Research Group, a prominent firm that tracks films' success, faced growing competition for its services, which focus on the methods of test screenings and telephone polling. In contrast, another firm,

Market Cast, relies on information from exhibitors. Lieberman Research and Gallup are also recently arriving participants in the testing and market research for films. Others include MovieFone, which produces CompetitorReport, and Entertainment Data, Inc. (EDI), founded in 1976 and bought by AC Nielson in 1998.[2] EDI, whose regular column analyzing the performance of movies appears in *Variety*, among other publications, collects its box office data by daily phone calls to thousands of theaters and provides other forms of industry tracking, including distributors' release schedules.[3] In addition to the increased availability of statistical portraits of the movie business and its audiences, the broad newsworthiness of the workings of the film industry expanded in the 1980s, a symptom of which was the explosion of entertainment journalism as typified by syndicated programs like *Entertainment Tonight*, first broadcast in 1981, and the magazines like *Entertainment Weekly*, launched in 1990. To be sure, something transpired to propel this organization of the gathering and packaging of industry data and analysis, as well as its growing significance for larger numbers of people. Though often blended with celebrity gossip virtually indistinguishable from that of earlier decades, a new phase has been reached in the everyday popular knowledge of entertainment.

The presumption of audience involvement with what are ostensibly industry measurements of performance equally alters the way film distributors and exhibitors conduct their operations. *Variety* editor Peter Bart offers this characterization of the use of weekend box office:

> By Sunday morning the distribution chiefs, having filled in their colleagues, start calling key members of the press to spread the word. Often the process of achieving the number one position becomes a test of gamesmanship. A distribution chief, for example, may call *Variety*'s box office reporter, Andrew Hindes, and inquire what his rivals at other studios have reported. If his film is running neck-and-neck with a competitor, he will offer a higher number. Not until Tuesday morning were the official numbers announced by a company called Entertainment Data, Inc., which based its estimates on hundreds [*sic*] of phone calls made by its employees directly to theaters. By that time the ads would already be in the newspapers claiming that the film in question is "the number one movie in America." Given the herd instincts

of the moviegoing public, this information helps build momentum, even if the basic data itself may be exaggerated. The machinery of hit-making had been set in motion.[4]

Bart's low opinion of cinemagoing audiences and underestimation of the extent of EDI's survey methods notwithstanding, his insights into the procedures of data collection and the jostling for position among distributors reveal an internal culture that actively produces the "truth" of a film's popularity. This "truth" is predicated on the availability and legibility of such measures.

Thus there is a visible, and provisionally accurate, financial dimension to contemporary commercial cinema that contributes to a routine knowledge of cinema culture. "How was *your* weekend?" relies on a popular recognition of box office revenue as a gauge of success and currency. It also reveals not only the role of opening weekends in the release strategy of films but a general appreciation of that role by film audiences. And popular appreciation of economic forces is a salient dimension here, showing that these measures of product activity and revenue generation are no longer strictly the purview of industry analysts. Carrey's reference marks a brand of popular "insiderism" where it is entirely likely that a wide audience *did* follow his self-conscious boasting. In this way, his brief performance is emblematic of the formation of a popular knowledge about the business of entertainment.

For Canadian audiences there was the added delight—or embarrassment, depending on one's predilections—in seeing a local hero circulating among the highest ranks of the international film world. By the end of 1997 *Liar Liar* made $181,410,615 in domestic box office revenue, making it the third or fourth highest grossing film of that year (depending on the source), then the biggest box office year of all time.[5] The standard measures of Hollywood's domestic box office include both Canada and the United States, so even at the level of industry economics there is confusion in the distinction between foreign and domestic. Treated on its own, Canada has represented the second largest export market for U.S. theatrical releases. Taking 1989 figures for illustration purposes, only Japan's 15 percent export market share for U.S. majors exceeded Canada's 11.3 percent. The next three were France (9.5 percent), West Germany (8.7 percent) and UK/Ireland (8.6 percent).[6] Canada's long-standing and substantial share of the U.S. film market frequently goes unnoticed, leaving it a surreptitious presence in industry data. The conflation of U.S. and Canadian figures is a sign of the close historical connections between the two countries' respective film cultures. Here is how *Playback*, a Canadian film and television trade publication, puts it:

> How does the Canadian market compare? Answer: splintering the Canadian market out of the North American equation is about as easy as separating the yolk from the white after the egg has been baked into a Felix & Norton chocolate macadamia. Old news: the Canadian theater scene is essentially the northern piece of a North American marketplace, and attempting to drag box office numbers specific to the Canadian marketplace is usually an exercise in futility.[7]

This entwinement, whose impossible separation the quotation metaphorically compares to the un-baking of cookies, is one of the historically stable qualities of these two national cinemas. Developing unevenly but in tandem, Canadian and American cinemas have actively hidden away their interrelationship, which has included the migration of talent and film shoots in addition to market access. The dynamic of unequal association should be highlighted as a defining feature of both U.S. and Canadian cinematic life. Virtually every time a U.S. newspaper cites the domestic box office for an opening weekend, buried in this figure are the Canadian box office returns for U.S. distributors. Researchers who talk about U.S. distribution and exhibition, yet do not acknowledge that another country is included in those figures, are misinterpreting their data or at worst performing a brand of imperialism by neglect.

However, rather than making claims about the impossibility of absolute accuracy, box office numbers are best understood as one terrain on which industry, policy, scholarly, and popular practice takes place. They serve many functions, many arguments, and they mean different things for producers, policymakers, and audiences. For instance, these figures act as a currency among cinemagoers for being up-to-date with respect to popular cinema. For Canadian fans, watching Jim Carrey, then, might extend the pleasure of confirming a secret understanding and call up narratives of career achievement that "winning" box office figures represent. His success is a minor, and sanctioned, form of Canadian participation in U.S. culture, however cynical and trivial that incursion may be. Some may not see this as a source of pride but rather as evidence of the complete hegemony of the U.S. industrial structure, whose very terms of operation are collapsed into the everyday popular pleasures of Canadians. In any case, both the measure itself and familiarity with the weekly rankings are examples of the blurred borders between national and international film worlds. In light of abundant discussion about the globalization of culture, it is worth remembering that the U.S. *domestic* industry, for all intents and purposes, encompasses two national cinema cultures and has in this respect always already been transnational.

Even the Academy Awards ceremony offers a study of the state of international film and the popular circulation of a business's image. It is a televised window on an industry event, garnering audiences in the billions, as the on-air commentators frequently remind us. Some in this audience conduct their own miniceremonies at home in conjunction with the official broadcast, fashioning a sort of virtual participation in the glamorous proceedings. The 62nd Annual Academy Awards, presented on March 26, 1990, acknowledged an emerging logic in Hollywood by "going global." The theme of the show was the international impact of film. Satellite feeds allowed awards to be presented live from various locations, including Sydney, London, Moscow, Buenos Aires, and Tokyo. An honorary award went to Akira Kurosawa, who accepted via a satellite appearance. The resulting image was of a worldwide business effortlessly touching ground in diverse and distant locations.

The global reach of cinema is not new. From the earliest moments of the initial settlement of a cinematic apparatus over a century ago, film's role in international commerical and cultural exchange was set for exploitation. But the sense that a new phase of globalization was upon us is such that, in early 1996, *Boxoffice*, an exhibitor's publication that began as *The Reel Journal* in 1920 and adopted its current name in 1931, went from referring to itself as "the business magazine of the motion picture industry" to "the business magazine of the *global* motion picture industry" (my emphasis). Globalizing efforts have become a more complete and relied on dimension of conventional practice over the last decade for essentially all facets and locations of the audiovisual industries, in varying degrees. So totalizing has this been that audiences—and scholars, for that matter—have had to recalibrate their understanding of relations between local and global film cultures.

This book explores the industrial and popular *discourses* about contemporary commercial cinema and its patrons that have become common sense. The term "discourse" refers to language in action and in performance that circulates to produce understandings about phenomena. The relationship between those two particular sets of discourses—the industrial and the popular—is such that in recent years we have seen the adoption of the language of the film business by popular film culture. This gesture of "being in the know" has coincided with changes in the film business itself, as it has been reinvented—yet again, as any glancing encounter with film history would confirm—as a global industry.[8] These changes include the movement of sites of production and the seeking out of markets further afield. So highly developed are the changes that they challenge the very "Americanness" of Hollywood, a fact brought home more completely in light of the international ownership of several of the major studios, as with the Australian holdings in Twentieth Century-Fox and MCA/Universal's successive Japanese, Canadian, and French ownership. One could continue by noting the presence in the United States of powerful stars, directors, and producers from around the world who alternately accelerate, steer, or halt a film's production. This behavior announces that Hollywood is part of a transnational idea of a talented individual's rising value and influence. We might ask, to what extent has the "dream" of Hollywood been deracinated from the United States?

Some wonder about the effects internationalization has had on the material produced and circulated. Paul Hirsch suggests, "In global consolidations in which U.S. firms become one among many, the presumption is a loss in their power to dictate stories, contract terms and artistic judgments."[9] Further, the very location of Hollywood becomes a matter of disputation as production activity scatters over such cities as Wilmington (North Carolina), Sydney, and Vancouver. Apprehensions about California's economic losses due to runaway film shoots have been growing, which has propelled some to denounce efforts to take advantage of the mobile film business. In an unusual reversal of the cultural imperialism argument, these efforts have painted countries like Canada and Australia as nefarious forces, feeding unfairly on California's proprietary right to the American film industry. This situation leads Rod Carveth to advise, rather worriedly, that "it has become evident that the United States is in danger of losing its competitive advantage in the international media marketplace."[10] With the growing involvement of other cinemas internationally, he goes on to point out that in the 1980s it became clear "that the United States would no longer have the same freedom to operate in the international marketplace."[11] A demand, therefore, existed for new ways of exporting U.S. film and dealing with diverse film markets and audiences abroad, as well as new ways of understanding what we mean when we use the term "American film."

For industry agents, an easier mobility of production can make available inexpensive sources of labor and new sites of technological skills and facilities. Economic forces of this nature have material effects for the many employed, whether set dressers, celebrity actors, caterers, or financial advisors. Toby Miller et al. draw attention to the way in which the growing "placelessness" of audiovisual industries produces a "new international division of cultural labour" (NICL). They recommend special consideration of "how Hollywood reproduces and regulates the NICL through its control over cultural labour markets, international co-production, intellectual property, marketing, distribution and exhibition."[12] Sketching a rough model of the uneven distribution of power represented by these divisions, they propose three international spheres of control: "first, a world center: second, intermediate zones nearby of secondary importance; and third, outlying regions of labour subordinate to the center. . . . These three foundations could be seen as, respectively, Hollywood; Western Europe, North America and Australia; and the rest of the world."[13] While this is certainly not a stable set of zones—and one must recognize the various hierarchies of cultural and economic power operating within each—their proposal has the advantage of highlighting the interconnectedness of an international audiovisual industry, one whose consequences are more far-reaching than what we can detect in appearance of the film texts themselves.

In concert with this internationalization, Joseph Turow notes the opportunity seized on by industry analysts and investors, especially as offered by new distribution channels ranging from pay-per-view television to videotape: "Executives saw the globalization of mass media activities that accelerated during the 1980s as providing yet another incentive for managing many distribution channels."[14] Turow highlights the growing understanding of synergies among media, which produced further consolidation of ownership. Additionally, attention to far-flung cultural consumers encourages "global branding" by advertisers as they aim to market products throughout the world. The international and intermedia tendencies of entertainment corporations have altered conceptions of their markets and audiences. A movie trailer announces the imminent arrival of a new film as well as a soundtrack, merchandise, a videotape, a DVD, a Web site, and so on. Just as this envisages a consumer who moves between media, there exists an idea about an international cinemagoer, one whose cinematic interests are not bound by local or national limits, and who looks instead to a globally circulating popular film culture. This imaginary cinemagoer might be seen as having similarities with other popular film audiences in assorted geographical locations, sharing elements of pleasure and diversion. Most importantly, a notion of the global cinemagoer has become part of industrial practice, helping to steer how the industry responds to the forces of internationalization. Emphasizing this dimension is not to claim that there is a standardized global movie patron but that there is an array of assumptions about points of commonality across national boundaries, acted on by producers, distributors, and exhibitors of popular film.

It is my intention to trace the emergence and significance of the reigning discourses of film in a global context, identifying the rationales and consequences of seeing similarities among widely differing cinemagoing populations. My focus is on the production of an industry common sense, among those international and intermedia corporations, concerning out-of-home film consumption. In order to fully understand the impact of this international and intermedia environment, and while concentrating on the U.S. industry, I will make reference to another national context, Canada, inserting its related debates and permutations. As a nation rife with cultural contradiction, Canada is an ideal case for such attention. Historically both inside *and* outside of the U.S. industry, Canada has been taken both as part of the United States in terms of film distribution and as an international territory with an elaborate policy framework of cultural protection. After years of invisibility, independent box office figures for Canada began to appear regularly in *Variety* in 1993, along with those of other countries, a change signaling the mounting prominence of the Canadian industry and an overall interest in international markets. Interestingly, this meant that Canada was, in effect, counted twice for a time, appearing as both domestic and international. This reporting became increasingly sporadic in the late 1990s, and Canada has disappeared into domestic charts once again in the first decade of the twenty-first century. Importantly, its treatment has been inconsistent. The Motion Picture Association of America (MPAA), the powerful U.S. industry lobby group, counts rentals earned in Canada as international, while the major distributors count them as U.S. domestic.[15] When something as basic as the definitional distinction between domestic and international film markets is problematic, it is safe to conclude that we are confronting a peculiar situation. Thus a certain struggle of Canadian nationhood is evident among the indicators of the economics of globalization. Add to this Canada's unsuccessful attempt in 1991 to get European status and become a member of the European Film Distribution Office,[16] and we begin to get an impression of a rather malleable sense of national identity. With illustrations like these, it's no wonder that Richard Collins described Canada as a "pre-echo of the post-national condition, one that is becoming increasingly generalized."[17]

As will be described below, one of Canada's national particularities has been its formation through a long and complex history of engagement with international culture. This engagement bears traces of its colonial past and has produced a sense of selective openness to culture from other locations as well as a sense of general popular disdain for, or at least extra close scrutiny of, work produced at home. With an abundance of laments for the lack of an indigenous popular cinema culture, or outright denouncements of what popular texts appear, few can avoid acknowledging a situation in which an international, and primarily U.S., popular cinema is "at home" in Canada and nearly monopolizes the cinemagoing of Canadians. Conversely, with some notable exceptions, in particular some aspects of the cinema culture of Quebec, Canadian cinema is somewhat "foreign" to and distant from the popular. This paradox of the unfamiliar local and the amply familiar international culture may be more broadly taken as a defining feature of the "global audience," and it is a characteristic I wish to consider further, though not to decry it from the start as a monstrous creation of cultural imperialism. Rather, there is a need to consider the ramifications of such an organization of popular taste, and to take it seriously, asking what meanings, sentiments, and affiliations it generates. In the Canadian context, a conventional view continues to hold sway, seeing the popular merely as a site of lost national potential and only as a site of ideological colonization. Little has contributed to an understanding of the everyday of Canadian cultural contradictions or to what it means to live with what critics see as the failings of nationhood. The view I take here is that popular culture is a crucial site at which social factions form and struggle and where the structures of life in relation to changing notions of national and global community arise, regardless of the origin of the text consumed. To begin requires giving the engagements of the popular priority before judging it as a weakening of national fortitude.

While this book includes a case study of Canada, complemented by examples from world cinema culture that will run throughout, the prime focus is on a phase in the internationalization of the U.S. film industry, or more precisely, a phase in industrial and popular "talk" about internationalization. In the background of this analysis of discourse is an epistemological inquiry. How are ideas about popular culture, about its audiences, about nationhood, and about internationalism fashioned and acted on? How are some ideas taken and circulated as a form of common sense, coming to be assumed and unquestioned? To respond, this study draws from the insights into the operations of knowledge and power made by Michel Foucault, who insisted that attention to hierarchical organizations of power alone was insufficient to explain the intricacies of modern society. Instead, power in its elemental form is "a relation of force."[18] It is not just about repression but about bringing conditions, behaviors, and understandings into being. As an implicit critique of the thesis of dominant ideology in that no single population can be said to exercise power over all others nor to claim ownership of reigning ideas, organizations of power operate rather like engines coordinating social and subjective relations. Though he wrote about uncovering subjugated knowledge, Foucault focused primarily on examples in which particular discursive apparatuses formed the basis of new institutional structures. He was interested not merely in how these things are talked about generally, but in how they are talked about by authorities, experts, moral leaders, and so on, attempting to pinpoint regimes of knowledge as they became solidified into institutional apparatuses. Simply put, he sought out for study those moments at which a discourse becomes a basis for the organization of institutional power.

Discourses have an effectivity; they yield spaces, practices, and understandings and offer a provisional "truth" to phenomena. Even the everyday and ordinary sites that surround us, and the activities associated with them, have at their heart discourses that organize them. The discourses of moviegoing have material effects. Deploying accepted forms of understanding about audiences, investors make decisions about where to build cinemas and what services should be available there, producers green-light certain projects and kill others, exhibitors look forward to certain films and dread others, and audiences internalize a view of their own tastes and pleasures. Thus we might ask what elements of language and logic assemble how we think about public film consumption, how we comport ourselves in cinemas, and to what consequence for social life.

My approach to the study of popular culture involves what Stuart Hall characterized as "a recognition of things we already know."[19] This begins with an exercise in stock-taking. What images, sounds, ideas, and metaphors circulate, pertaining to a particular subject and appearing repeatedly in a variety of locations and media? What sort of repetition or redundancy is apparent? Where and when do some sets of assumptions become the background on which future actions are taken and decisions are made? As Antonio Gramsci's famous dictum recommends, "The starting-point of critical elaboration is the consciousness of what one really is, and is 'knowing thyself' as a product of the historical process to date which has deposited in you an infinity of traces, without leaving an inventory. Such an inventory must therefore be made at the outset."[20] Ultimately, the objective of this book is to expose some recent historical traces that have formed an *episteme* of popular entertainment and the global audience. Around talk of national culture, global culture, new media, the entertainment business, and leisure pursuits are layers of sedimented images, sounds, ideas, and metaphors. These are not only a list of artifacts but also practices appended to those artifacts. Sedimented traces include the spaces and rationales for the ordinary operation of institutional structures. And in the most extreme instances, common sense is understood to be an incontestable truth, a sort of popular science of the everyday. On this, Gramsci remarked, "Common sense creates the folklore of the future, that is a relatively rigid phase of popular knowledge at a given place and time."[21]

Taking stock of images, sounds, ideas, and metaphors must equally engage an assessment of their resonance and relative power, not merely frequency. Doing so necessitates a conceptualization of where, for whom, and when that relative power functions, as provisional as any response may in fact be. In other words, assessing import requires a sensitivity to *context*. When concentrating on the present phase of globalization, the conventional definitions of the borders of social phenomena—nations, populations, ethnicities, countries, and so on—become ever more elusive; new and unforseen organizations of social categories appear. What are the interpretive and critical limits to charting the effectivity of popular and institutional knowledge given the blurred boundaries between national and international cultural life? More generally, how can we define context if a central characteristic is instability and ever-changing nature?

Significantly, Gramsci conceived of the social as fragmented since there cannot be said to be any determinant that guarantees forever the form and distribution of power in society. The "essence" of society cannot be reduced to a generalizable explanation, for instance, the economy or class. Hence his writings offer a stance against the overreliance on political-economic analysis. Gramsci argued that there are always multiple relations of force producing cultural and social domains. This view forms the basis of *conjuncturalism*, which recommends that cultural and social analysis should confront the precise contexts in which those forces have effects and are experienced, even as the contexts themselves are in the process of being made. Stuart Hall echoes this by proposing that there is "no necessary correspondence" between signs and their social or meaning effects.[22] Signs provisionally linking with meanings, populations, and ideologies forge an *articulation*, a process that occurs under the determining weight of the economic, though not under this weight alone.

As a flexible way to grasp context for cultural investigation, Gramsci's concept of the national-popular has been invaluable. In Andrew Ross's study of intellectuals and popular culture, the national-popular is understood to be a "taken-for-granted" mode of cultural activity, which in the United States is primarily a popular commercial enterprise. For his part, Gramsci was investigating the concept of the national-popular to understand the role of international culture. Ross picks up on this, suggesting that American popular culture offers a *multinational-popular*.[23] This means that for countries around the world, each with multifarious commitments to an international popular culture, their own national life is shaken up as it confronts culture that is shared extraordinarily widely. With this in mind, the national-popular becomes a contingent patchwork of the "elementary passions of the people,"[24] read from texts and practices springing from a myriad of sources. The pertinent issue is, as stated by Gramsci, "When can the conditions for awakening and developing a national-popular collective will be said to exist?"[25] How is one to identify those commonsensical elements, those popular passions, in light of the current phase of internationalism? It is worth remembering that Gramsci's writings on the topic began with the observation that Italy did not have a national-popular culture in the early part of the twentieth century, and that it had consequently developed an intricate relation with U.S. culture. This is fascinating inasmuch as it aptly describes the worries of many nations today as they toil to eke out a place in an international cultural context still dominated by U.S. cultural forms.

John Clarke tenders a concise take on hegemony and the questions it poses for cultural analysis, in a comment directed at a strain of British Cultural Marxism from the 1980s "New Times." He writes of the contradictions evident in national-popular's relation to hegemony:

> Those contradictions emerge around a number of different lines of force. The first involves the distinction between sedimented and emergent cultural forms . . . with the need to consider how the old is articulated with the new. The second concerns Gramsci's distinction between the "good" and "bad" sense of common sense: the need to politically evaluate the field of cultural practices and forms of identity to assess where progressive political connections can be forged. . . . Finally, there is the necessity of assessing the political balance of forces—lines of domination and subordination—within the field of national-popular.[26]

Three dichotomies—sedimented and emergent cultural forms, "good" and "bad" common sense, and lines of domination and subordination—offer a way to examine and dissect culturally and historically specific phenomena, or conjunctures. Yet, in fact, Clarke's argument, massively inspired by Raymond Williams, is to draw our attention to the fashion in which cultural studies, especially New Times, has fetishized the conjunctural at the expense of the organic.[27] He encourages us to read continuity, stabilization, ossification, and reinforcement where many have found discontinuity, destabilization, randomness, and chaos. In many quarters of cultural theory, it appears that the immediate and the "moment" have had an unavoidable attraction. Instead, ongoing connections are as central to the formation of contexts as new ones and hence deserve a prominent place in our thinking. In all cultural analysis we might pose the question: What is the relationship between the emergent and the residual and between the appearance of novelty and of repetition?

For the present study, I take cues from Marcia Landy, among others, who understands that a Gramscian approach to cultural critique in general, and to film analysis in particular, is not to prescribe but to interrogate and "map popular taste."[28] It is to produce a historical portrait of the dynamic relations between dominant and subordinate forms and practices, with the ultimate goal of knowing how to intervene, whether to disrupt, to target policy, to create alternative forms, or to act wisely from within existing institutions. To my mind, this means, as a first step of immeasurable importance, taking seriously the commitments and skills of popular audiences, however asymmetrically disturbed those skills might be. Such an approach requires an inventory of contexts, sites, dispositions, and knowledge that make up the everyday life of popular film culture in our historical situation. The discourses in question are evident in promotional material, in entertainment news, in trailers, in trade publications, in consultancy reports, in economic commentary, and in fan culture. They produce and reproduce not only the cultural forms themselves— genres, stars, films—but also the spaces in which these forms are engaged— multiplexes, video stores, living rooms. Indeed, it is a chief contention of this book that an essential location at which discourses of global audiences are being worked out and applied—one that has been overlooked by the swelling industry of scholarly work on global culture—is the motion picture theater. With this theoretical framework, I want to ask the following: What current discourses of audience and entertainment, specifically concerning popular film culture, are circulating? What is emergent and residual in these discourses?

How have they been instrumental in restructuring and promoting a sense of a global industry? What happens when national industrial and popular discourses of culture bump up against and become revised by these same internationally powerful *epistemes*? Can we still talk in terms of the dominance of global film culture over the subordinate national cinema cultures? Or has the "success" of international culture meant that it is no longer efficacious to ask about a national-popular version?

In what follows, I chart the modes of popular experience proffered, enforced, and regulated at the cinema, tracing their relation to streams of national and global cultural life. In no way is this study a comprehensive survey of all facets of cinematic culture. It is an examination of a thin, but tremendously visible, band of practices that we designate "commercial," "mainstream," "popular," "conventional," "dominant," "mass-oriented," even "Hollywood." While I address earlier and later developments, the heart of the study is bracketed by the years 1986 and 1998, a period beginning with the recognition of problems with existing film exhibition spaces and practices, during which there was rising agreement about the changes needed, and ending with a growing sense that this phase of exhibition had its own limitations. This periodization shows that the associated changes in cinemagoing were a product of two broad forces: first, the return of Hollywood majors to exhibition starting in 1986, and second, Hollywood's increasing reliance on global markets throughout the 1990s. This reliance includes the exportation of certain approaches to cinemagoing, and special cinema spaces, to select locales around the world. As will become apparent, a settlement formed around the improvement of theaters in the early 1990s. This settlement appeared in the form of an industrial common sense—again, which is not the same as "good" or even accurate sense—saying that cinemagoing required revisions and that in particular the site itself had to be "upgraded" in order to accommodate a new phase in the globalization of filmed entertainment. This "agreement" included a characterization of the special qualities of the contemporary cinema space, its status as a destination offering a range of leisure options, and a clear relation to or fit with other sites of audiovisual consumption. The most emblematic product of these changes was the *megaplex,* a multiplex cinema typified variously by its large auditoriums, its large number of screens, and the activities it sold in addition to film spectatorship.

Interestingly, even as many megaplexes continue to open, reports begin to surface in 1998 about their "failure." These coincided with a growing interest in digital projection technologies for film, a development that serves as a closing bracket on this period and demonstrates, yet again, the ever-changing nature of exhibition and distribution.

The industry endeavors described, and their repercussions for audience practice, are not unique to the years central to this study. Throughout the history of cinema, there have been ongoing efforts to shape cinemagoing and the space of public projection. At times, these efforts were explicit in their design to introduce taste and class distinctions at the site of the theater. One instance of the "elevation" of film to respectable middle-class entertainment was the rise of the movie palace in the 1920s, with its appropriation of high theatrical forms and its investment in the grandiose that contrasted working-class and immigrant cinema environments. Also significant is the way that cultural capital for cinemagoing was architecturally embodied in the scale and ornamentation of the movie palaces. Structures of space, and the associated spectator comportment, marked a shift in cultural hierarchies as well as changes in business practice. On the topic of exhibition, Douglas Gomery provides a fine composite of the industrial and economic forces that form and alter the activities of film audiences throughout U.S. cinema history.[29]

As Miriam Hansen describes early cinemagoing, "The neighborhood character of many nickelodeons—the egalitarian seating, continuous admission, and variety format, nonfilmic activities like illustrated songs, live acts, and occasional amateur nights—fostered a casual, sociable if not boisterous, atmosphere. It made moviegoing an interactive rather than merely passive experience."[30] The binary active/passive is a loaded one. Here, Hansen associates the still, contemplative body of the sound film spectator and of the movie palaces with passivity, and the vocal, unruly body of silent film and nickelodeons with activity, thus presenting an argument of cultural valuation that she in fact claims to be contesting. Nonetheless, she rightly declares that modes of activity, of cinematic engagement, differ. Competing regimes of behavior and bodily disposition characterized the shifts through the nickelodeon to the movie palace. Importantly, such dispositions are sometimes linked to social position, forming the basis of social distinctions. Hansen further argues that this shift involved the domestication of working-class public behavior, ultimately producing a standardized, predictable, middle-class audience, one that would not vary from one film performance to the next. This domestication "would subdue social and cultural distinctions among viewers and turn them into a homogeneous group of *spectators*,"[31] a view useful to standardizing operations of the film industry itself.

Similarly, Clarke writes that Roy Rosenzweig's study of U.S. leisure at the turn of the twentieth century "highlights the 'cultural work' which went into broadening the class basis of the film watching public to include the middle-classes in terms of the changing content of films, the new architecture of the cinema, and the assertion of decorum over the social behaviour of the cinema audiences themselves, involving the suppression of forms of collective sociability which had characterized working-class participation in the nickelodeon."[32] Simply put, such historical developments require work. Instead of either historical spontaneity or mechanical causality, the idea of *cultural work* accents the variety of forces and determinations that construct correspondences—or articulations—here between practices, expectations, sites of public cultural consumption, and presumptions about activity at those sites. Without asserting singular origins or intentions, people and audiences in a range of social positions are enlisted in service of formations of cultural practice. The work involved produces and reproduces the parameters and possibilities of social existence in general, in this case pertaining to business practices and to one form of public space. Thus, beyond the casual engagement of pastimes, the organization of how, when, and under what conditions people congregate is a fundamental dimension of social life. It may be but one brand of shared cultural experience, nonetheless, cinemagoing is part of the patchwork of practices and experiences contributing to senses of neighborhood, civic, national, or transnational cohorts. An examination of this role in the imagination of large communities, in the end, begins to uncover the contours of national-popular life.

Extending the historical and theoretical analyses of Gomery, Landy, Hansen, and Rosenzweig, I intend to demonstrate that shifts and reformulations of space and cultural practice similar to other periods of cinema history have been underway since the mid-1980s. In brief, I submit that a new common sense about popular cinema, globalization, and everyday life had been in process between 1986 and 1998. Further, the related concepts of popular cultural practice in a global context have a commanding impact on how we conceptualize, and act within, a national cultural community. I suggest that an examination of the economic and discursive transformation in the film industry itself reveals some of the forces propelling these changes and helps us to understand their implications for cultural policy and audience formations.

In order to do so, I focus on those venues that circulate ideas about cinematic life. These constitute a cross-section of media sources and genres, including advertising, feature articles, newspaper and magazine reporting, editorials, corporate publicity, government documents, and industry reports. I contend that the splintering of the film industry away from a single location has made industry organs like *Variety, Boxoffice,* and *Playback* more important as vehicles of debate, analysis, and information. They provide a point of intersection for an increasingly dispersed industrial sector. Further, the rise of hybrid industry-popular entertainment news means that trade publications are a source of reigning ideas about cinematic life for audiovisual producers and cinema consumers alike. Frequently a front page article in *Variety* will be taken up over the next few weeks in daily newspapers and weekly magazines.

The present examination followed the gathering of substantial amounts of articles and data from the early 1980s to the early years of this new century, with extra efforts to be comprehensive about material inside the thirteen-year temporal bracket 1986–1998. I repeatedly read the thousand-plus articles, with the most representative or informative cited in this text. The process revealed contradictions and slightly aberrant reports but eventually provided evidence of consistency and repetition. This consistency appears in a variety of forms through business and popular contexts. As such, it is maintained that industry strategies, audience expectations, and cultural policies rest on an apparent agreement about ideas, metaphors, and claims, which could typify the conditions of and issues facing public motion picture presentation or establish assumptions about the taste, activity, and interest of cinemagoers.

I want to be unambiguous here. It is not the aim of this study to weigh the accuracy of these reigning ideas. Nor am I someone who has privileged access to the process by which these ideas are put to use, never having worked for the film industry proper nor acted as an ethnographic observer of it. Industry participants have other sources and experiences on which to base their actions, unavailable to me. There is a considerable knowledge and marketing apparatus internal to the film industry consisting of high-priced reports of economic data and analysis selling for anywhere from a couple hundred to a couple thousand dollars apiece (which places them beyond the reach of those of us at public institutions). I had only infrequent and inconsistent opportunity to examine these works, which have limited circulation, though their observations can filter through into public sources. Similarly, though I am an avid (perhaps obsessive) film fan, the multitudes of cinemagoers have their own experiences and understandings to draw on, to which I do not presume to have full access. The material discussed in this book is important not because it is beyond challenge but precisely because it is public, it is available, and, hence, because it plays a considerable role in the kinds of claims that build up and are made about cultural life and cultural industry.

Where Jim Carrey's "And how was *your* weekend? Mine was *good!*" marks a condition of international "insiderism," with its implied access to measures of industry achievement, it equally registers a view of star biography, in the narrative of his rise from obscurity in Ontario to the highest ranks of Hollywood success, and of cultural practice, in the very idea of cinemagoing on the opening weekend of a film. One might add that Carrey accents a connection between the internationalizing industry and one's own home community, between the workings of a star machine and the everyday life of fans and audiences, between the Shrine Auditorium and one's local multiplex. There is a poetics of cultural distance in the traffic in images from elsewhere and their proximate, if temporary, residence in one's everyday locality. As passing as his joke may have been, it signaled a condition in which relations between industrial and cultural practice, between text and the quotidian, and between imagined and lived spaces had been reconfigured. Considering these changes and the conjuncture in which they took place, the following chapters begin a theoretical and empirical discussion of the forces propelling the formation of entertainment spaces and their audiences in a globalizing context.

CHAPTER TWO

Traveling Cultures, Mutating Commodities

"Films with legs," an industry term, refers to a couple of circumstances. In one usage, the traditional one, it refers to films that will last a relatively long time at theaters, that is, films that offer extended runs. The other use is to describe films that can travel well, that move easily from one market to the next. It characterizes how well exhibitors and distributors expect a film to do as it is released successively in new cities and towns, marking, in *Variety*'s lexicon, "stamina at the box office." Today, though, lengthy runs are not necessarily signs of success, and the selective and gradual release of films, called "platform" releasing, is not as common as it was in the past. Now, most box office revenue is expected within the first few weeks of release. For example, for wide releases of 600 screens and more in 1997, 37.3 percent of their box office revenue came from the first week.[1] Thus, though still frequently applied, the term "films with legs" does not designate the same qualities it once did because the industry context has been so radically altered. Saying that a film will travel well to new markets can no longer encompass only cinemas in different city locations but also movement to other national contexts and the inevitable transition to various other media forms. I confess to being drawn to the colorful image the phrase conjures up. Giant film canisters with long spindly legs, like the bugs in *Starship Troopers* (Paul Verhoeven 1997), scuttle crablike between cities, criss-crossing paths until they settle in to feed at a multiplex. Whatever fantastical notions "films with legs" may spark, the term does cast our attention toward the mutability now expected of film commodities. The contemporary moment demands a series of afterlives for cultural texts. To continue with the bug metaphor, a process of metamorphosis moves culture through a life cycle of commodity forms, from film to video, pay-TV, television, DVD, and so on, and at each stage the form migrates across geographical territories.

A. D. Murphy noted that the international box office success experienced in 1989 came at a time of expanding new media, demonstrating once again that "post-theatrical markets have stimulated theatergoing."[2] He continued, "on a global basis, it's been validated that the theatrical market is indispensable to launching films into the expanding film universe. Theater film rentals a decade ago accounted for about 80% of total distributor revenues from all media; nowadays that proportion is down to about 30%."[3] Peter Bart wrote in 1991 that domestic theatrical rentals account for about 20 percent of revenue, with international theatrical rentals adding another 15 percent. The remaining 65 percent, then, comes from video, cable, television, and other secondary markets.[4] Put differently, since the 1980s there has been the parallel evolution of multiple windows of exhibition and distribution for filmed entertainment and the globalization of both markets and ownership structures of the corporations involved. Table 1 presents one snapshot of the breakdown of the 1994 revenue sources for the majors (including Canada and the United States). By these figures, domestic and international theatrical releasing are equally important to major distributors. Notably, home video accounts for a greater slice of the revenue pie, with international video even exceeding domestic theatrical revenues. In other words, this is a situation in which the space of public film consumption resides alongside other venues of consumption, as well as in relation to international contexts. Table 2 shows the rising importance of home video revenues with respect to box office and television internationally, with 1988 as the first year in which home video surpassed the others as a revenue stream. Over those years, television revenues hovered around 23 percent.

Just as theatrical releases account for a dwindling percentage of distributor revenue, expanding windows of exhibition effectively splinter audiences while extending the lifespan of a filmed commodity. The rising centrality of the intermedia migration of texts, as the tables set out, indicates that the full financial and cultural significance of any single work can only be gauged across its media incarnations. So-called box office disasters may well gather steam as they

TABLE 1   Revenue Sources for Major Distributors, 1994 (as percentage)

Domestic theatrical receipts	16
Domestic home video	26
Domestic television	11
International theatrical receipts	16
International home video	19.9
Licensing, merchandising, theme parks, and rides	11.1

SOURCE: Leo Rice-Barker, "Industry Banks on New Technology, Expanded Slates," *Playback,* May 6, 1996, 19.
NOTE: Domestic refers to the United States and Canada.

TABLE 2   Share of Distributors' Worldwide Revenues by Media

Year	Box Office Rentals (%)	Home Video (%)	TV (%)
1986	40.2	35.9	23.9
1987	39.6	36.9	23.5
1988	35.5	40.6	23.9
1989	36.7	42	21.3
1990	36.1	41.7	22.2
1991	34.5	42.6	22.9
1992	32	45.1	22.9

SOURCE: Veronis, Suhler and Associates, Inc., "Filmed Entertainment Growth: A Five-Year Forecast," *Boxoffice,* October 1992, 42; Veronis, Suhler and Associates, Inc., "Filmed Entertainment Growth: A Five-Year Forecast," *Boxoffice,* November 1993, 62.

subsequently appear on DVD, videotape, and TV, or as they move on to other markets. Conversely, impressive ticket sales the opening weekend may fail to register any cultural impact over time, and those films may drop below the surface without a ripple. Textual migration also means that works move to meet audiences in wide-ranging places (cinemas and bedrooms, airplanes and living rooms, suburbs and city centers). What I wish to emphasize here is that the intermedia dimension, as it splinters aggregate audiences, also multiplies locations of consumption. Thus, motion picture spectatorship is put into contact with an expanding array of other social and cultural practices. This cross-media migration of texts is part of a popular cinematic knowledge, guiding decisions about cinematic encounters. The now-routine advertising proclaiming a film available "only in theaters" is a gentle nod that this exclusivity is temporary, and also reveals the ordinariness of this knowledge. Where and when motion picture "events" occur has been cracked open. The very idea of the location of film, that is, what we presume about how, where, and when film is engaged, is put into question. One result is that the theatrical context sits more securely as a recognizably "big screen" experience.

Globalization operates to similar ends, shaking our certainty about the location of film consumption. While a range of historical markers might be deployed to characterize the contemporary context, let me refer to a key turning point that has circulated in the trade periodicals: 1993 was the first year that international rentals for Hollywood films exceeded domestic.[5] In other words, major U.S. film corporations received more revenue from the films they had in theatrical release abroad than they did from those in the United States in that calendar year. The split through the 1990s tended to be about 50/50, though by 2000 the figures had returned to the late 1980s proportion, reflecting stronger domestic rentals, as evident in table 3. In 1996, global box office revenue hit a new record,[6] with international rentals accounting for the majority (51 percent).[7] Table 4 presents the significant increases enjoyed by distributors from cumulative international box office revenues through the late 1980s. Klady observed, "International exhibition has been a consistently profitable business, and further growth appears certain."[8] Table 5 shows the gradual tilt of domestic and international share of distributor revenue for box office, television, and home video through the latter half of the 1980s. For the majors, in 1996, 41 percent of theatrical, television, and home video revenue originated from outside the United States.[9] Thomas Guback refers to evidence that more than half the revenue of majors' films came from international circuits by the 1960s,[10] casting suspicion on the industry sources' claim that the experience of the 1990s was historically unique. His source appears to be an address to the House of Representatives by then MPAA president Eric Johnston. However, Guback does not indicate whether his data describes the ratio for a single year or for individual films over time. Regardless, though the elevation of 1993 to landmark status might be premature, that year has been taken up as an indication of the expanding international purview of the U.S. industry.

Table 6 provides an illustration of how overall distributor revenues changed

TABLE 3   Domestic (U.S.) and International Share
of Distributor Box Office Rentals (as percentage)

Year	Domestic	International
1989	56.9	43.1
1995	51.4	48.6
1996	49	51
1998	52	48
2000	55.6	44.4

SOURCE: A. D. Murphy, "Globe Gobbling Up U.S. Pix in Record Doses; Worldwide Rentals to Yank Distribs Shattered Marks in '89; Japan Key," *Variety*, June 13, 1990, 10; Don Groves, "Boffo Year for O'seas Markets," *Variety*, April 21–27, 1997, 9; Don Groves, "BO World Is Flat; Local Pix, Strong Dollar Hurt Yanks O'seas," Variety.com, June 11, 2002 (last accessed June 25, 2002).

TABLE 4   Distributors' Revenue from Worldwide
Box Office Rentals (in millions of dollars)

Year	Box Office Rentals	% Change from Previous Year
1986	$2,701	
1987	2,958	9.5
1988	3,338	12.8
1989	4,006	20
1990	4,544	13.4
1991	4,629	1.9

SOURCE: Veronis, Suhler and Associates, Inc., "Filmed Entertainment Growth: A Five-Year Forecast," *Boxoffice*, October 1992, 40.

from domestic to foreign in the late 1980s. It shows that total revenue more than doubled in the space of seven years, and that international sources accounted for a great proportion of that increase than domestic in every one of those years. The largest discrepancy appears in 1987, when domestic revenue rose 4.2 percent from the previous year while international revenue leapt 23.9 percent. Most sources continue to attribute the year of *Batman*, 1989, as a watershed moment for global Hollywood box office and revenues, and table 4 shows a full 20 percent increase in distributor revenue from worldwide admissions. Table 6, however, points to 1988, which witnessed unusual growth, with domestic and international revenue rising 20.6 percent and 34.1 percent respectively in what

Traveling Cultures, Mutating Commodities   **27**

TABLE 5   Domestic (U.S.) and International Share of Distributor Revenues (TV, Box Office, and Home Video) (as percentage)

Year	Domestic	International
1986	65.0	35.0
1987	60.9	39.1
1988	58.4	41.6
1989	56.9	43.1
1990	54.6	45.4
1991	53.2	46.8

SOURCE: Veronis, Suhler and Associates, Inc., "Filmed Entertainment Growth: A Five-Year Forecast," *Boxoffice*, October 1992, 40.

TABLE 6   Distributor Revenues (in millions of dollars)

Year	Domestic (% Change)	International (% Change)	Total (% Change)
1986	4,366	2,355	6,721
1987	4,550 (4.2)	2,919 (23.9)	7,469 (11.1)
1988	5,486 (20.6)	3,913 (34.1)	9,399 (25.8)
1989	6,214 (13.3)	4,708 (20.3)	10,922 (16.2)
1990	6,875 (10.6)	5,719 (21.5)	12,594 (15.3)
1991	7,132 (3.7)	6,286 (9.9)	13,418 (6.5)
1992			14,500 (8.1)

SOURCE: Veronis, Suhler and Associates, Inc., "Filmed Entertainment Growth: A Five-Year Forecast," *Boxoffice*, October 1992, 40; ibid., *Boxoffice*, November 1993, 62.

could be seen as an early indication of the changes to come and of the alterations in the sources of revenue for distributors. Nonetheless, table 7's fairly steady increase in domestic box office receipts, excluding the drops of 1985 and of the recession of the early 1990s, represents a substantial 306 percent increase from 1980 to 2001.

These changes, evidence of a still powerful domestic box office, of the additional importance of other revenue streams, and of a rising global market, have propelled the industry to take further advantage of this circumstance. The push toward global film commodities has led distributors to begin to synchronize international promotional campaigns and releasing strategies, including open-

TABLE 7   Domestic (U.S.) Box Office Receipts (in millions of dollars)

Year	Box Office Receipts	% Change from Previous Year
1980	2,749	
1981	2,966	7.9
1982	3,453	16.4
1983	3,766	9.1
1984	4,031	7
1985	3,749	− 7
1986	3,778	0.8
1987	4,253	12.6
1988	4,458	4.8
1989	5,033	12.9
1990	5,022	− 0.2
1991	4,803.2	− 4.4
1992	4,871	1.4
1993	5,154.2	5.8
1994	5,396.2	4.7
1995	5,493.5	1.8
1996	5,911.5	7.6
1997	6,365.9	7.7
1998	6,949	9.2
1999	7,448	7.2
2000	7,661	2.9
2001	8,412.5	9.8

SOURCE: The years 1980–1991 are from Veronis, Suhler and Associates, Inc., "Filmed Entertainment Growth: A Five-Year Forecast," *Boxoffice*, November 1993, 56; the years 1991–2002 are from Motion Picture Association of America, "2001 U.S. Economic Review," http://www.mpaa.org/useconomic review/2001Economic, last accessed June 22, 2002.

ing dates scheduled over a condensed period of time.[11] Another consequence has been the increased involvement in the production process of the agents who sell the international rights to films, with a voice and control previously unheard of.[12] Here, agents who buy and sell films in particular countries are receiving an unusual amount of attention as local informants.

These signs aside, it is important to remind ourselves how selective this process of globalization actually is. Evidence points to a continuing presence of key international locations. In November 1995, as measured by the American Film Marketing Association, seven countries or territories had been in the top ten markets for U.S. film consistently for the previous decade: Australia/New Zealand, France, Germany, Italy, Japan, Spain, and the UK. Revealing how important only a few countries are to this so-called globalization, the top ten markets in 1995 accounted for in excess of 75 percent of sales in all media. During that period, Canada made that list only once, as in other years it was treated as part of the U.S. market.[13]

The selectivity of globalization in the mid-1990s was evident in the ranking of top international markets a full decade earlier, making clearer that this "new phase" may in fact be the solidifying and intensifying of longstanding routes of cultural commerce. In 1985 the five largest export markets for U.S. major distributors were Japan, Canada, France, West Germany, and the UK. These five accounted for approximately 51 percent of all export rentals. The top fifteen markets totalled 81 percent of the export market.[14] In 1987 this concentration reached a 25-year high, with the top 15 accounting for 83 percent,[15] increasing again to hit 85.2 percent in 1989.[16] In terms of the straight dollar figures, international rentals were $2.43 billion in 1988, followed by a 28 percent increase to $3.13 billion in 1989.[17] In this year, the international/domestic split was 43.1 percent to 56.9 percent, a ratio that would soon begin to tip in the other direction.[18] Beyond the increasing scale of the global film business, these figures show the kind of concentration that has existed for internationalization. One can see how even minor trade barriers in one of those key markets, for instance France and Canada, would have a significant impact upon U.S. distributor revenue.

In concert with this evidence, it is worth keeping in mind that the United States has been notoriously unreceptive to international film. Where most countries live with some sort of everyday understanding of and encounter with an international popular film universe, even if a good deal of this import culture may be American in origin, the United States has been less engaged in this quintessentially modern experience. As Martin Short put it, explaining the sharp satirical edge of SCTV, "Americans watch television, but Canadians watch American television." The visibility of international media traffic is a familiar, if fraught, dimension of the contemporary world, one in which U.S. popular audiences have been less than full participants. Despite the unusual popularity of non–English language features, including *Like Water for Chocolate* (Alfonso Arau 1992), *Life Is Beautiful* (Roberto Benigni 1998), and *Crouching Tiger, Hidden Dragon* (Ang Lee 2000), U.S. distributors and exhibitors have historically acted as ideological isolationists. Toby Miller points out how this is in contrast with U.S. harping about closed markets abroad. He writes, "Washington/Hollywood/New York preside over the most closed television and cinema space in world history."[19]

Some industry measures are clearly designed to reflect global concentration by ignoring the work of smaller distributors. Analyses of the hundred top-grossing films for the year, not surprisingly, end up showing that the biggest companies handle the biggest movies. An article in 1996, "BO with a Vengeance: $9.1 Billion Worldwide," reveals the increasing revenue-generating might of the top hundred films, showing that twelve distributors control 96 percent of global activity, and that Hollywood firms, in particular, represent 99 percent of domestic box office and 87.5 percent of international. This seems to be stunning evidence of the prowess of those twelve companies, though of course it is not a measure of all film activity, but only the hundred top revenue-generating movies. The article actually reveals the extent to which distributors have been able to retain distribution rights as they move films into other countries, presumably squeezing out local distributors who may have been seeking the most lucrative films for themselves. While the article points out that an increasing number of non-Hollywood majors are part of this list of 1995's leading films, in the form of coproductions and international films, the circular logic of this ranking assures a continued, and inflated, sense of global influence among fewer corporations.[20]

This bid for precision is not to suggest that the globalization of the film industry is not happening. On the contrary, I would argue that the consolidated entertainment business is a flagship for the organization of late industrial capitalism more generally. The multinational entertainment corporation has become, in many ways, one vehicle through which nations negotiate their participation in transnational economies. As manufacturing sectors account for smaller proportions of the entire economy than they did in the past, the "new" economy of entertainment, Internet, and knowledge-based corporations represents a movement from the factory-installation capital of Fordism to the flexible accumulation of post-Fordism. But the selectivity of internationalism just described forces us to confront the reformation of a center of gravity for the flow of cultural and economic capital and the structures of claims, assumptions, and logic that exist about the very process and experience of globalization. With respect to this second point, if we are to begin to understand our cultural environment we need an accounting of the kind of intellectual production that occurs within industrial ranks, however unchecked or ultimately illogical the result may in fact be. What exactly is this globalization that we have agreed is occurring and whose certain existence guides so many of the practices of producers of filmed commodities? Ideas about culture do not only take form and circulate among industrial contexts. They are acted on, forming the basis of decisions concerning production and distribution. Some of these ideas also are reconstituted as vernacular understanding. Hence institutional industrial knowledge about globalization—among distributors, exhibitors, and producers—becomes embedded and sedimented, calling for the brand of archaeological research Foucault pointed us toward.

Currently, understanding what gives a film revenue-generating longevity— that is, its "legs" over time at the box office, across geographical regions, and through media formats—entails the idea of the multifaceted audience. The mobile, dispersed, global audience is an abstract entity. We can see an imagined unity being made, even though we are living in an era of the splintering and scattering of aggregate audiences. Significantly, commercial cinema venues, those specially constructed spaces intended to appeal to wide audiences, are one site at which the various struggles over globalization are being played out, sometimes concerning economics, but also concerning national legal structures, the future role of various levels of government, the selective mobilization of people, the uncertain continued existence of older cultural forms and practices, and so on. Andrew Higson's seminal reconsideration of the idea of "national cinemas" elaborates this view, taking account of the implications internationalization has for the national film cultures. For Higson, a text- and industry-based definition of films from a national location does not capture the depth and variety of a country's cinematic existence. He proposes that a national cinema encompasses not only the structures of production but also those of consumption, which comprise (1) all films, whether domestically produced or not, and their various exhibition contexts; (2) the forms and practices of audiences; and (3) the critical and institutional apparatuses that manufacture understandings of "art," "entertainment," and "national character."[21]

The geographic mobility of cultural commodities has been described as a loss of cultural specificity by commentators of various political stripes. One reading of what creates "films with legs" is the notion of the *cultural discount*.[22] This view holds that a film that hobbles itself with cultural specificity will not last as long nor travel as well as one with "degree zero" particularity. One sees versions of this argument in the assertion that U.S. film has tapped into a universal popular language and accordingly floats above historical and cultural specificity. For instance, Scott Olson writes that because of the textual *transparency* of its dominant cinema "the United States has a competitive advantage in the creation and global distribution of popular taste."[23] He continues,

> *Transparency* is defined as any textual apparatus that allows audiences to project indigenous values, beliefs, rites, and rituals into imported media or the use of those devices. This transparency effect means that American cultural exports, such as cinema, television, and related merchandise, manifest narrative structures that easily blend into other cultures. Those cultures are able to project their own narratives, values, myths, and meanings into the American iconic media, making those texts resonate with the same meanings they might have if they were indigenous.[24]

Following the logic of the cultural discount, or transparency, the deficiency of Canadian cinema has been that it is too Canadian, it has not been universal in its film language, and therefore it is ill suited to an interconnected audiovisual world. Such a proposal, however, is based on several mistaken assumptions. First, the cultural discount erroneously equates internationally popular forms with an absence of particularity. But how can we claim, conceptually speaking, that the specificity of *Titanic* (James Cameron 1997) is nil and that of *Exotica* (Atom Egoyan 1995) is high? To Olson's credit, he makes efforts to designate the characteristics of the transparent text, including open-endedness, virtuality, circularity, ellipticality, archetypal dramatis personae, verisimilitude, and high production values, though they are so broad as to appear to be an itemization of common attributes of the cinema as a whole. Second, the cultural discount implies that culture is fixed and made up of stable texts, effacing the possibility of people actively involved in cultural consumption. As a result, the concept cannot see culture as historically produced nor that all artifacts themselves have histories, hence, like all semiotic packages, they have their meanings altered and determined by contexts. Instead, with the cultural discount, texts have an inherent "value," to be measured somehow, indicating competitive advantage. Third, even if we accept transparency's limited definition of culture, it cannot account for the possibility that signs of cultural specificity may be precisely the qualities prized by international audiences, for example, signs of Australianness, Irishness, or Hong Kongness. What the discounted and the transparent texts see as "neutral" films into which people can freely situate their own cultural make-up may be, in actuality, films that are seen and negotiated as American. The cultural discount, then, is in fact a version of content analysis, a necessarily anticultural term designed to accommodate models of accounting and quantitative evaluation. Indeed, its authors wish to turn the cultural discount into a measure of how cultural difference affects the market value of cultural commodities.[25]

Nonetheless, the cultural discount is worth critical attention, because it, perhaps unwittingly, does capture the kind of knowledge about international culture produced in the industry itself: a core belief that the relative mobility of films can be measured or predicted and that there are cultural forms that transcend specificity. Put differently, the cultural discount and its parallels in the logic of entertainment investment circles contend that there are cultural versions of the ethereal and instantaneous mobility of global finance: nationless, rootless, obeying the forces of the market only, and able to disintegrate borders (or at least avoid trade barriers) through the evasive paths provided by technological infrastructures.

In order to explain this critique further, let's look at a particularly prized genre. More than any other form, it is the action film that is taken as best accommodating the qualities of mobility and mutability. Again and again, claims are made in trade publications, in popular sources of entertainment information, and in critical writing that the action film—and, more broadly characterized, film violence—is a prime case for the post-Fordist film commodity. It is as though there is something about the visual lyricism of screen violence, the dance of aggression, the spectacle of property demolished, and the presumptions of male spectatorship that makes it most mobile and that offers an easy translation for cinemagoers in diverse locations and circumstances. Action films are taken as one foundation in the formation of global film taste. After a fashion, the discourse of the global audience—that is, a primary target for those leggy films—is rooted in an agreement about genre, irrespective of the reliability of such assessments. Note Leonard Klady's surprise that, in 1999, "Comedies, long considered poor travelers, are proving every bit as viable (and considerably more profitable) as special-effects actioners."[26] Or compare this to the way in which the personal film, the director's cinema, is seen as specially connected to notions of national cinema, or at least the imagining of such. There are exceptions in contemporary Hong Kong cinema, the hybrid genres of India, and, of course, American cinema. Still, genre films in general, and action in particular, are often (erroneously) understood by scholars and critics as the ripping apart of the national cinema designation.

Star power is frequently cited as the defining feature of transnational action films; a cohort of action stars includes Jean-Claude Van Damme, Arnold Schwarzenegger, Sylvester Stallone, Mel Gibson, Jackie Chan, Bruce Willis, Chow Yun Fat, Nicholas Cage, and Wesley Snipes. These figures help to "pre-sell" a film. The desire to do so coincides with a requirement to reduce the risk of investment by offering recognizable and readable star texts, especially important in the context of skyrocketing costs of production and promotion. Interestingly, it is often said that similar demands of predictability led to the establishment of genre forms in the old studio system. As with any set of premises about the film business, counterevidence circulates. Some measures challenged the presumption that action films are best suited to international audiences. Four years before his assessment of comedies, noted above, Klady wrote that "the biggest increase in foreign box office over the last few years has come to comedies and intimate dramas—two genres previously thought to be hard sells in non-English-speaking countries."[27] Further, *Titanic* should continue to be cited for the way it rocked so many assumptions, including its use of low-level star personas and a heavily romantic theme, though the second half of the film moves into more conventionally recognizable action territory.

Simon During's article "Popular Culture on a Global Scale: A Challenge for Cultural Studies?"[28] takes account of some of the developments of global culture. His project is to describe a Gramscian field of political agency for international contexts, or what others have referred to as a transnational public. He characterizes cultural globalization, and the related possibilities for a global popular, as a pressing problem for many of the assumptions of cultural studies, contending that one brand of self-ethnography is truly a partner in the globalization process. During maintains that particular action films, ones featuring the muscular male body and a broad range of special effects, are crucial to understanding ideas about global audience formations. He discusses Schwarzenegger in Paul Verhoeven's *Total Recall* (1990) in detail.

During characterizes the action film as having the attributes of a "cinema of attractions," using Tom Gunning's ubiquitous phrase describing the foundational appeal of wonderment, surprise, and shock for audiences of early non-narrative cinema.[29] Doing so, During positions Schwarzenegger in a long history of strongman/circus shows, highlighting residual elements and traces of earlier cultural forms. He treats the film's careful attention to Schwarzenegger's body as a sign of masculinity that always reminds us of the training it requires. His body—the pain he can inflict with it, and the pain he can endure—is a shaped and constructed artifact. According to During, such a pumped-up form connotes an "idea of training," acting as an allegory of personalized labor and of work.[30] In this way, Schwarzenegger presents an ideological and performative fit between the place of action films in the global popular and the conditions of globalization, where a meeting point for widely differing peoples and cultures is an individuated (masculine) body that is both the source and product of labor. On this, During concludes that a film like *Total Recall* "market[s] the cultural and infrastructural conditions of its own success,"[31] which includes a simultaneous erasure of difference and its exponential growth through a kind of bodily empowerment.

For During, the very concept of the global popular is ostensibly culture that is popular in many places at once, or what might be called geographic blockbusters. This is not necessarily a Gramscian popular, which has to do with the formation of a historic bloc and with the "take up" of cultural positions and alliances. During is cautious, avoiding an equivalence between signs in and signs of the global popular, in which cultural globalization—that is, the internationalization of the industry—would be equivalent to other forms of transnationalism, a classic misapprehension in many studies of culture. We need to keep in mind that forms of globalization do not run synchronously. Why must the images and sounds produced by one form of global hegemony be instances of consensus and acquiescence across sectors? Even in the context of the conglomeration of media businesses, and the horizontal and vertical integration of the cultural industry, all possible consequences for experience and signification cannot be accounted for in advance. Ien Ang asserts, "It would be ludicrous . . . to try to find a definitive and unambiguous, general theoretical answer to this question—as the theory of cultural imperialism has attempted to do . . .— precisely because there is no way to know in advance which strategies and tactics different peoples in the world will invent to negotiate with the intrusions of global forces in their lives."[32] My approach is explicitly in contradistinction to work that takes international culture, popular or otherwise, as a sign of the *failure* of nation, of particularity, and of meaning. And such work is abundant and has formed an unfortunate clichéd rhetorical stance about the homogenization and the leveling-down of culture. Instead, in accordance with conjunctural critique, following Ang and others, I see it as essential to identify and dissect the forces and implications of globalizing culture, and then to begin to conceptualize how one lives and makes meaning in that context, without judging it as inappropriate, insufficient, or uniform in advance. This is not a call for the neoliberal "empowerment" readings During critiques so well. It is to challenge a continued impulse toward general models—in particular, crude forms of political economy—which can offer indispensable economic portraits and explanations for U.S. prominence in popular entertainment, but which, without a theory of consumption, may only hamper our ability to respond in a politically timely and resonant fashion. Our historical circumstance requires analyses that identify specific articulations of different global hegemonies, including geographic blockbusters and their local impact.

Some work on global culture makes the classic error of textual critique: images of power are taken as powerful images, or as evidence of the application of power. What if we were to see exactly the inverse, arguing that the popularity of the archetypal form and function of a figure like Schwarzenegger, with its exaggerated emphasis on an image of strength, is a symptom of weakness, of frailty, and of dwindling possibility? "Weakness" need not be an assessment of masculinity specifically, though some have explored that avenue.[33] Such figures can be a way to compensate for the overall vulnerability people feel in a global system, hence, paradoxically, they refer to people's sense of inconsequentiality and puniness. Figures of bodily power equally allude to general cautions and suspicions about that global system. One need only look at the way the inhumane global corporation has become an increasingly conventional element in the transnational action film. A paradox such as this—global cultural products presenting the dastardliness of global organizations—immediately deflates many of our critical skills. It means that "leisure's unstable status," as During refers to it, designates not only its mutability but popular culture's dialectical place in a transnational public, as the muscle building it up *and* tearing it down.

During's is one of the more compelling dissections of international culture. Far removed from the ahistorical "cultural discount" thesis, it becomes apparent that his reading works equally well as a critique of cultural analysis and its merits in treating the global popular. He directs us to the unpredictable possibilities of how global culture might be understood. And this is exactly the broader point I wish to emphasize. It does not make sense to be for or against globalization, which are the limited conceptual and political options that many versions of cultural imperialism persist in offering up. Accepting that crude binary reasoning effectively reads one site of critique, for instance, one global hegemony in the realm of the economic, as represented by centralized media ownership, into others (affect, ideology, sociability, representation, signification, etc.), sidestepping the challenging problem of correspondence (i.e., what combination of forces produces the cultural environment in which we live?). Alternatively, it erases the differential judgments of cultural traffic in which some, like an international art cinema, are signs of sophistication and others, like popular genres, are signs of conquest. Or such either/or approaches to the politics of globalization ignore the manifestly varying situations in which a single work appears, which simultaneously extends and multiplies the kind of cultural work texts and practices do. To be blunt, general theories of the global risk simplifying phenomena to the point of unrecognizability.

How the global popular is to be read remains a vital project for contemporary cultural theory. To start, it is unmistakable that claims *are* being made in the name of this popular, whether it is about genre, taste, identity, or political expression. While we may debate the possibilities of forming a democratic transcultural popular, it is already being actively emptied of its politics, as is the case with the concept of the cultural discount. In response, a global cultural analysis should examine the "micropolitics" of culture, that is, the diverse and provisional nature of ideology and power as it appears in and has effects on the structures of social life. When we are this far from a stance that sees ideologies of culture as guaranteed through an examination of textual or economic determinations in isolation, the context of the phenomenon under consideration becomes of the upmost importance. And if we assume that culture must be contextualized, then we must respond to Jennifer Slack's caution that "more often than not 'context' is invoked as a sort of magical term, as if by claiming to take context into consideration, one could banish the problems of specificity."[34] Those "problems of specificity"—that is, of conjuncture—deserve close, careful, and unpredetermined assessment. Here, to reiterate John Clarke's assertion, the vicissitudes of political assessments mean that critics need to examine the traces of residual and emergent cultural forms, the wavering formations of common sense, and the tensions between dominant and subordinate forces.

The political indeterminacy of global culture implicated in the "global audience" cannot be assessed without attention to location, especially as those locations and occasions continue to multiply. Research operating with an a priori assertion that loss and colonization characterize the global, and global film culture, ostensibly detours around the complexity of our current situation, opting for quick judgments and polemics. In this tendency, much work continues to assert an unfortunate dichotomy between the local and the global. Unrealistically imagining we have but two conditions to account for, the former has come to be associated with the immediate, the concrete, the real, the political, and the site of agency, where the latter is the distant, the abstract, the ethereal, the corporate, and the site of containment. As such, these conceptual articulations have facilitated a rather rapid, and mistaken, critical closure around the local as the site of politicized difference and the global as the ideological production of homogeneity.

Recent work has begun to examine and expose the theoretical pitfalls as well as the political limitations of this thinking. For instance, Doreen Massey reminds us, "Those who conflate the local with the concrete . . . are confusing geographical scale with processes of abstraction in thought."[35] Lawrence Grossberg concludes his critique of that binary by proposing an alternate model that sees power relations as always in the process of destroying and reconstructing hierarchies. He writes, "It is no longer a question of globality (as homelessness) and locality (as the identification of place and identity), but of the various ways people are attached and attach themselves (affectively) into the world. It is a question of the global becoming local and the local becoming global."[36] Despite his ample reference to Deleuze and Guattari in this argument, Grossberg's emphasis on the affective attachments of people is reminiscent of Raymond Williams's insistence that cultural analysis look for patterns of lived experience. Williams argued that such patterns of culture were both ideals for and modes of living.[37] They constructed the dominant social character of a period but also offered people a way to organize their relation to that character. He called this interaction "structure of feeling" and described it as "the living result of all the elements in the general organization."[38] Of this proposal, many critiques of Williams allege that he gave experience, and textual access to it, too much weight, ideology and struggle too little, and Grossberg pays heed to them. Nonetheless, Grossberg maintains that affect complicates how we apprehend the structures of a global cultural environment, in that we also need to take account of structures of experience.

A productive avenue has been opened up by Arjun Appadurai, writing of a global sense of movement, one in which culture and people emerge from, return to, and exist "elsewhere." In the context of movement, "both persons and images often meet unpredictably, outside the certainties of home and the cordon sanitaire of local and national media effects. This mobile and unforeseeable relationship between mass-mediated events and migratory audiences defines the core of the link between globalization and the modern."[39] The condition of mobility coupled with an inability to guarantee trajectories and consequences is, perhaps, the most significant feature destabilizing to cultural theory, in particular the concept of the national-popular. For too long, an aesthetic and moral certainty has plagued many critical claims about international cultural life. In Canada, for example, a strain of policy and a reigning common sense continues to presume an ability to know, with absolute certainty, that U.S. culture is colonizing Canadians, advancing what one might call an *episteme* of emergency. The lack of examination of how this operates and of how Canadians live the contradictions such a statement implies has positioned the unpredictable effects of culture outside even casual speculation. Part of the Canadian contradiction, familiar to many other national contexts, is the simultaneous attraction to and fear of U.S. culture. In fact, Appadurai suggests that this may be a vital feature of the contemporary world, in which there exists a "free-floating yearning for American style, even in the most intense contexts of opposition to the United States."[40]

For Appadurai, focusing on human creativity, on the imagination, extends the possibilities of acknowledging the accomplishments of people as we struggle to find a way to live in the modern world. His project is to "show that the work of the imagination, viewed in this context, is neither purely emancipatory nor entirely disciplined but is a space of contestation in which individuals and groups seek to annex the global into their own practices of the modern."[41] In this use, the imagination is not an independent realm of free thinking, but a product of historical context. The range of practices produced, regardless of the source of texts, is for Appadurai the very definition of culture. He writes, "I suggest that we regard as cultural only those differences that either express, or set the groundwork for, the mobilization of group identities."[42] Notice that the cultural here refers not to the formation nor the expression of identity, but to the *mobilization* of identity. Further, this version emphasizes group and not individual identity. The human labor, the cultural work, of thinking, reasoning, believing, and feeling contributes to the mediation of reality and what we take as true and worthy. Appadurai reminds us of the political dimensions of such labor: "The transformation of everyday subjectivities through electronic mediation and the work of the imagination is not only a cultural fact. It is deeply connected to politics, through the new ways in which individual attachments, interests, and aspirations increasingly crosscut those of the nation-state."[43]

For Appadurai, this mobility of people and culture is a mark of the end of modern notions of the nation-state, and the end of a modern notion of the public sphere as the obligatory element for democratic political life. Instead, our global imaginations require a conceptualization of a transnational and diasporic public sphere.

> As the nation-state enters a terminal crisis (if my prognostications prove to be correct), we can certainly expect that the materials for a post-national imaginary must be around us already. Here, I think we need to pay special attention to the relation between mass mediation and migration, the two facts that underpin my sense of the cultural politics of the global modern. In particular, we need to look closely at the variety of what have emerged as *diasporic public spheres.*[44]

One aspect should be added here. There are, of course, forces entirely outside the imagination pushing the need for new senses of transnational publics. When Appadurai writes, "We need to think ourselves beyond the nation,"[45] we would do well to remember that in many ways it is already being done for us, and not always in our best interests!

And Appadurai is mistaken to think the nation-state is in a free fall. Indeed, the "post-national imaginary" is part of a current form of national life. It is not a contradictory claim to dress up in nationalist clothing to beg for international culture or demand policy assistance to garner advantage in international markets. As the organization of markets reveals, we continue to address *countries,* each with its own historically varying policy and legal structures. In this way, Appadurai's call for a post-national imaginary cannot productively be seen as a response to an end of the nation-state, but rather as a reminder of the human energy at the root of culture, energy that, once attended to, guards us against uniformity in our analyses and forewarns us to avoid reducing cultural life to simple dichotomies.

The contemporary film business is an industry and cultural practice built around and reproducing certain ideas about links between the local and the global. The movie theater itself is one waystation for the migratory audience that Appadurai argues typifies the global. It is a site at which there is a fleeting lull in the mobility of people and culture. An inevitable scattering awaits when the lights go up again, but the situation is primarily one of rest. A screening can be a shared experience, a communal pleasure, and the various arrangements and activities—the kinds of food, the codes of when and how to talk, the flow of trailers, etc.—are an expression of cultural management conventions as much as they are aligned with a technological apparatus. Imagined communities of fans, of audience members, of cinemagoers, of film producers, of actors, and of citizens are all part of the occasion. Importantly, the site of the cinema is a physical location. It is an assemblage of practices, people, technologies, times, locations, and ideas. This assemblage resembles what Appadurai calls for in any theory of globalization—a linkage between the mobility of texts and contexts, and one that is empirically grounded (as many uses of his work have neglected to do). He writes,

> The structure of contexts cannot and should not be derived entirely from the logic and morphology of texts. Text production and context production have different logics and metapragmatic features. Contexts are produced in the complex imbrication of discursive and nondiscursive practices, and so the sense in which contexts imply other contexts, so that each context implies a global network of contexts, is different from the sense in which texts imply other texts, and eventually all texts. Intertextual relations, about which we now know a fair amount, are not likely to work in the same way as *intercontextual* relations. Last, and most daunting, is the prospect that we shall have to find ways to connect theories of intertextuality to theories of intercontextuality. A strong theory of globalization from a sociocultural point of view is likely to require something we certainly do not now have: a theory of intercontextual relations that incorporates our existing sense of intertexts.[46]

Intercontextual and intertextual relations mold the life of the cinema space, prominent vectors of which are the international and the intermedia qualities of culture. The "inter" overload of the preceding sentence is sadly unavoidable as it helps us keep our eyes on the "betweenness" and relationality of our objects of inquiry. This relationality forms the conjunctures through which social existence comes into being. For a variety of economic, cultural, and political reasons, cinemagoing currently refers to a particular encounter with a national and international cinema environment in a clearly defined location, one at home in your own community. This meeting point of the equally abstract sites of the global, the national, and the local gives each term a grounded existence, a material and experiential quality. What does this particular encounter result in? What does it highlight, what does it mask, and how is it historically unique, or at least historically specific?

This chapter began with evidence of the mobility and mutability of film commodities. It proposed that this empirical demonstration of screen traffic runs parallel to a conceptual set of claims concerning the indeterminacy of culture, its significance and its audiences. In the end, globalization and the cross-media trajectory of popular texts confronts us with the limits of how we understand the location and effects of culture, challenging how we delineate contexts for audience activity. The best work reminds us of the affective and imaginative elements of cultural life, ones not readily condensed into standardized models of cultural effects. Thus, I put forward that a point of departure for cultural analysis must be a compilation of the tracks left by intercontextual and intermedia cultural relations. For the present project, these relations of contemporary cinematic culture include, in part 2, a discursive analysis of industrial common sense about globalization, and the response to this common sense in another national context, Canada. Each facet of this inventory includes discussion of the new conditions of spectatorship arising from the temporary settlement of distribution and exhibition practices. The final two chapters chart the connections between the conditions of exhibition—that is, the forms, time, and spaces—and a contemporary structure of feeling involving the negotiation and division of global, national, and city cultures. This structure of feeling can be conveniently identified as a form of cosmopolitanism, or "felt internationalism." But first I want to address the theoretical stakes involved with the practice of public film consumption—that is, cinemagoing—and its relation to the state of film theory.

CHAPTER THREE

Matinees, Summers, and the Practice of Cinemagoing

In 1994, one of the major theater chains in Canada, Famous Players, became part of Sumner Redstone's Viacom empire, when he acquired Paramount. Soon after, Famous Players began to rattle unions, weaken job security, and generally make its employees as mobile and replaceable as possible. For example, the corporation, despite its own and Viacom's soaring profits, demanded 60 percent wage cuts from its projectionists in Alberta.[1] A six-month lockout and a (not especially well respected) boycott of their theaters followed. On one occasion, no doubt inspired by rally speaker William Christopher (TV's Father Mulcahy from *M*A*S*H*), protesters made their way through a theater lobby in Calgary using what Famous Players called "goon tactics." While the projectionist union denied that any of its members entered the theater, the corporation claimed to have videotape evidence of an assault and property damage. No criminal charges were laid, though a cardboard cutout of Sandra Bullock was sadly trampled in whatever melee took place. The corporation unsuccessfully petitioned the Alberta Labour Relations Board for an injunction against picketing at their theaters, though the Board ruled that protesters must keep a minimum of six feet from entrances. In a simple, but effective, understanding of global capital, the projectionists expanded their demonstrations to another Viacom company, Blockbuster Video.[2]

I begin with this anecdote in order to remind us of an obvious fact: the motion picture theater is not just a site of leisure; it is also a workplace. It is, if you will, someone's shopfloor and, potentially, a site of public protest. A reminder is in order because so much scholarship on film, so much of its theory, assures that the struggles I have just alluded to, as well as a range of extrafilmic practices at cinematic venues, will be neglected.

Though it may be discounted as merely facetious, it can be asserted that the problem with film studies has been *film*, that is, the use of a medium in order to designate the boundaries of a discipline.[3] Such a designation assumes a certain stability in what is actually a mutable technological apparatus. A problem ensues when it is apparent that film is not film anymore. It does not make any sense—and perhaps it never did—to say that there is a film culture as absolutely distinct from television, video, music, and amusement park cultures. The relationship between them is often one not of conflict but rather symbiosis or relationality.[4] These blurred boundaries between forms of audiovisual culture can no longer be brushed aside, as evidenced by a growing discussion about postcinema, a point of investigation that frequently serves to construct a false unity to "real" cinema. As appealing as it is to proclaim new periods, we are not in a postcinema era. We are, however, in an age after the monopolization of the motion picture theater as a site for moving-image culture. A *postcelluloid* cinema culture exists, the height of which are forms of digital projection and satellite distribution for cinemas, a development that unsettles traditional notions of how we are to understand public film performances. But, as Kevin Robins comments, "What is important . . . is the common actuality and the interplay of different orders of images within a specific social space. The point is that there are not just new technologies, but a whole range of available image forms—and consequently of ways of seeing, looking, watching—all of which are actually being mobilised and made use of, and in ways that are diverse and complex."[5] Robins's spatial emphasis helps highlight the interconnectedness of media forms. And indeed, in response to such calls for intermedia study, we see film departments and scholarly societies shuffling their names, becoming film and video, media, even cultural studies programs and organizations. This move often includes compiling courses in what are seen as adjacent fields of concern. A course on television, for example, is a now fairly standard part of cinema studies. Such trading up in more contemporary names does not mean that the focus of research or even the concentration of course offerings shifts coincidentally. At times, the new name can conceal a continuing understanding of research priorities. Adding "media studies" to a title, for example, does not mean all media are given identical attention, let alone professional respect.

If the current "versioning" of cultural studies for film departments, which is well underway, is to make film scholars rethink their practice, it should ask the following question: What would it take for film studies to abandon "film" per se as an empirical certainty for anyone but archivists who are charged with the care of the physical object? Instead, film is a set of conditions, unfolding in time, as much as it is a sequence of images and sounds. The film performance varies across time and across consumption contexts and carries a degree of unpredictability with it. *No two screenings are absolutely identical.* The people involved will be different, the print will have aged and new scratches will appear, the time of day might change, one's seat might be at a different angle, the sound might be at a louder volume, the sound system might be worse, one might be eating something different or be in a different mood, and the auditorium might have more comfortable seats. Or one might not even be at a cinema but rather be watching at home, at a drive-in, in a plane, in a classroom, at a library theater, at a bar, or in an airport, all of which increase the chance that one will not see the film without distraction. This itemization might be continued by thinking of the manifold and imaginative ways in which film becomes part of a lived and ordinary culture, as informal background to gatherings, as excuses for close-knit groups to congregate, as objects of intense personal rapture. Some might protest that these are not all ideal conditions, nor are they how the film was meant to be seen. This counterargument, however, is utterly unsatisfactory for it willfully ignores the essential properties of the aging of texts, the unfolding of film in time, and the movement of film through space, or what Walter Benjamin described as film's "exhibition value."[6] These three qualities alone, by definition, introduce changing conditions to each film performance and undercut attempts to police the "right" kinds of viewing circumstances.

And yet it would be an equally grave mistake to assert that there is no connection or consistency between each of those viewing conditions. Indeed, a chief operation of the film apparatus has been to assure and promote this consistency. Industry agents, from marketers to cinema designers, have attempted to conceptualize an unwavering text and event, one that suits an image of a standardized and predictable cinema patron. Therefore, given the inherently shifting nature of the film performance, one place to begin is an analysis of how film is "made" to be whole and imagined as something unique and unified in scholarly and in industry endeavors. Nowhere is this project of imagining the wholeness and consistency of the film event more evident than in the concept of the spectator.

Miriam Hansen opines that film studies has moved beyond apparatus theories, typified by Laura Mulvey's "Visual Pleasure and Narrative Cinema," and that such technologically deterministic approaches to spectatorship themselves now invoke a sense of historical distance.[7] She goes so far as to say that psychoanalytic-semiotic theories of spectatorship are obsolete, having been replaced by more historically specific examinations.[8] But, for her purposes, it is especially important that spectatorship itself has mutated to a "post-classical" phase, and that "the historical significance of 1970s theories of spectatorship may well be that they emerged at the threshold of a paradigmatic transformation of the ways films are disseminated and consumed. In other words, even as these theories set out to unmask the ideological effects of the classical Hollywood cinema, they might effectively, and perhaps unwittingly, have mummified the spectator-subject of classical cinema."[9] The might of this statement raises questions of the discursive effects of film theory on the reproduction of spectatorial relations. In the dominant histories, the shift from silent to sound film denotes the moment at which a new cinema audience emerged (though Hansen dates this a little earlier). This narrative poses that new classical cinema subject as a resolution to an original rupture, and a bourgeois, apolitical one at that. These spectators, with a rising presumption of standardized comportment at the cinema, were effectively interchangeable and taken as undifferentiated across time and location.

Pointing to a contemporary interest in policing noisy audiences, to the multiple subject positions apparent in the "blockbuster" film, and to the transnational operations of popular film, Hansen claims that "we are witnessing the end of 'modern' mass culture," as characterized by standardization and homogenization of industrial cultural forms.[10] She rightly comments that the forms of global cultural diversity do not guarantee a corresponding political openness, though certain opportunities exist that previously did not. "At any rate, whatever political score one may assign to these developments, it is obvious that they require theories of reception and identification different from those predicated on classical Hollywood cinema and the American model of mass culture."[11] For her part, Hansen draws comparisons between the early preclassical and contemporary postclassical cinema, with special attention to the parallel formations of public life, and makes a case for the use of the concept of the public as a way to avoid excessive faith in the political agency of consumption. Her focus is on a version of Jürgen Habermas's rational public as the required element of democratic community, and, through Alexander Kluge, a model of the alternative public sphere.

As evocative as her observations are, she tends toward an overstatement of the connection by claiming that "pre-classical and post-classical forms of spectatorship give the viewer a greater leeway, for better or worse, in interacting with the film, a greater awareness of exhibition and cultural intertexts."[12] Such a statement rests on a presumption of relative passivity in the consumption of classical film texts. She continues, "Both early-modern and postmodern media publics draw on the *periphery:* then, on socially marginalised and diverse constituencies within American national culture: today, on massive movements of migration on a global scale which, along with the globalization of media consumption, have irrevocably changed the terms of local and national identity."[13] Consequently, a stable, unified classical spectator is the apolitical agent against which the more participatory and marginalized crowds of pre- and postclassical eras figure. Such an argument strikes me as close to the continued mummification of the classical spectator with which she opens her critique.

Still, Hansen highlights an invaluable aspect: the classical spectator first and foremost is the product of discourse. Moments of emergent forms, and instances of settlement, to be sure, mark the history of cinema and its relation to community life. And further, the shift to sound is absolutely central. But the tale does not stop there; the cinematic subject, the audience, has continued to be formed and re-formed throughout the history of cinema, a product of converging forces including the economic, technological, and textual. Film exhibition has never been a static enterprise. Various forces have assured a continued destabilization of spectatorial relations, and in this and the following chapters I will identify some of those contemporary forces propelling a reconstitution of the site and practice of cinema. The general point is that it is important to understand the way that film exhibition, as an industrial and cultural endeavor, is invested in a project of stabilization, of making audiences and making—or imagining—them as readable, predictable, and knowable.

CINEMAGOING PRACTICE AND THE EVERYDAY

Motion pictures have been coterminous with, and perhaps responsible for, a fundamental shift in how aesthetics and representational practices are understood. Work on the relation between early cinema and modernity demonstrates that new modes of visuality were key to the emergence of the modern era, as well as modernism, though cinema was not singular in this but continuous with a range of visual technologies, both popular and experimental.[14] After the broad dissemination and adoption of film as a popular representational form in the twentieth century, never again could the concept of mimesis be understood without reference to its influence. Among other developments, the simultaneous belief in and distrust of the moving image, that is, the faith in its facility as a recording medium and the expectation of distortion and manipulation of that record, have left us with a malleable and fluid notion of time and space. Indeed, it is odd to see pundits of digital media make similar assertions about new representational technologies in woeful ignorance of the historical precedents. In short, our world is one in which time and space are expected to be made and remade on an ongoing basis, and film figures as symptomatic and emblematic of that expectation.

So powerful have the representational aspects of motion pictures been in the reimagining of time and space that scholars and critics tend to neglect other equally significant consequences. The seductive moving image and the glowing wonders of public projections successfully captured the attentions of audiences and theorists, fans and philosophers, alike. While the historical connections to text-minded disciplines, including literary and art criticism, assure a similar focus for film scholars, it is worth remembering that foundational claims often begin with presumptions about the supposed nature of the large, public, moving image and a related imagined audience. In this, audiences have figured less as a sociological entity and more as a textual construction. Commenting on the dominance of this apprach, Janet Staiger cogently argues for a historical materialist approach to reception, one that responds to the continuing centrality of textual study.[15] Judith Mayne notes that despite an expanded scope considering groups of films, publicity, magazines, and other intertextual designations, the approach has remained essentially textual. Conversely, audiences vanish into the speculative. As she writes, "Spectatorship occurs at precisely those spaces where 'subjects' and 'viewers' rub against each other. In other words, I believe that the interest in spectatorship in film studies attests to a discomfort with either a too easy separation *or* a too easy collapse of the subject and the viewer."[16] With regard to historical methods, she contends that

> textual analysis has not been rejected but rather revised. For a common point of agreement in studies of intertextuality, exhibition, the cinematic public sphere, and reception is the need not to reject textual analysis, but rather to expand its parameters beyond the individual film text. Textual analysis thus becomes attentive to the intersecting and sometimes contradictory ways in which different forms of address function across different textual registers.[17]

As Mayne goes on to propose a nuanced but decidedly textual approach, I remain convinced by her initial point, that the liability has been a relegation of audiences to the realm of either neglect or speculation. From psychoanalytic to phenomenological approaches, it seems that film's effects and relations stem, at least initially, from the stylistic qualities and conventions of the unfolding, visually rendered text.

While wanting to continue a study of textual consequences, or what he calls a "commercial aesthetic," Richard Maltby challenges the premise of the classical Hollywood narrative by reasoning that such a focus cannot take into account the varieties of spectatorial conditions and industrial determinations, especially in the age of conglomeration. He writes, "the phenomena of multiple formats, repeat viewings and modularity question the centrality of narrative and the concept of a 'univocal reading' solicited by classical film. An alternative historical framework, privileging economic relations rather than product styling, would provide a different account."[18] To this excellent call for close examination of the economic forces guiding the contexts of film and audiences, we might add Douglas Gomery's interest in corporate strategies, that is, the sorts of decisions made in the process of "doing business," because this allows us to "better understand how the 'film industry' as business, social and cultural practice has continued to dominate mass entertainment image making."[19]

Aspects of film's culture of time and space beyond its textual embodiment require consideration, for film equally unsettles community time and space.[20] Mayne writes, "The relationship between specific social groups and how they identify themselves as participants in the public sphere of the cinema offers the opportunity to examine how cinema has played a crucial role in the very notion of community."[21] Just as motion pictures call for a new relation to the aesthetics of narrative and the conventions of realism, among other representational issues, so too does the very location, structure, and regulation of public screening venues question a modernist understanding and experience of public space, urban life, and cultural identity. Motion pictures did not introduce streams of moving images only. They also introduced new kinds of theaters, spectatorial conditions, and related activities. Investigations into cinematic culture require a consideration of the range of practices in specially constructed and managed spaces—in other words, film exhibition. An artifactual approach to film can only point to some of this. Instead, movies as assemblages of motives, memories, architectures, labors, habits, and governances signal supplementary dimensions.

Several histories have traced the shifting relations among film form, theater space, and cinematic technologies. Examples include the history of the nickelodeon, the movie palaces, the introduction of sound and various projection innovations, the drive-in and multiplex cinemas.[22] Other histories have focused on industrial structure, especially the economic relationship between production, distribution, and exhibition.[23] These important works of social history and political economy still leave a range of cultural forces, powers, and determinations to be taken into account, in particular the discursive construction of the abstract entity we describe as movie audiences. Among those doing strong work on exhibition culture are Kathryn H. Fuller[24] and Gregory A. Waller, both of whom effectively pick up where Rosenzweig leaves off. Waller explains, "I have taken 'the public dimension' to include not only what went on in theaters but also the way audiences were represented, the attempts to assert local government control over cheap amusements, the various religious and secular reform campaigns, and the influential role of the local press in promoting, reporting on, and editorializing about the movies."[25] For this question of the "public dimension" and representation of film audiences, the specificity of film exhibition is a crucial site of analysis. One might consider, for example, exhibition's "fit" with or relation to an array of other cultural practices, sites, and industrial determinants. Robert C. Allen incisively points out, in a move away from the conventions of film theory and film history toward cultural studies, that the question of exhibition should not be approached in isolation.[26] Instead, he proposes reception as the concept under which the intersecting components of industrial dimensions (exhibition), sociodemographic characteristics (audience), projection contexts (performance), and signification (activation) reside.

Similarly, Jeanne Allen, in an early expanded contextual approach, highlights different levels of determination that form a connection between film viewing and consumerism in general in her discussion of the interwar period. She writes:

(1) access to film viewing was a highly visible manifestation of participation in a rich consumer environment; (2) the physical conditions of film exhibition fostered a liaison between film viewing and consumer behavior— national chains, proximity to shopping districts, the splendor of the theater, the material splendor on the screen in a darkened hall; (3) the commercial relations between the film industry and other business[es] existed to produce commercial films or to exhibit commercial products in theatrical films.[27]

Allen submits these three aspects of cinemagoing's publicness, its location and architecture, and horizontal relations between film and other commerical enterprises as part of the necessity of considering a wider consumer environment. They neatly sum up contemporary developments as well.

In calling for long overdue attention to methodology in film studies, Jackie Stacey too finds the reigning paradigms of textual approaches have left us with an underdeveloped sense of cinema audiences. She turns to television and reception studies, especially the work of Ien Ang, Charlotte Brunsdon, and Janice Radway as models for the kind of research lacking in film studies.[28] Where film studies has yet to assimilate fully the theoretical contributions of cultural studies, not so for television studies. A number of excellent works examine television's context by tracing the shifting social and cultural relations of domestic space in light of changing configurations of technologies.[29] Except for some research on theme parks and some on late nineteenth- and early twentieth-century public amusements, few have brought the important theoretical insights of studies of domestic media to bear on out-of-home leisure, especially public film exhibition.[30] In the context of a continued reworking of the distinctions between public and private, and the theoretical challenges of the materiality of audiences, such investigations seem especially woefully missing.

The complexities of the interrelationship between everyday life and television are well theorized and equally well appreciated. Rita Felski evocatively describes the conceptual challenge as follows: "At first glance, everyday life seems to be everywhere, yet nowhere. Because it has no clear boundaries, it is difficult to identify. Everyday life is synonymous with the habitual, the ordinary, the mundane, yet it is also strangely elusive, that which resists our understanding and escapes our grasp. Like the blurred speck at the edge of one's vision that disappears when looked at directly, the everyday ceases to be everyday when it is subject to critical scrutiny."[31] We might ask, then, why this "blur" has been so well considered with television and not with film. One explanation for the comparatively slow taking up of film and the everyday might be the apparent rhetorical collapse in the distinction between the everyday and the domestic; in much scholarship, the latter term appears as a powerful trope of the former. It is as though no matter how ordinary film is, TV is more so. One consequence of this presumption has been the absenting of a myriad of other—if you will, extradomestic—manifestations of everydayness, unfortunately encouraging a rather literal understanding of the everyday. In effect, *the abstractions of the everyday are reduced to daily occurrences,* and the presumed status of film as more of an "event" and less frequently attended marks its break from the everyday.

This crude binary is a philosophically untenable proposition. It leads us into unproductive digressions about how frequent is the "everyday." Most assuredly, the intermedia relations among film, video, broadcasting, music, Internet, and so on should undo such received wisdom about fixed and stable media qualities. Instead, we need to address the place and occasion of cinemagoing in light of these intermedia meldings. Cinema culture is woven into daily life in a host of ways—marquees adorn our cities; video rental outlets dot local malls; star interviews and production news inhabit our television schedules; film posters decorate bedrooms, offices, and construction sites; promotional T-shirts are worn; entertainment sections occupy space in newspapers; celebrity gossip forms ordinary sociability; and stars' faces and styles hail us in commercial venues. Though for many the act of cinemagoing might occur less than once every few months, cinemagoing is but one enactment of the structure and expression of cinema culture. It is one detail in the pattern. In short, there is no reason why the points of departure for critical inquiry that have so completely and profitably informed television studies could not equally speak to out-of-home technologies and cultural forms, that is, other sites and locations of the everyday.

I am taken by the number of times arguments for cultural/contextual/audience research in film have been proffered. For instance, Robert F. Arnold claimed in 1990 "that an understanding of 'going to the movies' as a historically determined social practice is a necessary starting point for a theory of film reception."[32] Additionally, intermedia continuities make it essential to address not only what people see but where and when they see it. As windows of exhibition open up, audiences are sent asunder, hence demanding new understandings of location. As Robins puts it, the task of cultural analysis should not be cinema but "the interplay of different order of images within a specific social space." Developing just such a critique of film studies, James Hay proposes that instead of the discreteness of the cinema, we might understand

> film as practiced among different social sites, always in relation to other sites, and engaged by social subjects who move among sites and whose mobility, access to, and investment in cinema conditions is conditioned by these relations among sites. To shift strategies in this way would involve not only decentering film as an object of study, but also focusing instead on how film practice occurs from and through particular sites—of re-emphasizing the *site* of film practice *as* a spatial issue or problematic.[33]

In other words, treating the spatial and temporal determinations of film might point us to the specificities of location and practice, as challenging as this might be to our methods and theoretical presumptions. For example, even in an otherwise instructive discussion of questions of space and film between Karen Lury and Doreen Massey, an unfortunate binary emerges, with film associated with representations of space (discussions of particular films, for example) and television with the routines and flows of domestic life.[34]

In 1976 Michel Foucault wrote, "A whole history remains to be written of *spaces*—which would at the same time be the history of *powers* . . . from the great strategies of geopolitics to the little tactics of the habitat."[35] Given the subsequent rush to understand relations between space and culture, it would appear that Foucault's comments were prescient. Indeed, there now exist influential variations in cultural theory that could be described as spatialized critiques of power and practice. This is not to say that Foucault should be specially credited with this turn. Though important to the denaturalizing of space in theory, he was preceded by such diverse critics as Harold Innis and Henri Lefebvre.[36] The crucial component of contemporary theories of space is, as Doreen Massey succinctly puts it, "no spaces are stable, given for all time; all spaces are transitory and one of the most crucial things about spatiality . . . is that it is always being made."[37]

In the production of space, correspondences between human agency and economic apparatuses are made visible. Where Foucault wants to draw our attention to the question of scale, pointing out the spatial dimensions of both the everyday contexts and vast global designs, Michel de Certeau alerts us to a distinction between space and place, where "*space is a practiced place*,"[38] thus emphasizing the link between site and agency. Though some may see this as a proposal for typologies, more modestly he aims to highlight the ingenuity and diversity of human action. He does not offer programs for the identification and analysis of the coordination of such action and creativity, and this may be the root of some doubts about de Certeau's political import. Reading *The Practice of Everyday Life*, one has an image of bodies moving about, engaged and active; it presents a poetics of ordinary energy. It is about horizons of possibility in human endeavor, which, arguably, is a point of initialization for any reading of politics and ideology. For de Certeau, locality plays a strong role here; it is where those horizons appear and are felt. He discusses "theaters of action" as locations of fragmented, miniaturized, and polyvalent forms of social interactions.[39]

One path into the everyday nature of the film experience and forms of public spectatorship, after de Certeau, and to apply Hay's call for "re-emphasizing the *site* of film *as* a spatial issue," is to be alert to the fact that "watching" is not a singular nor straightforward activity; "watching" consists of a variety of behaviors, actions, moods, and intentions. De Certeau reminds us of the elaborate bodily actions involved in reading. He writes, "We should try to rediscover the movements of this reading within the body itself, which seems to stay docile and silent but mines the reading in its own way: from the nooks of all sorts of 'reading rooms' (including lavatories) emerge subconscious gestures, grumblings, tics, stretchings, rustlings, unexpected noises, in short a wild orchestration of the body."[40] In models of film spectatorship, these "wild orchestrations" are rarely if ever acknowledged. With conventional treatments of film viewing, one could get the impression that it is a state of being force-fed images and sounds, rather like Alex in *A Clockwork Orange* (Stanley Kubrick 1971), eyelids pried apart and head fastened in place (or for that matter, Joseph in *The Parallax View* [Alan J. Pakula 1974], or Steve in *Disturbing Behavior* [David Nutter 1998]).

Further complicating this is the observation that cinemagoing does not involve only film viewing, a fact that is being accented further in the context of the megaplex cinemas. Similarly, in his episodic narrative of shifting exhibition contexts, Kevin Corbett recommends treating the movie theater as a technology so that the components of design, cinema technology, lobby operations, and audience activity might all be considered part of an organic and functioning whole.[41] The public film experience involves other forms of media consumption, including magazines, video displays, trailers for coming attractions, advertisements, radio broadcasts, taped music, and video games. To understand the practice of cinemagoing, a configuration of media consumption and social activity beyond film consumption must be drawn in for examination.

Public movie performances are occasions for eating, for disregarding one's usual dietary strictures, for knowingly overpaying for too much food, for sneaking snacks and drinks, for both planned and impromptu socializing, for working, for flirting, for sexual play, for gossiping, for staking out territory in theater seats, for threatening noisy spectators, for being threatened, for arguments, for reading, for talking about future moviegoing, for relaxing, for sharing in the experience of the screening with other audience members, for fleeting glimpses at possible alliances and allegiances of taste, politics, and identity, for being too close to strangers, for being crowded in your winter clothes, for being frozen by overactive air-conditioning, for being bored, for sleeping, for disappointment, for joy, for arousal, for disgust, for slouching, for hand holding, for drug taking, for standing in lines, for making phone calls, for playing video games, for the evaluation of trailers, for discussions of what preceded the film and of what will follow, and for both remembering and forgetting oneself. One could continue this rapidly constructed list, perhaps to include more inventive, subversive, even criminal practices. But, I suspect there is a degree of recognition invited by the range of actions presented. Here, cinemagoing is banal, it is erotic, it is civil, it is unruly; it is an everyday site of regulated and unregulated possibility.

In other words, public film viewing must be apprehended as a cultural *practice*. The term "cinemagoing" conveniently captures the physical mobility involved, the necessary negotiation of community space, the process of consumer selection, and the multiple activities that one engages in before, during, and after a film performance. Anne Friedberg's work offers substantial promise for just such a framework. In her documentation of the analogous relations between the sites and practices of shopping and cinema, she describes "the new aesthetic of reception found in 'moviegoing' " as "mobilized visuality."[42] In the present context, this "mobility" of reception is partly a product of the fact that movie theaters no longer have an exclusive claim on film spectatorship; or conversely, a specificity to film spectatorship arises from the current circumstance in which movies can be seen away from the cinema.

To be sure, this alarms many film purists. As Mayne observes, "Like many film scholars, I remember with considerable nostalgia the neighborhood theaters where I saw virtually all of the films that remain the privileged texts in my own history as a film spectator, and I bemoan the growth of multiplex, shopping-mall cinemas and the domination of 'film' exhibition by the remarkable development of home VCRs that characterize contemporary film reception."[43] Self-reflexively, she continues to wonder about the impact this nostalgic stance has had: "there has been considerable reluctance on the part of film scholars to examine the extent to which their own memories and fantasies of the exhibition context shape their theoretical enterprise."[44] It is essential to confront the limitations placed on our scholarship by such laments for passing cultural relations. We might begin by acknowledging that the expansion of film culture to include the various television- and computer-related technologies has not marked a demise of cinemagoing. Instead, we have seen, and continue to witness, a reformulation of what it means to go to the cinema, that is, *a reconfiguration of the practice of cinemagoing*.

De Certeau comments on the inadequate dichotomy of representation and behavior, observing that "the analysis of the images broadcast by television (representation) and of the time spent watching television (behavior) should be complemented by a study of what the cultural consumer 'makes' or 'does' during this time and with these images. The same goes for the use of urban space, the products purchased in the supermarket, the stories and legends distributed by the newspapers, and so on."[45] For him, the movement and encounter with the ordinary cultural world described here are actually "procedures of everyday creativity."[46] To extend this approach, images, sounds, bodies, labor, and capital all flow through the space of the cinema. It is a site of social interaction, entertainment, aesthetic pleasure, boredom; it is a foundation for the organization of personal and collective memories. Taken in this way, the motion picture theater is a heterogeneous space in which the possibilities and limits of personal and social existence are encountered, assessed, and articulated to other practices, remembered and immediate. This implies that cinemagoing is a nodal point for meaning, memories, and activities. The practice flourishes in the shadow of a culture industry seeking to profit from the anticipation, organization, and distribution of popular desires and expectations, hence it is involved in the discursive construction of cinemagoing. I turn now to some of the more pronounced dimensions of the structured site and event of public motion picture presentations.

STREAMLINED AUDIENCES, EXHIBITION SITES, AND TEMPORALITY

As aspects of a culture industry, film exhibition and distribution rely on an understanding of both the market and the product or service being sold at any given point in time. Operations respond to economic conditions, competing companies, and alternative activities. Economic rationality in these strategic processes, however, only explains so much. This is especially true for an industry that must continually predict, and arguably give shape to, the "mood" and predilections of disparate and distant audiences. Producers, distributors, and exhibitors assess which films will "work" and to whom they will be marketed, as well as establish the very terms of success. Without a doubt, much of the film industry's strategies work to reduce market uncertainty; for example, the various forms of textual continuity (genre films, star performances, etc.) and the economics of mass advertising are ways to ensure box office receipts. Yet at the core of the operations of film exhibition and distribution remain a number of flexible assumptions about audience activity, taste, and desire. These assumptions emerge from a variety of sources to form a brand of temporary industry common sense, and as such are harbingers of an industrial logic.

Ien Ang has usefully pursued this view in her comparative analysis of three national television structures and their operating assumptions about audiences. Broadcasters streamline and discipline audiences as part of their organizational procedures, with the consequence of shaping ideas about consumers as well as assuring the reproduction of the industrial structure itself. Ang writes, "Institutional knowledge is driven toward making the audience visible in such a way that it helps the institutions to increase their power to get their relationship with the audience under control, and this can only be done by symbolically constructing 'television audience' as an objectified category of others that can be controlled, that is, contained in the interest of a predetermined institutional goal."[47] Ang demonstrates, in particular, how various industrially sanctioned programming strategies (strips of programs, "hammocking" new shows between successful ones, and counterprogramming to a competitor's strengths) and modes of audience measurement grow out of those institutional goals. And, most crucially, her approach is not an effort to ascertain the empirical certainty of "actual" audiences. Instead, she charts the discursive terrain in which the abstract concept of audience becomes material for the continuation of industry practices; from this another materiality—for instance, schedules, length of programming runs, alternation between show and commercial— results that provides the boundaries for audience consumption.

Ang's work tenders special insight to the study of film culture. As with the best of television scholarship, it directs us toward an exploration of the routine procedures and operations of both industry and audience. One dimension of these routines is television time and scheduling. David Morley points to the role of television in structuring everyday life, discussing a range of research that emphasizes the temporal dimension. Alerting us to the variability of television scheduling, he comments that we "need to maintain a sensitivity to these micro-levels of division and differentiation while we attend to the macro-questions of the media's own role in the social structuring of time."[48] As such, the negotiation of temporal structures implies that schedules are not mono-lithic impositions of order. Indeed, as Morley puts it, they "must be seen as both entering into already constructed, historically specific divisions of space and time, and also as transforming those pre-existing divisions."[49] Television's tem-poral grid has been addressed by others as well. Paddy Scannell characterizes scheduling and continuity techniques, which link programs, as a standardiza-tion of use, making radio and television predictable, "user friendly" media.[50] John Caughie refers to the organization of the flow of texts as a way of talk about the national particularities of British and American television.[51] Ann Gray's detailed interviews with women about VCR usage reveals unforeseen modes of consumption and unpredictable meanings of that technology as it became situated in their daily routines.[52] All, while making their own contribu-tions, appeal to a rigorous accounting for viewing context as part of any study of audience, consumption, or experience. Uncovering the practices of televi-sion programmers as they attempt to apprehend and create viewing conditions for their audiences is a necessary initial step in this direction.

As we have seen, the inherent temporal and spatial variability of the film performance assures that the audience itself reflects this fundamental incon-stancy. And yet efforts are made to streamline and apprehend film audiences nonetheless, whether on the part of industry, as it tries to know and predict markets, or audiences themselves, as they come to routinize their leisure prac-tices. In this manner, despite the intermedia characteristics of commodities and practices, cinemagoing emerges as temporally and spatially distinct from other sites and times of audiovisual activity, and recognizably so. My call is for the extension of this vein of television scholarship to out-of-home technologies and cultural practices. In so doing, we pay attention to extratextual structures of cinematic life; other regimes of knowledge, power, subjectivity, and practice appear. Film audiences as a site of inquiry require a discussion about the ordinary, the calculated, *and* the casual practices of cinematic engagement. Such a discussion charts institutional knowledge, identifying operating strategies and recognizing the creativity and multidimensionality of cinemagoing. *What are the discursive parameters within which the film industry imagines cinema audiences and their routine actions? What are the related implications for the structures in which the practice of cinemagoing occurs and is recognizable as distinct from other forms of audiovisual engagement?*

One set of those structures of audience and industry practice involves the temporal dimension of film exhibition and distribution. In what follows, I propose a typology of three vectors of the temporality of cinema spaces (meaning that I will not address issues of diegetic time). My observations, of course, emerge from relatively recent industrial discourse in the United States and Canada and are not intended as general characterizations.

First, the running times of films encourage turnovers of the audience during the course of a single day at each screen. These show times coordinate cinemagoing and regulate leisure time. Whether the film is a lengthy epic or shorter standard fare, a foundational aspect of cinemagoing is the planning it entails. Even in the most impromptu instances, one has to consider meeting places, ticket line-ups, and competing responsibilities. One arranges childcare, postpones household chores, or rushes to finish a meal. One organizes transportation and thinks about routes, traffic, parking or public transit. And during the course of making plans for a trip to the cinema, whether alone or in the company of others, typically one turns to locate a list of what's playing and the corresponding show times in newspapers or through telephone and online services. There are those who decide which film to see on site, and, anecdotally, some comment that they no longer decide which movie to see, but *where* to see a (any) movie. Indeed, one of the significant reworkings of cinemagoing in recent years has been the expansion of start-times made available in larger multiplexes. Still, a film's start-time figures as a point of coordination as much as the film itself and location of the theater do. The schedule is essential to the routinization of filmgoing and its imbrication with other media and social engagements, as schedules only ever exist in relation to other schedules, other organizations of time in our lives.

Knowing the codes of screenings and the time provided for seating, snack purchases, socializing, and departure means participating in an extension of a model of labor and service administration. Even with the staggered times offered by multiplex cinemas, schedules still lay down a template around which other activities have to be arrayed by the cinemagoer. As audiences move to and through the theater, the schedule endeavors to regulate practice, making us the subjects of a temporal grid as well as of the film itself. To be sure, one can arrive late and leave early, confounding the schedule's organizing force. However, even these vaguely unruly actions leave the temporal parameters intact, and perhaps even work to make visible the industrial efforts to standardize exhibitors' services.

Running times incorporate more texts than the feature presentation alone. Where in the past there were programs of features and short subjects, there are now advertisements, trailers for coming attractions, trailers for films now playing in neighboring auditoriums, promotional shorts demonstrating new sound systems, public service announcements, reminders to turn off cell phones and pagers, and the exhibitor's own signature clips. In the last few years it has not been uncommon for me to clock the ads and announcements preceding the feature at twenty minutes. A growing focal point for filmgoing, these introductory texts received a boost in 1990, when the MPAA changed its standards for the length of trailers, inflating it from ninety seconds to a full two minutes. It is worth remembering that the production of trailers is minor industry of its own. From the late 1960s on, studios sought out independent production for trailers, resulting in the roughly twenty main houses dealing primarily in trailers of the 1990s.[53]

This intertextuality built into screening times needs to be supplemented with a consideration of intermedia appeals. For example, advertisements for television began appearing with regularity in theaters in the 1990s, including trailers for movie features on TNT and news shows on ABC. To the claim that "TV and movies compete for the same viewers and thus movie theaters are slitting their throats by encouraging audiences to stay home," an ABC executive responded, "That's stupid."[54] Screenvision Cinema Network, a company that brokers advertising deals with chains for a range of products, tried to make its advertising look as much as possible like a movie trailer in order to overcome any resistance audiences might feel toward commercials in cinemas.[55] Another, National Cinema Network, sells "cinema billboards" that project slides for products.[56] Not everyone felt the special nonadvertising characteristic of cinemas should be eroded. For instance, Disney's refusal to allow commercials before its films, which took effect with the release of *Pretty Woman* (Garry Marshall 1990), was met with eventual acquiescence by the major chains, though Cineplex Odeon stubbornly held out.[57] Regardless, a general environment of advertising and media forms means that many lobbies and auditoriums of multiplex cinemas offer a variety of appeals, including video previews, magazines, arcades, and virtual reality games. The evidence indicates that motion pictures are not the only media scheduled by theater managers and that there is an explicit attempt to integrate a cinema's texts with those at other sites and locations.

Thus an exhibitor's schedule accommodates an intertextual and intermedia strip. In a limited fashion, this is analogous to Raymond Williams's concept of "flow," which he characterizes by stating, "In all communication systems before broadcasting the essential items were discrete."[58] Certainly, the flow between trailers, advertisements, and feature presentations is not identical to that of the endless, ongoing text of television. There are not the same possibilities for "interruption" that Williams emphasizes with respect to broadcasting flow. Further, in theatrical exhibition, there is an end-time, a time at which there is a public acknowledgment of the completion of the projected performance, one that necessitates vacating the cinema. This end-time is a moment at which the "rental" of the space (one's seat) has come due, and it beckons a return to the street, to the negotiation of city space, to modes of public transit, and to the mobile privatization of cars. Nonetheless, the schedule and running time constructs a temporal boundary in which audiences encounter a range of texts and media in what might be seen as limited flow.

A second vector of temporality is the length of the theatrical run, meaning the number of weeks a film plays in a theater before being replaced by a newer text. The ephemerality of audiences—moving to the cinema, consuming its texts, then passing the seat on to someone else—is matched by the ephemerality of the features themselves. Distributors' demand for increasing numbers of screens necessary for massive, saturation openings has meant that films now replace one another more rapidly than in earlier eras. Films that would have run for months now get weeks, with fewer exceptions. Wider openings and shorter runs have created a cinemagoing culture characterized by flux. As Disney executive Jeffrey Katzenberg said, "Thanks to the dictates of the block-buster mentality, the shelf life of many movies has come to be somewhat shorter than [that of] a supermarket tomato."[59] The acceleration of the turn-over of films has been made possible by the expansion of various additional markets for distribution, most vitally videotape, scattering where we might find audiences and multiplying viewing contexts. In essence, film texts *grow old elsewhere.* Speeding up the popular in this fashion means that the influence of individual texts can be truly gauged only via cross-media scrutiny. It also im-plies, as William Paul cleverly puts it, "Now, in effect, the word-of-mouth must exist before any moviegoer has actually seen the film, a peculiar situation to be sure."[60]

Short theatrical runs are not axiomatically designed for cinemagoers any-more. They can also be intended to attract the attention of video renters, purchasers, and retailers. Independent video distributors, especially, "view the-atrical release as a marketing expense, not a profit center."[61] In this respect, we might think of such theatrical runs as "trailers" or "loss leaders" for the video-tape market, with selected locations for a film's release potentially providing visibility, even prestige, in certain city markets or neighborhoods. This is made explicit in *Playback*'s description of the release strategy for *The Kingdom* (Lars von Trier 1995): "It is . . . hoped that the rep release campaign will boost video sales, sort of like running a trailer for video."[62] Distributors are able to count on some promotion through popular consumer-guide reviews usually accompany-ing theatrical openings as opposed to the passing critical attention given to video release. Consequently, this shapes the uses to which an assessment of the current cinema is put. Acknowledging that new releases function as a resource for cin-ema knowledge highlights the way audiences determine the difference between big screen and small screen films. Taken in this manner, popular audiences see the current cinema as largely a rough catalogue of future cultural consumption.

The other exhibition windows are major industry sectors in their own right, and not simply dumping grounds for film distributors. Television networks see movies as especially attractive because, as it is understood, they tend to attract young male viewers, and they do better in multiple broadcasts than made-for-TV movies. Further, because film distributors "pre-sell" them for their theatrical release, the films require less promotion on the part of broadcasters.[63] Part of the appeal, then, of theatrically released films for broadcasters is that cinemas, because of the promotion surrounding film openings, are highly visible venues at which people come to be aware of new cultural texts. Excepting the more exclusive environment of film festivals, cinematic releases initiate a long, intermedia lifespan of a popular work. Thus theatrical releasing harbors signs of the new and the novel in audiovisual culture.

The third vector is motion picture release and its relationship to the calendar. Releasing is part of the structure of memories and activities over the course of a year. It equally provides a rhythm to a week, with some days more regularly associated with moviegoing than others (much to the chagrin of exhibitors who strive to spread patrons through the day and week with discount pricing). New films appear in informal and ever-fluctuating "seasons." The concepts of summer movies and Christmas films, of opening weekends that are marked by a holiday, set up a fit between cinemagoing and other activities, among them family gatherings and celebrations. Industry measurement firm AC Nielsen EDI offers a service that compiles school holidays and enrollment data for districts across Canada and the United States, asserting that "motion picture distribution and exhibition entities have long had a need to know when students are out of school."[64] This fit between the operations of exhibitors, the release plans of distributors, and people's vacation schedules is resonant for both the industry and popular audiences alike, though certainly for different reasons. The concentration of new films around visible holiday periods results in a temporally defined dearth of cinemas. An inordinate focus on three periods in the year in the United States and Canada—the last weekend in May; June/July/August; and December—creates seasonal shortages of screens.[65] In fact, the boom in theater construction through the latter half of the 1990s was, in part, to deal with those short-term shortages and not some year-round inadequate seating.

Configurations of releasing color a calendar with the tactical maneuvers of distributors and exhibitors. Television arranges programs to capitalize on flow, to carry audiences forward, and to counterprogram competitors' simultaneous offerings. Similarly, distributors jostle with each other, with their films, and with key dates for the limited weekends available, hoping to match a competitor's film intended for one audience with one intended for another. Industry reporter Leonard Klady sketches some of the contemporary truisms of releasing based on the occurrences in 1997. He remarks on the success of moving *Liar Liar* (Tom Shadyac 1997) to a March opening and the early May openings of *Austin Powers: International Man of Mystery* (Jay Roach 1997) and *Breakdown* (Jonathan Mostow 1997), generally not seen as desirable times of the year for premieres. He cautions against opening two films on the same weekend, which amounts to self-competition, using the example of Fox's *Soul Food* (George Tillman Jr. 1997) and *The Edge* (Lee Tamahori 1997). While distributors seek out weekends clear of films that threaten to overshadow their own, Klady points to the exception of two hits that opened on the same date, December 19, 1997—*Tomorrow Never Dies* (Roger Spottiswoode 1997) and *Titanic* (James Cameron 1997).[66]

To reiterate, the vectors of exhibition and distribution temporarily are (1) the running time of individual film performances producing daily schedules, (2) the length of the theatrical run, and (3) the "programming" of openings. My discussion of these vectors has taken account of their reigning standards. Yet each settles into industrial strategies and conventions that vary between cinema cultures and across historical periods. Even a brief examination of cinema history will show that the ruling markers of the start- and end-times of a film performance vary wildly, and at times did not exist at all (for example, the continuous screenings prevalent in the past). Consideration of these aspects reveals just some of the forces streamlining filmgoers. What I have delineated are components of an industrial logic about popular and public entertainment, one that offers a certain controlled knowledge about and for cinemagoing audiences. These vectors of temporality shape the "current cinema" (with apologies to *The New Yorker*), a term I employ to refer to a temporally designated slate of cinematic texts characterized most prominently by their newness (i.e., films in theaters now). By the same token, the temporal structuring of screenings, runs, and openings provides a material contour to the abstraction of audience. This material contour functionally presents options for the *what* and *when* of cinemagoing, establishing the parameters within which audiences act, make decisions, and respond.

Following Ang's conceptual lead, industrial discourses establish the spatial and temporal boundaries of a field of cultural practice. Further, identifying that epistemic formation about and for cinemagoing audiences leads to a high degree of provisionality rather than some essential "truth" of spectatorship. Simply put, an audience member is a variable creature, having one life in the eyes of those who sell concessions, those who market film, those who distribute film, those who share the cinemagoing occasion, those who will buy or rent the DVD, and so on. Martin Allor investigates the term "audience" as it has been deployed in media studies to reveal its mediation of the distinctions between individual and society.[67] He draws parallels between "audience" and other terms that similarly imply conceptual unity, including "population," "public," and "mass." Allor maintains that the apparent totality of such concepts is the product of the work of theory, which includes the dominant theories of media studies—political economy, poststructuralist film theory, reader-response criticism, and postmodernism. He writes, "taking the abstract totality of audience (or similar conceptions) as a starting point, these critical approaches have tended to reproduce alternative abstractions that pivot around single planes of contradiction, such as gender, class, or subjectivity in general, rather than multiple determinations."[68] He opts, then, for an epistemological critique of the formation of "audience" as a unified and total category in theory.

Allor establishes a sound challenge to the presumptions of individual consciousness, or lack thereof, at the root of a good deal of media theory. For instance, he demonstrates how the "mass" becomes a simple and predictable entity in Baudrillard's postmodernism. He writes, "The 'mass' in postmodernism functions as a term that denies the possibility of any collective representation of individuals and as a theoretical condensation that allows the theorist to speak at the same time (and in the same way) of individual psychology, class action and social codings."[69] This absence of specificity means that there is a tendency in postmodern media theory to treat cultural consumption as passive, lifeless, and unselfconscious.

Instead, Allor avows, "The audience exists nowhere; it inhabits no real space, only positions within analytic discourse."[70] His critics seize on this statement, charging that Allor has taken the analysis too far and that he refuses to take seriously the possibilities of any empirical research.[71] In this way, his essay becomes the "outside" against which the materiality of certain forms of audience research imagine themselves as reasonable. Unfortunately, this interpretation ignores the power of Allor's critique, which is about the invaluable contributions of a self-reflexive approach to the loose band of borrowed methods we call "audience research." His call, rightly so, is for specificity, for examinations of the epistemological and social determinations of what we call audiences. Additionally, this call can equally speak to the operations of sense-making performed by media organizations themselves. Whether through survey or interview research, broadcasters and distributors attempt to construct portraits of their markets, "to know" their audiences; hence they are participating in an intellectual exercise. For the present purposes, the making of audiences is an enterprise engaged within the corridors of media corporations involving the construction of knowledge, assumptions, and assessments about conditions and taste in the entertainment environment.

In a statement made decades ago about the interconnectedness of people, media, and our thinking about both, we see an assertion analogous to Allor's. Raymond Williams neatly sums up the provisional nature of "mass audiences" by declaring that there are no masses, per se, "only ways of seeing people as masses."[72] The implications of this assertion are far from benign, for we typically witness sundry manifestations of the abstract category of the "mass audience." Regularly, reference appears to millions or billions watching particular television programs, attending films, buying CDs, and reading books or magazines. Often, these multitudes may be represented as individuals, as sales figures, as box office revenues, or as single commodity units. But whether delineated demographically or financially, "the masses" is a concept that portrays links between people and cultural commodities. And in the end, the "mass" is a representational convention, nothing more. Given the nonessential character of audiences, we must ask how people see themselves in relation to these abstract masses. How do people variously take up that position of implied connection to vast and unseen populations or refuse its call? Assuredly, the path from mass to people is never straight and obvious, contrary to the very confidence a term like "mass" seems to bestow on some to speak with certainty about many.

Returning to appraise the concept of mass, which now seems to carry a faint whiff of the anachronistic, is especially important. An idea of mass audiences is evident in a discourse of global audiences, as culture industries actively investigate and court international markets and broad aggregates. Interestingly, another reigning discourse is that of narrowcasting and fragmentation, in which massification becomes an outdated description, replaced by a supposed proliferation of choice and taste formations. Where one discourse—especially prominent in reference to television and computer technology—has constructed the impression of fragmentation and of individualism, another remains trained on the enlargement of cinema audiences. This is evident in the abundant talk that circulates around blockbusters. Efforts to niche-market films pale next to the visible concentration on film events for "everyone." As a result, where being global at home connotes an intimate and directed connection—the "network" is an oft-deployed term here—the popular cinema audience continues to be saddled with metaphors of loss and impersonal experience. Even with the secure, and unproductive, tradition of the denigration of television viewing, the multitudes engaged with popular cinematic genres and practices find themselves in a similarly lowly regard. It is no wonder that critics find it handy to take up commercial cinema audiences as the quintessential "mass" and "mainstream," with "Hollywood" as their solidly familiar metaphor. Paradoxically, these seemingly contradictory conceptualizations of massification and fragmentation in fact travel together given the cross-media migration of texts, as texts become other texts, other commodities, for other markets and purposes. The endpoint of a microscopic zoom from the mass cinemagoing market arrives at what might be understood as its cellular component: the single sales transaction or the single purchase of an admission ticket. In the final analysis, distinctions between broad audiences and specialized taste segments have less to do with actual demographic evidence than with an organization of knowledge about audiences, a hierarchy of taste, and a set of decisions concerning the marketing and circulation of cultural commodities.

The investigation of any formation of audience—whether mass, consumer, or spectator—involves an understanding of how an industry common sense is a crucial force in its existence. Required, then, is a genealogy of the logic that circulates and on which decisions of investment and of the allocation of resources, creativity, and capital are made. The outlines of such parameters of space and time have begun to be sketched above. As Allor puts it, "In order to take the social subject seriously, the heterogeneous practices that frame individuated engagements with texts, discourses, and ideologies need to be taken into account."[73] For the spatial and temporal dimensions of film exhibition, the organization of audience formation begins with a root concept: attendance.

THE CURRENT CINEMA AND PATTERNS OF CINEMAGOING

Where many theorists would accent the technological apparatus of cinema as its defining characteristic, I want to refresh a more expansive, and perhaps simpler, point of distinction: that cinemagoing, by its very nature, requires some condition of *public* spectatorship. As banal as this statement may appear to be, it has to be taken quite seriously inasmuch as there is no longer any essentially public dimension to the consumption of moving images. Cinemagoing continues to thrive, but it is alongside a range of audiovisual sites and forms. Thus attendance—being among others for a cinematic event—is a primary operation for the practice of cinemagoing. It follows that reading the effectivities of cinematic locations necessitates noting empirical trends in contemporary cinemagoing.

To begin, we would do well to remember that not so long ago many felt that cinemagoing was not only in a state of decline but was headed for oblivion. Cries about the "death of the cinema" continue, and many observers seem to agree that the availability of home video and pay-per-view, the increasing size of the television screen, the improving quality of its sound and image, and the competing entertainment options offered by computer-related technology spell the demise of the century-old activity of public moving image consumption. Why take the added time and expense of going out to a film when the options at home are wider, more convenient, and cheaper? In actuality, cinema attendance figures do not support the argument of demise. After years of decline, attendance stabilized in the late 1960s, and in fact made gains in the late 1990s, with box office revenue increasing and breaking records rather regularly since 1989. As table 8 presents it, though U.S. admissions rose and fell through the 1980s, the 1990s saw an overall climb. The combined U.S. and Canadian admissions for 1997 were the highest since 1966.[74]

To offer a comparative sketch of one country's similar experiences, 1997–98 marked for Canada a nearly two-decade record of attendance at drive-ins and indoor, or "hardtop," theaters, just shy of 100 million, which increased the following year, as shown in table 9. Considering only "hardtop" admissions, the 97.7 million attendance of 1997–98 was a thirty-six-year record. Nonetheless, we can be confident that attendance will never equal the peak of earlier decades. Statistics Canada recorded this peak as 1952–53 with 256 million admissions,[75] while other sources indicate 1953, a full seven years after the same turning point in the United States, 1946.

Any argument about the death of cinemagoing neglects to consider, from an industrial point of view, that there is substantial revenue to be gathered at theaters. Moreover, as is evident in tables 8–10, fluctuations in attendance do not account proportionally for the rise and fall of theater and screen numbers. The increase in screens is disproportionately larger than that of attendance. In this period, the rationale that ignites theater building, refurbishing, and closing sprees requires more than changing attendance numbers for support. Notice, too, in table 10 how the trend captured is a rising number of screens and a decreasing number of theaters. In the United States in 1995, 7,744 theaters held 27,805 screens, whereas in 2000 fewer theaters, 7,421, offered more screens, 37,396. Similarly, as table 9 shows, Canada had 659 theaters accounting for 1,808 screens in 1994–95, and over the four-year period to 1998–99, the number of screens rose to 2,574, in 692 theaters. This trend represents an increasing number of screens per site, meaning that there are fewer sites to which one can travel to see a film, but at a given location there are a larger number of auditoriums. The rising number of screens presents audiences with either a wider selection of films or a wider range of start times when a single film is playing on several screens at a given theater. The concentration of screens at fewer sites precipitated a downsizing of both full-time and part-time staff, as seen in table 11.[76] This downsizing in turn has contributed to increasing profit margins. Indeed, in Canada large theaters account for 94 percent of the exhibition sector's $83

TABLE 8   U.S. Domestic Box Office Admissions (in millions)

Year	Dollars	Year	Dollars
1980	1,022	1991	982
1981	1,060	1992	964
1982	1,175	1993	1,244.0
1983	1,197	1994	1,291.7
1984	1,199	1995	1,262.2
1985	1,056	1996	1,338.6
1986	1,017	1997	1,387.7
1987	1,088	1998	1,480.7
1988	1,085	1999	1,465.2
1989	1,132	2000	1,420.8
1990	1,057	2001	1,487.3

SOURCE: For the years 1980–1992, Veronis, Suhler and Associates, Inc., "Filmed Entertainment Growth: A Five-Year Forecast," *Boxoffice*, November 1993, 56; for the years 1993–2001, Motion Picture Association of America, "2001 U.S. Economic Review," http://www.mpaa.org/useconomic review/2001Economic, last accessed June 23, 2002.

NOTE: The MPAA figures are based on the year's average ticket price, whereas Veronis, Suhler and Associates use a combination of sources. The jump in attendance between 1992 and 1993 reflects a difference in measurement and not some unusual surge.

million in profit, likely also due to the extra concession offerings at megaplex locations.[77]

As attendance made slow gains through the mid-1990s, and as box office revenue topped previous records, the frequency of the public cinematic experience has been eclipsed by experience in other sites of audiovisual consumption. Generously, three movies a year marks cinemagoing as an extraordinary event, associated with a special evening out for Canadians.[78] The 1997 U.S. average frequency is significantly higher at a little over five films per year (see appendix 3). There are variations worth considering here. First the MPAA's data and categories indicate that, in 1997, Caucasians made up 70 percent of the domestic audience with Hispanics, African Americans, and others accounting for 13, 11, and 6 percent respectively. Though the MPAA provides no definitions of each group, these figures are a glimpse at those whom the industry sees as its primary audience. Second, cinemagoing data show that those ages 16–39, on average, go out to film 13 to 14 times a year,[79] a substantially higher than average rate. In

The Practice of Cinemagoing   **73**

TABLE 9   Canadian Motion Picture Theaters, Screens, and Admissions

| Year | THEATERS | | | SCREENS | | | Admissions (in thousands) |
	Indoor	Drive-ins	Total	Indoor	Drive-ins	Total	
1953							252,000[a]
1963							97,882[a]
1964							101,728[a]
1988/89	657	132	789	1,490	175	1,665	78,868
1989/90	650	123	773	1,555	168	1,723	82,018
1990/91	633	109	742	1,565	148	1,713	78,934
1991/92	620	103	723	1,611	143	1,754	71,625
1992/93	598	88	686	1,613	129	1,742	73,727
1993/94	581	83	664	1,601	126	1,727	78,812
1994/95	582	77	659	1,682	126	1,808	83,766
1995/96	584	74	658	1,773	119	1,892	87,304
1996/97	588	68	656	1,877	112	1,989	91,327
1997/98	617	71	688	2,186	115	2,301	99,894
1998/99	624	68	692	2,468	106	2,574	112,792

SOURCES: Patricia Thompson, ed., *Film Canada Yearbook* (Toronto: Cine-Communications, 1994); Statistics Canada, *Film and Video, 1992–93, Culture Statistics* (Ottawa: Ministry of Industry, Science and Technology, 1995); and Statistics Canada, *Movie Theatres and Drive-ins, 1997–98, Culture Statistics* (Ottawa: Culture, Tourism and the Centre for Education Statistics, 1999).

[a] *Quick Canadian Facts, 1966–1967*, 22nd ed. (Toronto: Thorn Press, 1966), 127.

1998 U.S. admissions were distributed among the following age groups: ages 12–24 (37 percent), ages 25–39 (27 percent), ages 40+ (37 percent).[80] Third, geographical measures indicate that for city dwellers the rate of attendance is significantly higher. The suggestion one might make is that cinemagoing has a special affinity with urban existence, that it is an activity associated more closely with city life. This affinity should increase, as cinema chains have focused on development in urban areas, closing small town sites with predictable regularity. Fourth, there is a variety of other ways to segment the practice of moviegoing. Table 12 is a snapshot of how people see themselves as frequent or infrequent cinemagoers, with significantly fewer willing to describe themselves as never going to the cinema in 1989 than three years earlier. Another technique is to characterize avid, occasional, and rare frequenters. If avids are defined as

TABLE 10   Number of U.S. Theaters and Screens

| Year | THEATERS | | | SCREENS | | |
	Indoor	Drive-ins	Total	Indoor	Drive-ins	Total
1980				14,029	3,561	17,590
1981				14,732	3,308	18,040
1982				14,977	3,043	18,020
1983				16,032	2,852	18,884
1984				17,368	2,832	20,200
1985				18,327	2,820	21,147
1986				19,947	2,818	22,765
1987				21,048	2,507	23,555
1988				21,689	1,545	23,234
1989				22,029	1,103	23,132
1990				22,774	915	23,689
1995	7,151	593	7,744	26,958	847	27,805
1996	7,215	583	7,798	28,864	826	29,690
1997	6,903	577	7,480	30,825	815	31,640
1998	6,894	524	7,418	33,440	746	34,186
1999	7,031	520	7,551	36,448	737	37,185
2000	6,909	512	7,421	36,679	717	37,396
2001	6,596	474	7,070	36,110	645	36,764

SOURCE: Motion Picture Association of America, "2001 U.S. Economic Review" http://www.mpaa.org/useconomicreview/2001Economic, 2001 (last accessed June 23, 2002).

seeing more than one film every two weeks, then in the United States they account for less than 8 percent of the entire population. And yet this 8 percent segment buys more than 50 percent of all tickets, and in the first two weeks of a film's release, it accounts for 75 percent of the audience.[81] These avid movie-goers are the "early adopters" who, potentially, will convey impressions of the film to less habitual attenders. In the context of shortening theatrical runs, the first weeks are crucial, which only accents the centrality of these regular audience members. For film distributors, an ideal is selling a film that breaks out of the select group of intense moviegoers to attract those who attend occasionally and rarely, in other words, the other 92 percent of the population. The conventional definition of a blockbuster is a film that does precisely that.

Among the internal operations of the film business, "avids" are not charac-

TABLE 11   Canadian Employment and Profit of Theaters

	THEATERS			DRIVE-INS		
Year	Full-time	Part-time	Profit[a]	Full-time	Part-time	Profit[a]
1993/94	1,305	8,323	10.7	133	762	9.8
1994/95	1,155	7,722	11	173	784	9.6
1995/96	997	8,132	10.6	163	782	12.3
1996/97	1,251	7,981	10.2	132	777	12
1997/98	1,274	9,168	11.9	102	727	13.6
1998/99	1,586	10,850	8.8	101	659	11.8

SOURCE: From Statistics Canada, *Movie Theatres and Drive-ins, 1997–98, Culture Statistics* (Ottawa: Culture, Tourism and the Center for Education Statistics, 1999); Motion Picture Theatres Association of Canada, "Canadian Statistics," http://www.mptac.ca/stats.html, 2001, last accessed June 23, 2002.

[a] Percentage of total revenue.

terized by genre but by a familiarity with film culture. For this reason, a temporally inflected designation of film is useful—the *current cinema,* as introduced above. Those who are immersed in contemporary cinema know the offerings at any given point in time. They expect releases, know the cinemas, know the directors and actors, and know background production news and gossip. The very notion of a tiny minority as the bulk of public film consumers is a powerful feature of contemporary film culture. Those who see more than twenty-six films in a year are a select community, and yet they drive a good deal of the box office of commercial exhibition. It is not the films themselves but the practice of cinemagoing that defines this population. Moreover, "avids" exert an exaggerated influence on the current cinema, as this discursively constituted population is the guarantor of the immediate success or failure of new releases.

It is at this point that we can return to the growth and selectivity of a popular expertise in the film industry, and the sense of being in the know about the current cinema, as mentioned in chapter 1. Cinemagoing is not only an occasional act but is one practice among many that consists in a set of everyday skills and ideas. The development of hybrid industry, gossip, critical, and fan publications brings together *Modern Screen, Variety,* and *Film Comment.* Examples of such hybrid publications are *Premiere, Entertainment Weekly, Movieline,* and *Scarlet*

TABLE 12   U.S. Cinemagoing Frequency (as percentage)

	1989	1988	1987	1986
Frequent (at least 1 per month)	24	20	23	21
Occasional (once in 2–6 months)	32	30	27	25
Infrequent (less than 1 per 6 months)	10	11	10	11
Never	32	38	38	43

SOURCE: In Richard Natale, "Hollywood's Got the Billion-Ticket Blahs," *Variety,* March 30, 1992, 10. Rounding figures means they do not necessarily add up to 100 percent.

Street. In Canada there is the relative success of *Take One, Point of View, Cine-bulles,* and *24 Images.* Television shows either entirely devoted to film or to entertainment news are ubiquitous, providing programming that often appears to be an extended trailer. To borrow from political analyst Sidney Blumenthal, who wrote about the never-ending campaigning of contemporary politicians,[82] we are in the era of the permanent *marketing* campaign, where the selling of an entertainment environment is ongoing, an activity punctuated by new commodity texts. The extension of film marketing is also a function of widening the life cycle for film texts, drumming up audiences as works pass from one territory to another, from one medium to another. While many have commented on entertainment news as tabloid or trash news, that is, as a sign of the demise of traditional journalism, I want to emphasize that the hybrid marketing/fan texts tender a seemingly closer and more intense encounter with media industries. Such information vehicles form part of an everyday cinema culture.

The current cinema includes a range of genres, international cinemas, and films of varying release patterns and budgets. This cinema is not one-dimensional and homogeneous, though conventions of representation and industry practice exist. It is unified, as it were, through its temporal coincidence: the landscape of contemporary cinema is represented by what is in the theaters now, that is, by a slate of new films. The current cinema, then, is a paradigmatic set of options; newspaper pages are devoted to announcing their arrival in various communities and encapsulating their contrasting appeals. It encourages us to pose the question of intertextuality in a synchronic fashion. What, for example, is the relation—in terms of text, ideology, taste, and so on—between the film on the screen and the one in the neighboring cinema? This is not merely a question of consumer decision-making; for distributors, a reading of a film's links to other current films is foundational to the design of a releasing schedule. But beyond industrial determinants, the current cinema is a designation of knowledge and difference for contemporary populations. As Pierre Bourdieu reminds us, taste is not solely a reflection of essential aesthetic characteristics.[83] As a structure of cultural consumption determined by class, gender, and ethnicity, among other factors, taste is dialectically woven into social position, hence it is a site at which to apprehend patterns of cultural power. In the Bourdieuian sense, the current cinema is a field of cultural production yielding social distinctions.

Where taste formation can point to the salience of aesthetic value as manifest in cultural texts, here one must think of the engagement with the current cinema itself, in its entirety. Knowing the current cinema—what will open, where it will play, production and star news, etc.—establishes a sense of being "in sync" with the business and with other similarly invested people. I would hazard that the regularity of self-reflexive movies about Hollywood life is a development associated with the circulation of an impression of industry transparency. "Avids" *resemble* participants in a community consisting of fans and producers, entertainment reporters and actors.

Operating within this field—its spatial frame of the cinema and the community location, as well as the current cinema's temporal frame of daily schedules, theatrical runs, and openings—audiences act and express what become semiorganized as "lifestyles," themselves consumer-inflected views of identity deployed by industrial managers, investors, and audience members. Accordingly, uneven involvement with the current cinema, and its consequences for differing patterns of attendance, has a semiotic value marking social and cultural distinction. As Mike Featherstone indicates, contemporary uses of the term "lifestyle" refer in part to "individuality, self-expression, and a stylistic self-consciousness."[84] He challenges the presumption that "a postmodern consumer culture based upon a profusion of information and proliferation of images which cannot be ultimately stabilized, or hierarchized into a system which correlates to fixed social divisions, would further suggest the irrelevance of social divisions and ultimately the end of the social as a significant referent point."[85] Instead, Bourdieu inspires him "to argue that the new conception of lifestyle can best be understood in relation to the habitus of the new petite bourgeoisie, who, as an expanding class fraction centrally concerned with the production and dissemination of consumer culture imagery and information, is concerned to expand and legitimate its own particular dispositions and lifestyle."[86] Put differently to suit my present purposes, the locations and occasions of cinemagoing are a product of industrial endeavor and subsequently produce reigning social factions, with taste and engagement as vectors of division. Advancing along these lines should not lead our thinking away from the fact that people *live* these expressions and exclusivities of social position. With an industrially produced and disseminated apparatus of imagery and information, populations struggle, with relative degrees of freedom, to build both self and community.

The analytical problem with "lifestyle" is that the correlations between sets of cultural preferences and class (or any other designation of social position) are provisional and are worked on by the dominant logic of industrial practice. Even something as straightforward as differential pricing structures for tickets establishes temporal if not total exclusivity. Indeed, the brilliance of lifestyle is exactly that it is able to disguise itself as the field—where certain freedoms and expressions are played out—when in fact it is a *habitus,* that is, an organization of inclinations and dispositions. As Featherstone puts it, the work of cultural entrepreneurs and intellectuals of the new bourgeoisie is not "promoting a particular style, but rather catering for and promoting a general interest in style itself, the nostalgia for past styles, the interest in the latest style, which in an age which itself lacks a distinctive style—what Simmel referred to as the peculiar styleless quality of modern life— . . . are subjected to constant interpretation and re-interpretation."[87] This statement likewise characterizes the current cinema, with its promotion of a general interest and involvement with the newness of cinematic texts as an expression of contemporary living. The permanent marketing campaign might "make sense" to industry actors, but it also becomes a mode of experiencing and understanding a wider environment of entertainment, and a world of new images, sounds, and specially fabricated sites.

An idea of "newness" is a root quality of the organizations of "lifestyle" expressions. There is a rate of speed associated with the turnover of cultural commodities, one that is experienced and must be made manageable by cultural consumers. The speed of the circulation of the "new" moves commodities from current to backlog, making it requisite for audiences to conduct their consumption accordingly. Choosing between the necessity of a "big screen, freshly released" cinematic experience or waiting for the "small screen, less novel" videotape in an operation of aesthetic judgment, presuming sufficient knowledge about the film in advance and available funds to spend on either. "Lifestyle" distinctions pertaining to the current cinema can be understood as a function of the velocity of cultural "newness." On this, Arjun Appadurai goes so far as to suggest that the "inculcation of the pleasure of *ephemerality* is at the heart of the disciplining of the modern consumer."[88] He continues by itemizing some evidence of this force, including "the short shelf life of products and lifestyles; the speed of fashion change; the velocity of expenditure; the polyrhythms of credit, acquisition, and gift; the transience of television-product images; the aura of periodization that hangs over both products and lifestyles in the imagery of mass media."[89] Appadurai's assertion works only if we understand it as a characterization of the newness of cultural materials. In concert with this dynamic is an ever-expanding repository of aging cultural commodities and artifacts, that is, residual material from back catalogue music to obscure film titles on videotape. Again, releasing patterns provide excellent examples of accelerated ephemerality. For this reason, we need to understand how movie theaters occupy a special place in popular culture as a location for the introduction of new motion picture texts, where one life cycle of cultural commodities begins, before they spin through successive incarnations. For frequent cinema patrons, the current cinema is an array of immediate cultural choices and expressions. For the occasional or rare patron, as argued above, the current cinema is a catalogue of future cultural consumption, a source of knowledge to be acted on at the video store or on television. Together, they constitute part of the everyday of cinema culture.

The history of commercial cinema has been one of a struggle to standardize attendance, spectatorship, and viewing contexts, one that has had instances of stability but that has also always been in process and flux. This struggle has taken place in industrial discourse, among industrial managers, between audience members and social factions, and in the development of cinematic technologies and the work of marketers. Statistical measures bring audience segments within the reach of entrepreneurs, who see target markets and under-exploited economic potential. Adjacent to the programs industry agents initiate are the cinemagoers who wend their way through the offerings that appear. The economic and industrial incentives to put forward an ephemeral current cinema are then negotiated by audiences, whose patterns of activity bring signs of distinction into being. In short, cinemagoing is one act among the many everyday expressions, skills, and ideas that make up intermedia, and intercontextual, culture. In the end, the practice of cinemagoing may be creative and expressive, but it is also a product and reproducer of certain knowledge formations. Ultimately, the formation and circulation of cinemagoing knowledge molds patterns of attendance and lodges cinemagoing as a visible lifestyle expression, that is, as a visible boundary of social and cultural distinction.

PART TWO

Structures of Cinematic Experience

CHAPTER FOUR

Crisis and Settlement in Exhibition and Distribution

Even the most casual cinemagoer cannot help but remark on the drastic changes that have taken place at motion picture theaters over the last decade. Suddenly, or so it appeared, auditoriums expanded, screen size grew, sound systems became clearer and louder, and food choices were more abundant. The tiny multiplex cinemas that swept through malls in the early 1980s were being consigned to the past, thankfully, as many movie fans would hasten to add. Local newspapers across the continent, indeed in Europe and Asia as well, covered the construction and design of new complexes, some of which reclaimed historic locations and helped revitalize previously depressed areas of cities. In tandem, newspapers published articles on the closing of beloved older theaters, lamenting the loss of long-standing hubs of community as the newer complexes took charge of cinemagoing culture. These new complexes were not just for film projection but trumpeted substantial space devoted to the latest high-tech arcade games, party and conference rooms, and restaurants. And even the most casual cinemagoer, no doubt, could not have avoided noticing the inflation of admission prices that accompanied these alterations.

Where the first part of this book documented some of the material changes to the international circulation and the cross-media qualities of contemporary culture, and explored the related theoretical challenges cultural studies presents to film theory concerning the formation of audiences and contexts, this part will detail the efforts made by industrial agents to make sense of a transitional circumstance. In what follows, I examine contemporary formations of knowledge about cinemagoers (audiences), cinemagoing (practices), cinemas (spaces and times), and their interconnection with other aspects of everyday life. Further, I pay attention to the manner in which this knowledge was acted on, in the final analysis producing seemingly novel locations for public film consumption and revising industry strategy. In this documentation of industrial discourse, as laid out in the previous chapter, we witness the epistemological operations of cultural practice as media corporations attempt to know their audience and as audiences attempt to negotiate the resulting parameters. We begin with a much-discussed early turning point in the history of distributors and exhibitors: the U.S. Supreme Court decision in 1948 on the Paramount case.

The Paramount decree, succinctly put, required the major studios to divest themselves of their ownership of theater chains, thus forcing a further separation between those who produce and market films and those who present them to cinemagoers. Among the many ramifications of this divorcement was a swelling animosity between distributors and exhibitors. A troubling dimension of industrial structure from the very beginnings of cinema, relations between distributors and exhibitors have wavered between cosy, especially when their parent corporations were one and the same, to vexatious for studios without theater chains and for independent distributors without the clout wielded by Hollywood majors to dictate demands for the treatment of their films. By the time the Paramount decree took effect, and divorcement began in earnest in the 1950s, latent tensions became visible. In a nutshell, theaters need the films provided by distributors, and distributors need theaters to accumulate audiences and collect box office receipts. Each, in turn, sees a portion of revenue siphoned off by the other. At times, their interests are diametrically opposed. For instance, typically, the longer a film plays, the larger the percentage of the revenue that goes to the exhibitor. A conventional deal awards the distributor 90 percent of box office receipts in the first week, leaving only 10 percent for the exhibitor; the following two weeks sees this change to 70 percent for the distributor and 30 percent for the exhibitor, followed again by two weeks at 50/50.[1] Therefore, distributors have an incentive to pull films faster, and exhibitors have an incentive to want them to play longer, assuming they continue to draw patrons. Adding to the complexity, the terms of the revenue split can be renegotiated on a week by week, film by film, basis.

Thomas Guback describes the power over their respective operations as follows: "While theater operators have varying degrees of control over ticket and refreshment prices and operating expenses, they have almost no control over the supply of pictures available to them and the strategies for their release."[2] Exhibitors, as much as distributors, rely on hit films. For example, as a result of *Godzilla*'s (Roland Emmerich 1998) disappointing box office, Carmike Theaters expected a "sharp decline in quarterly earnings," an assessment based on the performance of a single film.[3] As distinct as they are necessary to each other's operations, considering the demands of each is crucial to understand the entirety of the motion picture industry. They both drive and direct the movement of the traffic in film. The way in which they negotiate these tensions between themselves shapes the context of film culture in general.

Guback notes some contradictory trends in the film business of the mid-1980s. Primarily, he begins by observing that the expansion of theater chains seemed counterintuitive in light of the growing availability of other ways to see films, including home video and pay-per-view television, and the absence of any increase in attendance figures.[4] Here, Guback emphasizes the role of shopping mall developers for whom the presence of a movie theater is a way to attract people to a location. Many of the new theaters were the product of leasing arrangements with developers, which meant that the capital required by the chain itself in order to open another site was minimized. Guback's conclusion points out that the rising number of screens cannot be accounted for by audience demand but by a changing industrial structure, epitomized by the return to the exhibition business of distributors. The growth he recorded was partly spurred by an increased willingness to circumvent the 1948 decree in the mid-1980s.

The tension between the presenters and suppliers of film is only one factor shaping the climate of the movie business. One must also consider the competition that exists between parties in each sector, pitting exhibitors against exhibitors. For instance, part of the exhibitor's challenge is to manage periods in which film releases come close together, organizing the scarce resource of screen time to accommodate and take advantage of what distributors are offering. Though the absence of a rival chain nearby is usually beneficial, it also could mean that distributors may make impossible demands, insisting that all of their films be presented. This could have the effect of shortening profitable runs, as newly released films replace ones that have been in circulation only a few weeks.

The legality of some competitive strategies used by distributors is not always crystalline. Bidding on films sight unseen, called blind bidding, is one such ambiguous gray-zone practice. In turn, exhibitors have developed their own strategies to respond to distributor demands as well as competition from other exhibitors. John Izod describes the three ways exhibitors have tried to avoid both blind and open, or unrestricted, bidding, marking the power of larger theater circuits in the 1970s as compared to independent theaters. First, chains put somewhat exclusive claims on cities, which eliminated bidding competition, and demanded *clearances,* in which a print would not be made available to another theater operator for a specified period of time within a certain radius. Second, chains had *first look* arrangements with particular distributors, allowing them to claim the more desirable films, leaving lesser works for independent theaters. And third, the practice of product *splitting* appeared to be widespread. In this practice, exhibitors would effectively divide a distributor's films between themselves, and not bid on each other's releases.[5] Not only did these tactics help to assure a chain's business, and squeeze the films available to smaller chains and independent operators, they also gave exhibitors a way to make demands of distributors, assuring better terms for the rental of films and access to the more financially attractive features. In an attempt to ease these differences, many places have replaced competitive bidding for films between exhibitors with an allocation system. In this model, exhibitors agree to share a film or to employ "a random alternative title arrangement."[6] The distributor only has to assure that a limited number of prints is made available in a given market. Despite these, and other sundry tactics and agreements, distributor/exhibitor relations are among the most mercurial elements having an impact on the organization of the motion picture environment.

As this depiction should make clear, the strategies of distribution and exhibition involve negotiating the temporal (when and for how long) and spatial (where and how proximate to the next location) exclusivity of film releasing. As a territorializing enterprise, theaters map out the locations for cinemagoing, shaping a landscape for the current cinema. As an industrial structure, they establish channels of access and limitation. For example, John Belton describes the industry response to suburbanization and changing leisure habits in the 1950s as leading to the rise of the independently owned drive-ins and efforts to attract audiences to the downtown cinemas with projection innovations, including Cinerama and Cinemascope. Exhibitors pursued these options over other alternatives, such as the construction of suburban circuits.[7] These chains arrived later, with American Multi-Cinemas (AMC) building suburban cinemas in the 1960s. Izod notes the continuing urbanization in the construction of cinemas in the 1970s and 1980s "with the difference that the new cinemas were predominantly not of the old downtown type."[8] The eventual suburbanization of cinemagoing shifted sites from rural areas and downtown cores to the burgeoning edge cities.

As an example of how geographically uneven cinemagoing can be, for two decades prior to 1986 there were no first-run theaters in Harlem. It was only with the efforts of the Harlem Urban Development Corporation that a five-screen multiplex opened in December 1986.[9] A decade later, AMC, along with the Economic Resources Corp., established "the first African-American owned-and-operated first run theater circuit," Inner City Cinemas Corp.[10] Magic Johnson Theaters, a joint venture with the basketball player and Loews Theaters, opened its first complex in Baldwin Hills in Los Angeles in 1995. Since then, other exhibitors have begun to build theaters in traditionally neglected black neighborhoods. Inner City Cinemas built theaters in Chicago with Cineplex Odeon, and National Amusements expanded into black communities in New York.[11] This development is an example of the possibility of highly localized success for films, especially with the high population density in urban areas.[12] This potential had been ignored. John Pierson describes the initial box office success of Spike Lee's first film as driven by cinemagoing in African American neighborhoods. He writes that "an amazing 87 percent of the first $6 million gross on *She's Gotta Have It* (Spike Lee 1986) came from only twenty markets, half from the Northeast Amtrak corridor, and a full third from the New York metropolitan area. Even more remarkably, half the total gross was generated by just twenty individual theaters."[13] The period of the absence of first-run cinemas is not only an example of the geographical dimensions of uneven development, as determined by the physical location of theaters. It equally exposes the selective designations of Hollywood's audience.

While the zones of cinematic life form unevenly distributed sites of cinemagoing, a certain internationalism of architecture and design is intended to express universal and placeless qualities of the auditoriums. The multiplexes before 1985 were largely generic and interchangeable. "Decor is deliberately bland to stay attractive beyond the life of any particular fashion; it is neither too modern nor too old-fashioned, so as to offend neither the old nor the young."[14] Izod refers to Gary Edgerton's commentary that theaters had moved from being dream palaces to retail outlets.[15] Izod ends his history of almost a century of Hollywood with a lament for the malling of film glamor. He writes, "While the entertainment on the screen seeks sometimes honourably, sometimes not, to work on the emotions, the shopping mall multiplex does not engage the imagination. Rather its interior reassures, soothes the senses, and directs them to trivial means of immediate further gratification—which require more spending."[16] Whether or not one agrees with this rather conventional assessment of the culturelessness of mall life, exhibition was about to take a dramatic turn in another direction, one that would rewrite the axioms of relations between exhibitors and distributors, as the latter began to exert even more control over the former. It seemed no consensus existed about whether or not the United States was overscreened, though some sources indicate that Canada has traditionally been seen as underscreened.[17] There did seem to be an agreement that both countries were in some way inadequately screened, that their screens were in the wrong location, and that they were equipped with archaic technology and design.

THE RETURN OF CONSOLIDATION BETWEEN
EXHIBITION AND DISTRIBUTION

The traditional conflicts between exhibitors and distributors were a dominant theme of ShoWest 1986, in Las Vegas, an annual meeting of the largest theater chains. MPAA head Jack Valenti's keynote address intended to smooth the ground between the two interests.[18] But this act of appeasement did not tone down the criticisms leveled at theater owners by the major film distributors. Fox reported that 40 percent of its trailers were being removed from prints, that only 35 percent of their stand-alone previews were even screened, and that most of their posters were never displayed.[19] Both Paramount and Lucas Films presented survey results showing extensive damage done to prints by exhibitors, the former claiming damage to 87 percent of its 70mm prints, and the latter finding that 57 percent of its films were marred on opening days.[20] The problem was not only the disfigurement of their film prints. The distributors expressed concern over a deterioration of the public film environment itself. These criticisms suggested that exhibitors were not only failing to serve those providing them with films—the distributors—but that they were also slack in their own operations— the public exhibition of motion pictures. Warner Bros. executive Barry Reardon issued the ultimate threat by declaring, "Unless you take the lead you might force us back into the exhibition business, just to protect ourselves."[21]

Reardon's statement was not an idle challenge. The subtext to the airing of these tensions was the then recent initiation of MCA/Universal's purchase of 48 percent of Cineplex Odeon, the major Canadian-based and -owned theater chain.[22] By the end of the year, 1986 saw a monumental upheaval of the relations between exhibition and distribution, with over 4,377 screens being bought and sold for a total of $1.62 billion.[23] *Variety* summarized, "In 1986, the year of revolutionary realignment, the motion picture industry returned to the origins of its pre-television growth and prosperity in the most massive marriage of distribution and exhibition since the 1948 Paramount consent decrees forced major studios to sell off their theater circuits."[24] ShoWest 1986 was ostensibly one of the first forums addressing the anxieties and expectations of what this particular example of industry consolidation would mean for its participants and investors. And, by all accounts, distributors were on the offensive, implying that they deserved what MCA/Universal was in the process of acquiring: increased control of the treatment of their films in cinemas. The members of the National Association of Theater Owners (NATO) met in October 1986 and echoed the themes of ShoWest, asking, "How can exhibitors and distributors— two longtime adversaries—peacefully co-exist?"[25] *Boxoffice,* describing the two factions as "oil and water, cats and dogs, Hatfields and McCoys," then noted "a truce" marked by the distributors' purchase of chains.[26]

Distributors demanded two things from exhibitors at ShoWest 1986. First, theater owners were to sell the film industry in general, and cinemagoing in particular, rather than promoting individual films, in effect a proposal for a permanent marketing campaign. In March NATO and the MPAA, through their new Exhibitor/Distributor Council, announced a $22 million joint effort to sell moviegoing as a whole.[27] Second, and related, chains were to improve the actual sites they occupied. A model for this improvement was already in formation: Disney vice president Richard Cook offered the "Disneyland model," one of providing "a clean, well-staffed and courteous environment." Cook claimed "that the majority of Disneyland's mail consisted of letters referring to cleanliness and courtesy of the staff, not to the bang-zoom of the ride attractions."[28] The theme park, introduced as a model of efficiency and service oriented primarily toward family use, is, moreover, an enclosed entertainment space, founded on an idea of "total entertainment," that is, a location combining a variety of activities. In this vision, sites of cinemagoing are not sites of cinematic spectatorship alone but carefully defined edifices that blend other leisure options. The suggestion here was that the films did not require refinement; the context of cinemagoing did. Any recommendations for improvement pertained to control over and an integration of the activities offered to patrons. Instead of a comprehensive portrait of the film landscape, this ShoWest meeting advanced a view of an industry agreement about the state of the business and its future directions: a fledgling "common sense" concerning motion picture exhibition and a feeling that the theme park might provide a model for the cinema.

It appeared that Cineplex Odeon took the lead in these recommendations. By April it announced that it would discontinue its discounted admissions, show all trailers attached to prints, and display posters for films even if they were not booked at that theater. *Variety* reported that these decisions "stemmed from distributor annoyance detected at ShoWest."[29] Of course, such an offer of appeasement to distributors cannot be seen outside of MCA/Universal buying into the Cineplex Odeon theater chain. An era of agreement between exhibitors and distributors was in actuality an empowerment of distribution operations and a vertical extension of ownership structures.

For their part, distributors saw the financial benefit of consolidating operations with exhibition. Guback characterized four potential advantages of consolidation for distributors: the ability to set admission prices, to have an increased slice of box office revenue, to maintain closer management of the merchandise sold in cinemas, and to increase control over release patterns.[30] This echoed *Variety*'s own analysis, which indicated that the alignment of distribution and exhibition offered more control of releasing and presumably more complete accounting of box office receipts. The lucrative concessions would also be made available to distributors.[31] Another commentator noted the ability to keep a film showing even after the opening box office has disappeared, and the possibility of having access to box office receipts immediately rather than waiting thirty days to collect them.[32] The former is only an advantage if it is part of a broader pattern of release; otherwise, longer runs favor exhibitors not distributors. *Boxoffice* observed, "By owning theaters, studios will be in a position to nurture films that require word of mouth publicity or specialized marketing campaigns. They could run these films in their own theaters longer, without the pressure to pull them out of circulation a week or two after their release. Studio-affiliated exhibitors also would be able to discount these 'sleeper' films to make them more attractive to audiences."[33] In *Variety*'s assessment, the objective for Hollywood majors was not to secure complete control of exhibition but to have "behind the scenes clout when it comes to operational policy and the allocation of playing time."[34]

One should keep in mind that large corporate mergers in many industries typified the 1980s, with the restructuring of global media conglomerates securing much popular and regulatory attention. There was an abundance of talk about efficiencies and affinities between media sectors. As Stephen Prince points out, before distributors returned to exhibition, many were part of corporations that had expanded into home video or premium cable markets.[35] Frederick Wasser itemizes the early efforts of Hollywood studios to seize the developing VCR industry by forming their own home video divisions, buying others, and establishing distribution partnerships. Between 1977 and 1982, Twentieth Century-Fox, MGM/UA, Columbia, Orion, Warner, Paramount, Disney, and MCA/Universal had all extended into this new area.[36] Thus integration between media, from music to publishing, coincided with ownership control of new windows of exhibition. In this way, consolidation of distributors and exhibitors in the mid-1980s was a continuation of investment practices that have been developing for years.

A prevalent issue centered on the place of independent distributors and exhibitors in relation to the consolidation among majors. *Variety*'s year-end summary of 1986's upheaval in exhibition stated,

> While no one argued during 1986 that these theater buys were illegal, it remains an open question whether they ultimately constitute a lessening of competition. Besides offering a safe haven for exhibition of a producer-distributor's own product, particularly titles which might not be strong enough to get good bookings at arm's length, owning one's own theaters is a very important bargaining chip in obtaining playtime at theaters owned by a fellow distributor/exhibitor, especially on a regional basis.[37]

The decline of independent distributors, and with it a lessening of competition for the majors, was already in evidence. Their share of domestic box office had reached just 7 percent for 1986, down from 20–25 percent in the early 1970s, though the demise of traditional indie venues like adult cinemas, drive-ins, repertory and ethnic theaters was cited as a precipitating factor.[38] Still, the consolidation of exhibition and distribution among the majors was expected to threaten independent theaters directly, negatively affecting the operations of independent distributors even further.

Some exhibitors were defiant about the looming encroachment of distributors on their business. Sumner Redstone publicly swore that a studio would never acquire his National Amusement, and, indeed, a few years later he bought a studio, Paramount.[39] Yet, in 1986, though NATO officially opposed the acquisition of theaters by distributors, not all of its members agreed, including the largest U.S. chain at the time, General Cinema.[40] By the following year, NATO as a whole shifted to this position, backing the reintegration of the U.S. film business.[41]

Were the film environments actually deteriorating? Anyone who remembers the wave of cramped screening rooms of the multiplexes that mushroomed across the United States and Canada in the early 1980s may well agree that audiences desired some improvements in cinema environments. True or not, this only tells us so much. Why were these sites of public exhibition recognized as shabby at that historical instance and not earlier? What struggles between industry sectors were being played out? How were assessments of consumer activity and new technology influencing the steps taken? Profits and stock prices push the work of corporations; still, there are rationales and assumptions that guide the decisions they make. It takes more than the discovery of untapped economic potential to redirect industry investment and planning on a massive scale. How and why did "cleanliness and courteousness" become the qualities marked for improvement? The qualities of the counterpoised terms "deterioration" and "improvement" are realized only in precise historical circumstances. In short, the manifest nature of public film exhibition carries the assumptions of a particular time. It is an ideologically invested marker of cultural and public life. An array of forces, intentions, determinations, and logics produces the semblance of the inherent taken-for-grantedness of industrial and cultural practice. Unpacking the forces underlying the process of that production here entails the concepts of a spatially and temporally defined pastime, city development zones, exhibitor/distributor relations and changing audiovisual entertainment.

But a starting point, a foundational determination, is a set of assumptions about the free-market economy in which the merger of major communication and cultural industries "made sense." It is not hyperbole to suggest that we continue to live in the shadow of decisions made by the Reagan Justice Department, whose actions (though not singlehandedly) with respect to industry ownership changed the U.S. economic terrain. Many of these actions, more alarmingly, have since been exported as the "unavoidable" conditions of globalization. In the film business, any expectation that the mergers and acquisitions of the mid-1980s would result in antitrust action and legislation, as expressed by *Daily Variety* editor Thomas M. Pryor, underestimated the power of the swing toward deregulation.[42] What was deemed monopolistic practice in the past came to be seen as a natural and logical development to accommodate changes in technology and market forces.[43] Instead, one should keep in mind that claims about the synergistic or converging tendencies of media industries have as much to do with business practices and policy as they do with technological capability.

In December 1986, when Tri-Star Pictures acquired Loews Theaters, they filed a motion asking for an overturning of the consent decree.[44] In an important instance revealing its shifting position, NATO offered its support to Tri-Star.[45] As it appeared that Tri-Star's request might be granted, some independent theater circuits complained they were unable to show some major releases and were being forced out of business.[46] One independent exhibitor commented that "when distribs advertise that a pic is opening 'at a theater near you,' it could mean 30 or 300 miles away."[47] Yet, in the face of these concerns, the Justice Department sent a memorandum to the judge presiding over Tri-Star's case in favor of the distributor's right to book its films in Loews Theaters.[48] In a later ruling, the Justice Department supported a distributor's prerogative to select "which theater is the best theater in a given area for that picture," regardless of the theater's ownership, if ownership is not used as a basis of discrimination.[49] Further, according to Wasser, the Justice Department reasoned "that home video and cable made film distribution diverse enough to re-allow vertical integration of theatrical exhibition and distribution."[50] While the Reagan Justice Department did not amend the consent decree of 1948, indeed proclaiming in February 1985 after several years of study that the decision would remain in place unchanged,[51] it was also apparent that the department would not act to limit reintegration either.

While industry consolidation was returning power to Hollywood majors, the operations of exhibitors were under scrutiny. Sumner Redstone attacked the Justice Department "for refusing to recognize that not all product splits are predatory,"[52] splits being one of the tactics available to exhibitors to limit competition among themselves and to respond to the demands of distributors. He was referring to Justice's "crusade" against splits, which was seen as a reversal of the department's 1977 pledge not to pursue product-splitting cases until the matter was resolved civilly.[53] The groundswell of activity Redstone noted followed the Supreme Court's 1985 refusal to hear the appeal of a product splitting case won by the Justice Department in 1980, essentially authorizing the legitimacy of the view that splits violated antitrust laws.[54] One such antitrust case was ongoing in Arizona,[55] a ten-year-old antitrust case from Harkins Amusement Enterprises of Phoenix that had its hearing in court in 1988. Owner Dan Harkins, who was also president of the Arizona Theater Owners Association, charged that his independent chain did not have access to the forty top-grossing films during the period 1973–1977. The court accepted the allegations of product splitting, bid rigging, and circuit-wide bidding on the part of several major chains and distributors, but dismissed other charges including unlawful clearances, moveovers, blind bidding, and monopoly practices.[56] As this case reveals, Redstone's complaint had as much to do with competition between major theater chains and independents as it did with tensions between exhibitors and distributors.

Though the Justice Department ordered a grand jury investigation, it did not hinder the process of merger and acquisition and would eventually relax its attention to possible splitting practices. A significant backing away from its investigations was the department's voluntary withdrawal of a product-splitting case against Pacific Theaters and Syufy Enterprises in California in 1986.[57] The case was withdrawn though the two parties continued to agree not to bid on each other's desired films, reasoning that the legality of splits had not been determined—this despite the fact that Justice had indeed viewed the practice as criminal in the past and had successfully won plea-bargained cases against General Cinema, Mann, Plitt, AMC, Cobb, Consolidated, and Carmine circuits.[58]

Less ambiguous was the laissez-faire attitude toward the consolidation of exhibition and distribution, which continued apace. Coca-Cola, through Columbia, bought the tiny 12-screen Walter Reade circuit in 1986 for $17 million, a tentative foray. By comparison, MCA's action was far more confident, shaking up the industry with its $159 million purchase of almost half of Cineplex Odeon, then controlling 1,176 screens, in May of the same year. As a condition of this purchase, Cineplex Odeon had to complete its purchase of Plitt Theaters.[59] Cineplex Odeon continued to acquire chains, as table 13 shows.

Though the MCA/Cineplex Odeon deal was widely recognized as the spark that ignited the rapid move back into exhibition, the 1948 consent decree did not apply to MCA's Universal Pictures, because at that time Universal had no theaters in the United States.[60] Instead, the strategic implications of their consolidation, coupled with the hands-off policy of the Reagan Justice Department, prompted other major distributors to initiate consolidation plans as well. A flurry of copycat acquisitions followed: Paramount bought Mann The-

TABLE 13 Cineplex Odeon's Major Acquisitions from 1985 to 1987

Date	Acquisition	Number of Theaters/Screens
November 1985	Plitt Theaters	211/607
April 1986	Septum	13/49
May 1986	Essaness Theaters	13/41
July 1986	Neighborhood Theaters	25/75
September 1986	RKO Century Warner Theaters	39/93
December 1986	Sterling Recreation Organization	38/114
June 1987	Walter Reade Organization	7/11
December 1987	Washington Circle Theaters	20/75

SOURCE: "Major Cineplex Acquisitions from 1985," *Variey,* April 26–May 2, 1989, 47.

aters' 360 screens for $220 million in October, then Festival's 91 screens and Trans-Lux's 21 screens for $65 million; Tri-Star/Columbia purchased Loews. Warner Bros. acquired 50 percent of Paramount's theaters for $150 million, creating a jointly owned chain to be renamed Cinamerica in January 1988.[61] USA Cinemas announced a merger with Cinema National's 288 screens in August 1986.[62] By the end of the decade, in 1990, the majors' ownership of chains accounted for 10.7 percent of the 23,000 screens in the United States.[63] Barry Litman and Anne Hoag chart the concentration differently, showing that it extended beyond the involvement of the major media corporations. They indicate that the top four and top eight exhibitors increased their share of the total number of screens from 1983 to 1988, and that their share did not increase from 1988 to 1993; it jumps significantly over the next five years, as presented in table 14. In any case, Litman and Hoag's evidence lends support to the claim that the buying and selling of chains led to fewer hands controlling a larger share of all screens. In other words, the more aggressive movement of the majors into exhibition coincided with widespread consolidation as exhibitors bought up chains themselves.

Mergers and acquisitions were not the only method of expansion. A building boom was also underway. In August 1986, U.S. screens totalled 22,384. Expectations—substantially inflated—were that expansion would take the total up to 30,000 by the end of 1987, though in November it was actually 22,721.[64] The U.S.

TABLE 14 Concentration of Screens among the Top Four and Top Eight Exhibitors

Year	Total Screens	Top Four (% of total)	Top Eight (% of total)
1983	18,884	18	25
1988	23,129	30	40
May 1993	25,626	27	40
1998	34,186	35	57

SOURCE: Barry Litman and Anne M. Hoag, "Merger Madness," in *The Motion Picture Mega-Industry*, ed. Barry Litman (Toronto: Allyn and Bacon, 1998), 101–102; 1998 figures use data from "Fabulous Fifty," *Boxoffice*, January 1999, 24.

screen count continued to increase, pushing numbers well above those of the past. One front page headline in *Variety* described it as an "expansion frenzy."[65]

Even at the 1987 ShoWest, the new president of NATO, Malcolm Green of Hoyts Cinemas, used his keynote to call for calm, assuring that "the massive return of distribution to theater ownership is no cause for the exhibition industry to push the panic button."[66] Buddy Golden, vice-president of domestic distribution for Orion Pictures, talked of "the spirit of *glasnost.*"[67] Thomas Moyer, president of Luxury Theaters, was even more optimistic, seeing the buying spree as an indication of the strength of exhibition. He stated, "Tomorrow will truly be the age of the motion picture industry. Why else would the film companies want to buy our theaters?!"[68] ShoWest 1987 heard continued concern that "audiences, because of sophisticated options in the home, are becoming increasingly demanding and selective in their theatergoing habits."[69] The convention featured concessions to an unusual degree, revealing trends toward various forms of bite-size candies, including M&Ms and Gummi Bears, and other more "upscale" offerings.[70] Attention to extracinematic dimensions was further accented in the years to come at this and other gatherings of industry personnel.

Garth Drabinsky, CEO of Cineplex Odeon, whose activities charted the way for larger multiplexes, observed that the future of cinemagoing relied on the distinctiveness of the event and site. This meant, he argued, that all exhibitors benefit from the "upscaling" of cinemagoing and that efforts in this respect might be best undertaken industrywide. He suggested there was a certain "ur-

Crisis in Exhibition and Distribution **99**

gency" in the need to create "the most felicitous motion picture viewing ambience that the present technology and the most creative architectural designs will permit."[71] To this end, he looked to movie palaces as "inspired solutions to the problem of how to attract audiences."[72] Additionally, Drabinsky argued that "a superbly educated and prepared work force is our single most important strategic weapon."[73] He recommended that in the context of a service industry like motion picture exhibition, morale and training are invaluable areas in which investment must be made, an opinion echoing the earlier advice of the Disney vice-president at ShoWest 1986.

Similarly, a special report on exhibition trends in *Boxoffice* asserted that transportation into film fantasy "in a safe, comfortable environment of a darkened auditorium has been a foundation for America's love affair with the movies and the experience of going to a theatre to see them."[74] Significantly, this romance was being recalibrated in light of other competing options, most notably home video. "Consumers, in short, are constantly reassessing whether the theatrical film experience is worth the extra cost, or whether they can wait a bit longer to obtain the same product in their homes at a lower price."[75] Indeed, by the time of the first combined NATO and ShoWest meetings in 1989, talk of "recapturing the movie palace magic" was explicit. Exhibitor Allen Michaan wrote that "to the audiences of today who have become accustomed to the sterile and unadorned multiplex cinemas that dominate the exhibition marketplace, visiting these special theatres has become a desired treat."[76] For this era of building and refurbishment, no metaphor was more frequently deployed than that of the "movie palace." Regardless of its imprecise point of reference, it is apparent that an idea of the movie palace continues to hold a prominent place in popular and industry ideas about cinemagoing elegance and prestige.

With the majority of theater chains outside the ownership of distributors, grievances and protests from both distributors and exhibitors were ongoing. At ShoWest in February 1988, independent circuits still worried that major chains were constructing oligopolies in exhibition, claiming that six or seven circuits commanded in excess of 85 percent of box office revenue.[77] They also had complaints concerning distributors, calling for more "timely" availability of prints, so that they too could open films in their often smaller markets along with those theaters in bigger cities.[78]

In such times of reorganization, previously stable dimensions of the cinematic apparatus came under scrutiny, as in the 1950s, similarly a time of industry upheaval addressed in part by experiments in projection contexts. At NATO's meeting in Atlanta in the fall of 1987, the association's recommendations included changing the projection speed from 24 frames per second to 30; coating film for protection from scratches; transporting larger reels of 6,000 feet in order to eliminate handling by projectionists as they splice reels together; and encouraging the industry to respect the 1.85-1 aspect ratio.[79] Such ideas, some of which would be floated and at times implemented over the next decade, were directed at assuring that an improved and standardized film commodity reached audiences.

It is reasonable to assume that theater expansion was a response to reports such as the one that appeared in *Variety* in October 1986, which maintained that the average U.S. household spent $520 annually on leisure. Importantly, the main areas of growth, the article claimed, would be out-of-home entertainment, the main beneficiaries of which were live entertainment, legitimate theater, and cinemas.[80] At the time, such a view was a challenge to conventional wisdom that continued to emphasize a return to the home, to "cocooning," and the weakening of cinemagoing. It suggested that cinemagoing might reimagine itself as a special trip, as opposed to the habitual or ordinary outing. Alan Silverman, president of Essaness Theatres, argued that the theater environment had to be promoted, and that the goal was "to sell entertainment as an event, not just a movie."[81] The association with live entertainment and legitimate theater would be another way of establishing an idea of the "upscale." Fewer trips but more spending meant needing more, and more expensive, items to purchase, hence introducing a range of activities into theaters.

As expected, this acquisition frenzy rapidly exhausted itself, and by 1987 a number of chains could not find buyers, despite lowering prices.[82] Not surprisingly, the restructuring of the late 1980s was far from uniformly celebrated. *Variety* reported that, in 1990, Universal, Paramount, and Warner Bros. "may be dashing for the exits" and that MCA's involvement with Cineplex was "the most disappointing marriage of distribution and exhibition."[83] Restructuring was also blamed for an increase in ticket prices and rental fees.[84] Enormous amounts of energy and resources went into the closure, construction, and refurbishment of newly acquired chains. Even as the transformation of theaters was well underway, some analysts continued to suggest that the pace of expansion did not make sense and would not improve on the work of the traditional multiplexes.[85] It appears, however, that regardless of the economic logic involved, a broader rethinking of the operation of the motion picture theater was developing. In this thinking, the multiplex was seen as a problem and as part of an era preceding the contemporary chapter of vertical integration. As the industry resituated itself in relation to the prestige of other special entertainment venues, how could the shopping mall multiplex, with its overall impression of dinginess, possibly fit? Thomas Pryor "pointed to the seeds of cultural and physical obsolescence in the rush to multiplex America."[86]

NATO circulated the Theater Alignment Program to members in 1989, designed to create national standards for the improvement of theaters and cinemagoing. The main areas of focus were print standards, technical dimensions of sound and image quality, and general cinema maintenance. Revealing a move toward a new model for exhibition, the proposal called for procedures of evaluation "in which theaters would be graded like hotels."[87] AMC supported this plan, one that distributors Paramount, Buena Vista, and Warner Bros. all publicly endorsed.[88] This idea was a drastic shift from the generic vision of the movie experience represented in the multiplex, in which sites were interchangeable and without built-in distinction. The analogy to hotels reflected a view of cinemagoing as a special trip, a minivacation, and one that might be imbued with signs of luxury. The Theater Alignment Program, itself a project of building industry consensus, presented an articulation—or link—between cinemagoing and other pursuits that might be loosely described as touristic in nature. The proposal to rate theaters suggests that differentiation and predictability were objectives for exhibitors. The idea of four-star and two-star cinemas brought a discourse of taste and class structure to the project of establishing national standards. This discourse about "top-rated" cinemas was given fuller realization at ShoWest 1991, where NATO president William Kartozian proclaimed that the future of exhibition would no longer be multiplexes, but "a new generation of theaters . . . superplexes."[89]

The Theater Alignment Program is evidence of an industrywide effort to change the site of public exhibition through the standardization of certain technological requirements and the construction of distinctive locations. In

1990 *Variety* described a receding interest in what had been the dominant approach to exhibition for decades: the multiplex. As Lawrence Cohn put it,

- To many moviegoers, visits to "converted" and twinned multiplexes has meant small screens, cramped auditoriums and even sound leaking from a neighboring salle. Complexes built from the ground up have featured more comfort and state-of-the-art presentations.
- To distributors, multiplexes have spelled vast hikes in p&a [promotion and advertising] costs.
- To filmmakers, multiplexes have heightened emphasis on mass market pictures at the expense of specialty films.[90]

Cohn's reference to the multiplex's reduced access to specialty films is a marked contrast to the original speculation about multiplexes offering easier windows for unusual, nonmainstream films. In the U.S. version of exhibition history, Kansas City's Durwood family, whose operations would become American Multi-Cinemas in 1968, created the first multiplex, with two screens, at Ward Parkway shopping center in 1963.[91] In the Canadian version, the first is the Elgin Theatre in Ottawa, whose operations were "twinned" in 1948 under the direction of Nat Taylor, who would later become one of the founders of Cineplex Odeon. "Twinning" offers certain economies of scale to an exhibitor, where, with overhead already taken care of, the second theater is that much less expensive to run. The second auditorium adds flexibility to one's programming, such that the moment a film's business slows, it can be moved to a smaller theater next door, replacing it with a more attractive offering on the main screen. Taylor would later claim that he "gave the whole Cineplex idea away free in a 1965 keynote speech at ShoWest," and that only Stan Durwood of AMC was listening.[92] Though his characterization of the logic of multiple screen sites would have been new to U.S. exhibitors, Durwood had had his first twin in operation for two years.

It is noteworthy that despite the complaints about and the subsequent turning away from the shopping mall multiplex, the very idea of the multiple-screen site remained uncontested. Indeed, it appears ever more surely as a core concept of exhibition venues, providing choice in show times, if not films, to audiences and flexibility to site managers. Beyond remaining unchallenged, the multiple-screen location was expanded on as the move to larger numbers of auditoriums progressed with the megaplex. In this dimension alone we find a point of continuity with previous industrial practices and strategies, resulting in a deeper entrenchment—and not a rejection—of the multiplex as part of a common sense about the film environment and cinemagoing.

Some domestic chains emerged as dominant industry players by sticking to precisely that supposedly outdated model of suburban mall multiplexes. A case in point is Carmike, celebrated for its downsizing and recession strategy as well as its deployment of new technology to streamline operations. The demise of many retailers in shopping malls during the recession of the early 1990s allowed Carmike to acquire space cheaply. They targeted small cities in the South and Midwest, quickly building the chain to the fifth largest in the country with 1,400 screens in 1992. This strategy earned Carmike the name "the Wal-Mart of the movie exhibition business."[93] Acquiring 209 screens from Essantee in 1986, then 116 screens from Consolidated Theaters Inc. in 1989, Carmike added the most screens yet in 1991, 353 in a joint venture with Excellence Theaters, whose office it soon closed down.[94] Their attention to the precise details of revenue flow led them to adopt a computer system enabling the head office in Columbus, Georgia, to know "how many boxes of M&Ms (plain or peanut) were sold" at any multiplex the night before.[95] In 1995 Carmike overtook UA as the largest U.S. exhibitor with 2,478 screens.[96] Appropriate to their business, Carmike built what they called "econoplexes," which they saw as upgraded multiplexes that fit well in smaller cities, rather than megaplexes.[97]

Predictably, other attempts to improve the profitability of multiplexes involved challenging labor rights. For example, the Theater Association of California lobbied against the increase of minimum wage in that state and proposed to establish a shift work model in which theater employees could be asked to work more than forty hours a week without receiving overtime.[98] Yet another intermingling of business activities was the movement of exhibitors into distribution.[99] AMC Entertainment founded its own distribution wing, AMC Motion Picture Group in 1993, following comparable moves by United Artist Theaters, GC, and Cineplex Odeon, with varying degrees of success.[100]

An argument that the United States had too many screens implicated the multiplex as a culprit. In 1990, U.S. screens reached 23,689, even though attendance had changed little.[101] The drastic decline in attendance since the 1940s had not resulted in a similar reduction of the number of screens; the number of U.S. screens in 1948 was 18,631.[102] "Overscreening" was being identified as a problem by 1989, one of the consequences of the building spree of the mid-1980s.[103] The overscreening of the United States was a main topic of ShoWest 1991, with several chains announcing plans to close screens.[104] Counterintuitively, these announcements did not affect the building already in process in any substantial way. The problem with an excess of screens is that it cuts into the per-screen revenues and adds to distributors' costs due to the extra prints they have to provide. A classic example of an underscreened country is Japan, which had 1,887 screens for over 110 million people in 1997,[105] making for a surprisingly tiny ratio when compared to Canada's roughly 2,000 screens for 31 million. While the concept refers to the source and amount of revenues and expenses, overscreening also has a geographical dimension. Along with its corollary, underscreening, it is an assessment of specific locations, the density of population, and cinemagoing practices. The negotiation of the number and concentration of screens affects the constitution of public life and activity. The physical situation of theaters, and people's relative access to them, is a key determinant in the structure of a cinematic community. This relative access is doubly affected when one also considers the number of closings that invariably accompany construction booms. Responses to overscreening and underscreening change where people see films, and how far they expect to venture for the cinemagoing experience.

Continuing with the critique of the theater environment, MCA president Sidney Sheinberg told *Variety* in 1992, "The audience doesn't perceive of the motion picture experience as a good value for the money."[106] The same article also claimed that "the U.S. is one of the only countries that doesn't actively market the theatrical experience,"[107] restating an earlier and common complaint. Contemporaneously, "value" appeared in relation to the procedures of exchange in cinemagoing. For instance, AMC started to accept credit cards in 1989, the same year Cineplex Odeon and American Express struck a deal to offer special services to card users.[108] One experiment to establish a sense of exclusivity has been General Cinema's and Ticketmaster's service of advanced sales and reserved seating by telephone.[109] GC president Paul Del Rossi declared, "All of our market research with moviegoers shows that people are looking for more convenient ways to go to the movies."[110] In some U.S. cities in 1989, MovieFone began offering the moviegoer access to show times and locations without having to turn to the newspaper.[111] MovieFone then expanded to sell tickets in New York City for Loews, Cineplex Odeon, AMC, Mann, and United Artist Theaters, as well as GC,[112] and eventually sold reserved seating. In an attempt to replicate the seat selections individuals tend to make on their own, the system tried to leave empty seats between parties.[113] With an initial service charge of $1.50, it was not a uniformly welcome addition.

With the strengthening ties between distributors and exhibitors, primarily a consequence of the return of the Hollywood majors to the exhibition business, an effect of the concentration of exhibition ownership in general, and in reaction to the expansion of home video, the 1980s witnessed a rising agreement about the reconstruction of the space and practices of the motion picture theater. Upscaling, comfort, courteousness, cleanliness, total entertainment, and prestige emerged as qualities to be offered through the services provided and through the design of auditoriums. There was no sea change in attendance sparking the new investment in exhibition, nor did the augmenting attendance of the 1990s keep pace with the rising numbers of screens. Instead, the immediate access to the newest trend in cinema culture, that is, available seating for the first weekends of commercial releases in major and minor centers in the United States and Canada, was taken as a core feature of popular cinemagoing. This manifestation of a reworking of spectatorial conditions finds its most complete expression in the 1990s rush toward megaplex cinemas.

CHAPTER FIVE

"Here Come the Megaplexes"

While the realignment of exhibition and distribution percolated, cinemagoers confronted one resulting development: the transformation of theaters. Visibly altering the appearance of downtowns and suburbs, cinemas morphed into entertainment centers. Awkward terms like "superplex," "mega-multiplex," and "gargantuplex" tried to designate the cinema complexes characteristic of this phase in exhibition.[1] *Variety* heralded the distinctive nature of the mid-1990s boom and launched the most lasting neologism in 1994 with the front-page headline "Here Come the Megaplexes."[2] The article indicated that, despite complaints about overscreening, virtually every major exhibitor had plans for the construction of new giant theaters.[3] That same year, *Boxoffice*'s first feature on the development, "Megaplex Rising," described them as "free-standing, multi-application exhibition complex[es]" and linked them to the success of previously minor parallel industries, including IMAX and ride simulators.[4] Megaplex theaters were to offer a range of leisure activities and expanded menus. They boasted unobstructed sightlines, comfortable seating and improved sound from THX, Digital Theater Systems, Dolby's Digital, or Sony's Digital Dynamic Sound.[5] Other features, though not unique to these new complexes, included curved screens intended to reflect the light and color directly back onto audiences, making the image brighter, and screens with small perforations so speakers could be placed behind them.[6] Curved screens also allow for more precise focusing of the image. Cineplex Odeon executive VP Lynda Friendly said of the changes exhibitors faced, "The most important of these challenges is the aesthetics of the moviegoing experience; the necessity of meeting the demands of film audiences that are growing older, more sophisticated and more critical of the surroundings that the theater operator provides."[7] The industry's response was to "supersize" the cinemas, along with the concessions.

One source claimed that the megaplex was the "brainchild" of AMC, with the first being Dallas's Grand 24 screen site in 1995.[8] AMC, as *Variety* put it, "sends old ways to the exits, brings new ideas through the turnstiles," in direct reference to the megaplex.[9] Though the chain was an aggressive participant in the megaplex building spree, with thirty-eight in early 1998, the move to this giant cinema complex was part of an industrywide logic rather than the plan of a single entrepreneur.[10] Still others suggested that Howard Lichtman of Cineplex Odeon is a "megaplexing elder statesman," on the basis of that corporation's earlier Universal CityWalk complex.[11] Without a doubt, for several years in the late 1980s chains introduced larger multiplexes and increased screens, seats, and attention to design. Early examples were Luxury Theater's Portland ten-plex,[12] and Loek's Grand Rapids twenty-eight-screen complex, trumpeted as the world's largest in 1988.[13] But the designation of the particular nature of this development as "megaplexing" did not occur until 1994.

The megaplex wave was an international one, with large indoor theaters opening in urban centers across North America, Europe, and Asia. U.S. examples of complexes described as megaplexes include Sony Theater's Lincoln Square in New York City with twelve screens and an IMAX auditorium, United Artists' fourteen-screen Washington Township site, Carmike's fourteen-screen Nashville cinema, and General Cinema's fourteen-screen Mall of America theater in Minneapolis. In 1995 there were about twenty such locations in the United States, with twenty more planned.[14] As the 1990s closed out, the number of screens at megaplexes soared. AMC Entertainemt, with its Dallas complex, a twenty-screen in Mission Valley, California, and a thirty-screen revitalizing Kansas City's downtown core, announced plans for a similarly enormous complex to take over and convert the old Montreal Forum hockey arena into a twenty-two-screen theater as part of their move into Canada.[15] Among the most elaborate megaplexes are Regal Cinemas' FunScapes, the first of which opened in Chesapeake, Virginia, in 1995. These are large theme park structures based on a core of fourteen screens. Michael Campbell, Regal's CEO, called FunScape an "all-inclusive family-oriented entertainment park."[16] This includes large play areas, eighteen-hole miniature golf courses, franchise food services, high-tech arcades, and a Victorian theme featuring a small theater designed to look like a nickelodeon. General Cinemas Company tested a lobby CD listening station, at which cinemagoers could sample and buy CDs.[17] United Artists Theaters planned to introduce motion simulators attached to theater seats.[18] Trade publications covered the grandeur of the larger sites as a form of branding for theater circuits. For instance, the Lincoln Square complex was described as "Sony Theaters' giant new flagship."[19] (See figures 1 through 6.)

While many commentators characterized megaplexes as "postmodern," as "descendents of the opulent movie palaces of the 1920s and 30s," and "state-of-the-art,"[20] these theater complexes were more than sites of film projection. One critic described megaplex design as "a kind of bright and sloppy deconstructionism that often looks like the work of Frank Gehry's evil twin: wantonly curving and jagged bulkheads; brashly inorganic materials, especially metal and plastic; an absolutely bratty disregard for every tenet of purity, restraint, and functionalism held dear by modernists."[21] They were palaces of audiovisual technologies and conspicuous displays of newly realigned corporate ownership. The changes they represent were so drastic that it appeared the era of the multiplex, associated with cramped, uniform auditoriums and shopping malls, was drawing to a close. The age of the megaplex was beginning.

Or rather more accurately, an industry-sanctioned discussion about the unique qualities of the megaplex was amply evident. The following sentence opens a feature article on Famous Players' new theaters: "After years of trudging off to watch the movies on puny screens in boxy cinemas, a new era of filmgoing is suddenly upon us."[22] Regardless of the proud proclamations about substantial overhauls in industry and popular periodicals alike, it is surely a matter of contestation whether these sites offered anything especially innovative to cinemagoing audiences. Indeed, the changes were not so drastic as to make the sites unfamiliar, and the use of cinemas as locations for a range of activities other than film spectatorship has many precursors. At best, tidiness was perhaps the most salient quality, and in this way the megaplex was partly a veneer of newness applied to standardized practices. Nonetheless, it is indisputable that there was a discourse about a shift in the construction, operation, and practices associated with the site of motion picture exhibition.

▲ **FIGURE 1**
Famous Players
Paramount, Toronto.
By permission of
Famous Players.

▶ **FIGURE 2**
Famous Players
Paramount,
Montreal

◀ **FIGURE 3**
Famous Players
Paramount, Toronto,
Club Room. By
permission of
Famous Players.

▼ **FIGURE 4**
Famous Players
Paramount, Toronto,
front lobby

▲ FIGURE 5
Famous Players
Paramount, Montreal,
upstairs lobby.
By permission of
Famous Players.

▶ FIGURE 6
Cineplex Odeon
Cinescape at Eau
Claire, Calgary. By
permission of
Cineplex Odeon.

Aspects of the definition of "megaplex" have slipped around considerably during the term's short history. The number of screens required for a site to be legitimately labeled a megaplex has been especially imprecise. Though *Variety* has settled on sixteen screens or more as its benchmark for megaplexes, figures continue to vary, in other venues, from theaters with fourteen screens to those with twenty and up. One sees even wider variability in countries other than the United States, where unusually enormous sites did not suit many locations, whether due to smaller population density or less frequent cinemagoing. Despite its explicit definition, even *Variety* will describe a fourteen-screen site as a megaplex.[23] Such inconsistency suggests that a fixed number of screens does not provide the most accurate definition, nor does it fully capture the megaplex's difference from earlier formations of exhibition. Instead, new exhibition technologies, expanded leisure and entertainment offerings, large screens, plentiful seats, and a model of customer service characterize the megaplex. And, importantly, many of these attributes and innovations were evident in the refurbishment of smaller multiplexes that took place alongside the construction of megaplexes, where theater chains opted to devote an unusual amount of space to restaurants and game rooms rather than auditoriums. In other words, the megaplexes of the mid-1990s were the most visible product of the reconfiguration of industrial discourses about cinemagoing, discourses that equally had an impact on other locations of public cinematic life. With these sites, both megaplexes and refurbished multiplexes, there was an attempt to reconnect cinemagoing to other practices, just as earlier phases of cinema exhibition had done from the integration of film with live performance to the luxurious trappings of the movie palaces. While the megaplexes did include a larger, if imprecise, number of screens compared with existing multiplexes, specific to this phase in exhibition history was a view that encompassed other forms of contemporary cultural consumption as part of the cinemagoing experience.

Famous Players was the tenth largest chain in the United States and Canada at the end of 1997, with its 525 screens only in the latter.[24] It was one of the more aggressive participants in this boom, with lavish sites and large auditoriums, though not matching the massive number of screens per site seen in U.S. expansion. Table 15 presents the complexes opened between 1997 and early 1999,

TABLE 15 Famous Players Theater Openings, May 1997 to February 1999

Date	Theater	Number of Screens	Number of Seats
May 14, 1997	Famous Players Coliseum, Mississauga, Ont.	10[a]	3,459
November 7, 1997	Famous Players SilverCity, St. Catharines, Ont.	8	2,005
November 21, 1997	Famous Players Six, Prince George, B.C.	6	1,326
November 28, 1997	Famous Players SilverCity, Mississauga, Ont.	10	2,948
December 5, 1997	Famous Players SilverCity, Ancaster, Ont.	10	2,960
December 12, 1997	Famous Players SilverCity, Windsor, Ont.	12	3,286
December 19, 1997	Famous Players SilverCity Riverport, Richmond, B.C.	12[b]	4,534
March 6, 1998	Famous Players Eight, Pickering, Ont.	8	1,757
May 8, 1998	Famous Players SilverCity, Richmond Hill, Ont.	10[c]	3,776
July 3, 1998	Famous Players Coliseum, Ottawa	12	3,432
October 30, 1998	Famous Players Eight, Belleville, Ont.	8	1,792
November 7, 1998	Famous Players SilverCity Metropolis, Burnaby, B.C.	10	3,124
November 13, 1998	Famous Players SilverCity, Guildford, Ont.	8[d]	3,450
November 20, 1998	Famous Players SilverCity Yonge-Eglinton Centre, Toronto	9	2,841
November 27, 1998	Famous Players Coliseum, Calgary, Alta.	10	2,560
November 27, 1998	Famous Players Coliseum Scarborough, Ont.	12	3,688
December 11, 1998	Famous Players SilverCity, Kitchener, Ont.	12	2,728

December 18, 1998	Famous Players SilverCity, St. Vital, Winnipeg, Man.	10	3,044
December 18, 1998	Famous Players SilverCity, Coquitlam, B.C.	20	4,534
February 12, 1999	Famous Players Colossus, Toronto	18 (+1 IMAX)	5,300

SOURCE: Famous Players Corporation Web site, "Infokit, Historical Facts," http://www.famous players.com/fp_infokits.asp.2000, last accessed November 22, 2000.

NOTE: Seat totals include expansions.

[a] Expanded on July 22, 1999, to a total of 13 screens (+2 screens, 1 IMAX).

[b] Expanded on December 18, 1998, to a total of 19 screens (+6 screens, 1 IMAX).

[c] Expanded in June 1999 to a total of 14 screens (+4 screens).

[d] Expanded in spring 1999 to a total of 12 screens (+4 screens).

totaling 234 screens in twenty locations, showing the combination of larger flagship complexes with smaller but technologically up-to-date sites.

In conjunction with their interest in distinctive cinema locations and experiences, Famous Players announced plans to build ten 3-D IMAX theaters in Canada between 1998 and 2002, the first of which would be at Toronto's 4,300 seat Paramount Theatre.[25] Famous Players has gone further than many in their efforts to offer different lines of new multiplexes. They inaugurated four brands: the family-oriented SilverCity, the downtown Paramount (figs. 3 and 4), the futuristic Colossus, and the Roman-inspired Coliseum.[26] The distinctions between them seem to amount to loose design references, with their architecture connoting the fun and excess of theme parks.

Megaplexes have been characterized as "destination sites" and "themeplexes" with the inclusion of high-end video arcades, digital sound, cafes and bars, merchandising outlets, party rooms, elaborate video displays of coming attractions in the lobby, theaters with "bouncy" chairs and extra leg room, expanded concessions menus, and assurances that "a manager will be on hand at all times much like a concierge at a hotel."[27] Famous Players set up automatic ticket machines in their lobbies beginning in 1994, something AMC had initiated in 1990.[28] Plans to refurbish the sound systems in existing theaters would give 90 percent of the chain either Dolby Stereo SR-D or Digital Theater System (DTS) by 1998.[29] Cineplex Odeon's parallel services encompassed new sound systems, bigger venues, and their arcade division Cinescape—ironically suggesting an escape from the cinema (figure 6). Cinescape developed virtual-reality and motion-based interactive games with Sega GameWorks, itself a joint venture of Sega, DreamWorks SKG, and MCA.[30] Calgary's Eau Claire Market cinemas saw early tests by Cineplex Odeon, with the first Cinescape built there, though it had but five screens.[31]

The role to be played by expanded entertainment activities and this renewed aestheticism—that is, the impulse to decorate every corner of the cinema—was not always unequivocal. In May 1995, Rex Weiner's article "Bumpy Interactive Ride" presented interactive technology as a focus for "location-based entertainment" but appeared uncertain about what kinds of games and services best complemented the main feature, the movie.[32] Some chains, including initially AMC, held the view that elaborate game rooms simply took up valuable space in the theater and did not construct them. By contrast, and mirroring the comparable actions of most major chains during this period, General Cinema, in a deal with Sega, installed games developed for Cineplex Odeon's Cinescape, and Famous Players launched TechTown.[33]

The megaplex typically constructs a continuity between the lobby and the world of cinema, where the boundaries of the screen, film culture, and moviegoing appear fluid and permeable. A description of the lobby at Famous Players Coliseum in Mississauga, Ontario, highlights this: "The lobby is as much a feast for the eyes, decorated with such movie props as a model of the F-14 Tomcat Tom Cruise flew in *Top Gun,* the submarine from *The Hunt for Red October* and The Starship Enterprise from *Star Trek: Generations.*"[34] It is notable that these models become "movie props," as though they emerge from the films they signify, which they do not. The lobby did boast one artifact, a bit of Canadian content: the cloak worn by Dolph Lundgren in *Johnny Mnemonic* (Robert Longo 1995).

Spin magazine presented a two-page drawing of the new site of public consumption of motion pictures. It began with a declaration of the end of an earlier cinema era. "The neighborhood multiplex is over. Finished. Done. Instead, we'll soon frequent megaplexes—theme-park-size cinemas with dozens of screens."[35] The illustration dissects AMC's thirty-screen site in Ontario, California. In this rendition, the lobbies and exits allow the "smooth flow of traffic,"[36] and electronic sensors monitor the air quality and temperature. Seats are wider than usual, with cup holders, and all offer unobstructed views of the screen. Advertisements appear in slide shows before the trailers. AMC sells ad space on its soft drink cups, as well as movie merchandise in the lobby. Throughout the mall video totem poles present commercials for shops and restaurants as well as previews of films, and a giant video screen above the entrance presents clips of films currently playing. One auditorium, called "Cinema Avant-Garde," presents smaller budget films and offers adventurous moviegoers discounts on concessions. As the description reads, "To encourage the timid, an avant-garde 'greeter' meets potential art-filmgoers in the lobby, and talks to the audience before each film."[37] Popular science-fiction films, including the *Star Trek* movies, *2001: A Space Odyssey* (Stanley Kubrick 1968), and *Blade Runner* (Ridley Scott 1982), inspired the decor.

Most apparent are the advantages afforded by the ample number of screens, which effectively accommodate the wide release of films, ensuring that viewers will be able to see the new release in those crucial first weeks. Eventually scaling back the number of screens presenting a film and moving films between larger and smaller auditoriums is an efficient way to ensure that fewer seats are going to waste when a film either does not draw as expected or as it ages. The design of megaplex projection booths, usually a continuous corridor above the cinemas, is such that it is possible to have two screens presenting the same film with a single print. Exhibitors use the standard platter projection system, which requires reels to be assembled on arrival, attaching the various trailers and advertisements, after which they sit in their entirety on a platter. As the film plays, unspooling from the inside outward, the take-up platter winds it to a state ready for the next showing. This means there is no change of reels during a film performance and no rewinding afterward. Time and, importantly for exhibitors, labor is drastically cut. With starts and house lights controlled centrally by computer, a projectionist needs only to check a film at the beginning of a screening. Thus it is possible for a single projectionist to handle an entire megaplex of sixteen screens. Further, because of the relative ease with which this system might be learned, many of these tasks are taken on by theater managers themselves.[38] Of course, many would challenge the level of quality control in this operation, noting the ubiquity of focus problems and lack of troubleshooting expertise among these faux projectionists.

As these descriptions make evident, the expanded cinema of the megaplex involved a horizontal integration of leisure activities ranging from video games to food consumption, in addition to the economics of wide releasing. As such, it was partially an attempt by exhibitors to retrieve revenue lost to other establishments during the course of an evening of cinemagoing. One goal in the development of extrafilm activities was to entice people to stay on site longer. As marketing VP Roger Harris stated, "It's a broad strategy to try to get people to spend 3½ hours with Famous Players rather than 2½ hours."[39] The opening of Famous Players Coliseum in Mississauga was "part and parcel of an ambitious plan to draw Canadians to the theatre more often—and spend more money while there."[40] Other exhibitors talk of a "graying" of the cinemagoing population that has made quality control more important. As the share of teenage moviegoers diminishes, that of those over forty increases; in 1986 only 15 percent of moviegoers were over forty, and by 1994 that percentage was 36.[41] MPAA's statistics for 1988 noted a rapid increase for over-forty cinemagoers, moving from 1987's 14 percent to 22.3 percent of total admissions.[42] In essence, chains were trying to neaten up the stickiness of theaters, left by young moviegoers, in order to accommodate the return of the adult audience. A good deal of the refurbishment, then, was intended to replace the unruliness of teenagers with a brand of bourgeois civility. Here, parallels are evident with the movie palaces, which similarly worked to install an idea of tasteful spectatorship. A director of Famous Players Western operations provided a statement that the new cinema environments had an idea of a "general" audience in mind, avowing, "Movie going will become an event for the whole family."[43] The assertion, interestingly enough, betrays a belief that cinemagoing has not been a family affair for some time. The fact that a majority of cinemagoers continued to consist of younger people did not appear to impede exhibitors' focus on older adults. As the primary purchasers of home video, adult audiences form a crucial market further down the life cycle of a film product, hence they become important targets for the entry stage of new motion picture texts.

Perhaps the most pronounced, even startling, declaration about the changing face of motion picture theaters is evidenced in the frequent proclamation "You don't even have to see a movie."[44] While this cannot be taken as an even remotely accurate depiction of how audiences use the megaplex, without a doubt such statements indicate an attempt to redefine cinemagoing in relation to new arrangements of cultural practice. As sites for a range of activities (especially as designed for an abstracted notion of the bourgeois family unit), these theme-plexes are emblematic of the broader convergence of shopping, cinema, theme parks, and museums, a development described by John Urry and others as *dedifferentiation,* that is, the collapse of social realms previously seen as distinct.[45] Certainly this has implications for the way we think about and theorize spectatorship in a public arena. In Langley, British Columbia, the Southside Community Church began meeting Sunday mornings at the local Famous Players Colossus in an effort to modernize their approach. As the pastor commented, "That place is packed every Saturday night so why can't it be packed on Sunday morning?"[46] Cinema complexes are hubs of community and public life. They do not situate conditions of spectatorship alone; they also construct relations between public and cinematic practices.

The discourse about the new relations of cinemagoing was not solely the purview of industry. It was equally a popular discourse, one that was evident in mass circulation magazines, newspapers, and the theaters themselves. Evidently, this wave of cinemagoing's architectural reconstruction also made good copy for periodical editors. Reports on the trend toward megaplexes appeared for popular-culture fans in *Entertainment Weekly* in June 1997, for Canadian moviegoers in the on-site promotional publication *Tribute* during the same month, and for a general Canadian readership in *Maclean's* in August.[47] Discussions of the megaplex theater began appearing in the popular press in 1995. *The Globe and Mail* characterized "location-based entertainment centres," derived from the CityWalk model.[48] Headlines declared the wonders of the new cinemagoing era over several years: "Coming Soon—New, Mega Movie Experience," "Theatres Getting Facelift: Big Screens Making a Comeback," "Coming Soon! More Theatres, Screens!," "Movie Madness: 48 New Screens Are Coming to the Region, Complete with Curved Screens, Stadium Seats, Super Sound and Gourmet Snacks," and "More Cinemas! Beaming Down to a Suburb Near You!"[49] The interest continued with feature articles through 1997, with "Faith in Popcorn" and 1998, with "The Vast Picture Show."[50] Such journalistic feature stories are important means by which the new relations of exhibition are organized and explained. They help these relations become part of a naturalized decision making or economic context, rather than acting as informational notices between producers, exhibitors, and consumers.

According to a *Toronto Star* feature, these "cathedrals of the 21st century will be palaces of pleasure."[51] Two qualities stood out in the hybrid "location-based entertainment" centers. First, the reporter wrote, "A theme is key. A theme lasts longer than a trend and can tie a place together. It can transform a mere restaurant into an 'experience'."[52] The concept of "experience" as it is used here concerns distinctiveness, as though one can only experience something if one cannot experience it elsewhere. The article continued by criticizing Planet Hollywood as "branding," which pertains singularly to a readable identity for commercial locations. Instead, the new centers' successful "theming" forged links between activities, here characterized as an especially cultivated expression of taste, where one "will be able to shop at an upscale Loblaws, sip coffee and eat biscotti, then watch a movie in a theatre with stadium seating."[53] Second, quoting an interior designer, "The trick is that you have a completely controlled environment without people knowing it."[54] Importantly, "controlled" is simultaneously a reference to security and consumption. The regulation of the flow of people and exchange is taken as an issue of safety; it is also about the predictability of behavior, consumer activity, and market structure. While these dimensions are apparent in many megaplexing chains, another article oddly characterized some aspects of Famous Players' new complexes as "motion picture themed."[55] This is a perplexing description begging two comments: How can a cinema *not* suggest motion pictures, and how can "film" in general—not glamor, not Hollywood, not even production, but film—be a theme?[56]

An intriguing example of the circulation of ideas about the new film environment is a trailer of Famous Players, promoting some of the changes to its theaters and ending with the slogan "Famous Players. Big screen. Big sound. Big difference" (figure 7). It intends to draw attention to the special features of the newly constructed or refurbished environment—the digital sound system, the screen projection, and so on. While the phrase surely offers a reading suggesting indifference—big screen, big sound, big deal comes to mind—the arrangement of the claim hints at an equation, that is, big screen *plus* big sound *equals* big difference. The modifying attribute warranting this declaration, the concept of

FIGURE 7 Famous Players corporate logo and slogan. By permission of Famous Players.

big, is bound up in a relation between the gigantic, the loud, and the spectacular, and the presumption that these are desired values unto themselves. As noted above, the megaplex in many respects defines its existence in direct opposition to the scaling down of film exhibition as represented by the multiplex. According to Roger Harris of Famous Players, the plan was to construct only larger venues with 250-plus seating, in contrast to the small screens Cineplex Odeon and others built in the early 1980s. He reasoned, "we think it's important to have that large-environment feeling."[57] This included larger screens and louder volume.[58] A report on ShowCanada 1998, the main annual meeting of Canadian exhibitors, concluded that "size does matter in the future of movie theatres."[59]

But beyond historical reference to the waning of an earlier common sense about exhibition (i.e., the shopping mall multiplex), what "difference" does the "large-environment feeling," the "big," mark? The most apparent—the exnominated term—is the small, the quiet . . . the television. In its invitation to appreciate the surroundings of the film performance, "big screen, big sound, big difference" is part of an ongoing operation to assert, define, and police the boundaries of difference in film exhibition, spectatorship, and public space, including difference from the domestic, from television, from the street, from the shopping mall, and from other forms and sites of cultural engagement.

This is especially conspicuous given the integration of film, television, and other entertainment industries, a product of the recent history of mergers and takeovers that have forged intricate entertainment conglomerates. Several challenges to the teleological history of television as destroying the golden age of motion pictures are illuminating. John Izod summarizes by indicating that the declining film audience after World War II preceded the rise of television set purchases, and that the decline continued after sales of sets leveled off.[60] Further, with increases in ticket prices in the postwar period, some exhibitors actually did better than they had when audiences were larger.[61] As Izod illustrates, before 1953 only approximately a hundred films had grossed in excess of $5 million, while in 1953–54 alone thirty films hit that mark, a development he connects directly to the introduction of CinemaScope.[62] Even as early as 1950, the research of Leo Handel attacked the orthodoxy of deleterious competition between media. Though his empirical studies did not include television, he found that cinemagoing, newspaper reading, and radio listening were positively correlated: those who engaged in one were more likely to engage in the other two. He commented that "media actually stimulate interest in each other," and that "the ardent radio fan is the same type of person who would show a considerable interest in motion picture and current news events."[63] Tino Balio supports the claim that exhibitors saw certain compatibilities rather than threats from television early on, citing *Variety*'s claim that 1952 was the first year the industry understood "that theaters and TV could live side-by-side and survive—quite comfortably—in the resultant battle for the audience."[64]

In light of a historical economic convergence of industries, it is fundamental that we consider the intermedia linkages of texts, production, and reception and reveal the process establishing specificity and distinction in those three realms, whether publicly situated or not. Indeed, in a comparable development, an idea of the new and unique qualities of home theaters has arrived, often with appeals to the distinctiveness of the domestic context and intimations of the upscaling of the television experience. These appeals celebrate increasing the size of the screen and its volume and making living-room viewing more like a "real" theater.[65] Simply put, the broad logic of the megaplex, and the multipur-pose multiplex, articulates a set of ideas about the public consumption of motion pictures as different from domestic consumption given the actual en-twinement of those two sites from the perspective of both industry and au-dience. It is here that the Famous Players imperative statement about "differ-ence" belies an industrial and popular discourse on the making of technological and spatial design as a commodity relation, operating inside an array of com-modities, sites, and practices.

Among the many qualities establishing a distinction from the shopping mall's multiplex of the early 1980s is "stadium seating" designed to provide the viewer with ideal access to the screen. Such seating guarantees a perfect position from which to gaze on the unfolding projection, in much the same way that conventions of realist narrative cinema promise to provide the spectator "the best seat in the house." As Cineplex Odeon's promotional material asserts, these are "state-of-the-art cinemas with *unobstructed sightline seating* where everyone sees what they came to see" (figures 8 and 9). The accompanying image is a cartoonish drawing of four people in tiered seats, one behind the other, with their individual sightlines depicted as beams emanating from their eyes. It seems as though, literally, the film originates from their heads, that they are the source of four distinct projections. What would obstruct? Obviously, other people. As these high-beam spectators show, the trajectories of vision do not interfere with one another, and neither does the physical presence of the other audience members. What everyone comes to see, evidently, is his or her own film. The quality being offered is the possibility of experiencing, unencumbered by other distractions, one's own event. What everyone did not come to see is everyone—anyone—else.

Here, megaplexes and the reconstructed multiplexes share their designs with other innovations. Cineplex Odeon's Varsity Cinemas VIP rooms, in Toronto, integrate this idea of private-in-public. These are smaller, more intimate screen-ing rooms with larger, amply spaced seats, small tables between them, and personal food service from items selected on a menu card. The analogy might be the first-class section of an aircraft, and likewise one pays a premium for this extra service and sense of privacy. Whether in the VIP rooms or in the larger auditoriums, the unobstructed view is a bid to avoid the public while being in

FIGURE 8

Cineplex Odeon advertisement for stadium seating. By permission of Cineplex Odeon.

public. There, one can feel alone in the company of others. This notion of upgrading is articulated to a version of mobile privatization, or at least a transportable version of isolation.

By the end of the 1990s, the megaplexes and the freshly updated multiplexes were front and center in the operations of the industry. ShoWest 1998 included seminars on the consolidation of exhibition as well as workshops on "how to convert an older theater to stadium seating without rebuilding."[66] The megaplex, it was noted, "has ushered in wider openings and faster playoff for most pictures. It's also resulted in the erosion of the long-standing practice of zero clearances. Many of the majors play day-and-date with venues literally across the street from one another as opposed to a three- to five-mile radius between engagements that was the norm a few years ago."[67] As noted earlier, clearances were one of the ways exhibitors protected their markets. Their erosion was a sign of a weakening influence. Leonard Klady indicated that responsibility for the diminishing importance of clearances lies with the megaplexes. He wrote that some "insist a no-rules policy ultimately diminishes the grossing potential of pictures and theaters."[68]

This expansion pleased distributors, who saw it as necessary to attract greater audiences and to have places for the ever-expanding openings of films.[69] Indeed, those with investments in theater chains actively pursued this tack. *Variety* noted, however, that odd sites of intense competition, like Woodland Hills, California, Las Vegas, and North Dallas, had become absurdly overscreened "war zones," revealing that some, if not a significant amount, of this

FIGURE 9 Detail from Cineplex Odeon advertisement

expansion was a costly mode of competition between companies.[70] Some concern was expressed that such geographically close competition might effectively jeopardize a film's box office prospects.[71] Nonetheless, after years of declining attendance and interest in the late 1980s, ShoWest had become a trade fair, and was oversubscribed, inducing some talk of splitting the convention into two different events.[72] The shift in the role of ShoWest, one that has made it a showcase for distributors' upcoming releases, was one marking the rising power of distributors over exhibition.

Exhibitors had their own issues to manage. Martin Peers suggested that older chains, with older theaters including Cineplex Odeon and UA, were suffering more than the ones that had been building anew.[73] Whenever attendance fell at any given site, there was a ripple effect for exhibitors in a related decline in concession sales. While box office revenues may be larger than ever, a situation enjoyed by distributors and exhibitors alike, a slowdown in revenue at the snack bar is felt only by exhibitors.[74]

In short, some saw the building and reconstruction as indicative of the growing influence of distributors on theater owners. The whittling away at clearances, facilitating wider openings and encouraging shorter runs, was a consequence of the building activity that reduced the number of theaters but increased screens. The number of new screens in the United States and Canada in 1996 was 1,663, and 2,438 the following year. This broke down into 189 new sites and 56 new megaplexes, defined here as sites with 16 or more screens. Canada saw 172 new screens in 1997.[75] Table 16 presents a breakdown by the number of screens at each theater for the United States for 2001, showing that

TABLE 16   U.S. Theaters by Number of Screens, 2001

	Number of Theaters	% of Total Theaters
Single Screen	2,280	32
Multiplex (2–7 screens)	2,901	41
Multiplex (8–15 screens)	1,458	21
Megaplex (16+ screens)	431	6

SOURCE: Motion Picture Association of America, "2001 U.S. Economic Review," http://www.mpaa.org/useconomicreview/2001Economic, 2001, last accessed, June 23, 2002.

TABLE 17   Top Fifteen Theater Chains, United States and Canada, December 1990

Chain	Screens	Chain	Screens
United Artists	2,699	National Amusements	650
Cineplex Odeon	1,680	Mann	517
AMC	1,604	Famous Players	506
General Cinema	1,488	Hoyts (US only)	442
Carmike	963	TPI	383
Cinemark	867	Excellence	357
Loews	837	Syufy	314
Act III	651		

SOURCE: "Top 20 North American Exhibitors of 1990," *Boxoffice*, December, 1990, 18.

though the megaplexes are a new addition and account for a substantial number of the total screens in the country, single-screen and smaller multiplex sites did not disappear.

Exhibition chains continued to be bought and sold in 1997 with Loews and Cineplex Odeon merging, and Kohlberg Kravis Roberts and Warburg Pincus buying Act III and Cinamerica respectively.[76] On February 20, 1998, however, Hicks, Muse, Tate, and Furst suddenly backed out of its commitment to buy United Artists Theater Circuit when it could not get a reduction of the $850 million cost. The proposed purchase was part of a plan, with Kohlberg Kravis Roberts, to merge UA, Regal, and Act III to form a mammoth circuit with 5,347 screens. Despite the setback, they continued with a purchase of Regal and Act III,[77] which supplanted Loews Cineplex Entertainment after a few weeks as the largest exhibitor in the world. Table 17 shows the ranking of the largest

TABLE 18   Top Fifteen Theater Chains, United States and Canada, December 1998

	Screens	Sites	Drive-ins	New in 1998
Regal Cinemas	3,650	412	3	1,300
Carmike Cinemas	2,837	507		87
Cinemark USA	2,731	276		910
Loews Cineplex Entertainment	2,700	466	3	22
UA Theater Circuit	2,315	345		40
AMC	2,291	229		43
Hoyts Cinemas	1,542	193		517
General Cinema	1,263	172		96
National Amusements	1,235	122	5	58
Edwards Cinemas	775	96	1	179
Famous Players	569	105		14
Silver/Landmark	557	109		404
Century Theaters	527	58	10	27
Hollywood Theaters	523	50		13
Kerasoles Theaters	475	93		−1

SOURCE: "Fabulous Fifty," *Boxoffice*, January 1999, 24.

circuits in Canada and the United States at the end of 1990, table 18 the 1998 rankings, and table 19 the 2001 rankings. The two latter years include their operations abroad.

Despite the ongoing reconfiguration of industry practice, the success of the megaplex became a topic of debate, with the first serious reconsiderations of the model appearing in 1998. *Variety*'s year-end assessment of 1997 noted that interest in building megaplexes continued, "but they've yet to demonstrate that they actually increase the size of the audience."[78] The reasoning here was that despite the increase of audience numbers in 1997, the rate was only 4 percent over the previous year; given the amount invested in megaplexes, and the profound changes they were imposing on moviegoing, the expectation was that the increase should have been greater. The article did argue, however, that a significant transformation attributed to megaplexes was that they "redistribute where people see their movies."[79] And they had stabilized a popular and indus-trial definition of what a "state-of-the-art" cinema looked like. Though by 1999 Regal was cautious about larger multiplexes, it continued to expand building

TABLE 19 Top Theater Chains, United States and Canada, January 2001

	Screens	Sites
Regal Cinemas	4,472	413
Loews Cineplex Entertainment	3,010	387
Cinemark USA	2,922	271
AMC Entertainment	2,790	185
Carmike Cinemas	2,959	390
United Artists Theater Circuit	1,623	218
National Amusements	1,400	127
Hoyts Cinemas (U.S. only)	938	107
Famous Players	913	106
General Cinema	880	105
Edwards Theaters	850	90
Century Theaters	700	65
Kerasoles Theaters	525	81
Wallace Theaters	520	72
Marcus Theaters	482	49

SOURCE: "Fabulous Fifty" *Boxoffice,* January 2001, 40.

sites with the now-standard features of digital sound, stadium seating, and expansive food services.[80]

The effects such complexes have on city life in general was a point of discussion. For example, some reporting presented megaplexes as initiatives in the revitalization of downtown cores, as in AMC's involvement in the Power and Light District of Kansas City.[81] But the geographical redistribution of cinemagoing did not guarantee industrial stability. One of *Variety*'s characteristically assonant titles, "Exhibs Vexed by Wall St. Hex on Plex," concerning the Regal/Act III/UA and the Loews/Cineplex Odeon mergers, questioned the logic behind these massive circuits.[82] Martin Peers suggested that "the megaplex-building craze is eroding the industry's profitability" as they siphon off attendance at older cinemas and as the growth of screens has not been matched by a corresponding increase in patrons.[83] Of the two examples of dwindling profits, AMC and Carmike, the latter, interestingly enough, had not been significantly involved in the megaplex boom.

Where there may have been a crisis in the interpretation of what going to the cinema meant in the context of changing demographics and the popularity of home video and home theaters, with the megaplex and the upgraded multiplex there was a temporary agreement about the future. As a "solution" to a condition of technological and industrial upheaval, these sites offered a reimagining of cinemagoing, partly through connections to other forms of public cultural consumption. The reconfiguration of cinemagoing encompasses the normalization of wider openings and receding clearances, as the availability of the new becomes a more salient quality of commercial moviegoing practice. Even in moments of settlement, the consequent formation is not written in stone and reveals an inherent instability as rival forces batter its existence. Competing interpretations struggle to make sense of the implications, whether of an industrial or cultural nature. From 1994 to 1998, the megaplex and "improved" cinema environments expanded their place as an industry-sanctioned response to changing cultural and economic conditions pertaining to cinematic spectatorship. By 1998 the provisional status of this settlement was evident, and the megaplex, like the cramped multiplexes before it, seemed to have a limited life remaining. In other words, the megaplex was but one response to an ever-mutating set of conditions of screen traffic, one that, as with all others, will pass into history as a product of its time. We might want to ask what it will leave behind as the sediment on which future arrangements will be established.

CHAPTER SIX

Zones and Speeds of International Cinematic Life

There was once a time when you could walk through the downtown core of any major Canadian city and not be confronted with a film shoot. As unimaginable as this may be, Toronto, Vancouver, and Montreal were not always cluttered with trailers, crews, and portable "no parking" signs. Even smaller cities, like Regina, Winnipeg, and Halifax, have become noteworthy hubs of international film activity (at least for the time being). Though these Canadian location shoots might be indigenous productions or international coproductions, a good deal of the money spent comes from U.S. television and film companies. The crews may be local, one of the leads may be a Québécois soap star, and the postproduction may be done in Toronto, but these films are primarily U.S. motion picture commodities, destined to garner revenue for U.S.-based corporations.

Some critics have written of the "branch plant" industry that this promotes, where creativity, expertise, and employment may thrive but not in the service of the country's own concerns and debates.[1] Importantly, the branch plant model is not a specifically Canadian experience but rather a convenient description of the maddeningly intricate relationship many nations have with the presence of Hollywood production in their midst. This is complicated further by the fact that assorted national cinemas engage, indeed encourage, the transportability of cultural production. Even in Canada, where the odds are high that the film shoot you encounter is a U.S. one, you cannot be certain, for it just might be a French, German, or Chinese production, or combination thereof, through coproduction treaties.

It is evident that an internationally integrated apparatus of production and consumption is part of the standard practice of Hollywood film. This circumstance establishes "new international divisions of cultural labour," which Toby Miller connects to some of the paradoxical and cynically shifting arguments of cultural protectionism evident in trade agreements, especially the GATT negotiations.[2] Asu Aksoy and Kevin Robins chronicle the financial forces shaping the U.S. "global image empire," concluding that alternative and national film cultures are increasingly squeezed from prominent channels of distribution. They write, "If Hollywood is now everywhere, it is because of its increased mobility and flexibility,"[3] though they then go on to critique the speedy conclusion of post-Fordism that cannot account for the continuation of labor rights issues from an earlier era. A case in point is the bid to circumvent union regulations or to take advantage of currency exchanges and tax incentives by moving productions to a less carefully monitored labor environment. So-called runaway productions—a term that belies the presumption of a "natural" Hollywood home that shoots run away from—have become a normalized consideration for producers. The result has been the establishment of satellite production economies in various parts of the continent and beyond. There are industry expositions focusing on locations, to which city, state, provincial, and federal governments send film commission representatives to sell their scenic, technical, and financial advantage. A collateral outcome, runaway productions have contributed to a changing notion of where U.S. entertainment emerges from, partially decoupling an idea of Hollywood from its California base.

Frederick Wasser charts some of the consequences of film's transnationalization, suggesting that there has been a reduced consideration of U.S. viewers as producers eye global markets.[4] This argument heads toward a "cultural discount" claim discussed in chapter 2. I would add that transnationalization of production and consumption has allowed audiences, U.S. and non-U.S. alike, to claim a certain proprietorship of films whose crews disrupted local traffic, whose stars sparked local news coverage, and whose images capture familiar landmarks, however disguised or misrepresented by the narrative. It is insufficient to discredit, or to attack as misinformed, the fact that it is important to Canadian fans that the first seasons of *X-Files* were shot in British Columbia or that parts of *Good Will Hunting* (Gus Van Sant 1997) were shot in Ontario.

Though transnational corporations suck profit and talent into their placeless agendas, considering this "feeling" of ownership incorporates a sense of proximity to the world of popular-cultural production for scattered audiences as culture industries shunt both commodities and economies from one place to another. Put differently, runaway productions affect consumption as those works reappear as finished imports to some audiences.

With this depiction of the mobile film production, I intend to reiterate that the globalization of film must not be mistaken as another case of the unidirectional flow of cultural commodities and ideologies from the United States to the rest of the world. Arjun Appadurai and others apprehend evidence of the mobilization of culture as a call for "intercontextual theories," ones that challenge presumptions of home and away, of local and global. At this point, I want to emphasize that even at the level of participation in an economic machine, we do not find a single nationally bound organizational or ownership structure but rather an intricate international concentration. In 1986 *Variety* commented on the extraordinary international presence at the American Film Market, a site originally intended for U.S. films and distributors; 25 percent of the films for sale were from sources outside the United States.[5] In the early 1990s, an article, "Here Come the Global Moguls," noted that international investment in Hollywood was turning from buying existing companies to creating new ones. Among those moving into the U.S.-based film industry were Japan's Fujisankei, France's Canal Plus, Italy's Penta, and Holland's PolyGram.[6]

Briefly stated, multinational ownership structures result in divisions of cultural labor that do not follow traditional models of political economy based on competition between nations. Divisions of cultural labor arise within countries and might find affiliation with marginalized labor in unexpected locations abroad. At an anti-runaway rally in Hollywood, some participants wore T-shirts bearing the image of a maple leaf in a weapon's crosshairs, punctured by bullets.[7] Echoing this, the gift shop of Frank Capra Jr.'s Screen Gems Studio in Wilmington, North Carolina, has on display a T-shirt decorated with a bright red maple leaf with a red line through it. And yet, the North Carolinian worker who wears this shirt is not one who would fall in line with those advocating a strengthening of the California industry, having ostensibly benefited from a domestic runaway economy. In fact, the anti-runaway protests work to pit cultural laborers against each other, creating more easily exploitable pools of workers, where in fact their concerns are fairly similar across production centers. For this reason, and in an effort to sidestep the pitfalls of the traditional national/international binary of cultural politics, Miller et al. recommend "supranational cultural policy," especially concerning labor, which "would not only elevate the crucial issues of equitable working conditions, job stability and fair compensation, but bring a diversity of cultural affiliations to the exclusionary and taste-rigid bureaucratic boards which have dominated cultural policy decision-making."[8]

This phase of globalization had other specificities, among which were its initial claims to newness. The growing interest in global coordination of Hollywood's activities was substantial enough for *Variety* to declare that globalization would be the "gospel for the '90s."[9] Reporter Richard Gold sketched the implications as follows:

> For the Hollywood majors it means accelerating worldwide competition for talent, projects, and product for their distribution pipelines. For territorial distributors and independent sales agents it means retrenchment in the face of stepped-up competition from globe-girdling mega-companies.
>
> For producers it means new sources of financing and new pitfalls for backing the wrong projects. For exhibitors it means new opportunities for expansion, particularly in Eastern Europe. And for filmmakers it means achieving the fine balance between universality and individual vision.[10]

It used to be the case that some distributors saw international box office as the cream on top of existing profits. For example, in 1985, 1986, and 1987, a full 80 percent of production costs were recouped at domestic box office for major releases, meaning the success of a film was primarily determined without its export to other markets.[11] Such a view, however, masks the way in which overseas markets have been considered and assessed for decades. Tino Balio notes that the post–World War II Hollywood pursued international markets "but the transfer of dollars back home was stymied by currency restrictions instituted by foreign governments."[12] Nonetheless, as Lawrence Cohn plainly stated a decade ago, "no picture is expected to recoup its costs solely at the domestic boxoffice, as is often cited by uninformed writers in the consumer press. Rather, the domestic performance is a key ingredient in setting a film on the road to success."[13] As the reliance on international markets has increased, this statement is even more important to keep in mind.

Predictably, escalating attentiveness to international markets drew more curiosity about the cinemagoing habits of other countries. Market research and industry data tracking expanded into new areas, with AC Nielsen EDI collecting daily box office information in the UK, Germany, Spain, and France as well as the United States and Canada. EDI introduced overnight reporting of box office in Australia in 1998.[14] Another sign of the globalization of consumer and cultural industry data gathering is the consolidation of many such organizations, including Nielsen EDI, National Research Group, BPI Communications, and Entertainment Marketing Information Services, under the single parent corporation of VSU, a publishing conglomerate based in the Netherlands.[15]

The courting of cinema audiences abroad was also driven by a desire to arrest lost revenue. U.S. distributors became more vocal about the operation of black markets for their products, calling for stricter international copyright laws as well as more involvement and closer surveillance of various individual national economies. For example, an agreement to release home video versions of U.S. films simultaneously in Mexico was, in part, an attempt to cut into the bootleg market for those tapes.[16]

Variety noted Warner's international success with *Batman* (Tim Burton 1989) as an important mark of the turn to global marketing and releasing perspectives.[17] Here, uncomplicated access to theaters is an invaluable resource to exploit. In conjunction, the very idea of cinemagoing became the focus of marketing campaigns internationally. In Britain, the Motion Picture Export Association of America, supported by several Hollywood majors, produced a trailer for theaters to sell the cinema experience.[18] Distributors and exhibitors in Germany initiated a promotional campaign to market moviegoing with the slogan "Cinema is the greatest."[19] Such examples point to the international aspects of the "permanent marketing campaign," revealing the global coordination of an agreed-upon set of ideas about cinemagoing. It is this internationalized cinemagoing and its relationship to public space that I wish to concentrate on in this chapter, beginning with a sketch of the investment activity of Hollywood majors in international exhibition.

Reporter Daniel Pruzin noted in 1991 that "U.S. films now account for over 50 percent of the box office in every major Western European country, with the share in Britain and West Germany well above 70 percent."[20] Included here was a novel dimension: the early 1990s witnessed growing investments in theatrical exhibition in select global markets. This investment was significant enough for some to go so far as to attribute the rise in global box office to "the construction and acceptance of multiplexes."[21] In effect, the exportation of the multiplex served as a beachhead for globalizing distribution. As Balio opines, the industry accepted the assessment that "outside the U.S., nearly every market was underscreened."[22] Thus new theaters intended to respond to this perception of "underscreening," though the number of screens may in fact have been an adequate reflection of cinemagoing rates below those of U.S. audiences (see appendix 3). Lawrence Cohn commented that the purported rethinking of the multiplex model in the United States seemed ironic given that a similar model was being exported.[23]

Thus a powerful element in this phase of globalization has been the expanding attention to global markets of not only producers and distributors but exhibitors. Millard Ochs of United Cinemas International observed that the internationalization of exhibition followed the saturation of the domestic market.[24] Both he and Peter Ivany of Hoyts wrote assessments on costs and issues involved with the international building of theater chains on the occasion of the NATO/ShoWest meeting of 1992, encouraging unprecedented attention to this trend.[25] Intercontinental chains had some presence in earlier periods. In the 1930s, Paramount and Loews both had theaters in England and France, and Twentieth Century-Fox had ownership interests in England's Gaumont and Australia's Hoyts, as well as cinemas in New Zealand and South Africa.[26] Guback records a failed post–World War II attempt to build theaters in West Germany.[27] These precursors pale in comparison to the building and buying of the 1990s.

In the grandest plans for this particular wave, AMC declared its intentions to build and buy 3,000 screens in Europe, Asia, and South America.[28] Distinguishing the period was not just the level of investment, but the kinds of facilities that were being constructed. *Variety* noted a "multiplex building boom" throughout Europe in 1990, with U.S. majors providing the capital and direction for much of the expansion.[29] For some, this was specifically the "Americanization" of moviegoing, a phrase referring to a strengthened relation between shopping and cinema as manifest in multiplexes as well as ownership involvement. *Box-office* covered what it identified as the "multiplex invasion" of Europe in which a suburban American "idea . . . is just now revolutionizing exhibition practices along the rues, strasses and calles of Europe."[30] Cinema refurbishment and construction occurred in most European countries, including Italy, Spain, Portugal, Holland, Germany, Finland, the UK, and Denmark, as well as Japan, Australia, and New Zealand. The involvement of U.S.-based interests in these markets was a spark to similar investments by national exhibitors. Warner Brothers Theaters International made moves toward its goal of a 500-screen global circuit by 1995.[31] WB and the Paramount/Universal–owned UCI examined the Italian market, with the latter making plans for a circuit with department store chain Rinascente, of Fiat. Both built and bought cinemas in Germany. UCI moved into Spain and added to its screens in the UK and Ireland. WB developed in Portugal, added in the UK, and invested in Japan through a coventure with supermarket chain Nichii for thirty-five theaters in five years. And Cineplex Odeon planned to build twelve multiplexes in Turkey between 1998 and 2000,[32] though only two complexes were active in 2002. A *Variety* headline announced in 1994, "Multiplex Mania Hits Exhibitors" in Spain.[33] Austria's multiplex boom saw construction of eight- to twelve-screen theaters in smaller towns like Graz and Linz, as well as the larger centers of Vienna and Salzburg.[34] Greater Union, an Australian exhibitor, entered into a joint venture with Wolff Group of the Netherlands to build Dutch multiplexes in 1998.[35]

For observers of the European scene, multiplexing explained growth in attendance figures and revenues. Belgium has been credited in retrospect with the construction of the first megaplex with a 1988 opening by Kinepolis Group.[36] It was definitely early evidence of a continentwide increase in screens and in the number of screens per site. Exhibition expansion in the UK brought the number of screens up to 2,454 in 1998 from 1,242 a decade earlier, but the number of sites increased only to 748 from 655.[37] In 1997 Battersea Power Station in London was to be the largest cinema complex in Europe and "the UK's first state-of-the-art megaplex,"[38] soon to be surpassed by complexes elsewhere, like the WB 30-screen site in Birmingham. And as the first megaplexes began opening in the UK, Virgin trademarked the term.[39] France, a country where multiplexing was relatively slow to take off, experienced a decreasing number of screens over the same period.[40] Regardless, the rapid growth in most European countries led to concerns about "overscreening."[41] Italy witnessed not only a boom of multiplexes but updating and refurbishment of existing screens, which then offered "previously unheard-of conveniences such as gigantic screens, state-of-the-art audio, air conditioning, bars, restaurants and parking areas and no more intermissions."[42] In 1998 Spain saw a particularly lively building spree of multiplexes, with substantial participation of international exhibitors.[43] For Madrid, the trade magazine called it, yet again, "megaplex mania."[44] Newly merged Loews Cineplex Entertainment planned to increase its presence in Europe through a joint venture with Yelmo Films of Spain to build 175 screens.[45] Loews Cineplex stated that it expects 15 to 25 percent of its revenue to arrive from international circuits within a decade. Similar, though more cautious, multiplex construction appeared in Eastern Europe, particularly Poland, Hungary, Czech Republic, Slovakia, and Russia.[46] AMC introduced complexes, some scaled back from their 20- to 30-screen complexes to 11 to 16 screens, in Japan, Hong Kong, Spain, France, Sweden, and Portugal.[47] (See appendix 4 for a breakdown of European multiplexing.)

Prior to this activity, underdevelopment in some areas was indisputable. Appendices 2 and 3 show the exceptionally sharp drops in moviegoing for Eastern Europe and China after 1987, with corresponding reductions in the numbers of screens. Spain's film attendance decreased rapidly in the mid-1980s, a change predominantly attributed to video. The result was the closing of almost 2,000 theaters.[48] Similarly, drastic declines in the number of screens in Portugal ended only as multiplex expansion began.[49] Distributors complained of the decrepitude of Italy's 2,000 cinemas, where small chains did not have the capital for refurbishment, and where zoning to protect historic building made such changes difficult.[50] As one might expect, the stories of international corporate giants insensitive to historical settings multiplied as the forces of capital collided with local concerns.

But an industrial discourse of underdevelopment is not the only explanation for this level of activity. Some reasoned that the "multiplex revolution" in Europe was a result of the post-recession context coinciding with an increase in attendance. Significantly, this investment was helping to restructure existing distributor/exhibitor agreements. As one commentator put it, "the boom is breaking down the old cozy and restrictive relationships between distribs and the traditional circuits, and bringing family audiences back to the cinema. It is contributing to the wider release of major titles in Europe and an increase in marketing budgets."[51] In other words, the new organization of chains, and the new deals struck between local and international investors, prepared exhibition for a degree of global coordination. The push toward global film commodities led distributors to synchronized international releasing strategies, including similar opening dates and promotional campaigns.[52]

Multiplexing did not hit Europe alone. There was an "explosion" of new theaters in Southeast Asia, and multiplex building specifically helped that growth.[53] *Variety* announced "Exhibs Gear for Multiplex Era" in Malaysia in 1994.[54] Smile-UA Cineplex and Tanjung Golden Village, the latter a joint venture of Malaysian, Hong Kong, and Australian exhibitors, opened new theaters in Malaysian malls.[55] In Japan, the building of multiplexes continued through 1997, including those of Virgin Cinemas, Warner Mycal, and AMC,[56] with the latter also distributing its own films instead of relying on Japanese distributors.[57] Exhibition in India saw joint multiplex building by Modi and United Artists Theater Circuit.[58] UATC and Entertain Golden Village opened megaplexes in Thailand.[59]

As is evident from this inventory of investment, U.S. exhibitors were not alone in extending their global presence. Australian-owned Hoyts cinemas had 1,400 screens operating in the United States, Australia, New Zealand, Mexico, Chile, and Austria.[60] Their international theater expansion included a plan to open more than 150 screens in Argentina before 2001.[61] They, along with Australian chains Village Roadshow and Greater Union, were a powerful presence internationally, especially as participants in the European multiplex building boom of the mid-1990s.[62] South African exhibitor and distributor Ster Kinekor opened multiplexes in the UK and Ireland and planned expansion into Eastern Europe.[63]

Another sign of the internationalization of distribution and exhibition was the first Cinema Expo International, held in 1992 in Brussels, expressly for the "extended global marketplace" in the film business.[64] U.S. interests in international exhibition were intense enough to characterize the Expo as a mode of competition between exhibitors, in effect taking their rivalries abroad.[65] Universal multiplexing was far from being universally celebrated; some saw it as too haphazard and disinclined to give necessary attention to local situations. For instance, U.S. exhibitor National Amusements initially stuck to eight cinemas in Britain, because, as CEO Ira Korff put it, "People overspent, tripped over themselves and made a lot of mistakes" in continental Europe.[66]

While *Variety* and *Boxoffice* gave the impression of unfettered expansion, reports of struggles against this form of global influence surfaced as well. For example, concerns about "control from outsiders" eventually blocked a WB complex in a suburb of Calcutta, though the project had been approved by the government.[67] Charges of Hollywood majors enforcing block-booking practices began to resurface, with France striking a government investigation into the possibility.[68] AMC faced anti-American protests as it tried to establish multiplexes in Toulouse and Dunkirk.[69] Warner Bros. International Theaters, Village Roadshow International, and local developer Focus faced restrictions that applied only to megaplexes in Italy, defined as those with more than 1,300 seats, exactly the cinemas this joint venture intended to build. These restrictions included screen-time quotas for Italian and European films.[70] They later drew protests from some of Italy's top filmmakers with their plans to build a 21-screen megaplex at Rome's Cinecitta Studios.[71]

Yet, in 1997, construction was continuing.[72] One Sony Cinema Products VP proclaimed that Latin America had the highest building rate of new cinemas in the world.[73] UCI, Cinemark, National Amusements, General Cinema, and Hoyts all built theaters in Latin America, with the largest box office boost of about 50 percent seen in Mexico in 1997, and with the latter two consolidating their South and Central American chains the following year.[74] UCI, Cinemark, General Cinema, and Hoyts all focused on Brazil, underscreened with a population of 160 million and fewer than 1,600 screens.[75] *Variety* commented, triumphantly, that "in contrast to Europe, the region [Latin America] saw Hollywood's supremacy remain untroubled by domestic hits in most arenas" and that "Mexican production sank to its lowest level since the 1930s."[76] Such blatant imperialistic pride extended to the cinemagoing practices themselves, as "even the less well-off Costa Ricans and Peruvians are getting the mall 'n' movie habit."[77]

A range of changes in business practice affected Australia exhibition. In 1991 multiplexing was being taken as a crucial strategy for New Zealand exhibition and distribution.[78] The same year multiplexing in Australia was changing the distribution business.[79] Multiplexes were later credited with a surge of box office receipts in Australia,[80] and the record year of 1997 was said to be a consequence of a jump in the number of screens, from 1,251 the previous year to 1,431.[81] Distributors and exhibitors voluntarily agreed to a code of conduct, which included a tribunal to rule on disputes, largely under pressure from independent cinemas that claimed they were not being treated as fairly as the bigger chains.[82] With this code distributors "will be obliged to provide exhibs with written reasons for refusing to supply product and to furnish B.O. figures from competing cinemas."[83] In response to the overscreening of downtown Sydney, U.S. exhibitor Reading was under siege from Hoyts, Greater Union, and Village Roadshow, unable to get films for its new multiplex.[84] And Village Roadshow promoted its Cinema Europa as an "arthouse within a multiplex," which included such minor luxuries as small tables next to the seats and the screening of Australian shorts before features.[85] The first opened at Melbourne's Jam Factory complex. In the wake of such aggressive expansion, by the end of 1998 Hoyts was scaling back its planned growth by at least 20 percent.[86]

Variety reflected the ruling spirit, stating that global distribution was "entering a new golden age unlike anything seen since World War II."[87] United International Pictures president Michael Williams-Jones, whose company handles global sales of Universal, Paramount, and MGM/UA films, claimed, "Within five years ... the current B.O. ratio between domestic and foreign for Hollywood films of around 50–50 will swing to 30–70 in foreign's favor."[88] This highly exaggerated estimate that would not come close to being realized nonetheless typifies the global consciousness of the day. As support, however, Williams-Jones indicated that the construction of multiplexes in Europe, Southeast Asia, and Latin America was an "assuring" sign of this shift.[89]

In summation, in 2002 the U.S. exhibitors operating in other countries included Loews Cineplex [Sony] (Austria, Canada, Hungary, Italy, Korea, Spain, and Turkey); Cinemark (Argentina, Brazil, Canada, Chili, Colombia, Costa Rica, Ecuador, El Salvador, Honduras, Nicaragua, Mexico, Peru, and Taiwan); AMC (Canada, France, Hong Kong, Japan, Portugal, Spain, Sweden, and the United Kingdom); General Cinema [acquired by AMC in 2002] (Argentina,

Brazil, Chile, Mexico, and Uruguay); *Warner Bros. International* [AOL Time-Warner] (Australia, Italy, Japan, Portugal, Spain, Taiwan, and the United Kingdom); *National Amusements* [parent company of Viacom] (Argentina, Chile, and the United Kingdom); *United Cinemas International* [Viacom and Vivendi Universal] (Austria, Brazil, China, Germany, Ireland, Italy, Japan, Panama, Poland, Portugal, Spain, and the United Kingdom); *United Cinemas International Central Europe* [affiliated with UCI] (Czech Republic, Hungary, Slovakia, and Turkey); *Wallace Theaters* (Marshall Islands, Federated States of Micronesia, and Saipan); *Caribbean Cinemas* (Dominican Republic, St. Maarten); *Cinemastar Luxury Theaters* (Mexico); and *United Artists Theater Circuit* [part of Regal Entertainment Group, with Regal and Edwards chains] (Hong Kong, India and Thailand). The global expansion of popular cinema has led to the redrawing of financial commitments internationally and cooperation among the majors as they pool resources for international operations. Note that several of these chains are part of conglomerates that produce and distribute films as well (Loews Cineplex, UCI, National Amusements, Warner Bros.). Significantly, when we speak of the international dominance of U.S. motion pictures, we must bear in mind that globalization concerns not only the supply of films to existing domestic chains. It equally involves the construction of cinema spaces and the capitalization of theater building and reconstruction on the part of major entertainment corporations. As comprehensive as this chronology of investment might appear to be, it remains but a partial portrait, one that crucially pertains to just a fraction of the globe. For example, China, with its two-thirds quota for domestic films, was left untouched by this expansion and hence had relatively few multiplexes.[90] Further, and quite astoundingly, there is only slight record of activity in Africa, save the occasional mention of Morocco, Ethiopia, and South Africa. Taking the tabulation of screen numbers presented in appendix 2 as one portrait of markets that figure most prominently for industry agents, we are immediately confronted with several blindspots. Further, the majority of Asian countries, Cuba, Bolivia, and Ecuador are all absent, reminding us that industry charts reflect trade routes, themselves a product of ideological agendas and political will.

While North America, South America, and Western Europe saw an expansion of the number of screens, the majority of the rest of the world experienced

TABLE 20   World Screens

	1988	1998
Western Europe	20,400	22,252
Eastern Europe	164,443	5,400
North America	27,037	39,001
South America	3,382	3,640
Asia	183,130	86,756
WORLD	400,107	159,898

SOURCE: "World Cinema Fails to Keep Up with USA; Global Spending Now Close to $17 Billion," *Screen Digest*, September 1999, 22.
NOTE: The countries included in the definitions of continents here do not necessarily conform to geographical standards. Nor do the figures account for all countries. I have used them nonetheless as they do capture the way industry data gatherers segment the globe. Note too that the world total includes individual countries not captured by the continental tallies, though it still does not represent a complete number of world screens. Appendix 2 gives a breakdown by country and presents those included in and excluded from the continental totals.

a decline, with an overall world total plummeting. Table 20 presents a continental comparison. China accounts for a significant proportion of massive reduction in the number of screens, going from 161,777 in 1988 to just 65,000 ten years later; in tandem, China's average cinemagoing rate fell from the highest in the world to among the lowest, comparing 1987 and 1997.[91] And the figures in appendix 3 for Central and Eastern Europe document nothing less than a radical deterioration of cinemagoing culture. In the end, it was the following countries that experienced at least a 20 percent rise in the number of screens during the boom of the 1990s: Argentina, Australia, Brazil, Canada, Cyprus, Germany, Hong Kong, Iceland, Indonesia, Ireland, Jordan, Luxembourg, Malaysia, New Zealand, Singapore, South Africa, Spain, Switzerland, Turkey, The United States, and the United Kingdom (see appendices 2, 3, and 4 for details). The global expansion of screen traffic has been, in actuality, an extraordinarily selective process, one that involved a reinforcement of the center of gravity for the flow of international film culture.

Hidden by the tales of growth are, of course, the closure, demolition, and transformation of cinemas. As cinemagoing reconfigures to suit new arrangements of cultural life, so too do sites rise and fall. Among the material repercussions of these commitments is the spatial reformation of cities, reinvigorating certain zones at the expense of others, building new meeting places for cultural consumption and abandoning others. Here, the theoretical advice of James Hay, Kevin Robins, and Anne Friedberg, as discussed in chapter 3, helps elucidate the consequences of these economic forces for the cultural practice of cinemagoing. The sheer volume of cinema spaces has escalated in some areas and contracted in others, with the effect of rewriting the parameters of where, when, and how people participate in contemporary cinema culture. Further, these spaces are chains, literally and figuratively drawing links to other cinema spaces in other cities and to cinema culture in other countries, and conversely leaving other places out of the circuit. One might speculate on the full implication of what it means to "get the mall 'n' movie habit," as the trade publications characterized the multiplexing wave. The chain-links of cultural practice shift our attention from images, sounds, and narratives, which are overwhelmingly the focus of studies of globalization in film studies. Instead, one becomes aware of the spatial dimensions resulting from an increasing financial involvement of primarily, but not exclusively, U.S. major chains. The international multiplex/megaplex manufactures zones of global cultural flow, a flow almost exclusively associated with the life of a contemporary city. In the following section, I examine some of the ways in which new sites of a city's cinematic culture invigorate a rearticulation of the public and the private, in particular contending with reigning ideas about the dangers of moving through urban space.

HOME AND AWAY: PUBLIC SPACE AND SAFETY IN FILM CONSUMPTION

Consider the following remarks made by director James Cameron when he accepted Producer of the Year at ShoWest 1995:

> But here we are in the last decade of the second millennium, and things are changing at a dizzying rate. The world is speeding up logarithmically, and we are bombarded by a million shiny new ideas, bright as jellybeans, few of which will have lasting value. We're surfing fast and wobbly across a liquid landscape of new media, new delivery systems, whole new forms of entertainment made possible by the digital revolution.

Theatrical exhibition was threatened first by TV, then video, then cable, and soon will contend with digital video on demand, and satellite direct TV. Soon it will be pay-per-view premieres of major films, and who knows what is around the corner.

But the responsibility is on exhibition's shoulders to keep exhibition vital into the next century. Screen size, brightness, image quality, sound quality—these are things that must be fought for passionately, against the pressures to cut overhead and increase profitability.

Your main defense against the forces of darkness is showmanship. Showmanship is not logical. It comes from passion, and it appeals on an irrational level. People need that special, transporting experience in the theater, or they're going to stay home. And they're getting a lot more eye candy every day by staying home.[92]

Cameron's plea to owners and managers of theater chains is replete with metaphors of candy and brightness. He sees a world thrilled by the prospect of change, as propelled by new delivery technologies. This world will still hold a place for theaters, but it will be a different role, calling specifically for showmanship, however, illogical it may be, as Cameron claims. Interestingly, this new context of which Cameron speaks reiterates a familiar dichotomy of social realms, here presented as the shiny, passionate environment of public screens in contrast to the threat of darkness posed by the home.

Often emphasizing demographic evidence, the film industry had recognized and tried to accommodate the impression of a new context. By 1987, talk of an inevitable aging of movie audiences appeared in trade analyses, specifically encouraging distributors and exhibitors to keep apace of the life changes of the baby-boom generation.[93] In response, Mann Theaters in 1989 reintroduced specially designed soundproof rooms from which children and parents could watch a film without disturbing the rest of the audience, in Laguna Niguel, California.[94] These "cry rooms" had existed in the 1940s, and their more recent incarnation was a product of another "baby boom." As an amalgamation of the living room and the movie theater, providing parents with a place for sequestered spectatorship, cry rooms were one effort to integrate family practices in public spaces of film consumption. Supported by appeals to demographic measures, exhibitors redesigned cinemas by importing private spectatorship and with it appended domestic responsibilities like child minding.

The public/private binary is evident in much of the writing on the differences between film and television. John Ellis's rich discussion of the culture of moving images and sounds detailed the articulation between public-film and private-television.[95] As film in cinemas requires travel through the community, he proposed that film is a cultural event whereas television is a localized, domestic cultural form. One limitation of this argument, a product of the fact that it characterized a time before home video took off, is its primary interest in identifying distinctions based on the medium itself. Ellis's characterization saw film and the practices around it as unified, in some way, and distinct from television culture. And yet film is indisputably a part of television culture, especially through the rental and purchase of video. MPAA sources put VCR ownership at 91.2 percent of U.S. television households in 2001.[96] A decade earlier, in 1990 alone, Canadians bought 248,000 camcorders and 1.08 million VCRs.[97] A dramatic empirical illustration like this should shake any claim about television being a passive, noninteractive medium. The point here is that neither television nor film are stable, unified apparatuses. To slightly revise Ellis's propositions, it is not film that is a cultural event, but cinemagoing. And while a film may be the centerpiece of cinemagoing, it is not the only medium, text, or cultural encounter involved in that practice.

The intercontextuality among media and sites means that a subsidiary effect is discernible for every development and innovation. New technologies, forms, and commodities for *domestic* engagements produce and are produced by, in a dialectical fashion, corresponding technologies, forms, and commodities in *public* locations. More boldly, the interconnectedness of media and contexts contributes to the fabric of everyday life as experienced and negotiated habitually by people. The intricate codeterminations among media and contexts do not imply that some equilibrium is being sought out. On the contrary, the very dynamics of capital assure an ongoing destabilization, as new commodities vie for position among an array of competing products and practices. Simply put, alterations and additions to the site of public motion picture exhibition respond to, and propel, changing relations between public and private forms of media consumption. And yet the reconstruction of difference between the public and private may well transpire via characteristics borrowed from each other. Hence, the exhibitor's showmanship of which Cameron spoke is realized in advertising that accents the homey qualities of comfort, familiarity, and privacy to be found in the otherwise cluttered space of the megaplex, as seen in the mobile privatized spectators of the previous chapter.

There are many consequences of such a reorganization. Significantly, the international investment in movie theaters belies a remarkable confidence in the very idea of public image and entertainment consumption. This is in marked contrast to the worry that cinemas were part of a passing historical era, that stagnating attendance and the availability of cheaper and more convenient domestic options were the death knell for cinemagoing. The activity I have charted indicates exactly the opposite view. Instead, entertainment conglomerates understand the role of cinemas as a specific form of cultural engagement and as a key part in the life cycle of cultural commodities that extend beyond the cinema site itself. Industrial actors are cognizant of the associated activities appended to film attendance. The idea of "total entertainment" is manifest in the fact that the building of multiplexes accompanies campaigns to sell cinemagoing itself. Further, the development of new zones of cultural practice through the construction of movie complexes has an impact on the patterns of city life. As construction reshapes downtown and suburban areas, establishing or reinvigorating zones of cinematic life, exhibitors try to manage dominant understandings of what it means to travel to and inhabit one of those locations for a few hours.

A powerful dimension revealed by the study of industry discourse was an idea about a controllable public space, designed to waylay an equivocal fear of moving about in the city. This has at times translated into an overtly racialized definition of the urban threat to middle-class consumers. As captured in his keynote to the 1987 NATO convention, National Amusements's Sumner Redstone suggested that exhibitors had to compete not only with inexpensive and comfortable domestic entertainment but also the safety of the home where people are "free from the hazards of the city streets."[98] These "hazards" stem from fears of an imagined underclass, revealing exhibitors' interests in attracting a more privileged class faction as their audience.

At the Christmas 1987 opening of the stand-up performance film *Eddie*

Murphy Raw (Robert Townsend 1987), violence broke out in three different theaters in California. One was a "gang-related" fatal shooting, one a stabbing, and a third involved a generally "unruly" crowd, leading to the arrest of four University of Southern California football players and a fifth person. Some theaters canceled showings or pulled the film altogether, because, as a "gang expert" said, "gang members would be particularly attracted to the film because of Murphy's popularity among urban youth."[99] A few years later, in 1991, exhibitors reported thirty-five injuries and two deaths at screenings of *Boyz N the Hood* (John Singleton 1991). When nineteen theaters canceled bookings, Singleton accused exhibitors of "artistic racism."[100] In response to exhibitors' skittishness, or seeing an opportunity for publicity, the film's distributor, Columbia, offered to pay for additional security at cinemas.[101] *Variety* claimed that an increase in security staff for that film hit 600 percent in some locations.[102] The additional staff included off-duty police officers "who specialize in gangs" and who "can often identify members through appearance."[103] At the time, exhibitors also took to "pre-screening films for their off-screen violence potential."[104] Given that decades of media-effects research has yet to offer a reliable method to make those predictions, exhibitors obviously applied some other criteria concerning presumed audience membership in order to identify "off-screen violence potential."

Other incidents reported in industry sources, ones seen as precipitating a response of increased interest in cinemagoer safety, include violence in several locations across California at *American Me* (Edward James Olmos 1992),[105] in eight states at showings of *Juice* (Ernest R. Dickerson 1992),[106] at the *New Jack City* (Mario Van Peebles 1991) premiere in Westwood, California, and at the National Amusements' Sunrise Valley Stream Cinemas on Long Island screening of *Godfather III* (Francis Coppola 1990) at Christmas 1990.[107] General Cinema's response to these events was to improve crowd management by lengthening breaks between screenings and allowing patrons to enter earlier. The intention was to cut down on gatherings outside the cinemas.[108] Less subtle responses included the installation of metal detectors, first at AMC's Southfield cinemas in Detroit in 1989 following a shooting, then at National Amusements's Sunrise Valley Stream in 1991. *Newsday* covered the latter with the headline "Screening Starts Before the Movie."[109] In a bid to reassure audiences, National

Amusements took out an advertisement in the same newspaper describing the metal detectors and other security measures.[110] The reported cost of the new security operation, said to be the most elaborate of its kind in the United States, was one million dollars, which included two dozen video cameras surveying the theaters and the parking lots.[111] Others have followed suit, with video surveillance becoming more evident. As a *Variety* article reported, "All new Pacific Theaters contain visible video cameras in lobbies and public spaces. Some circuits have emphasized lighting in corridors and parking lots and moved boxoffices outside."[112] With the rising attention to cinemagoers' safety, and in light of the racial profiling performed by some exhibitors, at NATO/ShoWest 1992, several African American filmmakers, including John Singleton, Warrington Hudlin, and Robert Townsend, participated in a panel on the incidence of violence.[113]

In the wake of these events, commentators continued a preoccupation with security, hailing Universal City's CityWalk as a "prototype for *controlled* entertainment meccas around the globe."[114] As *Variety* described, the planners of the limited access eighteen-screen Cineplex Odeon complex, with its own shops and restaurants, "are intent on avoiding the sort of urban problems that ripped apart once popular trendy movie areas like LA Westwood district."[115] Thus "the intent beyond CityWalk was clear cut—designed and conceived to be a crime-free upscale environment, largely for locals who wouldn't dream of walking in a 'real' city."[116] For exhibitors, this also meant not booking films seen as either potential instigators of violence or as attracting potentially violent audiences. Held up for special scrutiny were films by black filmmakers, including *Posse* (Mario Van Peebles 1993) and *Menace II Society* (Allen and Albert Hughes 1993), and volatile audiences had been defined as "rowdy teenagers and gun-toting gangs."[117]

Peter Bart opened up a critical assessment of entertainment destinations by avowing that "CityWalk represents either a wondrous leap forward or a symbol of civic failure. It represents either bite-size reality or a retreat from reality."[118] Concerning one transparent function of CityWalk, Bart wrote, "Security men are omnipresent . . . the grand design is to avoid booking violent, racially themed pictures that would attract unruly minority crowds. In the new world of vanilla megamalls, the proprietors don't wish to mix flavors."[119] In his commentary, Bart understood this as part of a broader change in cinemagoing in which "the movie theater no longer seems to be able to stand alone on the urban landscape. People want more for their money." But he continued by highlighting an underlying interest in security as a fundamental force, or rationale, for these developments: "Most of all they want a non-threatening environment, even if it's utterly simulated and they have to pay more for it."[120] Despite the critique, Bart appears to confuse his point of reference. Those paying more are certainly moviegoing audiences, but those desiring such non-threatening environments are also exhibitors, not necessarily the African American patrons and people of color who are instead treated with suspicion and ultimately bear the brunt of these misplaced security initiatives.

Two months after Bart's article appeared, Cineplex Odeon delayed the opening of *Poetic Justice* (John Singleton 1993) at CityWalk in response to a murder and reports of violence at the film's premiere elsewhere. The Los Angeles city council called the exhibitor's decision racist, though Cineplex Odeon president Allen Karp maintained lamely, "It was simply an issue of safety."[121] Given the chronology of crime that circulated, the very idea of safety was indisputably racialized, appearing specially connected with black films, filmmakers, and audiences. Exhibitors and distributors mobilized "safety" to capture a prized audience, the middle-class family, with their "development of state-of-the-art theaters and 'protected' theater environments like Universal's CityWalk."[122] As complexes move back into city cores, exhibitors confront and reproduce the association of inner-city life with violence and danger. Again, this has virtually nothing to do with actual rates of violence. Thus CityWalk let slip out the telling, and in many ways shocking, model for such sites: the gated community.

Let me be clear on this point. Megaplex cinemas are not gated communities. However, a vector of industry discourse reveals that an idea analogous to the gated community circulates as one strategy for the management of separated public space and for the advertising of its safety, a strategy finding expression in new theater complexes. The parallels with other forms of "megashopping" are evident, but gating offers a particular point of continuity between the megaplex and the theme park. Both are areas of public leisure, in which attendance is selective and mediated by admission fees. The megaplex, like the theme park, is not a limitless site of public engagement but promises a fairly restricted range of possibilities, enforced by the site's own privately managed security. These locations harbor a fear of the unfettered public, an anxiety about the surrounding city or community context, and a related popular sense of inadequacy or distrust of public policing's ability to guarantee safety. The correspondences between megaplexes and theme parks will be taken up further in chapter 8.

Why should we expect that the crime rate at theaters would be any different from any other place of congregation? There is, however, a long history that forms a solid part of a popular common sense about representation, suggesting that there is some correlation between images, tone, and the actions of people. As complicated and unpredictable as the correlation may be, according to the practices of exhibitors, detecting the negative social impact of a film has as much to do with an assessment of populations as with texts themselves. Laura Baker's examination of the early 1990s' parallel emergence of a new African American cinema and increasing concerns about security suggests that there was a fundamental contradiction between courting black audiences on the one hand and mall-based theaters that required a steady flow of middle-class— hence, what marketers tend to imagine as white—consumers. She concludes, "The rise of black Hollywood and the production of commercial feature films for black audiences have been celebrated within and without the industry as evidence of the inherently democratic nature of the market, its nondiscriminating supply of product in response to demand. However, if the market has operated to create the foundations of a more multi-racial cultural sphere, it has hardly operated to create shared, multiracial public space."[123] Models of security and surveillance are particular conceptualizations of efficiency, quality control, and upgrading. The reworking of spheres of public and private inevitably leaves us with novel paths and places of social life. Not all paths and places are welcome equally, and some are taken as dangerous, at times exposing latent bigotry. When we witness this kind of emphasis, we can conclude that not only locations, but the discourses about social existence, speak.

THE ACCELERATED LIFE CYCLE OF MOTION PICTURES

James Cameron's appeal to showmanship is one for which "screen size, brightness, image quality, sound quality . . . must be fought for passionately." By implication, exhibitors are to keep up to date with technological change and to do so through cinema complexes that are unique, offering a situation of spectatorship irreproducible elsewhere, let alone at home. Manageable and controllable, the megaplex and the upgraded multiplex were to be distinctively safe and inviting. Where some exhibitors internationalized their operations, the cinema complexes exhibitors built and designed were themselves an appeal to reconfigured ideas about private and public sites of cultural expression. Additionally, the spatial manifestation of the current cinema meshed with the programming of distributors' release schedules. When Cameron makes such sweeping assertions as "the world is speeding up logarithmically," it is hard not to imagine that he is thinking specifically about the accelerated life cycle of theatrical releases. The apparent distinctiveness of the internationalized cinema complex coalesced with new standards in the process by which cultural commodities aged.

One vector of exhibition temporality identified in chapter 3 was the theatrical run of a film. The length of runs contributes to the shaping of the borders of the current cinema by presenting a range of options over a loosely understood limited time period. Release patterns equally implicate future sites and forms, as the expectation is that movies in cinemas will become videotapes and DVDs for sale and rental, then other television texts. Such patterns are a product of, and help reproduce, prevailing assumptions about the economic life of a cultural commodity. Films mutate, becoming CDs, books, videos, DVDs, television, video games, amusement park rides, and other forms of merchandising. The release of a motion picture into commercial cinemas is, in most instances, the point of initiation of an extended existence of a generator of revenue. This is not a fixed trajectory, and one need only be reminded of the way novels continue to act as progenitors of conspicuous narratives to be reworked as films. This aside, table 21 breaks down the sources for the films released by the majors in 1997, showing that most originated from ideas proposed or scripts written directly for the screen.

Books, comics, television programs, and legitimate theater all appear, but the majority were written for film specifically first, implying that the first version in which a popular audience encountered most of those stories was a motion picture. The categories of life rights (families allowing biographical movies), inhouse ideas, pitches, and unsolicited scripts written on speculation accounted

TABLE 21 Sources for the Films Released by Majors, 1997

Source	Number of Films
Spec scripts	62
Books	29
Pitches	18
Franchises/sequels	8
Comics/cartoons	6
In-house ideas	7
Remakes	5
TV shows	4
Legit plays	3
Magazine/Newspaper articles	2
Life rights	2
TOTAL	146

SOURCE: Dan Cox, "H'wood Hunts the Great Idea," *Variety,* February 2–8, 1998, 1, 52, 53, 54.
NOTE: Majors include Disney, Sony, Paramount, Twentieth Century-Fox, Warner Bros., New Line Cinema, Polygram/Gramercy, MGM/UA, DreamWorks, and Universal.

for eighty-seven of that year's major releases, or 59.6 percent. This is a conservative number, for some of the films in the remake and franchise categories may have originated from pitches or in-house proposals. Though this is not a hard and fast axiom, film is currently an important gateway for the introduction of new cultural texts in general. The mainstream commercial theater in particular bears the mark of the newness of film commodities. Indeed most offerings there possess that newness, unlike the television, the bookstore, and the video rental outlet, in which a backlog of sorts is maintained. Thus, new TV programs, books, and CDs sit among an immediate archive of texts. In contrast, one might see the theater as closer to the newsstand in this respect, as both rest on the short-lived freshness of their wares exclusively. The cinema is one key location at which "young" cultural texts appear, a role that has not yet been fully eroded by straight-to-video premieres, by films based on television programs, nor by made-for-cable features. That texts will "grow old" elsewhere suggests that the spatial distinctions of private and public, of living room and lobby, are points of temporal distinction announcing the passage of time.

Technological changes, its promotion by manufacturers, and its adoption by audiences unsettles the flow of revenue for distributors. The transformation of the life cycle of a filmed commodity, at first extended through television and home video, throws previously standard operations askew. Thomas Schatz reminds us that Hollywood "has been increasingly hit-driven since the early 1950s,"[124] and that the blockbuster is in part the foundation of a franchise. Hit films become sequels, videos, and television broadcasts and are the architecture of star personas that act as vehicles of recognition across various media.[125] The multiple packaging of a film extends as commercially viable forms change, the result of which is a corresponding modification in the life and cultural consequence of an entertainment commodity.

If the formation of audiences, and by implication the management of their cultural consumption, is a key operation of the film industry, any alteration is of paramount import. Changes might be driven by the acceptance of new technologies or might arise from a new understanding of the entertainment predilections of audiences. In either case, reconfigurations of industrial and business strategies follow. Further, such changes are not confined to a single medium but are evident across media as a relational fit between commodity forms and cultural practices is sought. One can understand the crisis initiated after Carolco announced plans to premiere some of its films on pay-per-view. Exhibitors responded with a threat to ban those films from theaters.[126] Transformations in a film's life cycle manufacture other spatialized results. For instance, as video release dates move closer and closer to theatrical openings, discount theaters and traditional second-run screens feel that their business is being left out of the picture.[127] In brief, modifications in a commodity's life cycle and the associated fracturing of audiences reignites efforts to reconstitute and stabilize cinemagoing's place and particularity.

For the audience's part, the negotiation of this life cycle involves such everyday decisions about whether or not to wait for the video or DVD, that is, to allow the fresh commodity to age a little if one is to confront it at all. Consequently, private and public viewing cannot be seen as independent, especially given the structures of ownership that have spawned a complementary treatment of films as they move through the various windows of exhibition. For instance, increased focus on older audiences, in effect an attempt to reconstruct an adult moviegoing public, does not necessarily mean that they offer better box office returns than teenagers: "while teens comprise close to half of the so-called 'frequent' moviegoers—those who go at least once a month—they are not the prime watchers of movies on cable or buyers of videocassettes. The dilemma is that those ancillary markets now exceed theatrical exhibition in dollars. Some argue that domestic theatrical is, in essence, the loss leader for big returns from later markets."[128] Box office is a measure of future success, yet that future success might rest on people who are not frequent cinemagoers. Massive advertising for the opening of a new film can be intended for those who will only ever see the work on videotape or DVD.

Oddly, private and public space continue to be seen as antithetical, and, as typical explanations argue, changes in one are struggles against the other. The unusually secure, and questionable, tale of television destroying the golden age of film, and their respective references to private and public spheres, provides a ready narrative of subsequent conditions. For example, Michael Posner's article in *Maclean's* on location-based entertainment presented the received idea about film struggling against the powerful appeal of television, announcing that "the contemporary urban landscape is marked by increasingly sophisticated attempts to entice consumers (and their wallets) away from their television sets. And it seems to be working."[129] Similarly, *Variety* reasoned as follows: "When today's moviegoers venture away from the VCR and into a theater, they expect an event, an experience they couldn't get at home. To satisfy the audience—and to remain competitive in today's crowded theatrical market—exhibitors must provide the latest in technological innovations."[130] As a conceptual wedge between the two sites, "event" is seen as essentially public in nature and technologically based, supporting John Ellis's dichotomy. In a counterargument, Daniel Dayan and Elihu Katz pursue the possibility that, however isolated viewership may be, television offers communal experiences of ceremonial or historical events through its liveness.[131] But for Ellis, "event" presents a noticeable and identifiable association with a particular location. And the now familiar phrase "only in theaters" is a minor attempt to offer event status and exclusivity to a film, again reaped primarily from its newness. The theming of public consumer space is an invitation to inscribe a context with distinctiveness and difference from the private, though to do so there may entail appropriations from domesticity. Generally speaking, such appeals are opportunities to reconstruct distinctions between private and public locations, even as they borrow presumptions about each realm for their own.

Without a doubt, the making of public and private spheres does not flow from some essential well of difference. Rather, we might be better off recognizing their irreducibility, then revealing the machinations of the distinction between those two spatially and temporally designated realms. What should be obvious is the conventionality of intermedia considerations within the ranks of industry, producing a field of cultural practice consisting of various locations and occasions. Assorted sites and times for consumption are typified by assorted expectations for the arrival of new texts and the availability of old ones. What takes place at one moment has consequences for what takes place elsewhere and "elsewhen," to borrow Anne Friedberg's term. Alternatively stated, splintered audiences and expanding locations and occasions of cultural life do not simply produce isolated and atomized spheres of practice. Instead, the fragmented particles of popular life are integrated and weblike in both audiences' minds and industry strategies.

The worry about home video cutting into the livelihood of exhibitors was being challenged in the early 1980s. After court challenges by MCA and Disney against Sony for copyright infringement, initiated in 1976, as Bruce Austin explains, "By 1980 virtually all of the major Hollywood studios had created divisions of joint ventures to manufacture and distribute prerecorded entertainment and offered selected movie titles."[132] Despite the continuing popular sense that VCRs hurt the film industry, it was fairly clear that a synergy, to use the buzzword for the process, was developing. For instance, General Cinema believed that VCRs created "more discriminating and more sophisticated" cinema patrons as home video helped immerse people more completely in film culture. GC found that 73 percent of its customers were VCR owners, which in 1986 was roughly twice the ownership rate of the U.S. population.[133] They were confident of this in 1985 when they acquired Super Video, a video rental outlet.[134] From this evidence, we should understand that parts of the industry did not see the relation between private and public film consumption as only antagonistic, and that the terrain of popular and industrial practice was transforming into a novel context.

From this approach, we might return to an astonishingly basic question:

what business does the film industry think it's in? Distributors treat theatrical releasing as something more than a way to get a film to its audience. It is also potentially a marketing expense and a trailer for the video or for the sale of broadcast rights. For exhibitors, it is a way to sell snacks, tickets, and games. Their film exhibition operations may be a part of the management of real estate investments. Conversely, exhibitors might not be interested in a film in particular but in a generalizable idea of public cultural consumption. In reference to its U.K. operations, Warner Theaters asserted that the construction of multiplexes was "not so much to generate profits as to encourage cinemagoing per se."[135] Further, it seemed taken for granted that "the cinema is by far the most important marketing tool for the lucrative operations in home-video and pay TV."[136] In other words, the film business is an intricate conglomeration of sites, times, and commodities in which motion picture spectatorship is a central, but not singular, practice. This issue is complicated further in an age of blurred boundaries between media. Reflecting the dominant ideas about synergy, producer and studio executive Peter Guber said, "The railroad industry made a big mistake in the 1930's when it saw itself as being in the train business instead of the transportation business. It would be the same mistake to view us as being in the motion picture business rather than the communications business."[137]

The timeline of the intercontextual and intermedia travels of a filmed commodity, thus, reveals a range of industrial commitments, locations, and spectatorial conditions. Commodity life cycles structure industrial practice, that is, financial investment as well as audience engagement. The conglomeration of film as a cross-media, cross-commodity enterprise means that for every distinction there may be between sites and texts, there is cross-marketing to exploit. Film audiences are potentially future book, CD, videotape, and TV audiences too. Sites of theatrical exhibition become billboards for other windows of exhibition, as well as for future cinemagoing. I suggest that while a splintering of audiences takes place, multiplying the situations of film consumption, the interconnectedness of these situations constructs a more sweeping environment of entertainment, promoted by the permanent marketing campaign.

The introduction of new film texts, that is, patterns of releasing, has altered to accommodate dispersed but linked audiences and commodity life cycles. Of all the revisions to releasing strategies, the most prominent development has been the focus on the revenue of opening weekends. Peter Bart commented that the idea of the summer movie, and the screen jam created as distributors release so many films in a concentrated period, did not exist in the early 1970s, a time in which the practice of saturation booking and the concept of megahit movies were yet to be invented.[138] Today, opening weekends usually equate with wide releases in a large number of theaters, but for shorter periods of time. William Paul commented on this change from earlier strategies: "This exhibition strategy turned out to be . . . a radical reversal of past releasing patterns, and with this reversal, the movie distributors effectively changed the way they had addressed their audience in the past. Up through the 1970s, distribution was based on principles of exclusivity. Virtually every major release was tiered through a series of runs, with each tier effectively inscribing a somewhat different audience."[139] Andrew Hindes confirmed the current conventionality of wide releasing: "A glutted marketplace, sky-high media costs and ancillary sales considerations are forcing studios to open virtually every film in wide release, regardless of box-office expectations. In an environment where only the strongest titles ever see a third weekend, studios feel increased pressure to capitalize on a picture's brief moment in the sun."[140] Describing the changes evident in 1996, Hindes continued, "Five years ago, 2,000-print releases were the exclusive domain of summer and Christmas blockbusters. In the first three months of this year, 11 films have gotten the 2,000-plus treatment."[141] Such wide openings mean that portions of the current cinema are available simultaneously to audiences across the United States and Canada. "The preponderance of prints allows megaplexes to screen blockbusters as often as every half-hour and gives secondary markets a chance to open day and date with big cities."[142]

The increasing numbers of widely released films between 1993 and 1997 matched an escalating number of screens for those releases, shown in table 22. As measured by the number of screens at a release's widest distribution, the average was a 26.5 percent jump in 1997 over 1993. This apparent rising presence of individual films on high numbers of screens did not correspond with overall screen time, as films "played off" faster, getting bumped by the next new release sooner. Additionally, there was evidence of even further reliance on the box office receipts of the opening week for such wide releases, with an average of 37.3 percent of cumulative box office being taken then in 1997. Exhibitors'

TABLE 22   Film Releasing (domestic)

	1993	1997	Change (%)
Total releases	354	425	20+
Wide releases (600+ screens)	145	151	4.1+
Average peak number of screens	1,493	1,888	26.5+
First week's box office as % of total box office	29.3	37.3	27.3+
Average weekly box office per engagement	$3,239	$3,382	4.4+

SOURCE: "EDI Box Office News: More Shelf Space for Films," *Variety,* January 5–11, 1998, 30.

weekly box office per film rose during the same period, after several years of zero or declining returns, from $3,239 to $3,382. Interestingly, note that wide-released films grew 4.1 percent, which did not keep pace with the 20 percent growth of total releases over the same period.

Table 23 presents MPAA's tracking of the films rated and released, showing the lower numbers from earlier decades (and tallies differing from EDI's in the previous table). The films released annually in the 1990s prompted Leonard Klady to write, "there's unquestionably a glut of product and there's no way for theater chains to effectively handle the avalanche of movies."[143] The strategy of opening more and more on a wider number of screens further compounded this glut, as did the bottlenecking of film releases around key holiday weekends. One effect was some changing practices on the part of distributors. For instance, clearances were not enforced fully. There was simply no need to do so within the logic that films had to appear everywhere at once, creating situations in which different chains showed the same film in a single market. These crunch periods also meant it was a more common practice for exhibitors to have two films share the same screen.[144] As noted in chapter 4, wide releasing does not necessarily provide an advantage to exhibitors. Hindes points out that "some theater owners complain that it dilutes the audience pool and shortens film runs."[145] Shorter runs are less favorable to exhibitors, whose percentage of box office increases the longer the film runs, as "in the first few weeks of release, the lion's share of box-office proceeds go to the studio. The formula gradually shifts over time so that the theater owners keep an increasing percentage of

TABLE 23   Number of Theatrical Films Rated and Released (domestic)

Year	Rated	Released
1950	n/a	483
1960	n/a	248
1970	n/a	306
1980	n/a	233
1990	n/a	410
1995	697	411
1996	713	471
1997	673	510
1998	661	509
1999	677	461
2000	762	478

SOURCE: Motion Picture Association of America, "2001 U.S. Economic Review," http://www.mpaa.org/useconomicreview/2001Economic, last accessed June 23, 2002.

receipts."[146] Lawrence Cohn provided a comparison of the three Indiana Jones films. The first, *Raiders of the Lost Ark* (Steven Spielberg 1981), played for 83 weeks, *Indiana Jones and the Temple of Doom* (Steven Spielberg 1984) played for 24 weeks, and *Indiana Jones and the Last Crusade* (Steven Spielberg 1989) was in first run for 20 weeks. This is a shift in favor of the distributor's share.[147]

Put differently, in the age of more intense distributor involvement in exhibition, distributors were able to wield additional power to dictate favorable terms for themselves. When the rapid move into exhibition began, Barry Diller commented contrarily that "a studio would have to be stupid to build or buy movie theaters in the U.S."[148] And a few years later it became apparent to many that this consolidation was not the financial treasure it had originally seemed to be. Nonetheless, the benefits were substantial, including lower film rentals costs, quality control of the location, and, importantly, an increase in the ability to orchestrate the release and run of films. As one industry analyst put it, "It gives the major studios a way to maintain quality control over the presentation of their product. . . . When one considers that the theatrical opening is still the main engine driving sales of a motion picture in ancillary markets, the importance of that control becomes readily apparent."[149] Another industry consultant commented on *Bugsy* (Barry Levinson 1991), which was "distributed by TriStar,

International Cinematic Life   **159**

whose parent, Sony Pictures Entertainment, also owns the 885-screen Loews theater chain. '*Bugsy* was down to about 500 screens.' . . . 'Now all of a sudden, with a slew of Academy Award nominations, they have increased distribution back to about 1,200 screens. It certainly helps to have some theaters handy to put it in immediately.' "[150]

This kind of coordination meant that by the early 1990s, with an emphasis on opening weekends, a 3,000 screen opening was no longer an extraordinary occurrence.[151] In the summer of 1989, Paramount opened *The Hunt for Red October* (John McTiernan 1990) on 6,401 screens in the United States and Canada, which was an industry record, to be broken in January 1990 by Universal Pictures with its 6,792-screen opening of *Tremors* (Ron Underwood 1990).[152] This figure represented approximately 27.8 percent of all U.S. and Canadian screens (assuming drive-ins would mostly be shut for the winter in January, and taking the indoor screen tally of 22,774 for the United States (1990) and 1,555 for Canada (1989/90)). In other words, this single film opened its run in over a quarter of all indoor commercial screens in those two countries, a ratio habitually apparent through the 1990s with wide openings. On this point, we must recognize that the current cinema is made up of a short-lived but massively visible core of new texts and consider how this shapes cinemagoing practices. *Variety* identified the first experiments in saturation releasing as *The Trial of Billy Jack* (T.C. Frank [Tom] Laughlin 1974), which opened on 800 screens, and *Breakout* (Tom Gries 1975), on 1,500.[153] Even the definition of a limited release was revised in 1997 to take account of the general swelling of film engagements, to 600 theaters, not screens.[154] Compare, for example, the "saturation" release of *Jaws* (Steven Spielberg 1975) in 467 theaters, seen as an innovation in releasing strategies at the time, [155] with that of *Lost World: Jurassic Park II* (Steven Spielberg 1997), opening in 3,281 theaters (and on 6,000 screens). Its release peaked at a record 3,565 theaters.[156] Or consider the example of *Con Air* (Simon West 1997), opening in 2,824 theaters in Canada and the United States, as well as 390 screens in the UK and Ireland, 25 screens in Hong Kong, 180 theaters in Mexico, and 28 in both Argentina and Israel. That opening week it was also the top box office grossing film in Chile, Colombia, Panama, Uruguay, and Venezuela. The following week, it opened in Germany, Austria, then Spain, Holland, and South Korea.[157] This is not an exhaustive list of the film's openings, but it does make perfectly clear that an emerging idea of global simultaneity, however selective this process actually may be, is increasingly part of the common sense of Hollywood. Further, it is worth noting that the increased expense on the number of prints required for saturation releasing has been a boon for production houses specializing in the duplication process.

The counterintuitive strategy of *Titanic* (James Cameron 1997) is worth noting, if only to remind ourselves that ruling practices are never monolithic. In its 800 theaters, certainly a wide release but not of the scale of other films in 1997 like *Lost World: Jurassic Park II* and *Men in Black* (Barry Sonnefeld 1997), it still grossed more than either, consequently being cherished by exhibitors who saw higher per screen returns.[158] Additionally, it reversed the usual direction by opening overseas first.

Big-budget blockbusters are not the only films treated in this manner. A high-profile film will also act as a centerpiece around which other films will be introduced, either by the same distributor or competing ones. In a type of counterprogramming, films that cater to a perhaps smaller audience faction appear at essentially the same time as the broader-appeal movies. Multiple-screen cinemas facilitate this tactic, exhibitors and distributors reason, allowing groups to arrive together but to select a film more attuned to their individual tastes. It made sense for MGM/UA to release *Flawless* (Joel Schumacher 1999) the same week as their Bond film *The World Is Not Enough* (Michael Apted 1999), and for Fine Line to open *Tumbleweeds* (Gavin O'Conner 1999) that week as well. A James Bond film would be referred to as a "tentpole" movie. Some, however, have reconsidered the effectiveness of tentpole movies in generating traffic for smaller films. For instance, Dade Hayes declared, "The theory behind megaplex building and aggressively targeted marketing was to make the film biz more closely resemble cable television, with options for every taste and audience. Instead, tentpole movies routinely suck the air out of the box office. Anyone still consoling themselves with outdated notions of 'spillover' crowds should look at how other pics did when 'Harry Potter' arrived."[159] He then pointed out how the practice in fact does persist, using the example of *About a Boy* (Chris Weitz and Paul Weitz 2002) opening alongside tentpole film *Star Wars: Episode II–Attack of the Clones* (George Lucas 2002), and successfully so. For our present purposes, the practice reveals the careful consideration of the current cinema as a slate of temporally designated films on the part of exhibitors and distributors.

The impact wide releasing has had on the landscape of our current cinema cannot be overestimated. We now have an ever more coordinated continental, and burgeoning global, cinema culture. The orchestration of film releasing offers an expectation of *simultaneity*, one that might be described as a material and imagined sense of the "everywhere" of current cinema, something with which moviegoers are amply familiar from the many trailers promising this ubiquity. And while there is a rising simultaneity for one strata of highly visible texts, there is an even wider gap in the appearance of more marginal contributions to the current cinema, which may take longer to arrive, if at all, on local screens. From the international building of multiplex cinemas to the orchestration of the appearance of new cinema commodities, from the reassurances of control and safety in public locations to the tacit acknowledgment of splintered audiences, the details offered in this chapter indicate that a tentative simultaneity—many spaces, same time—and revised life cycle narratives—many spaces, many times—are constitutive modes of connection between people and places. Though a product of business practices and ownership structures, the consequences extend to the very nature of being in this nominally global context. The international building boom of multiplexes, many of which were jointly financed by transnational entertainment conglomerates and local national development firms, presents us with an extensive network of landing pads for a current cinema that jets its way across the world. I now turn to examine the experience of another national context, Canada, asking how industry and audiences operate in light of the material and discursive determinants characterized above.

CHAPTER SEVEN

Northern Screens

"Welcome to Hollywood North" was a 1988 symposium in Los Angeles that intended to sell the merits of the Canadian film and television industry, its talented personnel, and the financial advantages of shooting in Canada. Its schedule included such Canadian industry and policy luminaries as Harold Greenberg, Astral Media founder and producer of the most financially successful Canadian film *Porky's* (Bob Clark 1981), the prominent producer and distributor Rene Malo, and the former communications minister Francis Fox. Organizers, however, canceled the symposium "due to lack of interest from the U.S. production community," as *Playback* put it.[1]

A decade later, Hollywood's interest in, and distress about, Canada had skyrocketed. Industry sources expressed worry that Canada and other countries were "pecking away at Hollywood's hegemony" by drawing more and more film shoots.[2] Attracted by combinations of favorable exchange rates, lower wages, government subsidies, tax breaks, and labor laws advantageous for producers, "runaway" productions, according to some estimates, had caused the loss of 125,000 jobs over ten years, though these numbers vary widely. This drain prompted calls for California tax incentives to keep films in that state and for retaliatory trade measures against Canadian-shot movies specifically.[3]

Successes at international festivals, regular and lucrative sales to international markets, more films, bigger budgets, profitable distributors and producers— without a doubt, Canada has entered an extraordinary stage in which it stands as a vibrant industry and market. "Second cinemas"[4] or "medium-sized cinemas,"[5] such as those of Sweden, the Netherlands, South Korea, Australia, New Zealand, and Canada, may not constitute a major portion of internationally circulating cultural forms. And yet they must be recognized as significant participants in the current organization of global production and consumption. However inconsistent or localized their participation actually is, they place commodities in an international market and are involved in the production, distribution, or exhibition of other country's commodities. Tom O'Regan asserts that "national cinemas routinely negotiate the extraordinary internationalism of the cinema. They do so from an unequal basis. National cinemas can expect to be no more than a junior partner to the dominant international cinemas."[6] Canada plays such a junior-partner role as a producer of work destined for international markets. The elaborate stock of coproduction treaties, which encourage international financing and facilitate access to other markets, is one facet of Canada's globalizing film and television sector. Not to be underemphasized, the sector is amply integrated with U.S. business, hence its characterization as a branch plant industry. Thus the current unprecedented strength of the sector is somewhat paradoxical given that what we call the Canadian film industry is frequently one that acts in the service of U.S. productions. This owes no small amount to the cheap Canadian dollar and tax breaks, making Canadian shoots and labor inexpensive for American investors. In 1994, $402 million was spent on film and television production in British Columbia alone, with approximately 75 percent of this coming from Hollywood.[7] By 1998 that figure was $1 billion.[8] Provinces and cities now compete with one another for pieces of this tasty influx of production activity.

It is possible that the entwinement of national cinemas is so elaborate that absolute economic and cultural differentiation is impossible, constructing new hyphenated creatures to designate a film text's place of origin (Canada-China, Canada-Portugal-France). The messy lines demarcating national cinemas, and the historically intense blending of U.S. and Canadian cinema cultures, can make for some curious situations. For instance, though the population is not seen as large enough to sustain fully a national cinema within its own borders, the concentrated French-speaking population of Quebec can propel a local feature into the top ranks of Canadian/U.S. exhibition. Two sequels, no less, *Elvis Gratton II* (Pierre Falardeau 1999) and *Les Boys II* (Louis Saia 1998), both ranked 191 and 203 respectively in *Variety*'s 250 top-grossing releases for 1999, both beating the likes of *Besieged* (Bernardo Bertolucci 1998) at 208, *Happy, Texas* (Mark Illsley 1999) at 210, and *Hideous Kinky* (Gillies MacKinnon 1999) at 224.[9]

The assessment of rising industrial might and market attractiveness of Canadian film and television extends new levels of confidence to investors and producers alike. Where it used to be the case that ambitions to work in popular forms drew talent to other locations, today it is possible to chart a career path in film and television that does not include permanent departure. This has been the case for internationally celebrated directors (David Cronenberg, Atom Egoyan, Lea Pool, Patricia Rozema, Robert Lepage), actors (Bruce Greenwood, Elias Koteas, Shirley Douglas, Mia Kirshner), producers (Robert Lantos, Rene Malo, Michelene Charest), and entertainment moguls (Garth Drabinsky, Moses Znaimer, Izzy Asper). Canadian feature films now display a full complement of generic and audience appeal: the sci-fi *Screamers* (Christian Duguay 1995), the children's hit *Air Bud* (Charles Martin Smith 1997), the Gen-X *waydowntown* (Gary Burns 2000) and *Eldorado* (Charles Binamé 1995), the rock'n'roll road movie *Hard Core Logo* (Bruce McDonald 1996), the historical drama *Margaret's Museum* (Mort Ransen 1995), the personal, director-driven *The Hanging Garden* (Thom Fitzgerald 1997) and *Léolo* (Jean-Claude Lauzon 1992), the lesbian romance *When Night Is Falling* (Patricia Rozema 1995), the international coproductions *Sunshine* (Istvan Szabo 2000) and *The Red Violin* (François Girard 1998), and the Oscar-nominated (for Best Director) *The Sweet Hereafter* (Atom Egoyan 1997).

Signs of artistic and industrial achievement aside, a sense of failure and missed opportunity nevertheless haunts Canada in considering its cinema, analogous to other "minor" national cinemas similarly struggling for international recognition and national particularity. One does not have to talk to filmmakers, policymakers, movie fans, or relatives for long before hearing something about the dull, strange, indistinct, or inaccessible nature of Canadian cinema and television. Where Canadian film culture sells extraordinarily well to broadcasters and distributors across the globe, making the country one of the most prominent exporters of motion picture commodities, a reigning "structure of feeling" of failure means that this situation goes unrecognized or is actively disavowed by critics. The sense of failure partly stems from the fact that Canadian commercial cinema has not functioned well or consistently as a meeting point for a national community. With notable exceptions, especially in Quebec, an absence of a strong and reliable Canadian popular cinema promotes an impression of the nonexistence of the cinema. One commentator proposed bluntly that Canada is "unique among industrial nations in its extreme lack of desire to watch its own movies."[10]

There are some powerful forces behind the conditions of invisibility of Canadian cinema. The disjuncture between industrial prowess and a sentiment of failure reflects the attention producers pay to the economies of global buyers. Courting markets abroad might mean accenting the "Canadianness" and polishing the recognizable qualities, in this way making "nation" a form of product differentiation on the international markets (*Jesus of Montreal* [Denys Arcand 1989] and the TV shows *Anne of Green Gables* and *The Beachcombers* all come to mind). At other times, producers and distributors work to conceal Canadian attributes and origins. For instance, Canadian distributor Paragon Entertainment acquired HandMade Films, of London, in expectation of the ability to hide Canadianness. According to CEO Jon Slan, one advantage was HandMade's international reputation and its European status. As he says, "I don't believe people look at these as Canadian films."[11] In either case, local cultural production might not necessarily be responsive or conducive to local cultural consumption.

Many countries face similar dilemmas. At stake is not only economic viability or artistic freedom but the very fabric of a national community, or what Philip Schlesinger calls "the interior of the national communicative space."[12] Addressing the variability of expressions of national cinema culture, O'Regan writes that in most countries "cinema-going, cinema distribution, cinema viewing and cinema criticism are not primarily oriented to local national cinema, but to the cinema more generally, and more particularly the dominant international cinema."[13] In the multiplicity of studies of national cinemas, these issues are foundational elements. Andrew Higson's oft-cited essay "The Concept of National Cinema" is a case in point. In a still relevant argument that "the parameters of a national cinema should be drawn at the site of consumption as much as at the site of production of films,"[14] Higson reminds us that this consists in an array of films that arrive from other countries. He notes, quite tellingly, that Hollywood is "an integral and naturalised part of the national culture, or the popular imagination, of most countries in which cinema is an established entertainment form."[15] Thus it is a gross miscalculation to expect that a national-popular, or the interior national communicative space, would be composed solely of local consumption of local work.

At the risk of short-circuiting an intricate dilemma, we would be well advised to note that "nation" cannot but allude to a matrix of multinational artifacts, whether in responsive, colonizing, or appropriative gestures. Many recent theorizations of national cinema advance the claim that the term invariably leads one to the transnational. Susan Hayward asserts that national cinemas exist in boundaries that slowly evaporate, leaving pluricultural and hybrid entities behind. Writing about national cinemas becomes a task of "exposing its masquerade of unity."[16] Andrew Higson concurs, writing, "the degree of cultural cross-breeding and interpenetration, not only across borders but also within them, suggests that modern cultural formations are invariably hybrid and impure."[17] Indeed, he suggests, if one argument for a national cinema is as a safeguard against global homogeneity, hence as a promoter of cultural diversity, then this might in fact be achieved through the importation of culture rather than nationally rooted production.[18]

Considering the economic and cultural impact of transnational film culture, two sets of questions are significant. First, what is the fallout of cultural enterprise and policy that encourages internationalization of the film and television industry? Is it reasonable to expect that the bolstering of the resumés of Canadian film crews working on U.S. shoots will contribute to a vibrant indigenous film culture? Or are Canadian personnel in danger, as David Ellis has noted, of becoming line producers, a position of little creative input or power?[19] Second, how can we take account of the forms of viewing and experiencing film offered by the junior partner and branch plant aspects of the Canadian film industry? Is it justifiable to seek out forms of national spectatorship, given the disorderly borders between national cinemas? Or are there new forms of multinational cultural encounters we must extricate?

Nothing is more frequently cited as a roadblock to the full actualization of a popular cinema culture than the overwhelming U.S. presence in Canadian movie theaters. Indeed, Canada's inclusion as part of the U.S. domestic market for theatrical exhibition enjoys an elevated status as the quintessential emblem of the struggles of Canadian cultural particularity. The U.S. economic command over Canadian movie theaters circulates as a symptom of the overall "americanization" of Canadian culture. The close ties of exhibitors' to U.S. corporations squeezes domestic film out of commercial exhibition channels, such that it occupies only 2 to 3 percent of the market.[20] Even in Quebec, where the local popular film culture is stronger than in the rest of Canada, domestic film captures only 4 percent of the box office.[21] Where U.S. popular cinema is unavoidably manifest on Canadian screens, Canadian films are by and large absent from those locations. On this topic, where Peter Harcourt wrote about "the invisible cinema" of Canada, he observed that the problem was not a lack of films but a lack of audiences for those films.[22]

A national presence on commercial screens has stood for a long time as a gauge of the health of the national cinema. Discursively, exhibition has been treated as a recurring problem to the point where it is taken as a defining feature of Canadian cinematic life. A review of film policy marked the thirtieth anniversary of Telefilm Canada, the primary federal film and television funding agency. To make feature film as successful as television production, proposals included increasing the number of features shot in Canada, ticket taxes, screen quotas for Canadian films, more support for international marketing of films, and a levy on theatrical receipts and incentives for international investment.[23] Important for the present argument, its report began with box office revenue as a mark of the dismal state of Canadian film and ended with the goal of increasing the screen time of Canadian film to 10 percent by 2004.[24]

The dependency theory model of U.S. cultural imperialism in Canadian cinemas is hardly the domain of political economists exclusively. Instead, it is repeated and expanded by journalists, editorialists, policymakers, government representatives, and others. One of the striking aspects of the state of Canadian film is the frequency with which popular periodicals report on its absence, invariably citing the "colonization" of theaters as evidence. An article on the Toronto Film Festival becomes a report on the uncertain future of Canadian film, especially when compared to the international success of Canadian television.[25] This thinking is reflected in the headline of reporter Robert Everett-

Green's article "Not Coming Soon to a Theatre Near You."[26] Even industry sources habitually begin with this claim. For instance, an article on distribution opens, "Theatrical distribution in Canada has long been plagued by problems of American domination. It's not just the universal story in which American product hogs a huge percentage of available screen time, Canada has been sold off for years as a piece of the North American market."[27]

These examples are more than status reports on a nation's film culture. They represent a discursive agreement about its meager existence. They are evaluations reflecting a particular history of film culture and criticism. Film absence has an unusual presence in the Canadian popular imaginary. While political-economic description is indispensable, there has been an overinvestment in its explanatory powers, such that the multifarious conditions and operations of a traveling U.S. cinema are reduced to economic and ideological invasion only. The meanings and experiences of culture are just as powerful and effective in shaping social existence as economic, and those meanings and experiences are not written unambiguously on even the most dominant forms and practices of the day. Canadian distributors, producers, and filmmakers struggle for minor accomplishments in the context of the overwhelming presence of U.S. film. This, however, cannot be a substitute for nor be taken as equivalent to the struggles of Canadian audiences who must live and negotiate the existing popular cultural scene. Examining industrial structure alone, there is little room to consider the affective involvement of the Canadian audiences with U.S. theatrical releases. Further, there is a tendency to deploy commercial screen presence of features as a way to measure not only the national cinema but the "quality" of the popular audience. Such calls for the "improvement" of popular taste have been documented in other countries, and to be sure, when movie theaters were the sole sites at which audiences and film texts might meet, focus on access to screens was fundamental to building a cinema culture. Yet, with that time long passed, today theaters instead function as a sign of prestige, often against the more everyday, "lowly" form of television. Currently, the focus on commercial exhibition can be at the expense of the rising importance of other locations for spectatorship. In summation, and as will be developed below, (1) Canadian national spectatorship might be best thought of in relation to sites of consumption other than those of traditional theatrical exhibition; and (2) Canadian popular cinemagoing culture is not absent, but rather consists of an engagement with an internationally circulating popular culture.

This chapter examines how one national context responds to and manages the global film environment portrayed in the preceding chapters. It is my contention that motion picture theaters are one key site for an encounter with international entertainment, and in this way cinemas and cinemagoing have been a battleground for definitions and distinctions of national spectatorship.

THE CHANGING FACE OF CANADIAN EXHIBITION

Concurrent with circumstances in other countries, movie audiences in Canada are facing a new landscape of cinemas. Two theater chains dominate cinema exhibition, Famous Players and Cineplex Odeon. Taking December 1998 rankings of U.S. and Canadian exhibitors, Cineplex Odeon, together with its U.S. counterpart Loews Cineplex, was the fourth largest chain overall, and Famous Players was the eleventh. Though Famous Players only operates in Canada, its parent corporation Viacom is owned by National Amusements, which was the ninth ranking chain in the United States and Canada.[28] Their prominence on the North American scene aside, these exhibitors represent a long-standing presence in Canada specifically, with Famous Players forming in 1920 and Cineplex Odeon appearing in 1984. The latter is a product of Garth Drabinsky's Cineplex, which began with the eighteen-screen Toronto Eaton Centre multiplex in 1979, buying the older Odeon chain, founded in 1941. A significant minority ownership share of Cineplex Odeon had been in the hands of MCA/Universal and hence became part of Vivendi Universal shortly after 2000. Along with Magic Johnson, Loews-IMAX, and Star Theatres, Cineplex Odeon became part of Loews Cineplex Entertainment in 1998, whose parent at the time was Sony, only to be acquired by Onex and Oaktree Capital in 2002 after it filed for Chapter 11. Cineplex Odeon's and Famous Players' enduring presence has bestowed them with well-tailored connections to major U.S. distributors, thus helping to sew up the flow of films to their screens.[29] Famous Players has had ongoing understandings with Buena Vista, MGM, Warner Bros., and Paramount, and Cineplex Odeon had special relationships with Columbia, Fox, and Universal.[30]

A fundamental consequence of their might is the high concentration of theater ownership in the hands of few chains, one that contrasts with the more dispersed ownership among more numerous major chains in the United States. The ill-fated merger in 1998 between three U.S. chains—Regal, Act III, and UATC—caused shock waves as it would have given them over 19 percent of all U.S. screens.[31] In Canada, that same year, Famous Players and Cineplex Odeon control approximately 30 percent and 43 percent of screens, respectively.[32] Some estimates claim that these two chains account for as much as 80 percent of the theatrical grosses of a film,[33] and by 1999 Famous Players held an incredible 47 percent share of the Canadian market.[34] This kind of near duopoly, unheard of in the United States, has been a fact of Canadian exhibition for decades. The remaining share belongs to regional chains, such as Quebec's Guzzo, Ontario's Stinson, and Western Provinces' Landmark, and Newfoundland and the Maritimes' Empire.[35] Even these at times enter into arrangements with the two major chains. For example, both Guzzo and Empire have relied on Cineplex Odeon to bid on films for them.

As the firm most frequently credited with leading distributors back into exhibition in 1986, then buoyed by the ownership involvement of MCA/Universal, Cineplex Odeon has continued consolidation at an international level with several industry-shaking illustrations. After an attempted merger with Cinemark USA in March 1995,[36] Cineplex Odeon announced a merger with Sony's Loews Theaters in September 1997.[37] The day following the announcement, Canadian Heritage Minister Sheila Copps insisted that for the deal to be approved the new corporation must make a commitment to screen more Canadian films.[38] It was also possible that Cineplex Odeon would have to divest its distribution arm, Cineplex Odeon Films.[39] Indeed, following Investment Canada's approval of the Loews–Cineplex Odeon merger, the restrictions on foreign ownership of distribution meant that Cineplex Odeon Films had to be sold.[40] Part of the merger plans, as they went before the U.S. Securities and Exchange Commission, involved closing theaters that were in unnecessary competition with one another or were not performing well.[41] By 1998 the merger created the exhibition giant Loews Cineplex Entertainment, then with 2,900 screens in 450 locations throughout North America and Europe[42] and 13 percent of the U.S. and Canadian market share.[43] By May of that year, the new corporation sacked almost all of the top executives at Cineplex Odeon in Toronto.[44]

As with the chains to the south, the two Canadian titans have been making substantial investments since 1994 in the construction of new theaters and the refurbishment of existing ones, introducing new technology, design, and decor. Some regional chains, like Empire and Guzzo, have been refurbishing and building multiplex cinemas, and a newly arriving chain, Galaxy Entertainment, was developing an exhibition circuit in smaller cities and towns, starting with Ontario.[45] But nothing compares with the extent of investment from the two national chains. With 475 screens at 107 locations in 1996, Famous Players' expansion brought it to 771 screens at 111 locations by the end of 1999.[46] Cineplex Odeon added 179 screens to its existing 621 in Canada within the same three years.[47] Table 24 captures the resultant ranking of Canada's biggest chains.

Despite the remarkable level of building in the mid-1990s, it is instructive to remember that the late 1980s were also a time of expansion. Famous Players CEO Walter Senior said that their three-year plan in 1988 was "the largest single construction project in the history of Canadian motion picture exhibition."[48] Purportedly, the source of the spark to its plans was a renewed interest in cinemagoing, with Famous Players announcing a sudden 16.2 percent increase in admissions in the summer of 1986.[49] Explaining these changes, Senior stated, "A successful theater must be a part of the community it serves," and observed that "modern-day moviegoers want an experience that takes them as far out of their living rooms as they can be. They want to become immersed in the public experience of motion pictures, and that means an adequately sized auditorium, and not just a screen."[50] Here we see yet again that by negotiating a division between public and private space, cinemas are about community life and a relation to other sites of cultural consumption. Such thinking was not Famous Players' alone. Cineplex Odeon planned a greater expansion of 200 screens from 1986 to 1988, proposing to get rid of its small "airline-type" screens and adding 300 in the United States.[51] This came after its CEO, Garth Drabinsky, criticized theater operators for "a lack of inspiration, a lack of creativity, in the way that theaters are being built and the way theaters are being managed and maintained."[52]

Cineplex Odeon's new cinemas were noteworthy as an early sign that the tiny multiplex cinemas were on their way out. As Douglas Gomery puts it, Cineplex Odeon shifted in the mid-1980s from "drab 'cookie-cutter' multiplexes" to "vast

TABLE 24   Canada's Top Twenty-One Chains, June 2000

Chain	Sites / Screens
Cineplex Odeon	122 / 828
(Alta., B.C., Man., Ont., Quebec, Sask.)	
Famous Players	108 / 804
(Alta., B.C., Man., N.B., N.S., Ont., Quebec, Sask.)	
AMC (Ont.)	5 / 122
Empire Theatres (N.B., N.F., N.S., P.E.I.)	18 / 118
Landmark Cinemas (Alta., B.C., Man., Sask., Yukon)	39 / 101
Guzzo (Quebec)	10 / 100
Caprice Showcase (B.C.)	n/a / 54
Cinema City (Alta., Man.)	4 / 40
Stinson (Ont.)	n/a / 37
Magic Lantern Theatres (Alta., N.W. Terr., Sask.)	10 / 37
Galaxy Entertainment (Ont.)	5 / 33
Tarrant Enterprises (Ont.)	n/a / 29
May Theatres (Alta., Sask.)	n/a / 26
Alliance Atlantis Cinemas (Alta., B.C., Ont.)	6 / 24
Cinemark (Alta., B.C.)	n/a / 24
Premier Operating (Ont.)	10 / 19
Golden Theatres (Ont.)	n/a / 15
A Theatre Near You (B.C., U.S.)	4 / 12
Harris Roads Entertainment Group (B.C., Man.)	n/a / 9
The Movie Mill (Alta.)	1 / 7
Festival Cinemas (Ont.)	n/a / 6

SOURCE: "Canadian Giants of Exhibition," *Boxoffice,* July 2000, 34, 35.

NOTE: These chains account for approximately 95 percent of all screens.

complexes of whimsical, postmodern 'picture palaces.' "[53] The corporation intended the art deco–inspired design of some cinemas to be "reminiscent of the
splendor of the movie palaces of the 1920s and 1930s."[54] An early example of the
turn to more lavish cinemas was the Egyptien in Montreal, opening in 1987
(figure 10). With its cryptlike entrance, the multiplex was a kitschy tomb from
ancient Egypt, complete with decorative pillars and hieroglyphic markings.
This theme cinema connoted not a former civilization but theme cinemas of the
past, for the referent was movie palaces, not Egypt. In the Egyptien, as in other

FIGURE 10 Cineplex Odeon Egyptien, Montreal. By permission of Cineplex Odeon.

elaborate cinemas about to be built, signs of opulence operated simultaneously as signs of cinematic nostalgia. They followed this with further efforts. "New attempts to woo customers" described Cineplex Odeon being saved by blockbuster movies, and by expanding concession snacks, or what was called "Project Popcorn," noting a growing interest in location-based entertainment.[55] The construction of megaplexes was not far behind for this and other chains. For instance, in Montreal alone, Cineplex Odeon built the seventeen-screen Quartier Latin; Famous Players converted an old department store into the thirteen-screen Paramount and built the suburban twelve-screen Coliseum, seventeen-screen SilverCity, and eighteen-screen Colossus; AMC occupied and transformed a vacant hockey arena into the twenty-two-screen Pepsi Forum; and in the suburbs Guzzo built fourteen-, sixteen-, and eighteen-screen complexes.

Arguments and assessments about this investment and reconfiguration of cinema spaces echo these of U.S. exhibitors and distributors. Economic rationales for the expansion varied from changing demographics to accommodating saturation releasing and the increase in the number of films released theatrically.[56] Most prominently, the "improvement" of the moviegoing experience entered as a prominent and accepted rationale for the wave of changes, something the ample press coverage repeatedly noted. At the 1997 ShowCanada convention of exhibitors, though several innovations attracted attention,[57] the "Service: Disney Style" seminar was the talk of the meeting, providing evidence of the continuing power of Disney as a model for out-of-home leisure. This model championed customer service above all other aspects of exhibition, or as it was put in the presentation, "Success in any business is 10 percent product and 90 percent service."[58] And as part of its plans for its megaplexes, Famous Players sent managers to Disney University, where they received training in the Disney approach to service and entertainment.[59]

An unusual aspect of the expansion of the 1990s and beyond has been U.S. exhibitors moving their operations northward. Cinemark opened discount screens in Edmonton and Winnipeg,[60] and smaller regional chains Golden Theaters and A Theater Near You are both U.S.-based. The most rapid and aggressive change has been the construction of a handful of AMC megaplexes in large urban centers, Canadian beachheads for the Kansas City exhibitor. These are among the largest complexes in the country, virtually overnight moving AMC to rank as the third largest chain.

From this account, it is apparent how familiar the terms of improvement and internationalization were for this wave of expansion. Some commented that the Canadian strategy was slightly inappropriate and might have been based on a misinterpretation of the direction of the industry. Though distributors generally considered Canada to be underscreened, especially when compared to the United States, the recent construction of theaters with eight to twelve screens was not commensurate with the massive sites being built elsewhere.[61] Further, extraordinary growth in some areas meant that chains created congested cinemagoing markets. For instance, Ottawa saw its screen tally rise from 69 at the end of 1997 to 111 when 1998 closed. In the familiar dialectic for urban environments, closings and divestment accompany building and investment. At one point in early 1997, Famous Players stated that its expansion plans included closing 75 screens.[62] Earlier, in 1988, Cineplex Odeon began to retreat from "secondary markets" of 50,000 to 100,000 people by selling 57 multiplexes across Canada, a strategy it employed with its U.S. screens two years later.[63] The expansion in Canada specifically initiated a process of urbanizing, and suburbanizing, moviegoing, resulting in many smaller communities losing the only commercial cinema they had.

The total number of indoor theaters decreased over a ten-year period—from 657 to 1988/89 to 624 in 1998/99—while screens jumped from 1,490 to 2,468.[64] This inverse direction typifies a cinema landscape consisting of fewer locations for cinemagoing. With fewer sites, more screens, and greater profitability, most assessments would mark the Canadian exhibition industry as a healthy, stable part of the cultural scene. And yet it continues to be treated as a problem, especially when considering the unchallenged dominance of U.S. films it screens. The restructuring and investment characterized above *did not change this in the slightest,* making the growth yet another phase in the international, and primarily U.S., orientation of popular cinema in Canada.

New and redesigned edifices where people go to the cinema, the more synchronized openings, the relative choice of films and show times afforded by multiple screens, and the expanded extrafilmic services are all outgrowths witnessed during this period. As beneficiaries of the emergent coordination of saturation releasing, urban and suburban Canadians count on openings for major films simultaneous with those in U.S. metropolitan centers. This period witnessed events such as Canadian distributor Alliance's opening *Scream 2* (Wes Craven 1997) in Iqaluit, Nunavut, on the same day the film premiered elsewhere across Canada and the United States. This was the first time Iqaluit had enjoyed a coinciding film opening.[65] This coordination does not extend to all regions uniformly nor to all forms of cinematic life. It might in fact mark a widening temporal gap between major and independent releases, in that there are some films for which one must wait even longer. But there is a speedier arrival of the biggest-budget Hollywood films than in the past.

The simultaneity of the current cinema and the upscaling of the multiplex, however, did not break the barriers to Canadian films at those sites. Nor were they expected to do so. On the contrary, policymakers have been historically reluctant to force exhibitors to present Canadian films. The maturity of commercial exhibition—which can be a code for a faltering policy response—means that attention has tended to turn toward more fledgling sectors. Over the last decade or so, the distribution sector has held substantial promise for Canadian cinema, reasoning that its viability might ignite the marketing of and demand for Canadian films.

THE MAGIC SOLUTION OF FILM DISTRIBUTION

Ted Magder reminds us that the federal government's feature film policy from 1968 onward was as much a problem for Canadian cinematic practices as the U.S. majors ever were. In particular, he points to the lack of a distribution policy, such that distribution was not a condition of support for publicly funded films.[66] This situation changed with the federal film and video policy of 1984, which, in Magder's words, "dealt with more (or less) than the question of distribution,"[67] though it did not recommend protectionist measures. Magder comments that the reluctance to challenge U.S. majors' presence was "as incredible as it was predictable."[68]

In recent years, policy action has been explicitly designed to produce sizable, vertically integrated film companies, with distribution becoming a fulcrum for programs. An industry consultant recommended "greater consolidation in the Canadian distribution and production industry and better collaboration between filmmakers and distributors,"[69] and somewhat dramatically, "distribution assistance policies should be based on weeding out the industry and consolidating companies, rather than simply maintaining them."[70] Undergirding these assessments is a conviction that Canadian distribution is essential to the invigoration of a Canadian popular cinema. The problem has been that when U.S. majors own domestic rights to distribute films, those rights encompass Canada. Robert Lantos, founder of the media corporation Alliance, observed that "Canada is a gift in return for getting U.S. distribution," thus limiting the operations of Canadian distributors and hurting film producers who lose the opportunity to make an independent sale to Canada. Lantos opined that both producers and Canadian distributors "stand to make more money if Canada were treated as a separate country."[71]

The most elaborate effort to split the two markets was legislation, announced in 1987, that would require Canadian distributors to handle the theatrical and video release of films for which U.S. majors did not have world rights.[72] In effect, this bill required that Canada be treated as a film market independent of the United States, though with exceptions for certain films, as its authors were cautious about attacking the U.S. majors directly.[73] With the U.S.-Canada Free Trade negotiations under way at the same time, filmmakers and distributors expressed concern that it would be watered down by the time the legislation was introduced,[74] and this is exactly what happened when the proposed Film Products Importation Bill C-134 finally appeared.[75]

Despite the policy agreement on the separation of the two markets as a solution, from the start some were skeptical about the desirability of this initiative. Industry observer Ian Mccallum felt that the goals of aiding Canadian distributors and increasing screen time for Canadian film would not be achieved without quotas at theaters and without attention to major as well as independent film.[76] Instead, he reasoned, other developments, such as Telefilm's investment in commercial films and the Canadian location shooting of U.S. productions, were more substantial and marked the maturity of the Canadian film industry.[77]

Bill C-134 may have been the right policy at the wrong time. Here was a protectionist proposal being debated alongside mounting discussions about reducing trade barriers between countries. At their next meeting, Prime Minister Brian Mulroney responded to concerns expressed by President Ronald Reagan about the effect the distribution legislation would have on U.S. film exports.[78] As expected, the main industry group promoting U.S. film in Canada, the Canadian Motion Picture Distributors Association, attacked the bill using right-wing research showing that the government's measures protect mediocre film "that would have trouble surviving in a competitive market-oriented environment."[79] A prefiguration of the bill's impact was already being observed. Victor Loewy of Alliance Releasing charged that Canadian distributors were being frozen out of sales at the Cannes festival because of a "fear of being punished by the Americans."[80]

In the meantime, the proposed bill, coupled with a new distribution fund at Telefilm, stimulated the formation of small distributors, many of which were not located in the film centers of Montreal and Toronto, a development described in *Variety* as "a silly regional split."[81] Canadian exhibitors also launched distribution arms, including Cineplex Odeon Films[82] and Famous Players'

C/FP Distribution.[83] This escalating activity of Canadian distributors continued in the 1990s, with the largest two, Alliance Releasing and C/FP, taking 10 percent of Canadian box office. Trade sources attributed their success to their national scope, their catering to both French and English markets, and, most importantly, their deals to handle U.S. films, the final one being a vital part of the strength of many Canadian distributors.[84] In this context, too, U.S. distributors began setting up shop. Gulf and Western, the parent of Paramount and Famous Players at the time, negotiated a joint venture with Astral Bellevue to establish a Canadian distribution company in 1986,[85] and Buena Vista, the Disney film distribution company, opened a subsidiary in 1988.[86] Certainly, this was not to circumvent the Film Products Importation Bill, because as distributors of their own material they would be exempted anyway.

Regardless of the apparent bustling activity in distribution, the bill died, a sacrifice to larger political agendas. Where NAFTA was certainly a contributing factor, a few years later, the General Agreement on Trade and Tariffs (GATT) in the 1990s stumbled on the issue of cultural protection.[87] France took the lead in this, defending its right to subsidize its film industry and to impose quotas on imports. With the support of many European countries and Canada against the calls for freer trade for cultural product from the United States, Robert Lantos criticized Canada for not being bold enough in its criticism and for effectively staying "hidden behind the French."[88] The attitude he noted had as much to do with the multiple stakes involved as it did with timidity. National culture industries in the process of establishing a foothold on the global cultural scene can be expected to seek out participation with, and favor from, the reigning exporting behemoth. Alliance Atlantis was the Canadian distributor of *Lord of the Rings: Fellowship of the Ring* (Peter Jackson 2001), *The Blair Witch Project* (Daniel Myrick and Eduardo Sánchez 1999), and *The Spy Who Shagged Me* (Jay Roach 1999), all of which were considerable revenue generators for the company.

In the end, it has been most lucrative for distributors to acquire and distribute U.S. independent or specialty films, effectively piggybacking on the marketing and publicity done by U.S. distributors, and to set their sights on other windows of exhibition for Canadian works. The dimensions of distribution, then, include alliances and integration with the United States, as well as the organization of involvement through the life cycle of a film commodity.

Links are forged between intermedia and international culture, that is, consolidation and globalization. Canadian film, per se, drops into the background as a focus. Crucially, the sturdiness of this national structure is a function of international participation. Confounding received ideas of national designation, a complex hybrid global entity emerges. Where people wrote of "Euro-pudding" film and television production, a blended transnational distribution sector equally rocks presumptions about what a national cultural infrastructure is to serve and how it is to function.

Efforts to bring in similar legislation in Quebec had some degree of realization.[89] Quebec's Bill 109 passed in 1983, a protectionist measure stipulating that distributors had to be Quebec-based, except for those already operating prior to 1982 who had produced or acquired world rights to a particular film. This effectively "grandfathered" Hollywood majors.[90] In addition, French-language versions had to be provided within sixty days of the original release, later shortened to forty-five. This policy favored Hollywood majors, whose economies of scale allow for the upfront dubbing or subtitling costs, at the expense of smaller distributors, which might not be able to afford such versioning early in a film's release. This affected most conspicuously English-language Canadian films. In 1986 MPEAA chair Jack Valenti signed on to Quebec's proposals, agreeing that U.S. major distributors would not handle films whose production they did not invest in substantially and whose distribution rights to other main areas of export, including the rest of Canada and Europe, they did not already have.[91] Valenti, in an uncharacteristic expression of cultural sensitivity, stated that this deal recognized "the unique and singular character of Quebec in the world."[92]

Perhaps it is no surprise, but it appears the Quebec Cinema Act has not fully achieved its objectives. U.S. films increased their presence in Quebec, while Canadian and international films lost ground.[93] Some argued that the faster availability of French-language versions of U.S. film was responsible for a significant drop in Quebec's share of its own box office, from 10 percent in 1989 to 3 percent in 1993.[94] Ironically, as Manjunath Pendakur puts it, "the power of the majors was strengthened by the agreement, foretelling a bleak future for the Quebec independents."[95] For distributors from the rest of Canada, the impact was even bleaker. Quebec's legislation also barred the operation of Canadian firms based outside the province and established after 1982.[96] When the policy became active, *Variety* ran the headline "All Canada to Play by Quebec's Rules; U.S. Bigs Exempt from Distrib Law."[97] *Playback* for its part ran "Quebec Law Has Distribs Angered."[98] Distributors in Ontario responded by lobbying for a similar bill that would prohibit Quebec companies from operating in their province.[99] The tensions with an "internal" national cinema—a second second-cinema—thus present policy and industry challenges much as the international cultural universe does.

An aspect often neglected here is that revisions to the Investment Canada Act in 1985 provided a version of the very protection that the Film Products Importation Bill wanted to guarantee, though the latter was more detailed in its treatment of film distribution specifically. Investment Canada requires review of investments in cultural industries and restricts new non-Canadian firms from film distribution unless they receive an exemption.[100] This implied that those distributors who already had established operations—i.e., Hollywood majors—were exempt yet again. The president of the Dutch PolyGram Filmed Entertainment, Michael Kuhn, attacked this review policy, which had blocked their attempts to set up a film distribution business in Canada, calling it "monopolistic" and "xenophobic."[101] Industry Canada had refused their exemption, despite their additional promise to reinvest revenue into the Canadian industry.[102] The European Commission took Canada's barrier to PolyGram's operations to the World Trade Organization in May 1997, suggesting that it contravened GATT and WTO provisions on limitations to free trade.[103] In the meantime, they continued to operate in Canada, able to distribute their own films, and were joined by newcomer DreamWorks who similarly set up a distribution office in Toronto to do the same.

Not surprisingly, given the fact that cultural protection is not directed solely against U.S. products and that there are many invested parties, some have challenged the very idea of barriers to international cultural enterprises, maintaining that laissez-faire approaches are preferable. Steven Globerman, for instance, has argued that foreign ownership of distribution or exhibition is not a barrier to Canadians having access to film in theaters, that U.S. majors contribute sufficiently to the Canadian industry, and that there is nothing preventing Canadian filmmakers from taking advantage of the mass marketing expertise of

U.S. majors.[104] He rightly points out that the proposed distribution bill would have helped Canadian distributors circulate international product, not Canadian film. Yet when he then tries to account for the difficulties Canadian films have getting distribution, he has to fall rather lamely on the insupportable claim that Canadian films are not good enough, a claim that reveals a set of assumptions about cultural value beneath the supposedly neutral measures of economic potential and market power. Globerman recommends that Canadians lobby for reduced barriers elsewhere.

In the end, film distribution has been an actionable area of influence for public policy unlike commercial exhibition. Nonetheless, the internal competition for and criticism of direct subsidy, and the highly politicized attempts to legislate treatment of Canada as an independent territory, have presented obstacles for policymakers and industry analysts alike. In the prevailing market-driven option, distributors' presence and power relies not only on international sales of their productions but on their ability, in effect, to import international culture.

HYBRID COMPANIES AND WINDOWS

The foregoing discussion makes it evident that issues of national cinema cultures in global contexts confound conventional wisdom concerning the direction of the flow of commodities, the adequate measures of response, and the identification of invested parties. Though one strain of antiglobalization equates with anti-Americanism, rarely is the situation so clear-cut, for the many agents and entities involved look for support and advantage in their immediate environment and those farther afield simultaneously. In light of the colossal influence of U.S. culture, local ventures compete with one another for degrees of participation with that global powerhouse. Hence it is not uncommon to hear nationalistic calls for access to international commodities.

Skirting the borders of U.S. dominance in theaters, we have witnessed the Canadian version of the hybrid conglomerate with its coinciding global and intermedia scope. In an era in which "size matters" has become a familiar refrain applied to all market conditions, it is little wonder to see Canadian film and television companies trying to bulk up. Globalization, so the mantra went, necessitated economies of scale. Where champions of "narrowcasting," for instance, saw the fragmentation of markets as a liberating, choice-driven cultural model,[105] fragmentation at the level of industrial structure and ownership was considered a sign of instability and weakness.

Commenting on this, Madger writes of the "emergence of core companies" in the early 1990s.[106] Though midsize by the standards of transnational media corporations, Canadian firms similarly established their contribution to global cultural traffic through cross-media ownership, closer ties between production and distribution, and international cooperation, often through coproduction treaties. With a tight market for domestic screens, firms have sought out other windows of exhibition. In the late 1980s Canadian distributors received only 5 percent of their revenue from the box office.[107] Rather than a revenue center, the theatrical release of films, in some cases, occurred only in order that they would qualify for certain public funding streams. Alternately, distributors intend theatrical release to spark awareness for other venues, like video.

The overemphasis on commercial exhibition as a symptom of the ailing status of Canadian film in public and policy discourse has led to a substantial misinterpretation of the "problem" of the national cinema culture. First, it discounts the significance of the actual cinemagoing of Canadians as misguided and ill-formed. It treats popular taste as something to be combatted for the way it suppresses some imagined ideal Canadian popular culture. Second, focusing on the space of the cinema ignores the fact that people see far more films in other locations. Indeed, Canadians see far more Canadian films at other locations. As David Ellis noted, a single broadcast of a Canadian film can expect to have an audience double those expected from theatrical release, pay-TV and home video combined.[108] Here, what might be seen as a film that is not appropriate for cinemagoing will be seen as perfect for a television-viewing context. Perhaps the film in question was perceived as not worth the ever-inflating admission price or as inconsistent with a "night out." If so, it was being treated exactly as a solid majority of the current cinema would have been, that is, assessed in light of future sites and occasions of consumption. Third, and related, it leaves aside the integration of other windows of exhibition. Distributors do not assess commercial release in isolation of the general aging of their works; they see box office as a receding measure of success of their movies when compared with the increasing importance of television, pay-per-view, and videotape as sources of revenue. Where previous chapters noted a decreasing percentage of box office revenue in relation to cumulative revenue from all sources, exploiting access to extratheatrical venues becomes a primary explanation for the rising presence of Canadian distributors.

From the mid-1980s, the Canadian distribution sector expanded, increased its share of the screen time at commercial cinemas, and extended its operations into other areas. This led to endeavors to construct larger, national operations, accommodating Quebec's special legislation as well as setting sights on distribution abroad. One consequence has been the disappearance of smaller firms;[109] by 1998, consolidation taking place in Canada was substantial enough to warrant comment in international trade papers.[110]

There is no better example of the environment of consolidation than the 1998 merger of Canada's two biggest audiovisual companies, Alliance and Atlantis, the latter primarily a television production company. Alliance was the largest producer-distributor by the end of the 1990s. Growing out of an independent film distribution company founded in 1972, Alliance launched a distribution arm, Alliance Releasing, following the purchase of Quebec-based Vivafilm, in early 1987, and continued to buy rivals and expand internationally, at times with assistance from Cineplex Odeon.[111] In the early 1990s Alliance distributed New Line, Samuel Goldwyn, and Sony Classics in Canada,[112] subsequently striking an exclusive, and extremely lucrative, deal to handle Miramax and October Films.[113]

The new Alliance Atlantis financed, produced, distributed, and broadcast television and film. *Variety* described the merger as "the perfect example of the new maturity of Canada's entertainment business, which for the first time features a number of well-capitalized companies who are making waves beyond Canada's borders."[114] While its largest segment is its international television production and distribution, it also has whole or part ownership interest of seven Canadian specialty channels.[115] Involvement with exhibition windows led it to embark on an unusual venture. Alliance and Famous Players announced plans for an art cinema chain in the summer of 1998. An Alliance VP explained that megaplexes can keep away "people who like more sophisticated, mature-theme films," so there is a need for "destinations dedicated to a discerning crowd that loves quality art films."[116] Just as baby boomers were seen as a prime target for the family-oriented megaplexes, so too are they conceptualized as those left out of that site, as that aging demographic seeks "a different, less loud moviegoing experience."[117] The "loud," here, is securely linked with the megaplex cinema.

While a fascinating development, Alliance Atlantis Cinemas is a product of a contemporary idea of what "independent" and "art" film is. The terms are malleable enough to include any film, regardless of budget, box office, or popularity, that does not come from the eight or so Hollywood majors. And in the era of diversified entertainment corporations, many of the majors have their "prestige" unit, distributing what they market as "upscale," "off-beat," or "director-driven" films, further complicating the categories. Universal has October Films, Disney has Miramax, and AOL Time Warner has Fine Line. Alliance Atlantis is the dominant distributor of these films, by its own measure accounting for almost 90 percent of the art film market in Canada.[118] Whether or not Alliance Atlantis Cinemas will change the kinds of films available on popular screens remains unlikely. It is clear, though, that it is not intended to be a chain specifically devoted to Canadian film. Toronto offerings in the summer of 2000 included the Canadian film *New Waterford Girl* (Allan Moyle 2000) and the Brazilian film *Bossa Nova* (Bruno Barreto 2000) along with saturation release *Chicken Run* (Peter Lord and Nick Park 2000), *The Patriot* (Roland Emmerich 2000), and *The Perfect Storm* (Wolfgang Peterson 2000). Alliance Atlantis Cinemas, then, seems to be less an innovation than an enterprise built on continuing access to a purportedly global film scene.

In short, far from a crystalline view of the state of Canadian film culture, in this detailing we see competing interests tugging in various directions. Distributors, producers, filmmakers, talent, crew, exhibitors, programmers, popular audiences, art film audiences, federal government, provincial governments, and so on rarely work in concert, despite an omnipresent nationalist rhetoric whose shape seems to bend handily to accommodate all situations. The result is a resounding blow to any assertion about the obviousness of the borders of national culture, even in areas as seemingly unassailable as the economic.

Canadian cultural life might be seen as a "flow-through" edifice, and the policy history has worked hard to make it so. Television relies on rebroadcasting, Canadian content requirements notwithstanding, and Canadian film distributors and exhibitors count on deals for profitable international products. In short, the policy issue is not, nor has it ever really been, protection from international culture. It has been the regulation of who reaps the economic benefits from that flow of cultural commodities, as well as the valorization of certain forms of international culture over others. While some may typify Canadian cinemagoing practice as an absence, such a view cannot account for the other locations at which audiences encounter Canadian motion pictures. We need to reconsider the relations among these locations, given that cinemas themselves are not singularly counted on for the economic viability of producers and distributors. What is the status of continuing calls for additional screen time for Canadian films at commercial theaters in light of the rising cost, exclusivity, upscaling, and selectivity of cinemagoing in the age of the megaplex? The so-called failings of the cinema culture better capture the lack of economies of scale for production and marketing. We might say that Hollywood continues to build on the residual relations of a studio system long past. In contrast, a Canadian film infrastructure stands on the ruins of public culture, decimated after years of funding cuts. The establishment of that public culture had many objectives, many linked to a fortification of national identity. One of its designs was to found a space for the exchange of ideas in service of a democratic order. But as Kevin Dowler comments incisively, the history of attention to technological infrastructures has left Canada an "empty space" in which its status as a democratic community is at best a "simulated civil society."[119] Simulated or not, what Dowler dissects is an enduring structure of Canadian life: growing industrial sectors without a clear sense of their contribution to public life. These are two different, though related, issues. On one hand are local cultural entrepreneurs engaging in the international trade in cultural commodities, and on the other are populations negotiating what this produces. Here, we must consider what it might mean to live in the context of this internationalized Canadian space.

PASSPORT TO HOLLYWOOD

The experience of cinemagoing in Canada can be a frustrating one. Though it offers a view of an alternatingly maddening and exhilarating world movie culture, moviegoing essentially takes you away from your national home. A seat in a Canadian theater is essentially a seat in supranational territory. It offers the experience of being "anywhere" and of cosmopolitan connection to other world film audiences. Cinemagoing does not offer an experience of national spectatorship in the conventional sense. Canadians watching images and narratives of Canada is a phenomenon infrequently realized on those screens.

The integration with U.S. cinema culture involves not only the films, and the industrial structures producing, distributing, and exhibiting them, but also the movie magazines, the television shows about movies, the advertising, the Hollywood press junkets, the star interviews, the awards ceremonies, the popular criticism, the scholarly analyses, and so on. To round out the participation, Canadians eagerly tap into the publicity machine of another country, from Barbara Walters to *Entertainment Tonight,* seeing what interests other world movie audiences and helping assess cinemagoing choices.

As Sam Wendt of Cinar Film says, "It is generally accepted that English-Canadian audiences pay attention to the opinions of American critics at least as much as they do to their own critics." In this respect, the sense of international engagement, the entwinement with the currents of another national location, are part of the everyday of Canadian cinema culture.[120] For example, the newspaper advertisements for *The Insider* (Michael Mann 1999) declared, "Only one motion picture has been rousing, stirring and uplifting critics and audiences all across Canada," followed by quotations from *Good Morning America, Newsweek, Time, Rolling Stone,* and Roger Ebert.[121] Not one of these is a Canadian voice, and yet Canadian audiences *do* access all of these sources to gauge cinemagoing choices. This absurd insensitivity to national difference is, at the same time, a speck of evidence demonstrating internationalist, or at least continentalist, orientation.

Exhibitors are not blind to such peculiarities of expressions of nationhood. They will don the garments of nationalism while finding rationales for the dismal invisibility of Canadian theatrical releases. Typical is Cineplex Odeon's Allen Karp, who maintained that exhibitors were doing their part in providing screen time for Canadian features but that "Canadian filmmakers must make more accessible films and distributors must make more efforts to market them effectively."[122]

Without necessarily having an impact on screen time, there have been attempts to foster a national presence with other dimensions of cinemagoing. In this way, "Canadianizing" cinemagoing has often taken place around the central draw of the feature. For instance, a 1994 deal between the Motion Picture Theatre Association of Canada and the Canadian Association of Film Distributors and Exporters created Canadian Project Pictures. In consultation with distributors, exhibitors selected a film whose trailers and promotion would then appear regardless of what chain was actually playing the film.[123] In another effort, Famous Players offered a scheme that would match the advertising and promotional dollars for Canadian films screened at their cinemas. Cineplex Odeon initiated a program to present specially commissioned works of Canadian art as permanent fixtures in some of its lobbies.[124] The advertisements and public service announcements preceding the features are another point of visibility. These include the nationalistic Heritage Minutes that present short, glossy (and propagandistic) reenactments of notable events in Canadian history. A first reaction might be that PSAs and commercials are insignificant, and perhaps demeaning, formats for the promotion of Canadian filmmaking. Nonetheless, they proffer a space for Canadian filmmaking in Canadian theaters, even if they are not the main attraction.

Of course, as "solutions" they sidestep the questions of screen time and box office. Sharing trailers addresses an underdeveloped popular cinema as a problem of insufficient marketing; Canadian-made advertisements in cinemas hint that support for a "minor" industry may eventually spawn more prestigious work; and Heritage Minutes and Canadian lobby art sees national culture and history as an environment, a decor, that produces if not affiliation then awareness. The paltry number of Canadian films in the theaters cannot be addressed directly, because, quite simply, the economic incentives tend to work against their attractiveness to exhibitors as well as distributors.

What manner of confrontation and engagement remains for audiences? To begin to respond, one must take seriously the observation that Canadian film culture is not a dominant part of the popular cinemagoing practices of Canadians. And judgment must be reserved about this, as Andrew Higson advises. As quoted earlier, he recommends instead an examination of actual cinematic consumption as part of any national cinema culture. Canadian audiences are not absent from theaters. Audiences for Canadian film, however, are typically sparse, a function of taste as much as economics. While Seth Feldman wrote that Canadian film is located between center stage and oblivion,[125] in the popular imagination it is far closer to the latter. The investment in a global cinema culture, and the experience of estrangement from one's own cinema, is familiar enough to popular film fans. Peter Harcourt has written that the first time he taught Canadian film was at York University in the mid-1970s, under the foreign cinema section of an introductory course.[126] Take, for example, Bronwyn Drainie's commentary on *Margaret's Museum* (Mort Ransen 1995): "It has been an extraordinary experience going to see *Margaret's Museum,* which I have done twice since it went into general Canadian release a couple of weeks ago. Extraordinary because for the first time I can ever recall in Toronto (outside the charged atmosphere of the annual film festival, that is), there was a lineup of people waiting in the February deep-freeze to buy tickets for an English Canadian movie."[127] Part of the pleasure of the film, and part of its exceptionalism, is the anomalous presence of other people in the cinema. Further, it is not at all unusual to find a Canadian film in the "Foreign" section of a Canadian video rental store. While part-time employees try to explain that the section actually denotes "foreign language" videos, when spotting Québécois directors there, I wonder when French became such in Canada! And the excuse does not wash very well once one discovers, as I have at various times, the work of such English-language Canadian directors as Guy Maddin, William MacGillivray, and Deepa Mehta among the Kurosawas, Truffauts, and Arcands. Not bad company, but such cataloging promotes a domestic cinema as a cinema of "strangers."[128]

Yet this estrangement is a banal fact of global cultural life, despite the horror it continues to ignite among many critics. Writing about Australian cinema, O'Regan comments, "The international cinemas are more naturalized parts of the cinema landscape than are the various local cinemas. Within most countries people experience the cinema more as another cinema than as their own national cinema."[129] In this respect, the "foreignness" of Canadian cinema connotes its association with an international art cinema. This use of "foreignness" does not designate a geographical distance from the national territory, but a distance from popular cinemagoing taste. It makes sense to talk about how "at home" U.S. movies are in Canada, and how "come-from-away" Canadian films are. While plenty of non-Hollywood texts, from James Bond to Mad Max, have made it into the mainstream of international popular culture, the expectation that the minor cinemas of the world will regularly contribute in this fashion is slim. And these exceptions carry substantial significance. For example, over the last few years there has been an insistent whine asking, "When will we get our *Full Monty?*" a plea that willfully forgets that Canada has had a number of prominent entrants to international popular culture, as with *Porky's* and *Meatballs* (Ivan Reitman 1979). Thus, the cry is not just for a popular blockbuster but for the "right kind" of hit (e.g., a humanist crowd-pleaser rather than a gross-out teen flick). The selective memory confirms a ruling sense of embarrassment about the popular cinema culture, reflecting how bound by taste these appeals for a "proper" national cinema are.

It is advantageous to consider a structure of difference in Canadian life that facilitates a distinct reception of that international culture. Though there is definitely not a unified resistance to U.S. culture, one thing that Canadians have in common with each other is the recognition that U.S. popular culture is an imported culture, however welcome it may be by most. Further complicating this awareness is the fact that some of this imported work might also be described as an export product of the Canadian industry (e.g., CBS television series *Due South,* and the made-for-TV *Joan of Arc* [Christian Duguay 1999] and *Nuremberg* [Yves Simoneau 2000]). The entwinement of the U.S. and Canadian industries is such that U.S. texts, made with Canadian labor, eventually return to their point of production. This blurred import/export culture makes for some odd appeals to viewers. For instance, a U.S. network made-for-TV movie called *How the West Was Fun* (Stuart Margolin 1994), starring the Olsen twins, was shot in Alberta. When the television advertisements for the show ran, the local cable operator flashed a message across the bottom of the screen: "Shot in Calgary, shot in Calgary." This is hardly a form of subversion, but it is a recognition of the everyday appeal of reading the U.S. product through the eyes of the local viewer.

Further to this, the presence of Canadian talent in the United States, both in front of and behind the camera, provides another level of connection. The U.S. industry plays a role in the measure of accomplishment for Canadian talent. As such, it offers a way for Canadian audiences to view that success, to read a film or television program as a mark of a Canadian achievement. There is a *star-system-in-exile*, as Canadian spectators watch local heroes in U.S. film and television, which both links and differentiates Canadian spectatorship to and from U.S. cinema. Some examples of southward-bound talent include Graham Yost, screenwriter for the movies *Speed* (Jan de Bont 1994) and *Broken Arrow* (John Woo 1996), director Norman Jewison, Matthew Perry of *Friends, VIP* star Pamela Anderson, actor Kate Nelligan, Hayden Christiansen of *Star Wars: Episode II—Attack of the Clones* (George Lucas 2002), and the astronomically expensive Jim Carrey. This often remarked-on presence requires consideration as a point of access to transnational culture. An affective element draws audiences into the texts if not for a sense of ownership then a glimpse of recognition. The fleeting connection to distant cultural life is widespread enough to have been parodied by the satirical television program *This Hour Has 22 Minutes*. The skit involved two Maritimers watching television, flipping through channels. They happen upon Kevin Spacey appearing at the 2000 Academy Awards, who tells a brief story about how he forgot his tuxedo in Halifax where he had been filming *The Shipping News* (Lasse Hallström 2001) and had Judi Dench retrieve it for him in time for the show. The Maritime characters scream gleefully, "He mentioned Nova Scotia, he mentioned Nova Scotia!"

John Caughie has noted that, with the saturation of global media with U.S. products, viewing tactics develop to manage the oscillation between estrangement from the national home and connection to international culture. For instance, Caughie proposes that appreciation from an ironic angle is a tactic used by those who are suspicious of, yet still attracted to, the shiny surfaces of U.S. popular culture. He writes

> television produces the conditions of an ironic knowingness, at least as a possibility, which may escape the obedience of interpellation or cultural colonialism and may offer a way of thinking subjectivity free of subjection. It gives a way of thinking identities as plays of cognition and miscognition, which can account for the pleasures of playing at being, for example, American, without the paternalistic disapproval that goes with the assumption that it is bad for the natives.[130]

Not only have some, including Linda Hutcheon and Kieran Keohane, pointed to irony as an especially Canadian literary tactic,[131] but arguably English-Canadians are especially good at masquerading as Americans. The value of Caughie's approach is that this is seen as a coping mechanism, one that opens up the possibility of reading culture for the complex ways it is integrated into daily existence, rather than as a moment of psychic invasion. Cultural consumption becomes the starting point of expression, creativity, and identity negotiation, and it would be astonishingly naive to attend to a narrowly defined set of ideological consequences only. Instead, we need to acknowledge the evidence of struggle it represents. For instance, as Richard Collins agues, it is possible to understand that the appeal of international culture may be a tacit challenge to internal cultural hierarchies, in effect, a rejection of the national officially sanctioned culture in favor of the more scandalous popular forms.[132]

To appreciate this situation, one must acknowledge the extended history of critical and policy attempts to respond to U.S. popular culture's omnipresence in Canada. Certainly a recurring directive has been to organize and develop Canadian culture in the service of democratic citizenship, this often against the everyday cultural consumption of Canadians.[133] Without official access to education or commercial culture, from the 1920s onward, many activists engaged alternate spaces of cultural life. Accordingly, they cultivated lecture circuits, traveling film projectionists, traveling art exhibits, radio forums, drama leagues, adult education, magazines, and conferences. In response to the seductions of U.S. culture, leisure was seen as a kind of work that built character, citizens, and nation. After years of lobbying the government for aid, the infrastructure of voluntary societies, along with its educative agenda, became embedded as part of Canadian cinematic culture with the formation of the National Film Board of Canada (NFB) in 1939. With the NFB, we see (1) an idea about cinemagoing associated with the lecture, the discussion, and the school, and (2) the promotion of certain film forms, in particular experimental and documentary film, over the conventions of popular narratives.[134] For all its extraordinary success, the NFB sought a particular disposition in its film audiences, that of the student. Ultimately, it along with other such agencies, helped establish a radical disjuncture between an imagined ideal national (educated) subject and the actual cultural life of the nation. Consequently, Canadian cinema has seldom encompassed a popular cinemagoing practice, and when it has, the films have been treated disparagingly by critics. Instead, Canadian cinema has thrived in parallel locations—the school, the film festival or retrospective, the exposition, the community hall, the library, and the museum—in this respect, building on the earlier work of the voluntary societies. Importantly, all are locations with cultural dispositions, that is, ways of approaching and appreciating culture, distinct from those of popular cinemagoing or videotape rental.

In light of the historical location of Canadian cinema culture in nontheatrical sites, in places parallel to commercial cinema, it can be said to demonstrate an "expo-mentality," an orientation to and for the special venue. The expo-mentality of Canadian cinema is fully rendered in the unique format of IMAX, which grew out of Montreal's Expo '67. It was largely the brainchild of people trained and working at the National Film Board of Canada, blending the experimental and documentary traditions of Canadian film into a distinct cinema apparatus and industry.[135] Further, an expo-mentality has led to the development of a lively and important circuit of film festivals. Much in the same way that many national cultures begin to cohere and appear whole at international festivals, Canadian film culture deploys the local festival to assert images of national participation.[136] And yet this disposition extends cinemagoing as an educational or duty-bound activity, hailing Canadian audiences as students primed for self-improvement and connoisseurs set to confront adventurous work.

As this case study of one country's engagement with global culture makes clear, the vexing concept of national cinema returns to questions of judgment that have advanced particular cultural dispositions—that is, certain kinds of cinemagoing practices—over others. In this vein, Pierre Bourdieu's notion of the *habitus* is illuminating, suggesting that there is a set of dispositions that structure the relations to culture; this set includes things like taste formation, knowing how you are expected to act as part of a particular audience, and knowing if you are invited to the show to begin with.[137] Cultural life has as much to do with the structures of consumption as it does with the economics of production and exhibition, or with the actual texts themselves.[138] As Bourdieu puts it, knowing the habitus is akin to having a "feel for the game."[139] One needs to ask what dispositions (involving both taste and criticism) are affirmed by the critically celebrated Canadian films, and why do so many Canadians not feel invited? This involves issues of exhibition, distribution, and marketing, that is, the economic explanation. One must also deal with a variety of other discursive and material conditions that act to position cultural products and our relations to them. The habitus of Canadian "expo-mentality" offers little to a popular disposition in which a U.S. popular cinema is quite at home in Canada. Cinemagoing may not be about film at all but about extrafilmic reasons (to start a weekend, to see movies "everyone" is seeing, to celebrate an event, etc.). Your pleasures and subsequent memories may have to do with the cinematography, the kind of ending you are in the mood for, the quality of the company you share, and how close you are sitting to the bucket of popcorn. As we have seen, the claim that the space of film culture is the cinema is an increasingly arcane suggestion, one that itself bespeaks a particular cultural disposition. And, as Bourdieu reminds us, all dispositions are correlates of cultural capital and serve to establish social distinctions through cultural consumption. This is not to say that there is a single national *habitus,* but that there has been an attempt to situate a set of dispositions as central to a national character. In the end, an *authorized language* about Canadian culture has papered over its own investment in certain forms of social distinction and rendered the everyday pleasures of popular culture an absent location.

It follows, then, to wonder about the kinds of cinemagoing left for audiences. What does this situation produce? What kinds of effectivities and practices does it facilitate? What modes of consumption emerge from these forces? Both economic and discursive conditions have forged a "flow-through" stream of popular culture. Though this is not the only current, it is a primary one, forging the parameters in which cinematic congregation transpires. Most assuredly, the massively visible presence of new "hit" films tenders a portrait of the role of international cultural forms in the everyday life of Canada. For what the current cinema reveals is not absence or invisibility; *it is the presence of simultaneity and currency in Canadian cinema culture.* This is the sense of event made possible by the augmentation of the day and date coordination of the appearance of new films in both major and minor centers across Canada and the United States. Thus the role of cinemagoing in contemporary life is, in part, made up of a special set of dispositions and strategies developed to accommodate the determination of this simultaneity and currency. Confronted with a production, distribution, and exhibition edifice vying for its own stake in global screen traffic, cinemagoing in Canada emphasizes a familiarity with and negotiation of novel international cinema events. Though constrained by economic forces, cinemagoing produces participation in cinematic cosmopolitanism, displaying degrees of immersion into international cultural life.

CHAPTER EIGHT

The Miniaturization of the Theme
Park, or After the "Death" of Cinema

In the fall of 1997, before the merger of Alliance and Atlantis, four executives left the former to establish Vancouver-based distributor Red Sky. An early boost to their operations was the securing of video distribution in Canada for PolyGram Filmed Entertainment. For theatrical features, they bid on "prestige" films, reasoning that aging boomers "are hungry for something other than Hollywood mainstream."[1] President Tony Cianciotta argued that the building of megaplexes means "there will be more screens to go around and, therefore, a more diverse movie menu."[2] As his words reflect, by the late 1990s distributors and exhibitors made bids to capitalize on the perceived potential of the megaplex, or, alternately, to stake unabashed claims to cultural legitimacy by defining their work in opposition to them. In direct counterpoint to the giant cinema complex, independent film distributors began talking about "microcinema," a small-scale version of roadshowing in which filmmakers take their films to various communities and organize screening events in nontheatrical venues.[3] And just as Alliance Atlantis Cinemas "themed" their screens as an adult alternative to the brashness of the megaplex, some marketing plans and release strategies were at odds with those large suburban complexes and saturation openings. The renewed focus on platform releasing in the wake of *American Beauty*'s (Sam Mendes 1999) critical and box office accomplishments is one such development that appeared to run counter to the initial logic of the 1990s building spree (even though that film's release was too wide and expanded too rapidly to be considered a perfect example of platforming). In actuality, the slow build of platform releasing has never really been discarded, and it remains a tactic allowing for good reviews and word-of-mouth to boost expectations for a film's arrival. December tends to see a high share of films released in this manner, when distributors assure their "quality" movies qualify for that year's Oscar nominations.[4] Gradual, multitiered release patterns are proficient mechanisms to establish expectations, elevating such films above the wide openers. Indeed, this status within the current cinema requires the supposed crassness of the sudden saturation release as its point of comparison. Most certainly, though the wide opening and fast play-off can be a hit-and-run technique for terrible films, one cannot discount the sense of exclusivity and preciousness garnered by films for which one must wait.

The prospects for a more varied cinemagoing environment have not been borne out. As with the multiplex before it, the argument that megaplexes would diversify the kinds of films that reach audiences is no longer being taken seriously. As Peter Bart wrote of 1998, "More and more, the blockbusters dominated the marketplace. The fond hope of a decade ago that the modern megaplex would offer a glint of light for art movies had been dashed."[5] This critique notwithstanding, by the late 1990s megaplexes had a secure position as a dominant form of cinemagoing in major cities on several continents. Even though *American Beauty* played at megaplexes and *Chicken Run* played at Alliance Atlantis's boutique venues, there remained a certain legibility of each location effectively defined in contradistinction to one another. Put differently, the sense that there is an appropriate distributor or venue for mature, prestige, and adult-oriented films implied a solid understanding of the megaplex as a multi-activity site for families and younger audiences.

Though megaplexes insist on largeness as one of their salient characteristics, they are rather like shrunken amusement parks. The theme park model for the megaplex parallels similar "theming" in other commercial venues. Of the Lincoln Square megaplex in New York City, Greg Evans wrote that "Sony's ambitious project does for theatrical exhibition what the Hard Rock Cafe and Planet Hollywood did for the restaurant biz."[6] Some of these transformations seemed to have had a receding relationship to film, moving instead closer to video game arcades. AMC created Centertainment to develop "entertainment-based retail centers."[7] Regal constructed its FunScape sites, combining theaters with amusement park rides and activities.[8] Playdium Entertainment, with Sega Game Works, has been responsible for the Famous Players TechTown centers in its theaters. They have also constructed independent sites in Mississauga and in downtown Toronto consisting only of video games and "movie rides," with the intention of attracting patrons older than the usual teenagers.[9] Without leaving screen-based entertainment behind, and including IMAX Ride films, in which audiences stand upright for short films, Playdiums are loud, colorful pavilions of games, music, and food, closer in style and appeal to the carnival midway than to the movie theater.

Cinema's allusions to amusement parks are not new and may be some of its foundational characteristics. Tom Gunning's phrase "cinema of attractions" attacks the myth of the naive film audience of early nonnarrative cinema, challenging theorists and historians "who envision audiences submitting passively to an all-dominating apparatus."[10] Gunning suggests that perhaps spectatorial agitation and astonishment was part of the "attraction" of cinema. He sees this as a parallel to wonderment about the speed and chaos of modern urban life, hypothesizing that cinematic attractions offered coherence, through "distraction," that was lacking in the everyday. Thus the cinema was both a symptom of and a way to deal with overstimulation. Audiences' reaction of terror and screaming at moving pictures "was the antipode to the primitive one: it was an encounter with modernity."[11] In light of early cinema's location alongside various rides and pavilions, Gunning's argument extends the function of late-nineteenth-century fairgrounds and expositions to cinema and its audiences.

This nonnarrative ridelike appeal continues today. Subsequent developments include *This Is Cinerama,* with its promotional images of thrilled spectators being transported to new locations all the while remaining in their theater seats. The industry of IMAX, the large-format cinema originally situated at museums and exposition sites, equally focuses on the virtual transportation of the audience. IMAX is noteworthy for its attempts to induce the physical sensation of movement through its ample use of point-of-view traveling camera shots. Like the early cinematic apparatus, IMAX is about wonderment and astonishment.[12] Further, recent textual manifestations of the "cinema of attractions" can be seen in the loose subgenre of action films called "ride films"—

Twister (Jan de Bont 1996), *Speed* (Jan de Bont 1994), *The Fugitive* (Andrew Davis 1993), the three *Die Hard* movies (John McTiernan 1988; Renny Harlin 1990; and John McTiernan 1995), *Con Air* (Simon West 1997)—which are typified by an underdeveloped, linear narrative structure designed to link a series of elaborate stunts. A newspaper advertisement for *Twister,* for instance, invited people to "Go for a ride you'll never forget!"[13] Here, the diegetic pull is effectively nonnarrative, where progression of conflict and character is secondary to the surprise offered by successive set-pieces. In this subgenre there is a direct association with transportation and movement. It harkens to amusement park attractions like the roller coaster as metaphoric points of reference. With the ride film, the disaster genre has been reinvigorated as a fun-house thrill.

Some films have made the connections to theme parks even more explicit. There are several examples of film tales exploring the idea of being trapped in theme-park, fun-house or ridelike environments: *Jurassic Park* (Steven Spielberg 1994), *Nothing But Trouble* (Dan Aykroyd 1991), *Rollercoaster* (James Gladstone 1977), *Empire of the Ants* (Bert I. Gordon 1977), and *Westworld* (Michael Crichton 1973). Some films appear to be amusement park rides or set in theme locations, though diegetically they are not: *Hook* (Steven Spielberg 1991), *Goonies* (Richard Donner 1985), *Explorers* (Joe Dante 1985), and the "contact" sequence of *Contact* (Robert Zemeckis 1997). Perhaps most compelling in the interrelationship of film and amusement park, as Susan Davis notes, is evidence that a film's development process can involve asking about its potential to be realized as a good theme park attraction. According to Davis, in a number of cases the criterion appears to be " 'Will this story be good to ride?' "[14] thus, revealing one way that entertainment corporations try to take advantage of what are seen as synergistic possibilities.

It is my contention that such intermedia promotion extends to the theming of theater space as well. The cinema complex is a cross-promotional machine in which audiences become familiar with future films, current attractions, new video game systems and software, upcoming home video release, star gossip and general entertainment news. This machine distributes magazines, plays local radio stations and taped music, hands out promotional material, tests the audience with trivia questions, presents video clips in lobbies, and runs trailers in the theaters. All these operations, combined with the entertainment advertising that appears in prescreening slide shows, in arcade games, and on concessions purchases, establish a complete and integrated environment replete with media and commodity forms.

Chapter 5 introduced points of continuity between the megaplex and the theme park, including their fairly restricted range of social possibilities and their assurance of security. Similar to the impulse of the gated community, to which they both invite comparisons, the megaplex and the theme park represent a degree of retreat from public life. The hybrid entertainment site has been described as "part theme park, part cineplex, with a splash of shopping mall and a high-tech veneer."[15] As a "mongrel" form, it is an unusual combination of diverse corporate entities.[16] Referred to as "urban entertainment destination projects" (UEDPs), again CityWalk appears as the prototype, as do three New York sites: Sony's combination multiplex, Virgin Megastore, and sports-themed restaurant in Times Square; Disney's renovations of the New Amsterdam theater; and the Chelsea Piers project.[17] The reasons for this dedifferentiation include

> Shopping center developers, having lost many of their anchor tenants over the past decade, are looking for a way to revitalize their industry, and see entertainment companies as rich in potential. Urban developers, having watched office construction creep to a halt, are grasping for projects. Public officials scrambling for ways to bring life back to crime-ridden inner cities see high-security UEDPs as a way to attract timid tourists and other shoppers. Entertainment companies like Disney and Universal hope to penetrate regional markets that can support more than a souvenir store but less—way less—than a full-scale theme park.[18]

As captured here, a mix of competing forces involving downtown revitalization, corporate growth, and security converge to support and give voice to this particular "solution" to out-of-home leisure endeavors.[19]

The growth of location-based entertainment, like the Playdium complexes, was positioned as a direct challenge to moviegoing. A feature article began, "Dinner and a themed, interactive, location-based entertainment attraction, anyone? While it may not have the ring of the traditional 'dinner and a movie,' some prognosticators believe the Friday-night-date routine is in for a high-tech shake-up."[20] With predictions stating that such venues will exceed the business of cinemas in five years, and with their location usually close to existing mega-plexes, the threat was taken as a serious one.[21] These elaborate arcades, with their restaurants, bars, and cafes, allow owners to keep 90 percent of their take at the door, unlike theaters, whose box office is largely returned to distribu-tors.[22] The very notion of entertainment-plexes was seen as one development that sparked the megaplex revolution; the rejigging of cinemas was partly a defensive strategy to match what these centers also promised. Fortunately for film exhibitors, the entertainment-plexes have found it difficult to attract more than a teenage male audience, despite efforts to court a family and adult au-dience. Consequently, it is maintained that these "experience zones" will not be able to come close to replacing cinemagoing exactly.[23] But the impression of conflict between exhibitors and UEDP sites was overstated, as many of these centers have opened with the ownership involvement of theater chains or their parent corporations.

At the height of industry enthusiasm for megaplexes, commentators saw the changes as a "new revolution that aims to meld the amusement park experience with that of going to movie theaters."[24] In particular, simulation rides of vari-ous sorts were to appear at local theaters, presumably to challenge the hege-mony of the feature film attraction. Several factors illuminate the industry's rationale for this vertical shift in operations. First, the smaller physical space required made simulation rides less expensive, and they did not necessitate the negotiation of zoning that amusement parks do. Second, "urban retailers are seeking to mix shopping with adventure," citing CityWalk as a model.[25] Third, there was thought to be public interest in high-tech games, and, fourth, chains sought to capitalize on the relative cost-effectiveness of producing the software for such game experiences. Here, it is worth pointing out that even as cinemas extended the arcade component of their lobbies, they did so primarily via simulation rides, visual technologies, and imaging software. In other words, the cinematic world was not left behind with this reconfiguration of space and operation but expanded.

The megaplex, the UEDP, and the theme park promise an array of entertain-ment and activities. Though a central attraction of the megaplex remains the film itself, its move toward the theme park is evident in the construction of bars, restaurants, elaborate video arcades, miniature golf, bowling, and party rooms as part of some complexes.

> "We want to change people's ways of thinking about movies, particularly at old tradition of arriving 10 minutes before the movie starts and running out the door as soon as it's over," says Roger Harris, vice-president of Famous Players' marketing and theatre management. "We want them to hang around, come early, stay late. Conceivably you could come and have quite a good time without seeing a movie, although that's not what we have in mind."[26]

The megaplex design encompasses a contained temporal arrangement of the visit—an evening, a day, a weekend outing—involving a series of activities and purchases, as compared with the more discrete purchase of a singular cultural commodity. Indeed, a prominent metaphor for the megaplex arising from this context is that of the hotel, in which cinemagoers are patrons, and a manager is a concierge. Comparable to the transitory nature of hotel and motel visits, the "rental" extracted by cinemas and parks means that the stay is fleeting; one does not truly become a "resident." In contradistinction to the purchase of a cultural product for private consumption, here we confront an ensemble of (presumably) related commodities and practices presented to the patron in a spatially and temporally designated area established explicitly for their consumption.

With this in mind, we might wonder who understands these various activities as coterminous. For whom is any strategic shaping of the spatial and temporal relations among commodities and practices an organic fit? For whom does any particular shaping of cultural life appear commonsensical? In the end, the curating of cultural offerings and the industrial forces producing material sites and encounters are an articulation of lifestyle and ultimately of class. The immersion into the process of public consumption—that is, the root definitional criterion for cinemagoing—marks the associated sites as more than service goods. They are relations *among* cultural commodities and practices, calling to audiences as particular kinds of consumers, with particular kinds of interests, tastes, expertise, and disposable income and time. For this reason, the public event of moviegoing activates a structure of everyday existence in which various forms of identity and community take shape. Here, the "upgrading" of cinemagoing is especially significant, for the intermedia and intercontextual nature of the cinema complex has its full realization in the production of a bourgeois (cinemagoing) subject. It is for this subject that the cross-media appeals and new technological ideals appear as naturalized, common-sense developments of the contemporary age. This, then, is the fortification of a particular lifestyle as a dominant motor—economic and cultural—for the re-configured relations among commodities and locations.

In light of the discourse of exclusivity and lifestyle in theming, how are we to understand the very idea of the theme as it becomes an ever more present defining feature of quasi-public space? One way to characterize the apparent convergence between cinema sites and theme parks is to see it as part of the ongoing naturalization of reigning discourses and ideologies of family, enter-tainment, and public space. Some may be tempted to grasp this specifically as the "Disneyfication" of the cinema. As has been documented in earlier chap-ters, it is indisputable that Disney had been held up as the template for the reconfiguration of the site of cinemagoing. As early as 1986, distributors "sug-gested the Disneyland model for running their [exhibitors'] screens."[27] How-ever, the term "Disneyfication" appears to house an agreed-upon critique, self-assured about the difference between industrial culture and more authentic forms, and for this reason I am dubious about its usefulness. The term imme-diately signals the artificial, the commodity, the inauthentic, and all that has been taken as the predicament of popular culture, hence its connotations are ostensibly negative. "Disneyfication" is a description and a metaphor; it is mythologized, in the Barthesian sense, and therefore carries its own analysis and conclusions. The neologism is shorthand for a mass society critique that remains presumptive of the operations of popular culture and the political implications of entertainment. The evocation of 'becoming Disney' is yet an-other instantiation of a long-standing assessment of the juvenile, retarded, and infantile qualities of popular culture and its fans. The term "Disneyfication" diminishes as it designates. In this respect, I contend that the critique reveals more of the intellectual and taste formation of the critic than it does of the actual phenomenon described, ultimately referring to the corporation's own branding rather than its actual operations. Consequently, despite its current ubiquity as an expression of dread about contemporary culture, "Disneyfica-tion" obfuscates more than it explains.

Moreover, the term is historically misleading, because it takes as contemporary the innovated pursuits of Disney from the 1950s. Reference to Disney can be a handy way to acknowledge the origins of the idea of "total entertainment/total marketing." In practice, however, the production of such consumer/leisure environments has been disarticulated from that corporation specifically. Lifestyle commodities and practices abound from sundry sources, and businesses large and small work to market whole experiences beyond single products. For example, soon after MCA acquired its part of Cineplex Odeon in 1986, they announced plans for a hybrid motion picture theme park and production facility, Universal Studios Florida.[28] In place of the simple genealogical critique of Disney, we need to see the broad complexity of the rise of the combination production/consumption site for audiovisual entertainment. Further, as a complex and integrated corporation, Disney has operated through a variety of other objectives and agendas. The description of total "entertainment" may describe an overall corporate ideal, one that is no different from many other media conglomerates. And yet it is impossible for even the most all-encompassing umbrella to capture the diversity of operations. Many of Disney's assets are not theme parks, and most of its television shows, films, and books are not for children. As an analytic concept, "Disneyfication" offers little relation to and does not help us understand films like *Pulp Fiction* (Quentin Tarantino 1994), television shows like *Ellen,* magazines like *Women's Wear Daily,* the ABC television network, or newspapers like the *Fort Worth Star-Telegram,* all of which have been part of the Disney universe.

The term often holds a powerful echo of Jean Baudrillard's simulacrum, presuming a degree of relevance for his reading. He too emphasizes Disneyland's appeal to children, declaring that its imaginary worlds assure the reality of social life outside the park. He writes, "It is meant to be an infantile world, in order to make us believe that the adults are elsewhere, in the 'real' world, and to conceal the fact that real childishness is everywhere, particularly amongst those adults who go there to act the child in order to foster illusions as to their real childishness."[29] The pervasiveness of variations of this claim—precisely the reason I deem it necessary to address directly—might best be seen as a sign of the "secularization" of Baudrillard, and hence of a particular view of postmodernity pertaining to the necessity of artifice for a working sense of social reality. One consequence of the loose application of this view to "Disneyfica-tion" is that it sidesteps an important argument about simulation and changing relations of the real and the copy, which had been pursued elegantly by Walter Benjamin some fifty years earlier.[30]

Susan Davis encourages us to think of theme parks as a form of mass media and to see them as "important parts—not just peripheral adjuncts—of what is becoming a global media system."[31] She suggests that the proliferation of theme parks internationally is part of an ongoing history of cultural imperialism, participating in the maintenance of a global U.S. cultural hegemony. They cater primarily to new classes and elites worldwide, helping to create an Amer-icanized internationalist sensibility.[32] For Davis, the globalizing theme park constructs new forms of sociability, new ways of understanding and behaving in the context of international media and, more generally, global capitalism. The contradiction for her is that "the quick spread of the theme park form is a new and effective take-off point for the penetration of multinational entertain-ment media in the non-multinational world."[33] Thus "Cross promotion, which the theme park exemplifies and ritualizes, is now the bedrock of consumer culture, and especially so for children. The promotional maze makes the possi-bilities for non-commercial cultural spaces seem remote."[34]

This promotional maze stretches beyond the parks themselves. Theming blends itself into various practices of shopping, dining, and even walking, a process that might be described as the *miniaturization* of the theme park. Edward Soja points toward this as a postmodern development in which you don't visit the theme park but the theme park visits you.[35] The Planet Hol-lywood restaurant chain is an illustrative case, its current financial difficulties notwithstanding, in the way its theme rooms and museumlike displays of "pre-cious" film artifacts are also interwoven with current film promotion. Among the film oddities—a page of the *Demolition Man* (Marco Brambilla 1993) script, a costume from *Die Hard,* a fake gun used in *Terminator 2* (James Cameron 1991)—the themes themselves offer at best vague allusions to memories of moviegoing experiences—a medieval room, a western room, and so on. Con-spicuously, here we see the dispersal of the film world and the movie publicity machine into everyday life.[36]

In moments of alarm, some critics worry that everything is being subsumed under the theme park ideal. Margaret Crawford, for instance, proclaims, "The world of the shopping mall—respecting no boundaries, no longer limited even by the imperative of consumption—has become the world."[37] And yet, on the contrary, though "theming" is evident in a wide range of activities, to apprehend its function and logic one must acknowledge that the process does not exist everywhere nor equally. Even as it is a fairly transportable idea about retail and service industries, even as it becomes more generalized, it remains associated with specific activities and locations. "Theming" may be an *episteme,* but it is one that is brought into relief variously.

In a contextual examination of retail gigantism, Will Straw writes of music superstores that have been part of an influx of capital to languishing city centers, similar to other "destination sites" including museums and megaplex cinemas. He sees the superstore as an attempt to construct retail order in light of the fragmentation of mass taste in music. He writes that "the record superstore is an architectural expression of the broader reordering which has gone on within the culture of popular music—one through which musical tastes and consumption habits have come to be fragmented, distributed across an expanding array of niches."[38] Straw's observations reflect a contradiction in music retail "between the offering of a potentially chaotic abundance and the marshalling of a variety of means for focussing consumer choice and producing order from amidst this chaos."[39]

Can this particular manifestation be transported to explain other modes of consumption and other public spaces? Does the ordering of consumer activity apply as a primary effectivity for further "theming"? To be sure, as the encounter with the theme location becomes more frequent, one may be tempted to suggest that it functions to offer definitions and a signifying order to the site and process of exchange.[40] It begs a generic reading of conventionalized signs, and hence an intertextual one as well, as themes allude to other cultural forms. In an expansive study of themed environments, Mark Gottdiener provides semiotic analyses of casinos, malls, restaurants, and theme parks and itemizes some of the most prevalent themes, including the tropical paradise, the wild west, and nostalgia. His argument takes an implausible turn early on with his assertion that modernist design was "responsible for the eradication of symbolic depth in contemporary cities," a depth that returns with theming.[41] On the contrary, an austere absence of ornamentation is not an absence of a signifying function nor of "symbolic unity."[42] The minimalist environment might connote, quite simply, "the contemporary" or "the international." Despite this misapprehension, Gottdiener makes a valuable contribution if only in his systematic treatment of his intuition—one that is borne out—that the semiotic clutter of our dominant commercial locations promotes certain kinds of communal experiences. Though his argument details the community of address presumed by theming, it points to reading formations making sense of the organization of signs. From this, the variability and unpredictability of reading must be taken into account. As Gottdiener shows, there is ample semiotic evidence of the coordinated deployment of allusions in order to organize space; there is no comparable evidence demonstrating that people adopt those meanings as designed. In the end, themes *suggest* readings of space, guiding our interpretations through a formal linkage with recognizable codes. In this respect, themes are the application of generic conventions to everyday life, along the way presuming a knowing readership. As such, they may serve as markers of participation inside certain interpretive communities.

Davis characterizes theming as follows:

> Within the industry, the verb "to theme" refers to this totalizing effort. Surface stylistic characteristics are highly coordinated in theming but, more importantly, the meanings the park contains are centrally produced and as non-conflictual as possible. The theme park produces the appearance of a rich variety of artifacts, cultures, histories, styles, texts, architectures and performances, within a framework of overall uniformity of message.[43]

Here, the theme is a structure of codes and comportment, effectively industrializing pleasure and prohibiting the possibility of the park becoming an open "theater of action." Davis's description addresses the design of the theme park and the intentions of its managers. The relation between this and consumption is not broached. Importantly, though theme-space is a practiced discourse, one must acknowledge that the theme need not be attended to directly. Susan Willis, writing about historical theme parks, goes so far as to suggest that the performative and interactive dimensions of historical theme parks can be tactics to break through the surface of branding and logos. She writes, using the popularity of such parks as evidence, "contemporary culture yearns for the recovery of use value."[44] She also asserts that theming can convert people into "passive theme builders and logo collectors—not narrators, but instruments of narration."[45] Where Willis develops this claim to capture the logic of the flow of commodities as narrativized by theming, there is little to indicate the semiotic effectiveness of the endeavor. Even the most overwhelming of thematic coordination can be sidestepped as a person focuses on a single element, reads the codes wildly, or selectively attends to the activity at hand. Though theme-space regulates allusions and signification, it does not enforce them; it offers a degree of interpretive freedom. Rather than functioning as a determining force, a theme operates as a backdrop and is perhaps more akin to theme music as a connotative soundtrack to public activity.

Constance Balides dissects this aspect of the rise of "themed entertainment," noting the multiple viewing positions offered by blockbusters as they move from megaplex to home theater environments. This multiplicity of spectatorial appeals includes criticism of the cultural commodity itself. She writes of *Jurassic Park*, "One of the ways the film negotiates its postmodern thematics is, surprisingly, by criticizing the commercialism and simulation of its theme park."[46] According to Balides, the very artificiality of all-encompassing themed spaces only draws attention to its role in a process of commodification. She writes, "Theming in the context of an immersion-effect involves a spectacle that is clearly an illusion."[47] Further, "the pleasures of immersion do not involve the straightforward substitution of real experience associated with a naive consumer."[48] Thus themed entertainment presents self-reflexive possibilities for a knowing postmodern public, however contradictory and circumscribed its operations may be. It follows to expect that the events consumed in such locations would mirror and provoke those impulses.

This immersion-effect can tender all manners of contradiction that breed further reading and subject positions. Themed spaces, whether cinemas, restaurants, or stores, are not necessarily executed in a coherent fashion. Often they are a mishmash of references loosely organized around a set of texts or topics, but which are rarely completely congruous. Toronto's Paramount megaplex is a panoply of colors and contours. Outside, a giant Rubik's cube juts from the building. A long escalator draws crowds up from the street into the main lobby area. There, neon and spot lighting, mosaic tile work, Dubuffet-like curved ceiling dividers and mirrors, video monitors in round white casing, and a general profusion of screens create a cluttered environment. Among the lobby advertisements for coming attractions are video posters, whose screens mimic the shape of conventional paper posters. Motifs of bar codes and computer fonts suggest "technology" though without specific periodization. Exposed bolts and chrome pillars lend a vaguely industrial feel. These relatively permanent features are joined by more temporary accoutrements of film promotion, all with their own genre-based, minitheme appeals. At one visit, tiki masks and fake bamboo added a Polynesian theme to the general technoindustrial hodgepodge.

Items chosen in a seemingly desultory manner usually have faint syntagmatic connections. Some sites describe themselves broadly as "movie" and "fun" themed. As one megaplex manager casually put it to me, his site's theme was "the 1920s, the year 2000, you know, the future." Internationally, many megaplexes reproduced ideas about a Hollywood of the past. For instance, AMC's Nakama megaplex in Japan is "a fantasy Hollywood street scene from the art-deco period."[49] Its megaplex in Dunkirk, France, was designed to be "reminiscent of a luxury liner."[50] Notably, the site is "reminiscent of," rather than a recreation of, luxury liners. The AMC Forum in Montreal, in an effort to memorialize the building's esteemed hockey heritage as the former home of the Montreal Canadiens, embedded several commemorative plaques in the sidewalk at one entrance and graphically reproduced center ice in the lobby. A light and multiscreen show plays across the vast atrium for both paying and nonpaying customers, presenting images of local hockey history (a production partially funded by the government of Quebec). And yet these flourishes intermingle with a documentation of the conversion of the building, the themes of other restaurants and bars, and the corporate branding of AMC itself. Leisure spaces such as these are shifty in their theming and lack the precision suggested by rooting design in connotative formations. The thematic intent is legible, but it is distant from simulation. These messy locations of color and plastic do not force an organization of specific meanings on patrons, nor do they encourage a supposition that one has truly entered the world described. They are puffed-up pavilions whose syntagmatic organization creates an atmosphere of leisure.

Fundamentally, they signal that one is entering a zone of entertainment and perhaps that's all. This would account for the abundance of movie/Hollywood themes, which have a powerful grip on the very notion of dream, fantasy, and amusement. For example, in Montreal, a local chain of restaurants called Moe's crams its dining rooms with artifacts, making it impossible to tell if the theme is sports, English pub, Montreal nostalgia, or celebrity culture. Perhaps the theme, in the end, is restaurants; it is a restaurant that is restaurant-themed. I suggest, then, that theming is predominantly a mode of beckoning meaning systems without asserting singular meanings; it is an idea about the making of a meaningful organization of space. The theme, perhaps, is best considered a metanarrative for public space. It is as though the process of theming is sufficient unto itself.

But sufficient for what, and called for by what forces? Arguably, this use of theme is a return to one of its more arcane roots: not as a topic or motif but as an administrative division. The Byzantine word *thema* indicated a division of government emerging from the army splitting into semi-independent corps associated with specific districts. Seen in this fashion, theming involves governance, coordination, and localized regimes of social organization. Contrary to the surface manifestations of textual distinctions, theming's prime function is not significatory; its purpose is not to give meaning to people, sites, and communities. Instead, theming gives *difference* to public life. Theming is a process of division for civic and commercial coordinating and structuring. Thus the current special articulation between gating and theming appears to comply with such a process and should be taken as a logical extension of an impulse toward civic organization. This articulation circulates as an emerging common sense about, and administration of, community, economic, and cultural life.

Michael Sorkin takes a different tack, claiming that the new city of "theming," while "rising levels of manipulation and surveillance over its citizenry . . . with a proliferation of new modes of segregation,"[51] essentially acts like television by treating all its textual fragments as equivalent. Sorkin writes, "The 'design' of television is all about erasing differences among these bits, about asserting equal value for all the elements in the net, so that any of the infinite combinations that the broadcast day produces make 'sense.' The new city likewise eradicates genuine particularity in favor of a continuous urban field, a conceptual grid of boundless reach."[52] On the contrary, the ideological forces that "theming" produces arise from the mechanism of the production of difference. Further, it would be a grave misapprehension to assume that the core vector on which difference resides is between the real and the imagined, or the authentic and the inauthentic. Such a line of argument, one that finds a sympathetic voice in Baudrillard, leads to the conceptual trap of seeing some produced cultures as less produced or more natural than others. Instead, Lawrence Grossberg sees difference as a primary motor force of capitalism. He writes, "the new abstract machine of capitalism produces differences at the level of expression; it is difference which is now in the service of capital. The new abstract machine makes capitalism into a technology of distribution rather than production by producing a stratification in which difference proliferates in a highly reterritorialised world."[53] In the end, the very nature of the audiovisual enterprise is the formation of difference among populations—different spaces and different times—as much as it is about the creation of motion pictures. Cinemagoing, then, is one drill among many that galvanizes difference and forges the cinema-agent as a member of a provisional, divided, consuming public.

The machinery of difference in and of itself sets the terms of exclusion and specificity. The qualities of the public that it brings to fruition tell us something of the historical context and the range of practices that might be possible. For example, Marshall McLuhan once noted pithily that Europeans go home to be alone and go out to be with people, while Americans do the opposite. Perhaps the "privatized" public space of the cinema complex extends the reach of this American sensibility. This simplified observation notwithstanding, the most forceful and universal consequence of the friction between senses and embodiments of public and private is the production of difference through discursive and material means. Alexander Kluge rightly summarizes, "It is just as important to produce a public sphere as it is to produce politics, affection, resistance, protest, etc."[54] Yet such an application is surely always already in process. And just as spatial and temporal boundaries for cultural practice wend their way from industrial common sense into the lives of millions, the participation of people fortifies and gradually rewrites those boundaries as various agencies and managers tinker with their operations. Every instant of engagement, every move on the cultural field, recreates the parameters of collectivity and separateness. The discourses of cinemagoing, then, account for some of the raw elements distinguishing modalities of cultural life, for these modalities are simultaneously the reconstruction of social unity and social division.

MEGAPLEX FALLING AND DIGITAL HORIZONS

The periodization that has organized this study should not be overemphasized. Rising and falling agreements, visible in industry practice and having effects on fields of cultural activity, are a regular feature of historical change. Arguably, identifying and typifying those agreements is a first step into a discussion of historical context. It would be a mistake to fetishize sea changes and make pronouncements about unprecedented shifts, for ample continuity is also apparent, as per John Clarke's reminder (of Raymond Williams's recommendation) that cultural analysis pay equal attention to the emergent and the residual in cultural life. Of a different period in film history, the 1940s, Janet Staiger wrote, "It is important to understand that the shift from studio mass production to independent, specialised production has not necessarily secured a significant change in the factors which could affect the films produced, distributed and exhibited by the U.S. film industry. In fact, the move to independent production was not 'outside' the dominant sectors of the industry."[55] Similarly, the modifications I have itemized have as much to do with a reconstitution, and at times a reorganization, of dominant industry participants as they do with an introduction of innovative film environments. On a grander scale, this study should point to the ways in which capitalist structures habitually reinvent themselves in order to assure their existence tomorrow.

Yet the coincidence of several powerful forces and the subsequent organization of consent about those forces helps to characterize the tone and particularity of an era. While the 1986 point of departure for this research is fairly widely understood as the beginning of a new stage in the history of the entertainment industry, 1998 is not so well acknowledged as a turning point. To be sure, it is no definitive end to the practices of the preceding thirteen-year period. In fact, most of the practices, from integrated cross-media entertainment products to global markets to "themed" leisure spaces, continue in some form or other. Nonetheless, I maintain that by 1998 there were rumblings that the agreement concerning space, entertainment, and cinemagoing of the previous decade habored some fatal flaws. As with instances of settlement before, there was a growing impression that this configuration would mutate into another.

By 1998 the whiff of failure was in the air, and one can find evidence of the falling away of some aspects of the industry settlement on the globalized megaplex and the upscaled multiplex. Stubbornly, at ShoWest 1998, the trade papers continued to note such dominant trends as the consolidation of theater chains, the rise of the megaplex, and the associated waning of clearances.[56] And yet, at this event, the recognition of these changes paralleled a ripening feeling that the megaplex model was doomed, and that the rush to build fast may have created unnecessary instability for many exhibitors, perhaps for the industry as a whole. In October 1997 AMC credited megaplexes for their mounting fortunes,[57] and a year and a half later the chain had reversed this claim, reasoning they had build too fast, too large, and would have to trim back its future plans.[58]

Even the taken-for-granted groundswell of globalization encountered some shockingly abrupt setbacks. Distributors had come to presume that courting audiences across the planet would naturally lead to a situation in which most of their theatrical business would be done outside the United States. Yet figures for 2001 showed that only 38.7 percent of rentals came from outside, while 61.3 percent originated in U.S. chains. This spread was explained by the strength of the U.S. dollar next to other currencies, which made international rentals worth less.[59] Experiencing such volatility, distributors faced a far less rosy portrait of international markets than that of only a few years earlier. They even began to question whether the advantages of simultaneous international day-and-date releasing had been overestimated.[60]

As this sense of disappointment grew, the inklings of a new agreement, a new settlement, were beginning to accumulate. This next "solution" to exhibition involved the age-old dream of eliminating the frustratingly material element of film; the digital projection and delivery of motion pictures arose as the most hotly debated and anticipated developments of the late 1990s. Replacing celluloid and film reels, digital projectors translate information into complete images and sounds for each screen. One of the most advanced DLP (Digital

Light Processor) from Texas Instruments (figure 11), uses a system of at least 1,310,720 million microscopic rotating mirrors to achieve a high-resolution image that is reportedly closer to the smoothness and richness of 35mm film than the more visually noisy video projection.[61] Hughes-JVC, Sony, and Kodak, among others, have been developing their own systems, making the adoption of an industry standard imperative (something that major U.S. studios have just established in principle).[62] With digital formats, the physical transportation of film canisters to theaters would be replaced by that of disks, satellite relay, or fiber-optic transmission downloaded onto hard drives in each theater.

This digital dream has been simmering for years, with the objective of pushing the technology of motion pictures away from its late-nineteenth-century mechanical roots toward a twenty-first-century electronic state. Television has figured especially conspicuously in such aspirations. At an early stage in its history, we witnessed efforts to configure television as an alternative to film in the arena of public consumption. William Boddy exactingly documents the investment and experimentation in the 1940s with theater television.[63] Anna McCarthy more expansively proposes that television was never only a domestic technology and has always had some incarnation as a medium of public spectatorship.[64]

The prospects for a broadcastlike alternative to the prevailing film apparatus gained earnest attention in the 1990s. Most promising appeared to be high definition television (HDTV).[65] Addressing an exhibitors' convention in Australia in 1991, the president of NATO California, Timothy Warner, stated that new technology needed to accommodate global distribution. The development of such "new delivery systems . . . will enable first run features to open simultaneously worldwide."[66] In 1992 a high-definition video version of *Bugsy* was sent from Sony Picture Studios to a screening room in Anaheim through a fiber-optic telephone line, though with only half the resolution of 35mm film.[67] Soon after, Eutelsat tested satellite delivery of features to twelve small theaters for video projection in France, seen as an experiment in the convergence of telecommunications, broadcasting, and theatrical exhibition.[68] The president of the Theater Equipment Association, Terry Yushchyshyn, supported such a course in 1994, declaring that "the inevitable joining of TV, telephones and computers" will extend to film so completely that "pictures will be entirely

FIGURE 11 Texas Instruments DLP. By permission of Texas Instruments.

photographed, edited and projected without a frame of film being used."[69] This last statement now seems quaint. Taken together, these examples illustrate that the interest in some sort of video-like theatrical event was not advanced merely in the interest of cost-saving. Just as important was the coordination of releasing and the convergent relations with other media.

The current phase of enthusiasm about digital projection, however, can be traced to NATO's semiannual board meeting in Denver in November 1998. At that gathering, members saw six digital projection systems that surprised them with their clarity. To their eyes the images were virtually indistinguishable from celluloid projections, or at least that was how *Variety* reported their response.[70] From this date in late 1998 on, industry and popular periodicals alike have proclaimed the immanent arrival of fully digitized cinema and the expiration of celluloid. ShowCanada 1999 featured sessions on digital cinema that demonstrated "how close electronic cinema is."[71] At Cinema Expo 1999 in Amsterdam exhibitors were readying themselves "for major biz upheaval," as "it's a question of when, not whether, to switch from film to digital delivery."[72] The sticking point, apparently, was not image quality. As one exhibitor put it, "you could

Miniaturization of the Theme Park **215**

project an HDTV image and 90 percent of the audience would accept it."[73] Instead, one question haunts the debate: who will pay for the conversion from conventional projectors to digital ones? Conversion financing dominated discussion at the exhibitors' convention ShowEast 1999 as well.[74] At around a quarter of a million dollars, but expected to fall below $150,000, digital projectors are still significantly more expensive than the $60,000 for the existing standard projectors.[75] In contrast to the anticipated short lifespan for a single digital projector, the standard platter-system projectors can be used for decades. Further, many of those platter-system projectors are fairly recent purchases from the building and refurbishing of the 1990s. Many factors have cooled this enthusiasm, especially the financial difficulties of exhibitors. At ShoWest 2000, commentators charged this issue with creating an uncertain time line for the digital introduction, then ranging from the next two to ten years.[76] Other barriers included the need for projection standards, control over scheduling, assurances against piracy, and negotiation of the enormous debt exhibitors racked up during their 1990s building spree.[77]

Nonetheless, an industrywide agreement was in process. Put differently, we were witnessing an industrial common sense in formation, one that had more to do with ideas and assumptions of standardized practice than some uncontested truth about technological progress or audience taste. On June 18, 1999, George Lucas presented *Star Wars: Episode I—The Phantom Menace* (1999) in an experimental digital format.[78] Since then, he and others have been investing in this technology and testing it on audiences in select locations. The first major film to attempt digital distribution was *Bounce* (Don Roos 2000), delivered via satellite from Tulsa to AMC's Empire 25 in New York City, where it was stored on hard drives for the film's run. The press conference that followed included a photo-op of corporate representatives from Disney, AMC, and Boeing Satellite Systems dropping metal film canisters into a garbage can marked "obsolete."[79] When *Boxoffice* asked cinema architects about the future of theater design in 2000, they referred to reducing the size of the megaplex, creating more adult-oriented environments, continuing the extension of lobbies, and most prominently, the shift to digital projection and delivery.[80] Another sure sign of a new settlement about film exhibition, the MPAA announced guidelines required of any new digital projection and delivery system before it would be accepted as a standard (see appendix 5). A policy statement from the MPAA declared, with more than a little hyperbole, that "the introduction of digital cinema represents the greatest opportunity for enhancing the theatrical film experience since the introduction of sound and the advent of color."[81] Their objectives call for high quality in the system for spectators, which the MPAA insists must match if not exceed that of 35mm, cost advantages to exhibitors and distributors, security in the transmission of movies, and global standardization for the technology. It is worth noting that the MPAA guidelines recommend flexibility in the transportation of works and state that "the system should accommodate a variety of secure content transport mechanisms, including electronic as well as a physical media delivery."[82]

Digital distribution and projection targets certain interests of exhibitors and distributors. Most prominent, the celluloid print, expensive to produce, heavy and vulnerable to scratches and mishandling, is seen as a troubling object. Digital projection would not damage the image, unlike celluloid, which accumulates markings with each showing. As wide openings necessitate ever more prints, hence increasing distribution cost, it is not surprising to see a coinciding push to find an alternative. Boeing, whose Cinema Conexion uses technology developed for the secure satellite transmission of banking and military information, estimates that the roughly $1 billion for distribution costs can be cut by 75 percent.[83]

If adopted, digital projection systems would eliminate the exhibitor's labor of assembling the film reels and appending the appropriate trailers for the platter projection systems. Currently, the familiar film canisters arrive at theaters, at which time the projectionist (who might actually be a theater manager or rapidly trained part-time employee) assembles them into a single large roll to be placed on the horizontal platter for the duration of the film's run on that screen. This assembly takes about an hour, during which time trailers, ads, and exhibitor's signature clips are also to be added. Sometimes the projectionist—using the term loosely—doesn't bother with this extra splicing. Distributors, who count on this advertising for their product, can feel that they simply do not know what happens to the prints once they are in the hands of exhibitors. In fact, distributors will send around checkers to see if their trailers have been included.[84] If there were no such handling by exhibitors, distributors could gain a certain amount of control over the intertextual flow of a film performance.[85] When exhibitors champion the conversion to digital, they mention the elimination of bulky platter-system projectors and the work area for print assembly, in addition to the related labor. They believe there will be a reduction of staff and smaller booths that do not necessarily have to be placed above and behind the auditorium.[86]

One must be wary of the truth-value of all such claims. For the most part, they are indicative of sets of assumptions and desired improvements, rather than some technological or procedural certainty. Contradictions are frequent and obvious. For example, the benefit of saving the hour it now takes to have employees assemble films willfully ignores that it currently takes up to five hours to download a film from the eighteen to twenty disks it arrives on.[87] Nonetheless, the fact that such blatant inconsistencies do not arrest the growing consensus, or are explained away with dismissive promises to "de-bug that glitch later," only makes the components of an industrial common sense that much more pronounced.

The digital coordination of distribution and exhibition sets in motion added flexibility to scheduled presentations, which would affect the temporal parameters of cinema culture. Whether satellite or cable delivery, the less expensive distribution in digital format means that there is an added incentive to replace films faster. Theatrical runs might be easily extended or shortened with minimal expense, the latter further reinforcing the existing drift toward the rapid turnover of films in cinemas. Ultimately, nothing would stop exhibitors and distributors from providing variety in their slate of offerings that would replicate programming scheduled by television broadcasters. And this is precisely what two trials demonstrated.

Famous Players has been most active in the testing of digital projection, being among the earliest to install two Texas Instruments' projectors (one each at the Paramount Toronto and SilverCity Riverport Vancouver in December 1999; for a list of digital theaters and digitally distributed feature films, see appendices 6 and 7).[88] The features they have presented in this format began with *Bicentennial Man* (Chris Columbus 1999) and continued with such films as *Toy Story 2* (John Lasseter 1999) and *Time Code* (Mike Figgis 2000). Testing the digital projectors has been but one avenue for assessing how audiences will integrate the changing cinematic apparatus into their cinemagoing habits. Famous Players periodically presents World Wrestling Entertainment (WWE, formerly the WWF) events. On February 27, 2000, at seventeen Canadian theaters, fans gathered to see the WWE's "No Way Out" on megaplex screens, paying $CDN17 for the four-hour show. These events do not use the new digital projectors, relying instead on conventional video projection.[89] However, these performances assess the effectiveness of satellite distribution and the aesthetics of television events for theater environments. Crucially, they experiment with what kinds of motion picture presentations can be offered at multiplexes. In this case, it is an event that is available at home on pay-per-view. The WWE advertises "blast areas," which are public venues authorized to sell tickets for its PPV shows, most of which consist of bars and arenas.[90] Considering them a reasonable success in drawing patrons into public venues to see television programming, the trade publication *Cinema Technology* included Famous Players' WWE shows, along with six experiments, in its global survey of the state of the conversion to digital systems by exhibitors. The journal reported that the exhibitor recorded a two- to fourfold increase in revenue for those days on which WWE events played and concluded that people could be drawn out to see what was available at home.[91] Despite the generally positive appraisals, the WWE presentation exposed a technical weakness particular to broadcasting, one with which cinemas would have to contend should such events continue. The satellite feed provider mistakenly switched signals, and for thirty seconds Famous Players inadvertently treated the predominantly teenage WWE fans in cities across the country to hardcore pornography (making front-page news in the process).[92]

Another experimental show was a concert "theatrecast"—as Famous Players called it—of the virtual band Gorillaz on February 24, 2002 (figure 12). Charging $CDN17.50 per ticket, six cinemas (one each in Montreal, Ottawa, London, Calgary, Edmonton, and Vancouver) used video projection to present the band's first North American live appearance in Toronto the day before. Judging from the start-times, there were actually two theatrecasts, one starting at 3:00 EST for the three western cities and then 4:00 EST for the other sites. Using satellite distribution created the distinct impression of a live concert, reinforced by the advertising declaring that this was a "Larger than Live" event, though the

FIGURE 12
Newspaper advertisement for
Gorillaz's concert "theatrecast."
By permission of Clear Channel
Entertainment.

concert had been previously recorded. The theatrecast included a half-hour documentary, hence offering a programming strip. The performance equally implied simultaneous presentation across the country, irrespective of the fact that its times varied slightly. As one journalist put it, "Imagine, a Canadian tour in a single concert!"[93] The band itself is a concept produced by a collaboration between Blur lead singer Damon Albarn and *Tank Girl* comic book artist Jamie Hewlett, so the original concert was more accurately a multimedia performance of cartoons before a live audience, with the band playing behind the screens. In fact, the theatrecast received scathing reviews for its overemphasis on images of the crowd, as well as its poor sound and image quality. One reviewer observed that the projection was blurry and the theater audience was bored. Following the show, a lineup for refunds gathered, though none were forthcoming. Outraged by their treatment, the reviewer called for patrons to avoid Famous Players cinemas altogether.[94] The promoter Clear Channel Entertainment, which lists the Gorillaz theatrecast as part of a series, says that such events will continue, though none are scheduled at present.[95]

What I want to highlight about these efforts is that any transitional moment in the cinematic apparatus may develop from new technological possibilities, but it additionally involves industry strategy and procedures, assumptions about audience practice, and ideas about relationships to other media (video/TV, popular bands) and to other sites of cultural engagements (the home, the live concert). In the case of digital projection and delivery, part of what we are witnessing is an increasing concentration of decision-making power with distributors, as well as a possible expansion of who is a distributor. Clear Channel and the WWE are not standard theatrical distributors. It is possible that the textual flexibility offered by this system might include advertisements sold by distributors. Some, like Toby Miller et al., are quite reasonably more suspicious: "When digital film delivery arrives, filmgoers should expect the industry to alter images surreptitiously for digital product and commercial message placement, as sport fans exposed to digital inserts on televised sporting events already see."[96]

John Belton strikes a welcome note of skepticism about the digital revolution, arguing that even if complete conversion transpires, digital projection will not give movie audiences a new experience.[97] This claim, however, considers only the look and sound of the moving image, which is a restricted conception of the cinematic experience. Modifications to the discursive and material parameters of the everyday in cinemagoing also encompass aspects of time. Digital delivery and projection may well fit easily with the existing space of the multiplex and megaplex, but it may rework the *when* of cinemagoing. Thinking of the vectors of cinemagoing temporality discussed in chapter 3, the prospects for digital exhibition and distribution include (1) performances that might expand the "limited flow" of cinema, taking as examples WWE's four-hour show and the intertextual strip of Gorillaz, (2) shortening runs, to the extreme of one-time-only events that immediately vanish from theaters, and (3) synchronized releasing with presentations opening in a range of geographically dispersed locations at roughly the same time (barring delays for time zones). In short, these amount to temporal experiments as much as tests of the acceptability of the projected image, which tends to receive the most popular and critical attention. Conversion is not just a technological or financial issue but one of procedures, genres, and practices; we might ask how we need to rethink the specificity of the cultural activity at the motion picture theater in light of such shifts.

Such planning for the timing and appearance of films is akin to the programming and scheduling decisions of network executives. And I will hazard to say that digital delivery and projection, in which texts could be beamed to cinemas via satellite, or could arrive through fiber-optic cables, rather than circulate in prints, will only augment this comparison. In this format, it is feasible that distribution could be more carefully tailored to specific cities or even theaters. Of course, just as the promise of a more varied range of film texts at the multiplex and megaplex did not materialize, so too could digital delivery's heightened coordination of cinemagoing events serve a more, rather than less, restrictive public film culture. In theory, in avoiding the expense of print duplication, there will be motivation to extend or shorten runs according to their performance, to offer a wider slate of films during any given week, and to schedule special events akin to current pay-per-view television. In short, with digital delivery and projection releasing could become that much more like television programming. In the least, I suggest it will be conceptualized as such. The decades-old negotiation between public and private motion picture consumption continues. Here, broadcasting (or the more recent term "narrowcasting") appears ever more powerfully as a progenitor of the next phase in cinema history. To the existing tendency for rapidly revised runs and openings we can expect the sense of immediacy and "liveness" of performance to be added. The simultaneity of the current cinema—"opening everywhere" is the ubiquitous promise—is entrenched further.

Some film critics lament this development as "the death of cinema" and see the closing distance between television and film as culturally and aesthetically suspect.[98] Godfrey Cheshire delineates prognoses for the technological apparatus of film ("sudden death"), the entertainment form of movies ("forced mutation"), and the art of cinema ("rapid decay"), all traceable to digital formats and the multimedia location of the "enormoplex."[99] Stanley Kauffman uttered outright fears for the future of film acting, expecting that technicians would be celebrated for their digital enhancements of the likes of Julia Roberts and Robert DeNiro.[100] Others, including Walter Murch, wondered if "digital, perhaps, may prove to be paper to celluloid's parchment."[101] Offering a dose of historical perspective, Doug Saunders noted that *Variety*'s headline "The Death of Film" did not appear in response to the current postcelluloid aspirations; it was a comment about the arrival of color television in 1957.[102] George Lucas is typical of many filmmakers who see the cost savings and potentially finer image and sound quality as reasons to be unsentimental about the passing of the celluloid film medium.[103] A representative of a projectionists union and AMC's own testing of the new DLPs concluded that audiences actually preferred the brighter image of the digital format.[104] Some even hold onto the belief that the reduced expenses will make it easier for smaller independent films to gain access to major cinema chains. One new company, Emerging Cinemas, is following the IMAX model and establishing a chain of exclusively digital cinemas at science and arts centers.[105] IMAX itself, seeing even more significant savings in light of their unusually expensive large-format prints, was an early investor, buying a company that was developing such technology, Digital Projection International.[106]

Digital projection and delivery has emerged as the most widely accepted avenue for the next reconfiguration of cinemagoing. Concurrently, another model for distribution and marketing has appeared: Web-based cinema. Sparked by the Internet buzz that supported the unlikely success of *The Blair Witch Project* (Daniel Myrick and Eduardo Sánchez 1999), Web sites began by presenting previews, advertisements, and specially produced films. Some discussion has circulated about a rising interest in short filmmaking, in addition to a rather predictable celebration of Web-based film's potential for independent filmmakers. Sites like Ifilm and Atom Films see their services as alternatives to commercial theatrical releasing. As the quality of the images improves, pay-per-view feature films online will become more common. Major studios, including Warner Bros. and Trimark, have sites, with the latter presenting entire features at CinemaNow.[107] The involvement of studios has been spurred on by the fledgling and growing piracy of features online, allowing bootleg copies of recent releases to be sold via the Internet and made into DVDs.[108] And the exploration of Internet distribution and exhibition converges with that of digital projection. Internet distribution/exhibition turning point for the major studios occurred on June 6, 2000, when a feature film, *Titan AE* (Don Bulth and Gary Goldman 2000), arrived from Twentieth Century-Fox studio in Hollywood to be projected at a telecommunications convention in Atlanta.[109] Not to be left behind, video retailers Blockbuster and Hollywood Video have invested in online video-on-demand services.[110]

Just as these novel complements to exhibition were being negotiated, some of the economic blindspots of the previous agreement resulted in an industrywide destabilization. Praise for the megaplexes' return of the grandeur of the movie palace continued to appear in August 2000. *New York Times* reporter Monte Williams cheerfully celebrated the showmanship and cinephilia of megaplexes, writing, "The megaplexing trend appears to be going as global as the taste for American movies."[111] However, by the end of that month Carmike, United Artists Theaters, General Cinemas, Edward Cinemas, Mann Theaters, and Resort Theaters would file Chapter 11. Loews Cineplex Entertainment, AMC, and Regal Cinemas renegotiated loans, had their corporate credit ratings lowered, or prepared to file for bankruptcy protection.[112] The slowdown in North American exhibition even affected IMAX. The corporation had put a substantial share of the business up for sale in July 2000 but then subsequently pulled it when it realized that the troubles experienced by exhibitors meant that a suitable buyer would not be forthcoming.[113]

While exhibitors put the blame on the poor slate of films in that year, two more reasonable explanations were evident: the overscreening of Canada and the United States and the overemphasis on building expensive megaplexes. NATO's figures indicate that from 1990 to 1999 attendance grew by 24 percent while the number of screens increased 56 percent.[114] On this evidence alone, something had been amiss in industry thinking; it essentially overshot the popular sensibility of immediate access to the new. As exhibitors ran into impossible financial straits and needed to get out of leases for theaters they intended to close, contradictions in the logic of the megaplex and its appended strategies of distribution and releasing revealed themselves. The "size matters" at any cost mode of competition among chains began to seem dated and out of place. The industry common sense that ruled the previous decade required reconsideration. Some commentators suggested that the "good" idea of upgrading theater spaces for adult and family audiences was both too expensive and not integrated fully with other activities, like the closing of traditional multiplexes, leaving many wondering if chains could avert disaster, "dodge the bullets and outrun the boulders."[115] Among other implications, the uncertainty brought on by overscreening and megaplexing meant that investing in what appeared to be the next major turn for exhibitors—digital projection systems—would not be as rapid as expected due to an absence of available capital.

Market analyst Moody's recommended that as many as one third of screens needed to be closed to return stable profitability to exhibitors,[116] and beginning in 2000 circuits did just that. Table 25 presents the 2000, 2001, and 2002 year-end total of openings and closings, showing a consecutive overall loss in the number of theaters and screens. Canada saw 23 of its theaters, comprising 94 screens, close in 2000, then 43 theaters and 231 screens do the same the following year.[117] Loews Cineplex Entertainment, in the wake of its losses in 2000, announced shutting down or selling 112 theaters (675 screens).[118] As shaky as these events were for chains, this economic setback was not an index of the "death of cinemagoing" as a practice or industry. It was, however, a sign that yet again new arrangements were to be sought out. For instance, one reason for this situation was the relative slow pace for closing older, unprofitable sites, often due to long-term leases for theaters. Filing for bankruptcy protection and Chapter 11 opens up the possibility of renegotiating those leases.[119]

In the meantime, Cineplex Odeon and Famous Players were under investigation by the Canadian Federal Competition Bureau for collusion at the end of 2000. The charges stemmed from claims of independent exhibitors, especially Quebec's Guzzo Cinemas, who argued that the two theater giants agreed to not bid against each other's films in especially competitive zones in which a third chain is present.[120] Such splitting of the most lucrative of U.S. films effectively assures that these films will not be acquired by the smaller chains. In earlier years Guzzo had paid Cineplex Odeon $300,000 to negotiate exhibition deals for them. When they broke free of this relationship, Guzzo found they could no longer secure the most attractive films,[121] and their charges of collusion followed. Famous Players and Cineplex Odeon argue that as chains whose roots go back to the 1920s and 1940s, respectively, they have been able to establish long-standing relationships with the most powerful distributors. To their way of thinking, there is nothing anticompetitive about "traditional allegiances that have built up in business partnerships where certain distributors and studios decide to play with certain exhibitors."[122] It seems ironic that the Competition Bureau agreed to examine these accusations at a time of turmoil

TABLE 25   U.S. and Canadian Cinema Openings and Closings, 2000, 2001, and 2002

	2000		2001		2002	
	Theaters	Screens	Theaters	Screens	Theaters	Screens
Openings	189	2,038	104	1,175	52	601
Closings	448	2,410	281	1,561	179	878

SOURCE: "EDI Box Office News: Inventory Falls for Big Screens," *Variety,* January 15–21, 2001, 34; "EDI Box Office News: Theaters Downsize in 2001," *Variety,* January 7–13, 2002, 22; "Nielsen EDI Box Office News: Late-Year Flurry from Exhibs," *Variety,* January 13–19, 2003, 26.

for exhibitors, initiated by too fast construction of megaplexes and too slow closure of older theaters, which some market analysts peg at $U.S.20 billion in losses.[123] This ostensibly made the argument of the disadvantage of the smaller chains less credible, at least temporarily, as larger chains filed for bankruptcy protection. One should note that, true to Canada's "flow-through" characteristics, this dispute had nothing to do with access to Canadian theaters by Canadian films, but rather with who gets access to the most economically attractive of international cultural commodities. It concerned who the industrial participants and beneficiaries of that "flow-through" culture will be.

As should be evident from this chapter, the financial ruin of some chains and the technological transformations of the film apparatus did not eradicate public motion picture spectatorship. The peals of the "death of cinema" have rung in earlier historical eras, proclaiming the irreparable damage wrought on the art form by social and technological change. Instead, the reconfiguration of the practice of "going to the movies" characterized throughout this study entails a realignment of corporate entities, technological apparatuses, and social activity. The mini-midway of cinema complexes, and the varying placement of a motion picture encounter therein, is consistent with an extensive history of public amusement, one that is pivotal for the very idea of modern communal existence. Fundamentally, buildings, technologies, and commodities—arranged spatially and temporally for popular engagement—generate difference among institutions and populations. Examining the movie theater and its appended industrial and popular practices reveals more than the historical context and

FIGURE 13 Cineplex Odeon Egyptien, Montreal, closed

periodization of the cinema. Cinemagoing is an institutional formation, rather than some stable technological, textual, or experiential apparatus. The activity is not only a function of a constraining industrial practice or of wildly creative patrons but of a complex inter-determination between the two. It likewise confronts us with the discursive and material production of difference constituting what people see and struggle with as social life.

Meanwhile, an abundance of large-budget special effects–driven films disappoint fans and critics alike, prompting responses like Dogma '95's retreat into neorealist mise-en-scène. Randy Cohen, whose column "The Ethicist" appears in the *New York Times Magazine,* received a letter wondering it if was okay to sneak into terrible studio films but to always pay for independent ones. The individual reasoned, "Given the quality of movies like *Mission to Mars* that leave me feeling as if someone stole my nine bucks, it is fair to say that until studios start making better films I may bend the rules?" Cohen responded by admiring the aesthetic grounds but found them insufficient to justify theft, and, besides, "anyone with a lick of sense [would] want to sneak *out* of a bad movie."[124] The mere existence of such everyday ethical dilemmas, and their prosaic recognizability, should reassure cinephiles everywhere that the practice persists even if we still dream of a more enriching cinema. Alexander Kluge spoke for many when he claimed, "I love to go to the movies: the only thing that bothers me is the image on the screen."[125]

CHAPTER NINE

Cinemagoing as "Felt Internationalism"

In his beautiful short essay "Upon Leaving a Movie Theatre," Roland Barthes describes the prehypnotic state one falls into at the start of a cinematic event.[1] He suggests that moviegoers get ready for dreaming, with the theater acting as a mechanism to keep us at the twilight between sleep and consciousness. Darkness helps promote that sense of bodily loss, one that keeps audiences prepared for the experience of departure from the ordinary. The film is a lure, he writes, for an ideological and unconscious process of organizing the world as we rest calmly before the screen. It is evident that it is equally a lure that moves populations from one location of their neighborhood and city to another, drawing people out to experience that intensely personal twilight together. The elaborate theme lobbies of megaplexes sustain the sense of departure initiated by the screen images. To be sure, they are not darkened environments in which one loses sight of the strangers in one's presence. But, even with their colored lights and cacophony, the intermedia turmoil of cinema complexes broadcasts their singularity and uniqueness. Here is a set of technologies, practices, and shared engagements that cannot be found anywhere else. A trip to the cinema, the passage through the lobby and the consumption of food, drink, and games, is part of the preparation for the screening—preparation for that filmic twilight—like an urban and architectural trailer for movie watching.

Production, distribution, and exhibition, as the broad divisions of the film-industry apparatus, present a narrative path for the film commodity as it moves from conception to consumption. Clearly, the mechanics of the film business involve not only the making of movies but also their delivery to an audience, the gathering up of that audience, and the provision of a site for the film encounter. The latter moment of consumption is a death of sorts. When its exchange value has been expended, so has a commodity's life from an economic perspective, hence the concurrent obsession with the various subsequent media "reincarnations" of the work. The path of a motion picture text molds each stage via a revisitation to earlier phases, so that a film gets "re-produced," "re-distributed," and "re-exhibited" time and again. As cross-media stakes intensify, whether through ownership or coventures, so too has the experimentation with commodity forms and the paths they take. Such a transmission or narrativized approach to the life of the film should not steer us away from the construction of that audience, that is, the making of the consumer, citizen, fan, and spectator. Delivery, distribution, and exhibition of film to some segment of the population might be understood best as the shaping of that segment. And as this book has contended, this shaping is not the province of textual conventions alone but of spatial and temporal ones. The "where" and the "when" of film are crucial components in the formation of audiences, whether imagined as the product of local practices or as manifestations of international popular taste. My concentration on the establishment of an industry common sense about this, and its ramifications for popular cultural life, stem in part from an impression that the powerful elements of the formation of the location and context of cinemagoing have been underplayed in film theory and analysis.

The organization of people at film events is evidence of communion. Miriam Hansen's use of Kluge's alternative public sphere is one example that takes the meeting of strangers at a film screening as holding the germinational potential of becoming a public. Moreover, some filmgoing events and habits offer a wedge of resistance unavailable to some populations elsewhere. Importantly, Hansen highlights the historical efforts to put a halt to the variability of film crowds and, in effect, to audiences' ability to transform themselves into a fully realized public. Indeed, the complexity of this question makes Oskar Negt and Alexander Kluge critical of the potential uses of the "public sphere," seeing the ephemeral qualities and locations of the contemporary environment as a mark of individuation rather than of community. In the end, they suggest that what we think of as the public sphere is in fact a relation to the sphere of production. They write,

> *it cannot be considered to be unified at all, but rather the aggregate of individual spheres that are only abstractly related.* Television, the press, interest groups and political parties, parliament, army, public education, public chairs in the universities, the legal system, the industry of churches are only apparently fused into a general concept of the public sphere. In reality, this general, overriding public sphere runs parallel to these fields as a mere idea, and is exploited by the interests contained within each sphere, especially by the organized interests of the productive sector.[2]

Furthermore, it is precisely the ephemeral nature of film audiences that makes them productive illustrations of contemporary social existence. People move through cinemas to sit momentarily in the presence of others, retaining thoughts of similar situations unfolding elsewhere, and move back through the streets to domestic life. The fleeting arrest of that movement is a point of imagined relation to an unseen population of resting, consuming bodies. Cinemas are sites for the mobility and flow of bodies, texts, and money. They are also sites for the materialization and conceptualization of shared ideas about mobility and flow. Looking at them in this way, we can begin to grasp the remarkable changes that have already installed themselves in contemporary civic life, as exemplified by the miniaturization of the theme park and its incorporation into the cinematic exhibitionary complex. Resting momentarily, balanced between the "safety" of home and the public of crowds, the film audience—that abstract creature of industrial and cultural discourse—might be apprehended as an intermediary between our private and public selves.

Often public spaces have been seen as infused with the possibility of messiness and unruliness. The cinematic sphere, contrarily, it would appear, offers the opportunity to glimpse the orderly and servile nature of a population. The policing of ushers, the presence of security cameras, the regiment of scheduling, and the overt appeals to decorum in film trailers (feet off the seat in front, no talking, cell phones and pagers off, etc.) are indices of the intense interest in encouraging civility and reducing the prospects for impromptu (and economically unproductive) interventions. Hansen has suggested that the 1990s saw an unusual amount of talk and enforcement of how one was to comport oneself at movies.[3] Famous Players has taken to having employees introduce each screening under a spotlight with a litany of "dos and don'ts." And probably the biggest budget announcement ever designed exclusively to install a code of silence played in Canadian theaters in the middle of that decade, produced by the agency Gee Jeffrey and Partners for Rogers Cantel Telecommunication (figures 14, 15, and 16). Winning Clio, Cannes, and Andy awards for advertising, other wireless communication companies used versions of the trailer, including BT Cellnet in the UK, Vodaphone in New Zealand, Telstra in Australia, and Telefonica in Spain. In a military setting, it presents a scene of emergency in which a young white hero arrives to dismantle a noise-sensitive nuclear device. He performs the delicate operation with sweaty-browed concentration, but something goes wrong. A beeping sound starts the countdown. Just before the device blows, obliterating the characters and presumably the entire city, the frantic hero demands to know the source of the sound that triggered the bomb. In his final words, his assistant states, "It came from the audience," to which the hero replies, "What kind of jerk lets their cell phone go off in a movie?"

The advertisement elicits a momentary confusion. It presents itself as a trailer for a coming attraction, using signs of high production values to evoke a big-budget action film, including sweeping lights, fast camera movement, and a relatively large number of extras to create the spectacle of nuclear panic. A patchwork of technological commodities, from cordless microphones to a laptop computer, provides a link with the primary object of attention, the cell phone. The breaking of its realism by the interference from the audience here results in nuclear devastation. It is a humorous—at least in the first viewing—depiction of the dire need for the regulation of cinemagoing behavior. It might not be criminal for a spectator to let a cell phone ring during a movie, but it might be explosive for realist narrative.

Every screening wants to announce itself as another exercise in bourgeois civility, or an individually embodied comprehension of a cooperative silent crowd. This is not to suggest that such efforts to police and propagate a discourse of comportment are successful. Given what appears to be an obsession in controlling and limiting social interaction during a cinemagoing event, one

FIGURES 14–16 Stills from trailer discouraging cell phones in cinemas. By permission of Gee Jeffrey and Partners, Rogers Cantel Telecommunication.

might conclude that the opposite is the case and innovative alternatives to "good" cinematic behavior abound. But the qualities of this investment by exhibitors and distributors are telling. As discussed earlier, one of the arguments about the formation of cinema spectatorship has to do with predictability and control, a sort of industrial standard of audience generation and comportment. In the current dominant incarnation of standardizing mechanisms, the themed cinematic institution of the megaplex or the upgraded multiplex, and the accelerated international cinema text, pursue knowable audiences across the globe.

This book has attempted to document how the impulse to seek out and shape an ideal standardized audience has been retooled yet again for a global cinema environment. In the process, the relations among media and contexts have been redrawn, one key element of which has been an augmenting sense of coordination and simultaneity across locations. One of the theoretical challenges advanced here has been the following: where are the spaces for agents of cultural politics in light of evidence of cultural simultaneity?

As has been put forward throughout, there is no necessary reason why simultaneity must equate homogeneity. The dispersion of spaces and sites, the intermedia mutations of cultural commodities, and the polysemic nature of signs all indicate that it would be a profound and presumptuous misstep to think that cultural artifacts harbor their own essential meaning effects. For too long, the speedy critical glide to this premise has made for some lazy claims about global culture. Instead, Ien Ang's discussion of capitalist postmodernity as a chaotic system is instructive. She points out that "chaos" does not signal an absence of structure or lack of order, but that our historical context, and our globalizing tendency, is one of radically indeterminate meaning.[4] The structures of theatrical exhibition contribute to global cultural economic forces as well as a *sensibility* about the global. There is, of course, work to be done to maintain and promote diversity in cultural life; attacking transnational culture as a matter of course, however, is a dead-end strategy.

Cees Hamelink twenty years ago warned about "cultural synchronization."[5] And yet, despite a passionate and detailed analysis, Hamelink's dependency theory cannot account for the variable functions of that international culture, concluding that the forces of synchronization must be arrested in order to promote cultural dissonance. Alternatively, Benedict Anderson indicates that a modern concept of simultaneity resides at the cultural roots of nationhood. He writes of how the novel and the newspaper provided a national communal consciousness that harbored a sense that events were taking place coincidentally, as was people's awareness of those events. He proposes, drawing from Walter Benjamin's "Thesis on the Philosophy of History," that "meanwhile" floats above such cultural forms, allowing people to grasp not only the words on the page but the way those words presume simultaneous consumption.[6] On these grounds, synchronization in cultural life *produces* forms of community, which for Anderson are nations. Contrary to Hamelink's assessments, international cultural simultaneity spawns new transnational communities that reside in people's imaginations and have material consequences for the organization of popular existence. I can think of no better embodiment of such transnational imaginings than cosmopolitanism.

The age of the megaplex has its antipode in earlier arguments for the perfect spectatorial situation. Peter DeCherney comments on the ideal movie theaters advocated by Seymour Stern and Harry Allan Potamkin in the 1920s and 1930s, which embraced a "streamlined continuity model as an alternative to the baroque designs and multimedia presentation of the palaces."[7] The clean, uncluttered auditorium with nothing to interfere visually with the viewer, they reasoned, encouraged a more immersive, individual relationship with the screen. Today, prestige screens (Ex-Centris in Montreal) and nominally adult venues (Alliance Atlantis Cinemas) adopt aspects of this, in which the tastefully sparse is a response to the megaplex clutter. And yet, as DeCherney mentions, Siegfried Kracauer responded differently, arguing that the elements of "supplementation" to the screen—music, illumination, live performance, and decor—help to create, in Kracauer's words, a "homogeneous cosmopolitan audience."[8] This supplementation served a productive function by distracting and interrupting the concentration of that cosmopolitan audience. As Kracauer wrote of the movie palaces' external and surface bombardment of the senses, "Like *life buoys*, the refractions of the spotlights and the musical accompaniment keep the spectator above water."[9] It is opportune to speculate on a similar affirmative potential for the oft-mentioned gaudiness and trashy muddle of today's cinemas. The supplementation of midway distraction one experiences at megaplexes might, like the movie palaces, pilot audiences away from individual interpellation toward wider senses of community. Just as the cinema complex stirred reconstitutions of public and private life, it also helps initialize a contemporary brand of cosmopolitan public to which Kracauer alludes in his essay on movie palaces. He reasoned, "in pure externality, the audience encounters itself; its own reality is revealed in the fragmented sequence of splendid impressions."[10]

Several cultural theorists approach cosmopolitanism as a point of entry into a model of political life. The concept captures a sense of competence with the contemporary and a connection or empathy with difference. The cosmopolitan person imagines a global breadth for his/her habitus. Ulf Hannerz writes, "Cosmopolitans can be dilettantes as well as connoisseurs, and are often both, at different times,"[11] and then wonders about how this alters when international movement is not necessarily a defining feature of cosmopolitanism any more. Moreover, cosmopolitanism is taken by some as a possible alternative to the restrictions of national or local communities. On this point, John Hartley describes a postmodern public sphere of media images and Arjun Appadurai wants to name a transnational public.[12] All are fairly careful to avoid a stable trajectory whereby the cosmopolitan culture lifts one out of the local; instead, the notion describes an importing, as much as an exporting, mechanism. But their reinvestment in the very term "public" is telling, reminding us that thinking of political agency requires some site—or imagined point—of commune. Here, Timothy Brennan's intricate study is particularly instructive. Detailing the mobilization of cosmopolitanism as an obstruction to emerging formations of nations and states, Brennan reveals the pitfalls such globalism has had for critical theory's ability to help us understand contemporary cultural politics. Where others have championed cosmopolitanism as a conceptual negotiation of new global political agency, Brennan cautions us about the way its current form may redirect us from other key struggles for community and may carry with it what are not international ideals but American ones.[13]

Such an indispensable lesson, one that essentially turns on scholarly discourse, can be supplemented by bringing cosmopolitanism as a structure of feeling—or a "felt internationalism"—into full relief. Steering away from the treatment of cosmopolitanism as a worldly view from above, Bruce Robbins compellingly imagines it as a "collective, engaged, and empowered" brand of internationalism, one characterized by continuities between local and global commitments.[14] Importantly, he questions a tendency to pit nationalism against globalism, as though the two are in battle for people's affiliations and emotional attentions. Rather, he proposes that "the forms of global feeling are continuous with forms of national feeling. This implies that, though the potential for a conflict of loyalties is always present, cosmopolitanism or internationalism does not take its primary meaning or desirability from an absolute and intrinsic opposition to nationalism. Rather, it is an extension outward of the same sorts of potent and dangerous solidarity."[15] A line of attack that runs through this book is a class critique of the misguided binary option of globalism and nationalism. He notes in close detail the operations of a jet-setting intelligentsia that result in a disparaging view of the nationalist commitments of the broader population. And yet he documents an emerging discussion of a "popular cosmopolitanism," a shared and easily accessible sense of worldliness, that holds significant weight in the everyday life of people.[16]

I can think of no more apt characterization of Canadian cinemagoing, where commercial screens inhibit for the most part a Canadian film presence but offer an encounter with an international scene. The Canadian national-popular, such that it is, includes a continuing reorganization and reappraisal of skirmishes with and glorifications of international culture. In the context of a sense of Canadian cultural absence, one of the strategies has been to present a cosmopolitan face, that is, to celebrate worldly sophistication, or, in effect, to live elsewhere. Here, I arrive at a general conclusion about the motors and effects of transnational culture, namely, that *popular cosmopolitanism needs to be taken seriously as a pervasive mode for negotiating and managing reigning ideas and experiences of global economies and cultures.* It is a structure of feeling about senses of allegiance and affiliation—about being in step—with imagined distant and synchronized populations. Popular cosmopolitanism can be continuous with, and can be incorporated into, senses of nationhood. It is a mode internal to existing national boundaries and obviously does not make them disappear magically. Where many critics can only see international popular culture engulfing and suppressing domestic expressions, there remains a rich popular knowledge about a contemporary multinational culture, or what Simon During might describe as a fledgling form of global popular, one that could serve dominant discourses of national community or could offer a foothold for an alternative.

The politics of such a turn are far from set in stone, for there is ample evidence of both rightist and leftist critique rooted both in forms of nationalism and internationalism. In this respect, while identifying the way cosmopolitanism *and* nationalism play into efforts to smooth the logic of world capital, Robbins perceptively highlights the overwhelming presence of anticapitalist convictions in the antiglobalization movement, itself a community with a highly developed international consciousness. He goes further in suggesting that the romance involved with a certain brand of leftist politics can become a dominant form of American nationalism, especially among a privileged class of intellectuals and scholars.[17] Similarly, Canadian critics have been notoriously uniform in their apprehension of popular cosmopolitanism as a problem to be attacked and ridiculed, yet they have actively championed other strains of international awareness. The result has been the domination of left critique by a narrow band of rhetoric, squeezing out other progressive possibilities that might give full due to popular practices and understandings.

Returning to the lessons of Gramsci on the national-popular is edifying, for among his writings is a battle with the implications of new forms of internationalism, especially for the making of a progressive historical bloc. He recommended that putting together a class of democratic political agents necessitates an engagement with the everyday language of people. This vernacular may consist in pieces of cultural life that spring from unlikely and far-flung sources. For pundits of an autonomous and authentic national culture, these popular pieces of cultural life may be seen as illegitimate, especially if those pieces arrive from other shores. Yet, and at times seemingly against his own better judgment, Gramsci advised a genuine scrutiny of the stockpile of materials that are part of popular everyday consciousness. Such an analysis will lay bare the thinking of a time and place and will provide the raw resources required to tap into that thinking. As Marcia Landy puts it,

> Gramsci's conception of language is divided between normative and "spontaneous" or "immanent" linguistic practices. The normative linguistic practices relate to traditional practices. The sources of conformism and of inno-

vation are identified by Gramsci as radiating from the schools, the church, elite and popular writers, theater and film, radio, popular songs, public assemblies, and local dialects. . . . Hence one must be aware of these many lines traversing and feeding into language in order to effect any change.[18]

From exactly these varied media sources emanates a widespread sentiment of connection and participation in a contemporary transnational moment. This "felt internationalism"—that is, the potential condition for a global popular—is not evenly distributed and has multiple appearances, but it exists as a powerful organizing feature of ordinary cultural life.

As an international and internationalizing formation, the contemporary film industry ignites the global circulation of culture. Among other outcomes, the apparatus of the lived space of cinemas arranges a localized encounter with a transnational commercial film culture. A moviegoing public seems to be beckoned into a cosmopolitan demeanor. What, then, are the implications of the public consumption of a slice of that global cultural traffic of images and sounds in those regulated cinema spaces? What relations of the local and the global are articulated in the megaplex? The cinema complex is but one urban and suburban intersection of the two, where the proximate and the distant collide. Emphasizing the metropolitan experience at the root of global culture, Saskia Sassen proposes, "globalization is a process that generates contradictory spaces, characterized by contestation, internation differentiation, continuous border crossings. The global city is emblematic of this condition."[19] The cinema entertainment complex is a now visible component of the global city environment. The examination of cities has appeared as an unsettling category between the abstractions of local, global, community identity, and national identity. Most certainly, as Sassen puts it, "A focus on cities allows us to capture not only the upper but also the lower circuits of globalization."[20]

Given the history of the relation between cities and cinema,[21] and in the context of the developments I have elaborated throughout this book, *megaplexes and the upgraded multiplex are among those lower circuits of globalization.* Corralling screens across continents into coordinated openings and closings of films paints an image in which the variegated traces of cultural expression connect people to geographically distant and temporally synchronized communities. Cinema complexes are sites for an encounter with one dimension of global cultural traffic. The "everywhere" of the current cinema accents this role of motion picture theaters further. Ulf Hannerz describes cosmopolitanism as "a mode of managing meaning" about city and national space in light of ideas about globalization.[22] "We often use the term 'cosmopolitan' rather loosely, to describe just about anybody who moves about in the world."[23] This feeling of movement has less to do with global mobility than an image of travel. "A more genuine cosmopolitanism is first of all an orientation, a willingness to engage with the Other."[24] So, what does it mean to be cosmopolitan without intercity mobility but instead with what Friedberg calls a mobilized visuality? Indeed, we have the exoticization of certain zones in the city, to which the megaplex is one contributor. Especially salient, here, is the fact that the "making special" of entertainment/consumption zones is a process employed by cities in disparate countries.

Importantly, moving from city to city in Canada and the United States, one expects to encounter essentially the same film events and similar show times, locations of theaters, and concession offerings. The consistency across city film cultures includes the conventionalized signs of "alternative" cinema culture (local repertory screens, cine-clubs, festivals, and film co-ops). Thus difference in one strata of continentalist film culture can be mapped more prominently *inside* a particular city than between cities. In this respect, the current cinema does not indicate geographical distinctiveness (e.g., between cities) as much as it does temporal particularity. We may want to think of the flexible landscapes of urban life, in which film texts and events appear as markers we share of various seasons, events, and memories.

The film landscape has a manifold semiotic operation. Theatrical releases and the cinema complexes themselves are billboards that promote the television broadcasts, videotape and DVD releases, repackaged novels, new game software, soft drinks, fast food, new music, and Web sites. Moreover, they reference the boundless range of human emotion (friendship, romance, pleasure, animosity, embarrassment, tedium, hopefulness, despair, and so on). They produce an atmosphere for social life, adorned with each new release. Advertisements for future commodity forms and situations for collective conduct share this atmosphere. Seeing the film landscape as a series of billboards allows us to identify the dual dimensions of consumer and cultural practice without collapsing the two together. Lawrence Grossberg and Meaghan Morris have elaborated on the billboard metaphor "to describe the multiple effectivity of cultural practices."[25] Grossberg continues,

> Billboards are neither authentic nor inauthentic; their function cannot be predefined, nor are they distributed according to some logic of the "proper" organization of space or the "proper" use of place. They follow what Morris calls a "logic of the next." And they perform, provoke, and enable a variety of different activities: they open a space for many different discourses and practices, both serious and playful, both institutional and guerrilla. . . . They manifest complex appeals that draw us down certain roads, open and close alternative routes, and enable us to be located in a variety of different ways at different sites and intersections where we can rest, or engage in other activities, or move on in different directions.[26]

Grossberg's argument draws us to regard the locations of culture as points of process and movement rather than containment. As that cultural landscape is itself in transit, any mode of critique is doomed if it does not address the everyday forces of volatility, as well as the everyday tactics to manage them.

Most striking is that what developed in exhibition and distribution after 1986 was not a radical departure but rather something that accented what was already percolating. The contemporary cinema complex is a suitable enframement of Raymond Williams's distinctions between residual, emergent, and dominant practices. Attention to this manifestation alerts us to sedimented cultural forms and practices in addition to freshly developing ones.[27] The industrial drive to coordinate, control, and mark off one site of cultural consumption from another relies on existing operating assumptions, leaving people with a recognizable field of cultural activity. Moments of upheaval in the cultural industries deserve close consideration not for their novelty but because they allow us to peek into reigning discourses; the critical intent is not to fetishize the newest technology but to take advantage of the shift in process to witness how industry agents make the argument for changes in their standard operations, with their objective of reconstituting and solidifying points of economic advantage.

Questions about these organizing features of film culture remain. What are the implications of living with cultural institutions that grow from and presume some imagined, internationally invested audience? What does it mean to live with a transnational cultural politic but to have to work politically with decidedly noncosmopolitan modes of governance (for instance, perhaps, municipal governments)? I want to speculate tentatively on two observations, ones that I think illustrate the contradictory and at times confounding situations with which we must tussle. The changing practice of "going to the movies" has generated some freshly dominant notions. For example, the industry's reliance on opening weekends as a rapid source of revenue and as a predictor of future success rests on a widespread acceptance of the value of such openings among cinemagoers. Exhibitors and audiences alike note, often with frustration, the uneven distribution of cinemagoing through the week, an inequality that initial release dates only accent further. If they tend to be the most crowded and the most expensive of cinemagoing occasions, why don't more people avoid opening weekends? The answer lies beyond the organization of the work week, if only because there are subsequent weekends for most film releases. I am convinced that there is added sign value that involves a collective sense of being up-to-date, being the first on the scene. Opening weekends allow the material and sensory experience of commune. One goes to the first showings of a theatrical release precisely to be with strangers and to be part of that crowd. The current cinema's coordination of release dates across the continent, and beyond, fosters an imagined and temporally bound sense of similar crowds elsewhere. It may be but a minority for whom this newness is salient and who have the means to act accordingly, but it is financially attractive enough to drive a dominant industry strategy. The added value of attending new releases stems from the possibility of being contemporary along with a large, dispersed population. The mass crowdings on opening weekends is not solely a symptom of the supreme loss of will to consumer agendas. Indisputably representing a consumerist "being in the world," the crowded opening is also an adjunct to "being in the know" about contemporary cultural life.

And yet, in contradistinction to this mark of sociability and collectivity, representations of moviegoing appear to signal the failure of that collectivity. The abandoned drive-in and the decaying movie palace have become clichéd signs of the passing of an era and of the betrayal of promises for a better community context. Recent depictions of cinemagoing emphasize the chaos of the practice. In a now-classic episode of *Seinfeld,* an evening out at the multiplex becomes a night of frustration as friends miss meeting one another, as they go into the wrong theaters, as they spend too much money, and as they don't even see the movie they wanted to see and end up walking out. The opening sequence of *The Trigger Effect* (David Koepp 1996) depicts the movie theater as a site of the breakdown of civic life and an intimation of impending violence, where the slightest encounter may turn into a physical confrontation. The threat of the movie house is taken even further in the opening of *Scream 2* (Wes Craven 1997), where a trip to the washroom at the opening of a horror film becomes a gruesome murder. *Poetic Justice* (John Singleton 1993) presents a drive-in drive-by assault.

These two sets of observations announce the correspondent inclinations toward affiliation and demise that cinemas signify. They may appear contradictory in the first instance, but they are perfectly consistent as expressions of hope and concern. The impression of collectivity betrays a reverie about, or a desire for, commune. And the expectation of an ensuing chaos heralds a sense that collectivity must struggle to exist and requires labor to come into being, and that social life is being hijacked by less than communitarian impulses, like the profit motive. Presently, cinemas can signify a feeling of loss and despair about public life. They linger as talismans of an alternative public sphere that might have been but has not developed as yet. Even so, with every expression of sociability as people seek out an encounter with that supposedly chaotic crowd, there is a dream of global collectivity. Such reveries are not idle distraction.

They are the notional sensibilities on which social and political life flourishes or withers. The experience of the moviegoing crowd, produced through the discursive constructs of industry common sense and new practices of cinemagoing, consists in a local subjectivity lurching toward a felt internationalism, however erratically and fitfully. What is to be made of this felt internationalism is another matter, one that has not been predetermined and written in stone.

As this study has underscored throughout, talk of globalization references the mobility of culture, capital, and people. And though this talk may present a sweeping and uniform impact of globalization, it is not a totalizing flow. In point of fact, this international mobility is just as responsible for new kinds of fixity and exclusion as it is for social and economic movement. Put simply, not all capital flows equally, not all people are set in motion across the planet in the same circumstances, and not all cultural forms enter the realm of global exchange. The industrial will to orchestrate commodities and markets leaves us with a multitiered environment as it unevenly circulates forms and establishes zones of consumption. This unevenness extends to the velocity of culture, such that audiences confront varying speeds for the arrival and departure of cultural forms. Consequently, these dynamics fix in place a core of popular texts, while other works find themselves as part of a "minor" cinema, eking out parallel, noncommercial and alternative venues. More broadly, a root impact of global flows is the production and administration of spatial and temporal differences in cultural life. Indeed, the content of the divisions, ones that set the parameters for the formation and expression of alliances among people, matters less than the sheer fact of the divisions.

The terms of the reconfiguration of cinemagoing charted here are an emerging international simultaneity in and acceleration of the current cinema, a revaluation of the space and time of new film events, an orientation of the cinema complex that responds to other occasions for audiovisual consumption, a dedifferentiation of zones of social activity and intermedia consumption, and, given the prominent place a range of "screen" technologies have in cinema locations, a public display value of new technology. The reconfiguration of cinemagoing has also included a reformation of the links between intermedia and international culture, and between those of the economies of industrial consolidation and the experiences of globalization. A dominant industrial discourse repeatedly proposes "family" as the principle orientation for the megaplex and the upgraded multiplex, and to this end we see some of the films themselves revealing an amusement park ideal. Consistent with the design and architectural embodiment of this ideal, the "ride film" has appeared as the presumed ideologically neutral narrative form suited to such an environment. The focus of this study, however, has not been on the textual ramifications in film but on issues of popular constituencies related to screen traffic. As entertainment destinations, cinema complexes play a part in the establishment of new lines of spatial and temporal difference in public life. Each aspect is a product of an industry common sense that informs a discourse of an international popular audience. The provisionally settled common sense produces, and is a product of, an image of community that articulates the proximate and the distant. Ultimately, this evidence has been read to suggest that a national-popular is not in opposition to international life but arises within an idea of a global-popular.

In closing, it is worth remarking on the nostalgic tone of megaplexes. They are rife with allusion to a golden era of the cinema[28] and of civic life, at times drawing analogies with "the main streets of old."[29] Behind the impressively lengthy escalators at Toronto's Famous Players Paramount, near the facilities reserved for corporate functions, and hence going unnoticed by most patrons, is a gentle note of historical awareness. There, a set of attractive architectural photographs dating from the 1920s of the Paramount Theater in Times Square, New York City, adorns the walls. Nearby is a section of the wrought iron railing, including the Paramount logo, from that site. Though the original theater has been shut, this relic has become adornment for a new megaplex, however much it may clash with the rest of the environment. As pronounced in the opening line of Disney's Family Channel film *Phantom of the Megaplex* (Blair Treu, 2000), "History can slam right into the present and totally blow your mind." The film follows the Andy Hardy–like exploits of a young assistant manager of a twenty-six-screen suburban megaplex preparing for a Hollywood opening night. Built on the site of an old movie palace, the megaplex appears to be haunted by an old cinemagoer who might have been trapped inside and killed when the original cinema was razed. The gentle high jinks of the phantom, and the presence of Mickey Rooney as a former employee who hangs around to "help out," remind the characters of an era in which the wonder of cinema held a central place in community life. But, of course, the film illustrates the continuation of that community as the megaplex becomes a place for youth employment, for dating, for dropping off children, for the volunteer labor of seniors, for meeting celebrities, and for generally rallying together to solve a mystery.

Such fantasies of community do not alter the fact that as contradictory spaces, cinema complexes are only ever semipublic and operate through a series of regimens of behaviors. Cinemagoing is not merely sitting and watching: it involves an application of a set of ideas about and skills in contemporary sociability. Yet, even as cinema complexes invite dreams of collectivity and agency, they are sites that survey, police, and discipline public comportment. They represent the dominance of ideas about partial gating and theming, safety and difference, in a space for the participation in and experience of global cultural life. Such zones mark a tacit agreement that public membership in a transnational context has a price for admission.

Screens per Million Population

Nation	1996	1997	1998
Iceland	191.0	186.6	165.2
Sweden	132.3	132.1	131.3
USA	113.5	119.9	128.3
Norway	90.8	92.0	89.2
Australia	69.9	78.2	86.1
Azerbaijan	93.0	89.8	85.8
France	78.1	80.0	81.1
Canada	67.9	76.0	81.0
New Zealand	77.5	81.2	78.1
Switzerland	69.7	73.8	75.8
Spain	60.1	65.4	75.4
Estonia	121.2	75.5	73.5
Ireland	60.9	65.2	70.6
Czech Republic	72.6	72.2	69.6
Finland	63.7	62.9	64.5
Denmark	61.7	60.9	62.7
Hungary	54.5	58.1	61.1
Austria	52.3	52.5	56.3
European Union	51.0	53.0	55.6
Slovakia	62.1	54.9	54.6
Slovenia	49.5	46.1	53.8
China	57.6	55.3	53.1
Germany	49.5	50.4	51.4

Nation	1996	1997	1998
Luxembourg	39.4	63.0	50.7
Israel	51.4	51.4	50.7
Belgium	43.4	46.8	48.9
Lithuania	48.5	48.6	47.6
Singapore	46.5	47.4	46.3
UK	37.9	40.6	44.8
Italy	40.6	41.9	43.7
Latvia	54.2	44.8	42.7
Portugal	29.3	29.7	35.9
Taiwan	36.2	34.8	34.6
Cyprus	32.8	31.1	33.4
Croatia	31.2	31.5	33.4
Netherlands	28.2	32.3	29.5
Hong Kong	28.9	29.1	29.3
Greece	26.8	26.7	26.5
Mexico	17.8	21.4	24.4
Argentina	14.7	17.7	23.2
Poland	21.5	21.5	21.6
Uruguay	21.0	20.3	19.5
South Africa	19.9	18.5	18.7
Romania	16.4	15.2	16.6
Japan	14.6	15.0	15.8
Malaysia	15.6	15.7	15.5
Philippines	14.7	14.3	13.7
Venezuela	12.3	13.6	13.6
India	14.2	13.9	13.5
Bulgaria	17.4	14.1	12.7
Serbia	13.0	12.0	12.4
Korea, Rep [S]	11.5	11.0	11.6
Chile	10.8	10.8	11.1
Russia	12.8	11.5	11.1
Brazil	9.6	10.0	10.9
Indonesia	11.0	10.9	10.5
Jordan	10.1	9.9	9.6
Bahrain	9.3	9.1	9.0
Turkey	6.3	7.8	8.2

Nation	1996	1997	1998
Colombia	7.7	7.9	8.0
Morocco	6.9	6.9	6.7
Qatar	7.1	6.9	6.6
Thailand	4.4	5.9	5.8
Yemen	5.3	5.2	5.1
Peru	4.8	4.6	4.8
Iran	4.6	4.5	4.3
Myanmar	3.7	3.7	3.6
Kuwait	3.4	3.3	3.2
Ethiopia	0.8	0.7	0.7

Source: "World Cinema Fails to Keep Up with USA; Global Spending Now Close to $17 Billion," *Screen Digest*, September 1999, 22.

World Screen Count

Nation	1988	1996	1997	1998
Western Europe				
Austria	416	421	424	454
Belgium	422	440	475	498
Denmark	381	322	320	328
Finland	344	325	322	331
France	4,819	4,530	4,661	4,762
Germany	3,246	4,035	4,128	4,244
Greece	675	280	280	280
Iceland	19	51	50	45
Ireland	145	218	234	256
Italy	3,871	2,326	2,401	2,500
Luxembourg	17	16	26	21
Netherlands	438	435	501	461
Norway	419	395	402	392
Portugal	378	303	322	370
Spain	1,882	2,354	2,565	2,968
Sweden	1,100	1,169	1,165	1,167
Switzerland	412	489	521	537
UK	1,416	2,215	2,383	2,638
Subtotal	20,400	20,324	21,180	22,252

Nation	1988	1996	1997	1998
Central and Eastern Europe				
Bulgaria	3,268	146	116	106
Croatia	—	145	147	150
Czech Republic	—	750	747	720
Estonia	709	180	111	110
Hungary	2,943	558	594	620
Latvia	—	137	112	106
Lithuania	1,284	180	180	180
Poland	1,656	829	829	841
Romania	617	373	345	379
Russia	—	1,900	1,716	1,650
Serbia	—	137	135	135
Slovakia	777	334	296	296
Slovenia	174	98	91	107
Subtotal	164,443[a]	5,767	5,419	5,400
EUROPE	184,843[a]	26,091	26,599	27,198
North America				
Canada	1,673	1,986	2,301	2,486
Mexico	2,130	1,639	1,955	2,329
USA	23,234	29,731	31,640	34,186
Subtotal	27,037	33,356	35,896	39,001
South America				
Argentina	647	499	608	810
Brazil	1,337	1,610	1,707	1,907
Chile	160	150	153	160
Colombia	468	276	286	295
Peru	320	113	110	115
Uruguay	85	67	65	63
Venezuela	365	252	284	290
Subtotal[b]	3,382	2,967	3,213	3,640
Asia				
Azerbaijan	—	696	677	650
China	161,777	69,000	67,000	65,000
Hong Kong	133	176	179	185

Nation	1988	1996	1997	1998
India	13,355	13,100	13,000	12,900
Indonesia	1,654	2,150	2,150	2,100
Iran	279	290	290	285
Japan	2,005	1,828	1,884	1,993
Korea, Republic of (South)	696	511	497	528
Malaysia	177	300	309	310
Myanmar	—	165	170	170
Philippines	1,200	980	970	950
Singapore	46	131	135	133
Taiwan	800	681	666	672
Thailand	584	268	360	360
Turkey	424	381	487	520
Subtotal[b]	183,130	90,657	88,774	86,756
Middle East/Africa				
Bahrain	6	5	5	5
Cyprus	19	24	23	25
Israel	175	281	290	290
Jordan	15	47	47	47
Kuwait	14	8	8	8
Qatar	4	3	3	3
Yemen	—	46	46	46
Ethiopia	—	40	40	40
Morocco	250	184	184	180
South Africa	375	750	768	793
Australia	712	1,264	1,422	1,576
New Zealand	145	270	285	290
TOTAL[c]	400,107	155,993	157,603	159,898

Source: "World Cinema Fails to Keep Up with USA; Global Spending Now Close to $17 Billion, *Screen Digest,* September 1999, 22.

[a] The 1988 European totals include unspecified screen numbers from several Eastern bloc countries, most significantly the Soviet Union.

[b] These are not comprehensive continental totals and should be read as an industrially defined accounting.

[c] This total includes only the countries and figures provided in this table. It is not an absolute number of world screens.

National Average Cinema Admissions per Person (annual)

Nation	1987	1997
India	5.89	8.45[a]
Singapore	7.56	5.97
Iceland	5.06	5.37
USA	4.46	5.16
New Zealand	2.59	4.40
Hong Kong	11.05	4.29
Australia	1.89	4.21
Canada	3.07	3.24
Ireland	1.47	3.21
Spain	2.21	2.66
France	2.45	2.51
Norway	2.94	2.48
UK	1.38	2.35
Switzerland	2.46	2.26
Belgium	1.63	2.16
Denmark	2.23	2.07
Luxembourg	1.61	2.03
Monaco	3.33	2.03[a]
Israel	2.88	1.87
Hungary	5.34	1.78
Italy	1.90	1.76
Germany	1.76	1.73
Sweden	2.12	1.70

Nation	1987	1997
Philippines	1.26	1.70
Austria	1.46	1.68
Slovenia	3.55	1.61
Bahrain	2.04	1.58
Yemen	—	1.47[b]
Taiwan	1.00	1.46
Portugal	1.70	1.30
Cyprus	—	1.26
Belarus	—	1.20[a]
Netherlands	1.05	1.20
Finland	1.32	1.14
Japan	1.18	1.12
Slovakia	3.72	1.05
Greece	1.95	0.99
Croatia	—	0.97[b]
Indonesia	0.76	0.93
Czech Republic	—	0.91
Mexico	2.98	0.89
Malaysia	1.45	0.79
South Africa	—	0.76
Qatar	—	0.75
Argentina	1.23	0.73
Korea, Rep [S]	1.17	0.68
Estonia	10.83	0.67
Poland	2.52	0.61
Ukraine	—	0.60[a]
Chile	1.11	0.58
Morocco	1.38	0.56
Colombia	1.91	0.53
Brazil	0.80	0.49
Thailand	0.20	0.47
Venezuela	0.57	0.42
Romania	7.02	0.41
Latvia	—	0.41
Iran	1.03	0.40[a]

APPENDIX 3 (continued)

Nation	1987	1997
Serbia	—	0.38
Kazakhstan	—	0.37[a]
Russia	—	0.37
Moldova	—	0.32[a]
Bulgaria	9.38	0.24
Kuwait	0.47	0.19
Turkey	0.67	0.15
Kirghizia	—	0.14[a]
Zimbabwe	0.23	0.14[a]
China	19.58	0.12
Macedonia	—	0.09[a]
Tadzhikistan	—	0.09[a]

Source: "Average Cinema Admissions per Head," *Screen Digest*, September 1998, 205.

[a] 1995.

[b] 1996.

Multiplexing in Europe (as of September 1999)

Screens per site	8–12	13–17	18+
Austria	8		
Belgium	9	5	2
Czech Republic	1		
Denmark	1	1	
Finland	1		
France	54	16	3
Germany	63	7	2
Greece	3		
Hungary	4		
Ireland	7		
Italy	7		1
Luxembourg	1		
Netherlands	4		
Norway	3	1	
Poland	1		
Portugal	5		1
Spain	52	4	4
Sweden	13	2	
Switzerland	2		
UK	92	19	2

Source: "Databox," *Screen Digest*, September 1999, 19.

MPAA's Goals for Digital Cinema (August 21, 2000)

1. *Enhanced Theatrical Experience:* The introduction of digital cinema must be used by the motion picture industry as an opportunity to significantly enhance the theatrical film experience and thus bring real benefits to theater audiences.

2. *Quality:* The picture and sound quality of digital cinema should represent as accurately as possible the creative intent of the filmmaker. To that end, its quality must exceed the quality of a projected 35mm "answer print" shown under optimum studio screening theater conditions. Any image compression that is used should be visually lossless.

3. *Worldwide Compatibility:* The system should be based around global standards so that content can be distributed and played anywhere in the world as can be done today with a 35mm film print.

4. *Open Standards:* The components and technologies used should be based on open standards that foster competition amongst multiple vendors of equipment and services.

5. *Interoperable:* Each of the components of the system should be built around clearly defined standards and interfaces that insure interoperability between different equipment.

6. *Extensible:* The hardware used in the system should be easily upgraded as advances in technology are made. This is especially important in evolving to higher quality levels.

7. *Single Inventory:* Once a consensus on digital cinema standards is reached and implemented, upgrades to the system should be designed so that a single inventory of content can be distributed and compatibly played on all equipment installations.

8. *Transport:* The system should accommodate a variety of secure content transport mechanisms, including electronic as well as a physical media delivery.

9. *Secure Content Protection:* The system must include a highly secure, end-to-end, conditional access content protection system, including digital rights management and content watermarking, because of the serious harm associated with the theft of digital content at this stage of its distribution life cycle. Playback devices must use on-line authentication with the decrypted content files never accessible in the clear.

10. *Reasonable Cost:* The system standards and mastering format(s) should be chosen so that the capital equipment and operational costs are reasonable. All required technology licenses should be available on reasonable and nondiscriminatory terms.

Source: Motion Picture Association of America, "Motion Picture Goals for Digital Cinema," http://www.mpaa.org/dcinema/dCinemaGoals.htm, 2000, last accessed May 1, 2002.

Existing Digital Cinemas, 2000

City	Cinema
Canada, Mexico, and United States	
Toronto, Ontario	Famous Players
Vancouver, British Columbia	Famous Players Riverport
Mexico City, Mexico	Cinemex Mundo E
Tlanepantla, Mexico	Cinemex Mundo E
Burbank, California	AMC Media Center North
Chestnut Hill, Massachusetts	General Cinema Theaters
Hollywood, California	El Capitan
Irvine, California	Edwards Irvine Spectrum
Lake Buena Vista, Florida	AMC Pleasure Island 24
New York, New York	AMC Empire 25 (2 screens)
Olathe, Kansas	AMC Studio
Plano, Texas	Cinemark Legacy
San Diego, California	AMC Mission Valley 20
San Francisco, California	AMC Van Ness
South Barrington, Illinois	AMC Barrington 30
Tempe, Arizona	Harkins Theaters Arizona Mills
Valley View, Ohio	Cinemark Valley View
Europe	
Brussels, Belgium	Kinepolis Ciudad de la imagen
London, England	Odeon Leicester Square

City	Cinema
London, England	Warner Village Finchley Road
Manchester, England	UCI, Trafford Centre
Paris, France	The Gaumont Aquaboulevard
Berlin, Germany	Berlin Zoo Palast
Cologne, Germany	Cinedom Cologne
Dusseldorf, Germany	Dusseldorf
Barcelona, Spain	UCI's Cinesa Diagonal
Madrid, Spain	Kinepolis Ciudad de la Imagen
Asia	
Chiyoda-ku, Japan	Japan Nichigeki Theater
Tokyo, Japan	AMC Tokyo Disneyland
Seoul, Korea	Seoul Cinema Town

Source: Motion Picture Association of America, "Worldwide Location of Digital Cinema Theaters," http://www.mpaa.org/dcinema/, 2000, last accessed April 30, 2003.

Digital Movies Released for DLP Projectors (as of 2001)

Title	Studio	Release Date
Star Wars: Episode I	Fox/LucasFilm	June 1999
Tarzan	Disney/Buena Vista	July 1999
Toy Story 2	Disney/Buena Vista	November 1999
Bicentennial Man	Disney/Buena Vista	December 1999
Mission to Mars	Disney/Buena Vista	March 2000
Dinosaur	Disney/Buena Vista	May 2000
Fantasia 2000	Disney/Buena Vista	June 2000
Titan A.E.	Twentieth Century-Fox	June 2000
The Perfect Storm	Warner Bros.	July 2000
Space Cowboys	Warner Bros.	September 2000
Crimson Rivers	Gaumont (France)	September 2000
Very Mean Men	Giants Entertainment	October 2000
Bounce	Miramax	November 2000
102 Dalmations	Disney/Buena Vista	November 2000
Nagasaki Bura Bura	Toei (Japan)	December 2000
Emperor's New Groove	Disney/Buena Vista	December 2000
Vertical Limit	Sony/Columbia	January 2001
Pay It Forward	Warner Bros.	January 2001

Source: "Digital Movies Released for DLP Projectors," *Film Journal International,* March 2001, 88.

ONE. GLOBAL AUDIENCES AND THE CURRENT CINEMA

1   Leonard Klady, "More BO Oracles Take up Trackin'," *Variety*, October 19–25, 1998, 9.

2   Ibid., 16.

3   Tom Matthews, "Playing the Numbers," *Boxoffice*, September 1989, 12.

4   Peter Bart, *The Gross: The Hits, the Flops—the Summer That Ate Hollywood* (New York: St. Martin's Press, 1999), 177–178.

5   Leonard Klady, "Top 250 of 1997," *Variety*, January 26–February 1, 1998, 17–18.

6   A. D. Murphy, "Globe Gobbling Up U.S. Pix in Record Doses; Worldwide Rentals to Yank Distribs Shattered Marks in '89; Japan Key," *Variety*, June 13, 1990, 7, 10.

7   Allison Vale, "Boffo Screen Build," *Playback*, May 5, 1997, 22.

8   For a close political-economic study of the international operations of the U.S. film industry through the first half of the twentieth century, see Ian Jarvie, *Hollywood's Overseas Campaign: The North Atlantic Movie Trade, 1920–1950* (New York: Cambridge University Press, 1992), and Kristin Thompson, *Exporting Entertainment: America in the World Film Market, 1907–1934* (London: British Film Institute, 1985).

9   Paul Hirsch, "Globalization of Mass Media Ownership: Implications and Effects," *Communication Research* 19, no. 6 (December 1992): 678.

10 Rod Carveth, "The Reconstruction of the Global Media Marketplace," *Communication Research* 19, no. 6 (December 1992): 707.

11 Ibid., 712.

12 Toby Miller, Nitin Govil, John McMurria, and Richard Maxwell, *Global Hollywood* (London: British Film Institute, 2001), 18.

13 Ibid., 54.

14 Joseph Turow, "The Organizational Underpinnings of Contemporary Media Conglomerates," *Communication Research* 19, no. 6 (December 1992): 687.

15 Don Groves, "Boffo Year for O'seas Markets," *Variety*, April 21–27, 1997, 16.

16   Suzan Ayscough, "Canada Wants Euro Status for Distribbing," *Variety,* April 15, 1991, 51.

17   Richard Collins, *Culture, Communication, and National Identity: The Case of Canadian Television* (Toronto: University of Toronto Press, 1990), xii.

18   Michel Foucault, "Two Lectures," in *Power/Knowledge,* ed. Colin Gordon (New York: Pantheon, 1980 [1976]), 89.

19   Stuart Hall, "The 'Rediscovery' of Ideology: Return of the Repressed in Media Studies," in *Culture, Society, and the Media,* ed. Michael Gurevitch, Tony Bennett, James Curran, and Janet Woollacott (London: Sage, 1982), 75.

20   Antonio Gramsci, *An Antonio Gramsci Reader: Selected Writings, 1916–1935,* ed. David Forgacs (New York: Schocken Books, 1988), 326.

21   Antonio Gramsci, *Selections from the Prison Notebooks of Antonio Gramsci,* ed. and trans. Quintin Hoare and Geoffrey Nowell Smith (London: Lawrence and Wishart, 1971), 326.

22   Stuart Hall, "Signification, Representation, Ideology: Althusser and the Post-Structuralist Debates," *Critical Studies in Mass Communication* 2, no. 2 (1985): 91–114.

23   Andrew Ross, *No Respect: Intellectuals and Popular Culture* (New York: Routledge, 1989).

24   Gramsci, *Selections from the Prison Notebooks,* 418.

25   Ibid., 130.

26   John Clarke, *New Times and Old Enemies: Essays on Cultural Studies and America* (London: HarperCollins, 1991), 172.

27   Ibid., 173.

28   Marcia Landy, *Film, Politics, and Gramsci* (Minneapolis: University of Minnesota Press, 1994), 12.

29   Douglas Gomery, *Shared Pleasures: A History of Movie Presentation in the United States* (Madison: University of Wisconsin Press, 1992).

30   Miriam Hansen, *Babel and Babylon: Spectatorship in American Silent Film* (Cambridge: Harvard University Press, 1991), 61.

31   Ibid., 66.

32   Clarke, *New Times and Old Enemies,* 75; Roy Rosenzweig, *Eight Hours for What We Will* (Cambridge: Cambridge University Press, 1984).

TWO. TRAVELING CULTURES, MUTATING COMMODITIES

1   "EDI Box Office News: More Shelf Space for Films," *Variety,* January 5–11, 1998, 30.

2   A. D. Murphy, "Globe Gobbling Up US Pix in Record Doses," 7.

3   Ibid, 7, 10.

4   Peter Bart, "View From the War Room," *Variety,* May 27, 1991, 3.

5   Don Groves, "Boffo Year for O'seas Markets," 16.

6   Don Groves, "Megahits Push Global BO to Record High," *Variety,* December 16–22, 1996, 9, 14.

7   Groves, "Boffo Year for O'seas Markets," 16.

8   Leonard Klady, "U.S. Exhibs Discover the Joy of Plex O'seas," *Variety,* April 8–14, 1996, 9.

9   Leonard Klady, "MPAA Trumpets Pains, Gains; BO Take of $5.91 Bil Hurt by Cost Rise," Variety.com, March 5, 1997, last accessed June 26, 2002.

10 Thomas Guback, *The International Film Industry* (Bloomington: Indiana University Press, 1969), 10.

11 Richard Gold, "U.S. Pix Tighten Global Grip: Major Studios Speed Up Their Foreign Openings to Synch with U.S. Push," *Variety*, August 22, 1990, 1, 96.

12 Adam Dawtrey, "Is Planetary Pic Peddling Passe?," *Variety*, October 30–November 5, 1995, 182.

13 Andrew Hindes, "Study Marks Global Shift," *Variety*, October 30–November 5, 1995, M44.

14 A. D. Murphy, "Recap of Top Foreign Markets: Japan Nudged Canada from 1st," *Variety*, October 22, 1986, 52, 154.

15 A. D. Murphy, "Majors' Global Rentals Boffo: Soft Dollar Boosts 87 to a Record," *Variety*, May 18, 1988, 1, 30.

16 Murphy, "Globe Gobbling up US Pix in Record Doses," 10.

17 Ibid., 7.

18 Ibid., 10.

19 Toby Miller, "The Crime of Monsieur Lang: GATT, the Screen, and the New International Division of Cultural Labour," *Film Policy: International, National, and Regional Perspectives*, ed. Albert Moran (New York: Routledge, 1996), 76.

20 Leonard Klady, "B.O. with a Vengeance: $9.1 billion Worldwide," *Variety*, February 19–25, 1996, 1, 26.

21 Andrew Higson, "The Concept of National Cinema," *Screen* 30, no. 4 (1989): 345–347.

22 Colin Hoskins and Rolf Mirus, "Reasons for the U.S. Domination of the International Trade in Television Programmes," *Media, Culture, and Society* 10, no. 4 (1988): 499–516; and Colin Hoskins, Stuart McFadyen, and Adam Finn, "The Environment in Which Cultural Industries Operate and Some Implications," *Canadian Journal of Communication* 19, nos. 3/4 (summer/autumn 1994): 353–376.

23 Scott Robert Olson, *Hollywood Planet: Global Media and the Competitive Advantage of Narrative Transparency* (Mahwah, N.J.: Lawrence Erlbaum, 1999), 5.

24 Ibid., 5–6.

25 Hoskins, McFadyen, and Finn, "The Environment in Which Cultural Industries Operate and Some Implications," 371–372.

26 Leonard Klady, "Blockbusters Trigger Box Office Record O'seas," *Variety*, January 25–31, 1999, 18.

27 Leonard Klady, "Foreign BO Beckons: Comedies, Dramas Get More of the Action . . . ," *Variety*, August 28–September 3, 1995, 1.

28 Simon During, "Popular Culture on a Global Scale: A Challenge for Cultural Studies?," *Critical Inquiry* 23 (1997): 808–833.

29 Tom Gunning, "An Aesthetic of Astonishment: Early Film and the (In)Credulous Spectator," in *Viewing Positions: Ways of Seeing Film*, ed. Linda Williams (New Brunswick: Rutgers University Press, 1997 [1989]), 114–133.

30 During, "Popular Culture on a Global Scale," 818.

31 Ibid, 821.

32 Ien Ang, "Cultural Studies, Media Reception, and the Transnational Media System," in *Living Room Wars: Rethinking Media Audiences for a Postmodern World* (New York: Routledge, 1996), 143.

33 Yvonne Tasker pursues this argument in "Dumb Movies for Dumb People: Masculinity, the Body, and the Voice in Contemporary Action Cinema," in *Screening the Male: Exploring Masculinities in Hollywood Cinema,* ed. Steven Cohan and Ina Rae Hark (New York: Routledge, 1993), 230–244.

34 Jennifer Slack, "Contextualizing Technology," in *Rethinking Communication, Volume 2: Paradigm Exemplars,* ed. Brenda Dervin, Lawrence Grossberg, Barbara J. O'Keefe, and Ellen Wartella (London: Sage, 1989), 329.

35 Doreen Massey, "The Political Place of Locality Studies," *Environment and Planning* A 23, no. 2 (1991): 270.

36 Lawrence Grossberg, "The Space of Culture, the Power of Space," in *The Post-Colonial Question: Common Skies, Divided Horizons,* ed. Iain Chambers and Lidia Curti (New York: Routledge, 1996), 185–86.

37 Raymond Williams, *The Long Revolution* (New York: Columbia University Press, 1961), 47.

38 Ibid., 48.

39 Arjun Appadurai, *Modernity at Large: Cultural Dimensions of Globalization* (Minneapolis: University of Minnesota Press, 1996), 4.

40 Ibid., 174.

41 Ibid., 4.

42 Ibid., 13.

43 Ibid., 10.

44 Ibid., 21.

45 Ibid., 158.

46 Ibid., 187.

THREE. MATINEES, SUMMERS, AND THE PRACTICE OF CINEMAGOING

1 Similar demands have been made of other projectionist unions across the country. Famous Players locked out projectionists who refused to agree to a wage cut in Winnipeg. See "Famous Players Locks Out Staff," *Winnipeg Free Press,* February 13, 1995, B2. In June 1995, B.C. Projectionists Union accepted a 16.3 percent wage cut; see "Movies Keep Rolling as Projectionists Accept Pay Cut," *Vancouver Sun,* June 17, 1995, A5. Cineplex Odeon locked out its projectionists who similarly refused a 50 percent wage cut; see Harold Levy, "Projectionists Locked Out by Cineplex," *Toronto Star,* October 27, 1996, A4. Famous Players and Cineplex Odeon both locked out projectionists in December 1998; see "Locked Out Projectionists Picketing Vancouver Film Fest," *Globe and Mail,* September 25, 1999, C6.

2 Mario Toneguzzi, "Famous Players Dispute Locks Out Projectionists," *Calgary Herald,* January 16, 1995, A1; Gordon Jaremko, "Chain Wants Picketing Limited," *Calgary Herald,*

February 7, 1995, A13; Rick Mofina, "Unionists Videotaped at Rally for Locked-Out Projectionists," *Calgary Herald,* April 8, 1995, G8; Dave Pommer, "Picketing Limit Denied," *Calgary Herald,* April 21, 1995, D6.

3   This claim is not as outrageous as it may appear at first, especially given the frequency with which it is now made. Panels on the death of film and the field seem to have become a staple of film studies conferences over the past few years.

4   For a detailed discussion of the links between the television and film industries in the 1950s, see Christopher Anderson, *Hollywood TV: The Studio System in the Fifties* (Austin: University of Texas Press, 1994), and William Boddy, *Fifties Television: The Industry and Its Critics* (Champaign: University of Illinois Press, 1990). For additional historical scope, see Tino Balio, ed., *Hollywood in the Age of Television* (Boston: Unwin Hyman, 1990).

5   Kevin Robins, *Into the Image: Culture and Politics in the Field of Vision* (New York: Routledge, 1996), 5.

6   Walter Benjamin, "The Work of Art in the Age of Mechanical Reproduction," in *Illuminations,* ed. Hannah Arendt and trans. Harry Zohn (New York: Schocken, 1968 [1936]), 217–251.

7   Miriam Hansen, "Early Cinema, Late Cinema: Permutations of the Public Sphere," *Screen* 34, no. 3 (1993): 197–210.

8   Ibid., 198.

9   Ibid.

10   Ibid., 199.

11   Ibid.

12   Ibid., 210

13   Ibid.

14   See Anne Friedberg, *Window Shopping: Cinema and the Postmodern* (Berkeley: University of California Press, 1993), and Leo Charney and Vanessa R. Schwartz, eds., *Cinema and the Invention of Modern Life* (Berkeley: University of California Press, 1995). For the prehistory of changing spectatorial regimes, see Jonathan Crary, *Techniques of the Observer: On Vision and Modernity in the Nineteenth Century* (Cambridge: MIT Press, 1990).

15   Janet Staiger, *Interpreting Films: Studies in the Historical Reception of American Cinema* (Princeton: Princeton University Press, 1992).

16   Judith Mayne, *Cinema and Spectatorship* (New York: Routledge, 1993), 37.

17   Ibid., 68.

18   Richard Maltby, " 'Nobody Knows Everything': Post-Classical Historiographies and Consolidated Entertainment," in *Contemporary Hollywood Cinema,* ed. Steve Neale and Murray Smith (New York: Routledge, 1998), 27.

19   Douglas Gomery, "Hollywood Corporate Business Practice and Periodizing Contemporary Film History," in *Contemporary Hollywood Cinema,* ed. Steve Neale and Murray Smith (New York: Routledge, 1998), 47.

20   Miriam Hansen, *Babel and Babylon,* explores the interconnections here extensively.

21   Mayne, *Cinema and Spectatorship,* 67.

22   For instance, Bruce A. Austin, *Immediate Seating: A Look at Movie Audiences* (Belmont,

Calif.: Wadsworth, 1989); John Belton, *Widescreen Cinema* (Cambridge: Harvard University Press, 1992); Douglas Gomery, *Shared Pleasures;* Kathy Peiss, *Cheap Amusements: Working Women and Leisure in Turn-of-the-Century New York* (Philadelphia: Temple University Press, 1986); David Nasaw, *Going Out: The Rise and Fall of Public Amusements* (New York: Basic Books, 1993); Steve Neale, *Cinema Technology: Image, Sound, Color* (Bloomington: Indiana University Press, 1985); Melvyn Stokes and Richard Maltby, eds., *American Movie Audiences: From the Turn of the Century to the Early Sound Era* (London: British Film Institute, 1999); Barbara Wilinsky, *Sure Seaters: The Emergence of Art House Cinema* (Minneapolis: University of Minnesota Press, 2001).

23   For instance, Thomas Guback, "The Evolution of the Motion Picture Theatre Business in the 1980s," *Journal of Communication* 37, no. 2 (1987): 60–77; Douglas Gomery, "U.S. Film Exhibition: The Formation of a Big Business," in *The American Film Industry,* rev. ed., Tino Balio (Madison: University of Wisconsin Press, 1985), 218–228; Douglas Gomery, "Building a Movie Theatre Giant: The Rise of Cineplex Odeon," in *Hollywood in the Age of Television,* ed. Tino Balio (Boston: Unwin Hyman, 1990), 377–391; Barry Litman, *The Motion Picture Mega-Industry* (Toronto: Allyn and Bacon, 1998); Janet Wasko, *Hollywood in the Information Age* (Austin: University of Texas Press, 1994); Frederick Wasser, "Four Walling Exhibition: Regional Resistance to the Hollywood Film Industry," *Cinema Journal* 34, no. 2 (winter 1995): 51–65; Kevin J. Corbett, "The Big Picture: Theatrical Moviegoing, Digital Television, and Beyond the Substitution Effect," *Cinema Journal* 40, no. 2 (2001): 17–34.

24   Kathryn H. Fuller, *At the Picture Show: Small-Town Audiences and the Creation of Movie Fan Culture* (Washington: Smithsonian Institution Press, 1996).

25   Gregory A. Waller, *Main Street Amusements: Movies and Commercial Entertainment in a Southern City, 1896–1930* (Washington: Smithsonian Institution Press, 1995), 259.

26   Robert C. Allen, "From Exhibition to Reception: Reflections on the Audience in Film History," *Screen* 31, no. 4 (1990): 347–356.

27   Jeanne Allen, "The Film Viewer as Consumer," *Quarterly Review of Film Studies* 5, no. 4 (fall 1980): 482.

28   Jackie Stacey, "Textual Obsessions: Methodology, History, and Researching Female Spectatorship," *Screen* 34, no. 3 (1993): 260–274.

29   David Morley, *Television, Audiences, and Cultural Studies* (New York: Routledge, 1992); Roger Silverstone and Eric Hirsch, eds., *Consuming Technologies: Media and Information in Domestic Spaces* (New York: Routledge, 1992); Lynn Spigel and Denise Mann, eds., *Private Screening: Television and the Female Consumer* (Minneapolis: University of Minnesota Press, 1992); Lynn Spigel, *Make Room for TV: Television and the Family Ideal in Postwar America* (Chicago: University of Chicago Press, 1992).

30   Susan G. Davis, "The Theme Park: Global Industry and Cultural Form," *Media, Culture, and Society* 18, no. 3 (1996): 399–422; Michael Sorkin, ed., *Variations on a Theme Park: The New American City and the End of Public Space* (New York: Hill and Wang, 1992); Anna McCarthy; *Ambient Television: Visual Culture and Public Space* (Durham: Duke University Press, 2001).

31   Rita Felski, "The Invention of Everyday Life," *New Formations* 39 (1999): 15.

32 Robert F. Arnold, "Film Space/Audience Space: Notes Toward a Theory of Spectatorship," *Velvet Light Trap* 25 (spring 1990): 46.

33 James Hay, "Piecing Together What Remains of the Cinematic City," in *The Cinematic City,* ed. David B. Clarke (New York: Routledge, 1997), 212.

34 Karen Lury and Doreen Massey, "Making Connections," *Screen* 40, no. 3 (1999): 229–238.

35 Michel Foucault, "Questions of Geography," in *Power/Knowledge,* ed. Colin Gordon (New York: Pantheon, 1980), 149.

36 See, for instance, Jody Berland, "Space at the Margins: Critical Theory and Colonial Space after Innis," in *Harold Innis in the New Century: Reflections and Refractions,* ed. Charles R. Acland and William J. Buxton (Montreal: McGill-Queen's University Press, 1999), 281–308; Henri Lefebvre, *The Production of Space,* trans. Donald Nicholson-Smith (Oxford: Blackwell, 1991).

37 Karen Lury and Doreen Massey, "Making Connections," 231.

38 Michel de Certeau, *The Practice of Everyday Life,* trans. Steve Rendall (Berkeley: University of California Press, 1984), 117.

39 Ibid., 125.

40 Ibid., 175.

41 Corbett, "The Big Picture."

42 Friedberg, *Window Shopping,* 3.

43 Mayne, *Cinema and Spectatorship,* 65.

44 Ibid., 66.

45 De Certeau, *The Practice of Everyday Life,* xii.

46 Ibid., xiv.

47 Ien Ang, *Desperately Seeking the Audience* (New York: Routledge, 1991), 7.

48 Morley, *Television, Audiences, and Cultural Studies,* 265.

49 Ibid., 266.

50 Paddy Scannell, *Radio, Television, and Modern Life* (Oxford: Blackwell, 1996), 9.

51 John Caughie, "Playing at Being American: Games and Tactics," in *Logics of Television: Essays in Cultural Criticism,* ed. Patricia Mellencamp (Bloomington: Indiana University Press, 1990), 49–50.

52 Ann Gray, *Video Playtime: The Gendering of a Leisure Technology* (London: Routledge, 1992).

53 Faye Brookman, "Trailers: The Big Business of Drawing Crowds," *Variety,* June 13, 1990, 48.

54 John Brodie, "Coming Soon to a Theater Near You: TV Trailers," *Variety,* August 31, 1992, 20. Even earlier, AB.C. did some theater advertising for its miniseries *Roots* in the mid-1970s. For a more complete discussion of this topic, see Kim B. Rotzoll, "The Captive Audience: The Troubled Odyssey of Cinema Advertising," in *Current Research in Film: Audience, Economics, and Law,* ed. Bruce Austin (Norwood, N.J.: Ablex, 1987), 72–87.

55 Marcy Maglera, "Advertisers Crowd onto Big Screen," *Advertising Age,* September 18, 1989, 14, 15.

56 Ibid., 15.

57 Claudia Eller, "Theater Giant Warms Up to Disney's Big Ad Chill," *Variety,* March 28, 1990, 7.

58 Raymond Williams, *Television: Technology and Cultural Form* (New York: Schocken, 1975), 86–87.

59 "The Teachings of Chairman Jeff," *Variety*, February 4, 1991, 24, quoted in William Paul, "The K-Mart Audience at the Mall Movies," *Film History* 6 (1994): 494.

60 William Paul, "The K-Mart Audience at the Mall Movies," 495.

61 Andrew Hindes and Monica Roman, "Video Titles Do Pitstops on Screens," *Variety*, September 16–22, 1996, 16.

62 Mary Maddever, "Kingdom Targeted the Rep Circuit," *Playback*, June 17, 1996, 11.

63 John Dempsey, "Theatricals Rate Second Look," *Variety*, September 20–26, 1999, 33, 39.

64 AC Nielsen EDI, "School Holiday Calendar," www.entdata.com, last accessed June 23, 2002.

65 Leo Rice-Barker, "Industry Banks on New Technology, Expanded Slates," *Playback*, May 6, 1996, 20.

66 Leonard Klady, "Hitting and Missing the Market: Studios Show Savvy—or Just Luck—With Pic Release Strategies," *Variety*, January 19–25, 1998, 18.

67 Martin Allor, "Relocating the Site of the Audience," *Critical Studies in Mass Communication* 5 (1988): 217–233.

68 Ibid., 219.

69 Ibid., 227.

70 Ibid., 228.

71 For instance, James Lull, "Critical Response: The Audience as Nuisance," *Critical Studies in Mass Communication* 5 (1988): 239–242; and S. Elizabeth Bird, "Travels in Nowhere Land: Ethnography and the 'Impossible' Audience," *Critical Studies in Mass Communication* 9, no. 3 (1992): 250–260.

72 Raymond Williams, "Culture Is Ordinary," in *Studying Culture: An Introductory Reader*, 2d ed., ed. Ann Gray and Jim McGuigan (New York: Arnold, 1997 [1958]), 11.

73 Allor, "Relocating the Site of the Audience," 229.

74 Leonard Klady, "H'wood's BO Blast: '97 Admissions Highest in Three Decades," *Variety*, January 5–11, 1998, 1, 96.

75 Harvey Enchin, "Canadians Going Back to the Movies," *Globe and Mail*, July 11, 1996, B1.

76 There were, for example, 15 percent fewer full time employees at theaters in 1994–95 than in the previous fiscal year. Enchin, "Canadians Going Back to the Movies," B1.

77 Statistics Canada, *Motion Picture Theatres Survey* (Ottawa: Culture, Tourism, and the Centre for Education Statistics, 1999). The same source indicates that the number of smaller theaters dropped by 52 and larger ones grew by 29. The argument that larger theaters are more profitable runs counter to a growing industry feeling that megaplexes have not been as successful as they were expected to be, as evidenced by Loews Cineplex's financial troubles in 2000.

78 Enchin, "Canadians Going Back to the Movies," B4.

79 Gayle MacDonald, "The Vast Picture Show," *Globe and Mail*, January 17, 1998, B5.

80 MPAA, quoted in Philip Jackman, ed., "Movie Marketing Hits $25-Million per Picture," *Globe and Mail*, March 11, 1999, A22.

81 Quoted in Howard Lichtman, with Harriet Bernstein, "Marketing Canadian Feature Films:

A Perspective," in *Selling It: The Marketing of Canadian Feature Films,* ed. Joan Irving (Toronto: Doubleday Canada, 1995), 8.

82 Sidney Blumenthal, *The Permanent Campaign: Inside the World of Elite Political Operatives* (Boston: Beacon Press, 1980).

83 Pierre Bourdieu, *Distinction: A Social Critique of the Judgement of Taste,* trans. Richard Nice (Cambridge: Harvard University Press, 1984).

84 Mike Featherstone, "Lifestyle and Consumer Culture," *Theory, Culture, and Society* 4 (1987): 55.

85 Ibid., 55–56.

86 Ibid., 56.

87 Ibid., 66.

88 Arjun Appadurai, *Modernity at Large,* 83.

89 Ibid., 83–84.

FOUR. CRISIS AND SETTLEMENT IN EXHIBITION AND DISTRIBUTION

1 Christopher Grove, "Programming Screens is Multi-complex Task for Theater Managers," *Variety,* March 16–22, 1998, 46. Exhibitors in the United States and Canada conventionally take between 10 and 20 percent for operating expenses off the top, called the house nut. In other countries, this amount is more likely to be between 40 and 60 percent, meaning that those exhibitors stand to fare better in this respect. "Distribution Revenue Rising," *Screen Digest,* June 1998, 134.

2 Guback, "The Evolution of the Motion Picture Theatre Business in the 1980s," 66.

3 Peter Bart, *The Gross,* 201.

4 Guback, "The Evolution of the Motion Picture Theatre Business in the 1980s," 60–77.

5 John Izod, *Hollywood and the Box Office, 1895–1986* (New York: Columbia University Press, 1988), 193.

6 Leonard Klady, "Exhibs Fight Screen Demons," *Variety,* July 31–August 6, 1995, 16.

7 Belton, *Widescreen Cinema,* 71–76.

8 Izod, *Hollywood and the Box Office,* 196.

9 Dan Gilroy, "Harlem Unveils New Multiplex; First Theaters in Two Decades," *Variety,* December 10, 1986, 28.

10 "AMC Skein to Add Sites in Inner Cities and Globally," *Variety,* September 21, 1992, 15.

11 Monica Roman, "Exhibs Adding Fuel to Urban Renewal," *Variety,* April 21–27, 1997, 9, 16.

12 Ibid., 16.

13 John Pierson, *Spike, Mike, Slackers, and Dykes* (New York: Hyperion, 1995), 75.

14 Izod, *Hollywood and the Box Office,* 197.

15 Gary R. Edgerton, *American Film Exhibition and an Analysis of the Motion Picture Industry's Market Structure, 1963–1980* (London: Garland, 1983), 141 as noted in Izod, *Hollywood and the Box Office,* 197.

16 Izod, *Hollywood and the Box Office,* 197–198.

17 Assessments of over- and underscreened areas tend to export, and thus naturalize, U.S. rates of cinemagoing. In this way, they can be seen as another instance of cinemagoing's Americanization.

18 "Valenti To Take on Exhib-Distrib Tensions as ShoWest Keynoter," *Variety*, February 5, 1986, 7.

19 "Distribs Exhort Exhibs to Try to Increase Viewer Satisfaction," *Variety*, February 19, 1986, 11.

20 Ibid.

21 Ibid.

22 Paul Noglows, "Studios Stuck in Screen Jam," *Variety*, March 9, 1992, 73.

23 Will Tusher, "Distribution's Theater Buys Near Peak, '86 a Watershed in Acquisitions," *Variety*, January 7, 1987, 3.

24 Ibid.

25 Kris Turnquist, "NATO '86: Exhibitors Come to Grips with Their New Partners—Distributors," *Boxoffice*, February 1987, 12.

26 Ibid.

27 "1986 Chronology of Major Industry Events," *Boxoffice*, April 1987, 13.

28 "Distribs Exhort Exhibs to Try to Increase Viewer Satisfaction," 11.

29 Will Tusher, "Cineplex Odeon Declares Support for Distribs in Policy Statement," *Variety*, April 9, 1986, 20.

30 Guback, "The Evolution of the Motion Picture Theatre Business in the 1980s," 74.

31 Tusher, "Distribution's Theater Buys Near Peak, '86 a Watershed in Acquisitions," 24.

32 Thomas M. Pryor, "The New Exhibition Mania," *Variety*, August 6, 1986, 5, 31.

33 "Strategic Trends in Theatrical Exhibition: The Independent Exhibitor's Survival Guide," *Boxoffice*, July 1989, 16.

34 Hy Hollinger, "Merger Mania Facing Congress: Democrats May Pressure Justice Dept., Sec," *Variety*, January 14, 1987, 1.

35 Stephen Prince, *A New Pot of Gold: Hollywood Under the Electronic Rainbow, 1980–1989* (Berkeley: University of California Press, 2000).

36 Frederick Wasser, *Veni, Vidi, Video: The Hollywood Empire and the VCR* (Austin: University of Texas Press, 2001), 96.

37 Lawrence Cohn, "New Economy of Scale in Hollywood: Majors' Buys Wide-Reaching," *Variety*, January 14, 1987, 44.

38 Lawrence Cohn, "Overproduction Hurts Distribs: But Theatrical Playoff a Must for Credibility," *Variety*, February 25, 1987, 3, 86, 98.

39 Tusher, "Distribution's Theater Buys Near Peak, '86 a Watershed in Acquisitions," 24.

40 Will Tusher, "GCC Prez is not Concerned over Distributors' Return to Exhibition," *Variety*, June 18, 1986, 7, 26.

41 "NATO Changes Stance on Theater Ownership," *Boxoffice*, October 1986, 21.

42 "Daily Variety Editor Predicts Exhib Crisis," *Variety*, March 2, 1988, 8, 114.

43 Jon Lewis makes a convincing argument for Kirk Kerkorian's 1979 ownership bid in MGM and Columbia, and the Justice Department's failure to successfully pursue it as monopolistic practice, as an early precedent in the turn toward the megamergers of the 1980s and 1990s. Jon Lewis, "Money Matters: Hollywood in the Corporate Era," in *The New American Cinema*, ed. Jon Lewis (Durham: Duke University Press, 1998), 87–121.

44 "Tri-Star & Loews Seek Relief from Consent Decrees," *Variety*, April 8, 1987, 4, 24.

45　"Tri-Star Gets Nod from NATO in its Bid to Book Loews," *Variety,* May 6, 1987, 8, 579.

46　"Three Indie Exhibs Register Scorn for Demise of Consent," *Variety,* May 27, 1987, 5, 36.

47　Ibid., 36.

48　"Justice Dept. Memo Gives Insight into Agency's Distrib-Exhib Ideas," *Variety,* June 17, 1987, 3, 34.

49　Will Tusher, "Justice Dept. Says Customer Selection Okay for Distribs," *Variety,* December 21–27, 1988, 10.

50　Wasser, *Veni, Vidi, Video,* 136.

51　"1985 Chronology of Major Industry Events," *Boxoffice,* April 1986, 14.

52　Will Tusher, "Warners Mulls Franchise Option in Theater Deals," *Variety,* December 17, 1986, 106.

53　On the contrary, Guback, "The Evolution of the Motion Picture Theatre Business in the 1980s," 75, marks 1977 as the year the Antitrust Division opened the door to product-splitting cases, arguing that "splitting was a *per se* violation of the antitrust laws and no different from bid rigging."

54　Ibid. The defendants in the case, which concerned the Milwaukee market, were Capitol Services, Kohlberg, Marcus, and United Artist theaters.

55　"Arizona Exhib in Midst of Two Major Antitrust Offensives," *Variety,* December 10, 1986, 40.

56　Will Tusher, "Indie Exhib to Have its Day in Court: Harkins Circuit is Suing Majors," *Variety,* April 13, 1988, 3, 34.

57　"Theater Owners Win Antitrust Round: Justice Dept. Suit Dismissed," *Variety,* December 17, 1986, 3, 104.

58　Ibid.

59　Michael Cieply and Leonard Zehr, "MCA Agrees to Buy 33% of Cineplex for $106.7 million," *Wall Street Journal,* January 16, 1986, 8.

60　Hy Hollinger, "Merger Mania Facing Congress: Democrats May Pressure Justice Dept., Sec," 50. The terms of the consent decrees were not uniform across the studios. Stephen Prince comments on how this affected their relative eagerness or reluctance to return to exhibition in the 1980s, in *A New Pot of Gold,* 84–85.

61　Richard Gold, "No Exit? Studios Itch to Ditch Exhib Biz," *Variety,* October 8, 1990, 84.

62　"USA Cinemas Confirms Cinema National Merger," *Variety,* August 13, 1986, 3.

63　Richard Gold, "No Exit? Studios Itch to Ditch Exhib Biz," 1.

64　Will Tusher, "Exhibs Follow their Manifest Destiny: Not Dissuaded by Rise of Video Biz," *Variety,* May 13, 1987, 54; "NATO Puts U.S. Screen Tally at 22,721, Highest on Record," *Variety,* November 25, 1987, 6, 33.

65　Jim Robbins, "Exhibs are in Expansion Frenzy; Busy Month for Theater Acquisitions," *Variety,* July 1, 1987, 1, 33.

66　"ShoWest Keynoter to Settle Exhib Worries re: Distrib Acquisitions," *Variety,* February 4, 1987, 5.

67　"Roundtable: Distribution and Exhibition, The Ties that Bind," *Boxoffice,* March 1988, SW-28.

68　"Exhibition Looks to the Future," *Boxoffice,* December 1987, 36.

69   "Union and Exhibs Traded Praise at ShoWest Opening," *Variety,* February 18, 1987, 42.

70   John W. Quinn, "Exhibs Bellied up to Candy/Popcorn Bar at ShoWest's Trade Fair," *Variety,* February 25, 1987, 9.

71   Garth Drabinsky, "New Strategies for the Future: Two Challenges Facing Exhibition, Part 1," *Boxoffice,* February 1988, 10.

72   Ibid., 11.

73   Garth Drabinsky, "New Strategies for the Future: Two Challenges Facing Exhibition, Part 2," *Boxoffice,* March 1988, 82.

74   "Strategic Trends in Theatrical Exhibition: The Independent Exhibitor's Survival Guide," 14.

75   Ibid., 15

76   Allen Michaan, "Recapturing the Movie Palace Magic," *Boxoffice,* March 1989, SW-6.

77   Will Tusher, "Small Theaters Blast Circuits," *Variety,* March 2, 1988, 1, 9.

78   Will Tusher, "NATO Hears Indie Exhibs' Cries for Earlier Access to New Pics," *Variety,* November 23, 1988, 7.

79   "NATO Pushes for Print Changes," *Variety,* November 25, 1987, 7.

80   "U.S. Folks Are Big Spenders on Entertainment," *Variety,* October 8, 1986, 1, 160.

81   "Exhibition Looks to the Future," 37.

82   Jim Robbins, "Exhibitor Sees Falling Prices for Theaters," *Variety,* January 28, 1987, 1, 76.

83   Gold, "No Exit? Studios Itch to Ditch Exhib Biz," 1.

84   Ibid., 84.

85   Gayle MacDonald, "The Vast Picture Show," B1, B5.

86   "Daily Variety Editor Predicts Exhib Crisis," 114.

87   Will Tusher, "Theater Owners Assn.'s Plan Suggests Practices to Help Better Moviegoing Experience," *Variety,* May 10–16, 1989, 34.

88   "Strategic Trends in Theatrical Exhibition: The Independent Exhibitor's Survival Guide," 17.

89   Richard Gold, "U.S. Overscreened? Not for Mega-Hits," *Variety,* January 28, 1991, 60.

90   Lawrence Cohn, "Fewer Plexes but More Multi, Sites Down, Screens Up as Boom Fades," *Variety,* October 29, 1990, 1.

91   Ibid.

92   Sid Adilman, "The Man Behind the Multiplex, and Cineplex," *Variety,* April 26–May 2, 1989, 50.

93   Jay Blickstein, "Small-Town Dixie Chain on Exhib Fast Track," *Variety,* March 30, 1992, 51.

94   Jennifer Pendleton, "Chain Sees Possibilities in Midst of Recession," *Variety,* March 30, 1992, 60.

95   Blickstein, "Small-Town Dixie Chain on Exhib Fast Track," 64.

96   Martin Peers, ". . . And Threatens to Short-Circuit Exhibs," *Variety,* April 8–14, 1996, 1, 74, 75.

97   Carmike Cinemas, "Carmike Corporate History," www.carmike.com, 2002, last accessed July 10, 2002.

98   "ShoWest Keynoter to Settle Exhib Worries re: Distrib Acquisitions," 8.

99   John Evan Frook, "Chain Tests Distrib Waters," *Variety,* March 8, 1993, 50, 56.

100 Ibid.

101 Will Tusher, "Nation's Screen Tally Reached a New High in '90," *Variety,* January 28, 1991, 3.

102 Cohn, "Fewer Plexes but More Multi, Sites Down, Screens Up as Boom Fades," 76.

103 Jim Robbins, "Exhibition's Future: Too Many Theaters, Little to Put in Them, Predict Tradesters at Cinetex," *Variety,* September 27–October, 1989, 3.

104 Gold, "U.S. Overscreened? Not for Mega-Hits," 60.

105 Jon Herskovitz, "Japanese Biz Thriving in Face of Economic Troubles," *Variety,* November 30–December 6, 1998, 32.

106 Richard Natale, "Hollywood's Got the Billion-Ticket Blahs," *Variety,* March 30, 1992, 10.

107 Ibid.

108 John Quinn, "AMC's Plastic Plan Gaining after Slow Start in Kansas," *Variety,* April 5–11, 1989, 12, 16.

109 John Evan Frook, "Advance-Ticket Test Underway in Texas," *Variety,* May 11, 1992, 30.

110 Ibid.

111 "Interactive Service Moviefone, Now On Line in LA, Coming to Gotham; Offers Info on Screen Locales, Times," *Variety,* November 8, 1989, 30; Tom Matthews, "The Free Film Phone," *Boxoffice,* April 1990, 20.

112 Greg Evans, "Manhattan MovieFone Mania," *Variety,* January 24–30, 1994, 7, 19, 21.

113 Anthony Ramirez, "At Theaters Near You: Reserved Seating Comes to Manhattan Movies," *New York Times,* November 16, 1997, 41, 47.

FIVE. "HERE COME THE MEGAPLEXES"

1 "Mega-Multiplex for St. Petersburg." *Variety,* May 17, 1993, 34; "Edwards Gargantuplex," *Boxoffice,* April 1995, 124.

2 Paul Noglows, "Here Come the Megaplexes: Exhibits Usher in 24-Screen 'Destinations,'" *Variety,* August 22–28, 1994, 1, 65.

3 Ibid.

4 Louis M. Brill, "Megaplex Rising," *Boxoffice,* November 1994, 44, 46.

5 Sony's Digital Dynamic Sound is the most expensive to install, almost three times that of DTS, making it less attractive to exhibitors and less likely to become the industry standard. Adam Sandler, "Sound Systems Spar over Theater Sign-ups," *Variety,* August 22–28, 1994, 4.

6 Stephanie Argy, "High-Tech Add-Ons Usher in 'New Wave' of Filmgoing," *Variety,* March 16–22, 1998, 50.

7 Jim Robbins, "A $400-Million Strategy for Success: Cineplex Odeon Builds and Rebuilds," *Variety,* April 26–May 2, 1989, 70.

8 Andrew Hindes, "Megaplex Dominance Intact: Chain Fends off Rivals as Company Pushes for Bigger and Smarter," *Variety,* March 16–22, 1998, 39.

9 Ibid.

10 Ibid.

11 Brill, "Megaplex Rising," 48; Jimmy Summers, "Cineplex Odeon Launches a Dazzling New Flagship," *Boxoffice,* September 1987, 8, 10, 16.

12 Nancy Carter, "Tom Moyer's Luxury Theaters Opens Dazzling Ten-Plex," *Boxoffice,* March 1987, 88, 89.

13 Tom Matthews, "Jack Loeks' Studio 28," *Boxoffice,* August 1988, 18, 20, 24.

14 Susan Bourette and Michael Grange, "Mega-Complex Coming to a Theatre Near You: Famous Players to Unveil 'A New Level of Movie-Going Experience'," *The Globe and Mail,* August 28, 1995, B2.

15 Aaron Derfel, "U.S. Movie Chain for Forum," *Montreal Gazette,* August 13, 1996, A1, A9; Konrad Yakabuski, "AMC Targets Forum for 'Megaplex'," *Globe and Mail,* August 15, 1996, B1, B4.

16 Pat Kramer, "FunScape: Exhibition's New Landscape?," *Boxoffice,* September 1995, 16.

17 Pat Kramer, "A Busy Day in the Life of Exhibition," *Variety,* December 22–January 4 1997/98, 46.

18 Noglows, "Here Come the Megaplexes: Exhibs Usher in 24-Screen 'Destinations'," 66.

19 Alex Albanese, "The Shape of Things to Come?," *Boxoffice,* March 1995, SW-16.

20 Christopher Harris, "Faith in Popcorn," *Globe and Mail,* May 10, 1997, C3.

21 Adele Weder, "Architecture? Or Abomination," *National Post,* December 26, 1998, 4.

22 Harris, "Faith in Popcorn," C3.

23 Jon Herskovitz, "Virgin Bows 14-Screen Megaplex in Japan; Move Puts Exhib on Map," Variety.com, April 26, 1999, last accessed June 26, 2002.

24 Martin Peers, "Exhibs Vexed by Wall St. Hex on Plex," *Variety,* January 26–February 1, 1998, 1.

25 Robert Brehl, "Famous Players Signs Up for 10 Imax 3-D Theatres," *Globe and Mail,* February 5, 1998, B8.

26 Shlomo Schwartzberg, "Major Players," *Boxoffice,* May 1999, 34, 35, 36, 37.

27 Rebecca Eckler, "Curtain Set to Rise: Theatre Complex Hopes to Entice the Entire Family," *Calgary Herald,* July 17, 1996, C7.

28 "Automated Ticket Vendor, 1st in U.S., Bows on Coast," *Variety,* April 11, 1990, 13.

29 Brendan Kelly, "Loop Hums with High-Tech Sounds," *Variety,* December 9–15, 1996, 60.

30 Pat Kramer, "Cinescape Artists," *Boxoffice,* September 1996, 28, 29, 30; George T. Chronis, " 'Eau' Canada!," *Boxoffice,* April 1994, 24, 26, 28.

31 Monte Stewart, "Cinescape Ushers in New Era in Movies," *Calgary Herald,* August 22, 1996, C3.

32 Rex Weiner, "Bumpy Interactive Ride," *Variety,* May 22–28, 1995, 7, 14.

33 Chris Pursell, "Auds Lured by Virtual Arcades," *Variety,* December 22–January 4, 1998, 49; Pat Kramer, "Cinescape Artists," 28, 29, 30.

34 Harvey Enchin, "Famous Players Striving to Get More People Out More Often," *Globe and Mail,* Thursday, May 15, 1997, B7.

35 David A. Greene, "The Movie Mall: Selling Cinema at the New Megaplex," *Spin,* January 1998, 38.

36 Ibid.

37 Ibid., 39.

38 Johanna Scheller, "Focus on This: The Projector's on but Nobody's Home," *Globe and Mail,* January 15, 1999, A14. One consequence of the rise of the manager-projectionist has been that, as Scheller writes, "complaints received during a [projectionist] union man's shift are recorded in an incident report, whereas complaints during a manager's shift are not."

39 Brendan Kelly, "Marketers Make Most of Moviegoing Experience," *Variety,* December 9–15, 1996, 81.

40 Harvey Enchin, "Famous Players Striving to Get More People Out More Often."

41 Leo Rice-Barker, "Industry Banks on New Technology, Expanded Slates," 20; and Harris, "Faith in Popcorn," C3.

42 Paul Harris, "MPAA Puts '88 BO at Peak of $4.46-Bil; Aud Gets Older," *Variety,* February 15–21, 1989, 1, 4.

43 Eckler, "Curtain Set to Rise: Theatre Complex Hopes to Entice the Entire Family."

44 Ibid.

45 John Urry, *The Tourist Gaze: Leisure and Travel in Contemporary Societies* (Newbury Park, Ca.: Sage, 1990).

46 Sarah Schmidt, "Hold the Popcorn, Pass the Plate," *Globe and Mail,* February 14, 2000, R10.

47 Degen Pener, "Tyrannosauras Plex," *Entertainment Weekly,* June 6, 1997, 32, 33, 35; Jim Slotek, "Moviegoing in the Millennium," *Tribute,* June 1997, 34, 36; Michael Posner, "A Really Big Show," *Maclean's,* August 11, 1997, 38, 39.

48 Susan Bourette and Michael Grange, "Mega-Complex Coming to a Theatre Near You," B1, B2.

49 Sandra Rubin, "Coming Soon—New, Mega Movie Experience," *Calgary Herald,* August 29, 1995, D7; Wendy Stephenson, "Theatres Getting Facelift," *Winnipeg Sun,* August 30, 1995, 21; Paul McKie, "Coming Soon! More Theatres, Screens!," *Winnipeg Free Press,* January 13, 1998, A1, A2; Jay Stone, "Movie Madness," *Ottawa Citizen,* January 9, 1998, E1, E2; Brendan Kelly, "More Cinemas! Beaming Down to a Suburb Near You!," *Montreal Gazette,* December 4, 1999, D1, D2.

50 Harris, "Faith in Popcorn"; Gayle MacDonald, "The Vast Picture Show," B1, B5.

51 Christopher Hume, "All Roads Lead to FunCity," *Toronto Star,* November 1, 1997, M1.

52 Ibid., M16.

53 Ibid.

54 Ibid.

55 Stone, "Movie Madness," E1.

56 The function of themes is taken up in chapter 8.

57 Brendan Kelly, "Marketers Make Most of Moviegoing Experience," 81.

58 One consequence of digital sound technology has been a tendency to show off sound clarity at higher volumes. Far from being unanimously praised by audiences, it has provoked an increased number of complaints about the loudness, according to exhibitors. Pamela Swedko, "Theatre Executives Gather for ShowCanada Confab," *Playback,* May 5, 1997, 26.

59 Paul Willcocks, "Size Does Matter in the Future of Movie Theatres," *Globe and Mail,* May 15, 1998, D2.

60 John Izod, *Hollywood and the Box Office, 1895–1986,* 134.

61 Ibid., 135.

62 Ibid., 142.

63 Leo A. Handel, *Hollywood Looks at its Audience: A Report on Film Audience Research* (Urbana: University of Illinois Press, 1950), 155, 156.

64 "Pix-Video Wedding Closer," *Variety*, December 31, 1952, 19, cited in Tino Balio, *United Artists: The Company That Changed the Film Industry* (Madison: University of Wisconsin Press, 1987), 105.

65 See Barbara Klinger, "The New Media Aristocrats: Home Theater and the Domestic Film Experience," *Velvet Light Trap* 42 (1998): 4–19; and William Whittington, "Home Theater: Mastering the Exhibition Experience," *Spectator* 18, no. 2 (1998): 76–83.

66 Andrew Hindes, "ShoWest Boasts New Event Hosts," *Variety*, February 23–March 1, 1998, 30.

67 Leonard Klady, "Exhibs Trip on Glitz: Serious Issues May Get Lost in ShoWest Blitz," *Variety*, March 9–15, 1998, 9.

68 Ibid.

69 Leonard Klady, "Exhibs' Expansion Buoys Distribs," *Variety*, March 20–26, 1995, 7, 16.

70 Ibid., 16.

71 Klady, "Exhibs Trip on Glitz," 9.

72 Ibid., 16.

73 Martin Peers, ". . . And Threatens to Short-Circuit Exhibs," 1, 74, 75.

74 Charles Fleming, "Snackbar Slowdown Bitter Pill for Exhibs," *Variety*, January 21, 1991, 3, 93.

75 "EDI Box Office News: More New Screens in 1997," *Variety*, January 19–25, 1998, 38.

76 Martin Peers, "Consolidation Alters Face of Exhibition," *Variety*, December 22–January 4, 1997/98, 37, 52.

77 Martin Peers, "Hicks Nixes High-Priced UA Theaters Acquisition," *Variety*, February 23–March 1, 1998, 4.

78 Leonard Klady, "H'wood's BO Blast," 96.

79 Ibid.

80 Braden Phillips, "Chain Plans 1,000 New Screens in '99," *Variety*, March 8–14, 1999, 31, 32.

81 John Quinn, "Movies Make a Town Square," *Variety*, March 16–22, 1998, 58.

82 Martin Peers, "Exhibs Vexed by Wall St. Hex on Plex," 1, 83.

83 Martin Peers, "Mega Building Punctures Profits," *Variety*, June 8–14, 1998, 8.

SIX. ZONES AND SPEEDS OF INTERNATIONAL CINEMATIC LIFE

1 See, for instance, Michael Dorland, "Theses on Canadian Nationalism: In Memoriam George P. Grant," *Cineaction* 16, 1988, 3–5.

2 Toby Miller, "The Crime of Monsieur Lang," and Toby Miller et al., *Global Hollywood*.

3 Asu Aksoy and Kevin Robins, "Hollywood for the 21st Century: Global Competition for Critical Mass in Image Markets," *Cambridge Journal of Economics* 16 (1992): 1–22.

4 Frederick Wasser, "Is Hollywood America? The Trans-Nationalization of the American Film Industry," *Critical Studies in Mass Communication* 12, no. 4 (December 1995): 423–437.

5 Lawrence Cohn, "Overseas Pics Grow at L.A. Mart: 25% of Films from Outside U.S.," *Variety*, February 19, 1986, 3, 340.

6 "Here Come the Global Moguls; Newest H'wood Invaders Are Building, Not Buying," *Variety*, October 21, 1991, 1, 94.

7 Doug Saunders, "Maple Leaf No Hit at Hollywood Bowl," *Globe and Mail*, December 3, 2001, A10.

8   Miller et al., *Global Hollywood*, 108.

9   Richard Gold, "Globalization: Gospel for the '90s," *Variety*, May 2, 1990, S-1, S-104.

10 Ibid., S-1.

11 Lawrence Cohn, "It's Still Paying to Play the Movies: Majors Recouped Costs on '87 Pix," *Variety*, March 2, 1988, 3, 115.

12 Tino Balio, *United Artists*, 24.

13 Lawrence Cohn, "Big-Buck Scorecard, 1986–1988," *Variety*, January 11–17, 1989, 30.

14 Don Groves, "Reading Battles Aussie Biz in Multiplex Offerings," *Variety*, August 17–28, 1998, 16.

15 For an elaboration of this trend as a form of coordinated surveillance, see Miller et al., *Global Hollywood*, 181–194.

16 Adam Sandler, "Milestone in Mexican Video Biz," *Variety*, October 3–9, 1994.

17 Amy Dawes, "Global Batmania Lifts Warners to Foreign Mark; Success Mirrors 1989 U.S. Results; Firm Cites Euro Screen Proliferation," *Variety*, February 28, 1990, 7, 16.

18 "MPEA, Studios Promote Big-Screen Film-Watching," *Variety*, February 15–21, 1989, 48.

19 Miriam Hils, "Busy BO Propels Building," *Variety*, June 15–21, 1998, 52.

20 Daniel R. Pruzin, "The Americanization of Europe, Part I: How Hollywood Dominates the European Film Market," *Boxoffice*, February 1991, SW-56.

21 Leonard Klady, "Locals Boost BO: Plexes, Homegrown Heroes Pump Global 100," *Variety*, February 9–15, 1998, 30.

22 Tino Balio, "'A Major Presence in All of the World's Important Markets': The Globalization of Hollywood in the 1990s," in *Contemporary Hollywood Cinema*, ed. Steve Neale and Murray Smith (New York: Routledge, 1998): 60.

23 Lawrence Cohn, "Fewer Plexes but More Multi, Sites Down, Screens up as Boom Fades," 1.

24 Millard L. Ochs, "Cost Considerations in Developing the International Market," *Boxoffice*, February 1992, SW-16, SW-18.

25 Peter A. Ivany, "The Development of the International Market," *Boxoffice*, February 1992, SW-17, SW-19.

26 Douglas Gomery, *The Hollywood Studio System* (New York: St. Martin's Press, 1986), 35, 58, and 84.

27 Thomas Guback, *The International Film Industry* (Bloomington: Indiana University Press, 1969), 130–31.

28 "AMC Goes Global," *Boxoffice*, January 1993, 40.

29 Don Groves, "New Multiplex Building Boom May Reshape Euro Film Biz," *Variety*, June 13, 1990, 1, 20, 21.

30 Kim Williamson, "A Small World After All," *Boxoffice*, July 1994, 26.

31 Don Groves, "TW Announces Co-Ventures for European Hardtops," *Variety*, May 27, 1991, 35, 39.

32 John Nadler, "Cineplex Enters Turkey," *Variety*, April 27–May 3, 1998, 16; John Nadler, "Multiplex Mania Strikes Exhib Biz," *Variety*, May 18–24, 1998, 64.

33 "Multiplex Mania Hits Exhibitors," *Variety*, September 26–October 2, 1994, 55.

34 Cathy Meils, "Austria's Plexes Target Small-Town Expansion," *Variety*, January 5–11, 1998, 26.

35 Mark Woods, "Aussie GU Pacts with Dutch Exhib," *Variety,* March 23–29, 1998, 20.

36 Marlene Edmunds, "Kinepolis Keeps the Plexes Coming," *Variety,* June 15–21, 1998, 74.

37 Allen Eyles, "The Last Remaining Sites for UK Plexes," *Variety,* June 15–21, 1998, 49. For a useful detailing of the UK experience, see Stuart Hanson, "Spoilt for Choice? Multiplexes in the '90's," in *British Cinema of the 90's,* ed. R. Murphy (London: Routledge, 2000), 48–59. For an earlier expression of the concern vis-à-vis film exhibition, see Simon Blanchard, "Cinema-Going, Going, Gone?," *Screen* 24, nos. 4/5 (July–October 1983): 108–113. *Screen Digest* records the growth differently, with 1,416 screens in 1988 swelling to 2,638 in 1998 (see appendix 2).

38 Andrew Hindes, "Megaplex to Power Up London," *Variety,* June 23–29, 1997, 20.

39 Allen Eyles, "Megaplexing Comes to Great Britain," *Variety,* June 15–21, 1998, 50.

40 Nancy Tartaglione, "Arthouse Exhibs Fight Back," *Variety,* June 15–21, 1998, 49.

41 Miriam Hils, "Plex Mentality Causes Concern," *Variety: Global Media Report,* June 8–14, 1998, 10.

42 Jacqueline Christian, "Modernization Means Money," *Variety,* June 15–21, 1998, 56.

43 Stephen Mackey, "Foreign Exhibs Fuel Boom," *Variety,* June 15–21, 1998, 71.

44 Stephen Mackey, "Madrid's Megaplex Mania," *Variety,* April 20–26, 1998, 33.

45 Martin Peers, "Loews Lines Up World: Shugrue Tapped to Lead Exhib in Global Moves," *Variety,* June 15–21, 1998, 12.

46 Rick Richardson, "Underscreened Market Soldiers On," *Variety,* June 15–21, 1998, 78; John Nadler, "More Multis Mean More Magyar Moviegoers," *Variety,* June 15–21, 1998, 82; Cathy Meils, "Arthouses Hopping in Prague," *Variety,* June 15–21, 1998, 82; Tom Birchenough, "Slow Progress for Soviets," *Variety,* June 15–21, 1998, 86; Cathy Meils, "Politics Plays Havoc with Plexes," *Variety,* June 15–21, 1998, 86.

47 Pat Kramer, "Bold Design Drives Expansion," *Variety,* March 16–22, 1998, 40; Marlene Edmunds, "No Plex Unturned in Nordic Hardtop Frenzy," *Variety,* February 9–15, 1998, 66.

48 Linda Moore, "Spain: The Multiplex Pick-Me-Up Arrives Late But Strong," *Variety,* June 29, 1992, 62.

49 John Hopewell, "Portugal Ripe for Growth," *Variety,* June 26–July 9, 1995, 56.

50 Jennifer Clark, "Italy: Setting Houses in Order after Decades of Neglect," *Variety,* June 29, 1992, 62.

51 Adam Dawtrey, "Euros Go on Screen-Building Spree," *Variety,* February 6–12, 1995, 1.

52 Richard Gold, "U.S. Pix Tighten Global Grip," 1, 96.

53 "Exhibition Explodes in Asia," *Variety,* May 3, 1993, 37.

54 "Exhibs Gear for Multiplex Era," *Variety,* August 22–28, 1994, 41.

55 Baharudin Latif, "Chan, Godzilla Battle it out on Malaysian Screens," *Variety,* November 30–December 6, 1998, 36.

56 Jon Herskovitz, "Japanese Biz Thriving in Face of Economic Troubles," 32.

57 Gwen Robinson, " 'Plexes Proliferate amid Downward Box Office Trend," *Variety,* March 6–12, 1995, 49.

58 Don Groves, "Multiplying Multiplexes," *Variety,* June 12–18, 1995, 42.

59 Anchalee Chaiworaporn, "Thai Film Prod'n Suffers," *Variety*, November 30–December 6, 1998, 40.

60 Don Groves, "Mergers Boost Hot Hoyts," *Variety*, February 23–March 1, 1998, 34.

61 Beatriz Goyoaga, "Aussie Distrib Hoyts Enters Argentina," *Variety*, March 16–22, 1998, 19.

62 Don Groves, "Aussie Exhibs Stretch Abroad," *Variety*, June 15–21, 1998, 78.

63 Bryan Pearson, "South African Exhib Builds on Euro Stake," *Variety*, August 30–September 5, 1999, 45.

64 Larry Leventhal, "Cinema Trade Show Makes Euro Debut," *Variety*, June 29, 1992, 61, 62.

65 Don Groves, "Exhib Battle Goes Global," *Variety*, July 26, 1993, 23, 32.

66 Don Groves, "Boom Resounds Worldwide," *Variety*, June 29, 1992, 61.

67 Uma da Cunha, "WB Scraps Multiplex Project," *Variety*, September 11–17, 1995, 41.

68 Don Groves, " 'Plex Push Piques Overseas Exhib Ire," *Variety*, September 23–29, 1996, 17, 23.

69 Michael Williams, "Gauls to AMC: Yankee Go Home!," *Variety*, April 20–26, 1998, 14.

70 David Rooney, "Plexing of Rome May Feel Sting of Regs," *Variety*, November 30–December 6, 1998, 15.

71 David Rooney, "Mega Opposition: Italian Filmmakers Blast Studio-Lot Plex," Variety.com, April 6, 1999, last accessed June 26, 2002.

72 "Euro Screen Growth: Multiplex Boom Continues," *Variety*, June 23–29, 1997, 53.

73 Andrew Paxman, "Southern Renaissance: Corporate Ventures Multiply Region's Booming Multiplexes," *Variety*, March 23–29, 1998, 43.

74 Don Groves, "Hoyts, GCC Merge Latin America Ops," *Variety*, August 3–9, 1998, 22.

75 Marcelo Cajuiero, "Cinemark Targets Brazil with 6 Plexes," *Variety*, April 6–12, 1998, 17.

76 Andrew Paxman, "Latin BO Surges 13%: Regional Revs Up but Stock Market Blasts Brazil," *Variety*, January 19–25, 1998, 21; "The Multiplexing of Latin America," *Variety*, March 23–29, 1998, 68.

77 Paxman, "Southern Renaissance," 43.

78 Phil Wakefield, "Cinema Pins Hopes on Multiplex Solution," *Variety*, September 30, 1991, 59–60.

79 Blake Murdoch, "Multiplexes, Weak TV Scene Change the Distribution Map," *Variety*, April 24, 1991, 66, 74.

80 "Multiplexes Recharge BO," *Variety*, April 27, 1992, 64, 66.

81 Don Groves, "Boffo Year for Aussie Box Office," *Variety*, January 19–25, 1998, 21.

82 Don Groves, "Oz, Distribs, Exhibs Extract Peace Pact," *Variety*, August 3–9, 1998, 14.

83 Don Groves, "Pix Flash but Sides Clash at Oz Confab," *Variety*, August 24–30, 1998, 12.

84 Don Groves, "Reading Battles Aussie Biz in Multiplex Offerings."

85 Don Groves, "Art Pix Plex Plan: Village Roadshow Establishing a Global Brand," *Variety*, October 19–25, 1998, 26.

86 Don Groves, "Hoyts Trims Expansion," *Variety*, November 23–29, 1998, 14.

87 Don Groves, "Prexy Predicts Global Golden Age," *Variety*, September 11–17, 1995, 56.

88 Ibid.

89 Ibid.

90 Willie Brent, "China Opens but Film Supply Still Closed," *Variety*, November 30–December 6, 1998, 34.

91 "World Cinema Fails to Keep Up with USA; Global Spending Now Close to $17 Billion," *Screen Digest*, September 1999, 22; "Average Cinema Admissions per Head," *Screen Digest*, September 1998, 205.

92 James Cameron, "The Role of Exhibition in the Information Age," *Boxoffice*, October 1995, 11.

93 "MPAA Gives Pix Clean Bill of Health: Greying Audience Won't Crimp BO," *Variety*, November 25, 1987, 3, 33.

94 Marc Ramirez, "Crying Time Again? Moviegoing Parents Will Have a Refuge," *Wall Street Journal*, June 23, 1989, B4.

95 John Ellis, *Visible Fictions: Cinema, Television, Video* (Boston: Routledge and Kegan Paul, 1982).

96 Motion Picture Association of America, "2001 U.S. Economic Review," http://www.mpaa.org/useconomicreview/2001Economic, 2001, last accessed June 23, 2002.

97 Sid Adilman, "Canada Can't Get Enough Camcorders," *Variety*, April 8, 1991, 46.

98 "Redstone Decries 'Complacency' of Exhibs in Couch-Potato World," *Variety*, November 25, 1987, 32.

99 "Man Killed During 'Raw' Fracas; Film Is Pulled from One Theater," *Variety*, December 23, 1987, 7.

100 "Violence 'N the Hood'," *Boxoffice*, September 1991, 17.

101 Ibid.

102 Mark Becker, "Stepping Up Cinema Security," *Variety*, July 22, 1991, 13.

103 Ibid.

104 Ibid.

105 " 'American' Violence," *Boxoffice*, May 1992, 45.

106 "Violence Mars 'Juice' Opening," *Boxoffice*, March 1992, 24.

107 Becker, "Stepping up Cinema Security," 13.

108 Ibid.

109 Katti Gray, "Screening Starts Before the Movie," *Newsday*, March 31, 1991, www.newsday.com, last accessed August 20, 1998.

110 National Amusements, Inc., "An Open Letter to the Patrons of Sunrise Multiplex Cinemas," *Newsday*, March 28, 1991, www.newsday.com, last accessed August 20, 1998.

111 Gray, "Screening Starts Before the Movie," paragraph 7.

112 Becker, "Stepping Up Cinema Security," 13.

113 Jeff Schwager, "A Celebration of Our Industry: NATO/ShoWest '92 Generates Excitement," *Boxoffice*, April 1992, 14, 15.

114 Suzan Ayscough and Judy Brennan, "Will Movie Meccas Do the Right Thing?" *Variety*, July 12, 1993, 1 (my emphasis).

115 Ibid.

116 Ibid., 69.

117 Ibid.

118 Peter Bart, "Bite-sized Reality," *Variety*, July 12, 1993, 3.

119 Ibid.

120 Ibid., 5.

121 Army Archerd and Suzan Ayscough, " 'Poetic' Violence Surfaces," *Variety,* August 9, 1993, 14.

122 Leonard Klady, "Tracking a Lost Generation: Stunted Growth of Core Audience Frustrates Filmers," *Variety,* November 29, 1993, 1.

123 Laura Baker, "Screening Race: Responses to Theater Violence at *New Jack City* and *Boyz N the Hood,*" *Velvet Light Trap* 44 (fall 1999): 18.

124 Thomas Schatz, "The New Hollywood," in *Film Theory Goes to the Movies,* ed. Jim Collins, Hilary Radner, and Ava Preacher Collins (New York: Routledge, 1993), 9.

125 Ibid., 31.

126 John Evan Frook, "Exhib Bigs on PPV Pix: Not in My Theater," *Variety,* May 10, 1993, 26.

127 Leonard Klady, "Discount Houses Feel Freeze in Exhib Squeeze," *Variety,* November 4–10, 1996, 7, 14.

128 Klady, "Tracking a Lost Generation," 74.

129 Michael Posner, "A Really Big Show," 39.

130 Stephanie Argy, "Changes in Tech Toys Help Pix Look, Sound Their Best," *Variety,* December 22–January 4, 1997/78, 42.

131 Daniel Dayan and Elihu Katz, *Media Events: The Live Broadcasting of History* (Cambridge: Harvard University Press, 1992).

132 Bruce A. Austin, "Home Video: The Second-Run 'Theater' of the 1990s," in *Hollywood in the Age of Television,* ed. Tino Balio (Boston: Unwin Hyman, 1990), 331.

133 "Gen. Cinema Says VCRs Are a Help to Exhibition Biz," *Variety,* January 14, 1987, 7, 48.

134 Will Tusher, "Exhibs Follow Their Manifest Destiny," 54.

135 Terry Ilott, "Multiplexing Still Perplexing," *Variety,* January 4, 1993, 52.

136 Ibid.

137 Quoted in Nancy Griffin and Kim Masters, *Hit and Run: How Jon Peters and Peter Guber Took Sony for a Ride in Hollywood* (New York: Simon and Schuster, 1996), 297.

138 Peter Bart, "View from the War Room," 3.

139 William Paul, "The K-Mart Audience at the Mall Movies," 489.

140 Andrew Hindes, "Prints and the Paupers: Multiplex Mania Spurs Big Ad Buys, Wide Bows . . ." *Variety,* April 8–14, 1996, 1.

141 Ibid., 74.

142 Ibid.

143 Leonard Klady, "Screen Squeeze Sows Exhib-Distrib Discord," *Variety,* October 3–9, 1994, 13.

144 Ibid., 13.

145 Hindes, "Prints and the Paupers," 74.

146 Ibid.

147 Lawrence Cohn, "Fast-Lane Releases Are Short on Legs," *Variety,* July 12, 1993, 5.

148 Ibid.

149 Ibid., 69.

150 Ibid, 69, 73.

151 Richard Natale and Charles Fleming, "Distribs Say 'Open Wide!' " *Variety,* June 24, 1991, 1,

69; Leonard Klady, "Holiday Hits Ignite Fights for More Sites," *Variety,* December 9–15, 1996, 11, 12, 119.

152   "U Pix on 6,792 Screens, a Record," *Variety,* January 24, 1990, 12.

153   Lawrence Cohn, "Fewer Plexes but More Multi, Sites Down, Screens Up as Boom Fades," 76. Justin Wyatt notes *The Trial of Billy Jack*'s releasing strategy as a marked constrast to the innovative combination of four-walling and television advertising used to successfully exhibit *Billy Jack* (T.C. Frank [Tom] Laughlin 1971). Justin Wyatt, "From Roadshowing to Saturation Release: Majors, Independents, and Marketing/Distribution Innovations," in *The New American Cinema,* ed. Jon Lewis (Durham: Duke University Press, 1998), 64–86.

154   "EDI Box Office News: A Decade of Limited Releases," *Variety,* February 23–March 1, 1998, 42.

155   Lee Beaupré, "How to Distribute a Film," in *The Hollywood Film Industry,* ed. Paul Kerr (New York: Routledge and Kegan Paul, 1986 [1977]), 185–203.

156   "EDI Box Office News: Wide, Wider, Widest," *Variety,* January 26–February 1, 1998, 21.

157   Mark Woods, " 'Con Air' Flies to O'seas BO Highs," *Variety,* June 16–22, 1997, 14, 54.

158   "EDI Box Office News: Wide, Wider, Widest," 21.

159   Dade Hayes, "Grant vs. Goliath in Summer Gamble," *Variety,* March 10, 2002, 16.

SEVEN. NORTHERN SCREENS

1   "U.S. Symposium Nixed," *Playback,* May 2, 1988, 3.

2   Nick Madigan, "Runaways Inspire Taxing Questions," *Variety,* August 23–29, 1999, 7.

3   Ibid., 7, 9.

4   Stuart Cunningham, *Featuring Australia: The Cinema of Charles Chauvel* (Sydney: Allen and Unwin, 1991).

5   Tom O'Regan, *Australian National Cinema* (New York: Routledge, 1996), 89–110.

6   Ibid., 48.

7   Miro Cernetig, "Hooray for Brollywood," *Globe and Mail,* May 13, 1995, D1.

8   Doug Saunders, "Trouble in Hollywood North: Controversy Is Rising over Canada's Subsidies to U.S. Movie Moguls," *Globe and Mail,* May 13, 2000, A3.

9   "The Top 250 of 1999," *Variety,* January 10–16, 2000, 20, 22.

10   Doug Saunders, "We Want Flubber?," *Globe and Mail,* February 14, 1998, C1.

11   Brendan Kelly, "Canadians Finding Global Sales Respect," *Variety,* October 21–27, 1996, M20.

12   Philip Schlesinger, "The Sociological Scope of 'National Cinema'," in *Cinema and Nation,* ed. Mette Hjort and Scott MacKenzie (New York: Routledge, 2000), 24.

13   O'Regan, *Australian National Cinema,* 46.

14   Andrew Higson, "The Concept of National Cinema," 36.

15   Ibid., 39.

16   Susan Hayward, "Framing National Cinemas," in *Cinema and Nation,* ed. Mette Hjort and Scott MacKenzie (New York: Routledge, 2000), 101.

17   Andrew Higson, "The Limiting Imagination of National Cinema," in *Cinema and Nation*, ed. Mette Hjort and Scott MacKenzie (New York: Routledge, 2000), 67.

18   Ibid., 71.

19   David Ellis, *Split Screen: Home Entertainment and New Technologies* (Toronto: Friends of Canadian Broadcasting, 1992), 135. For an extended analysis of the implications of location shooting in Canada, see Mike Gasher, "The Audiovisual Locations Industry in Canada: Considering British Columbia as Hollywood North," *Canadian Journal of Communication* 20 (1995): 231–254.

20   *The Road to Success: Report of the Feature Film Advisory Committee* (Ottawa: Canadian Heritage, 1999), 3.

21   Ibid. A 1994 report put the breakdown of Canadian theatrical market share (excepting Quebec) at 96 percent United States, 2 percent other countries, and 2 percent domestic. Quebec's figures are 83 percent United States, 14 percent other countries, and 3 percent domestic. Secor Group, "Canadian Government Intervention in the Film and Video Industry," October 19, 1994, 24.

22   Peter Harcourt, "The Invisible Cinema," *CineTracts*, 1, no. 4 (spring–summer, 1978): 48–49.

23   Brendan Kelly, "Canada Sets New Pic Policy," *Variety*, February 9–15, 1998, 26; *The Road to Success*.

24   *The Road to Success*, 5.

25   "Doubt Clouds Canada's Film Future," *Calgary Herald*, September 9, 1997, C3.

26   Robert Everett-Green, "Not Coming Soon to a Theatre Near You," *Globe and Mail*, January 18, 1997, C2.

27   Pamela Cuthbert, "Distributors Post Record Results," *Playback*, February 13, 1995, P-6.

28   "Fabulous Fifty," *Boxoffice*, January 1999, 24.

29   Pendakur characterizes the demise of Allen Theatres circuit in 1923 and the rise of Famous Players as a good part of the roots of Canada's dependent relationship with the United States in film. At this point, distributors had virtually no option but to deal with this national chain. Manjunath Pendakur, *Canadian Dreams and American Control: The Political Economy of the Canadian Film Industry* (Toronto: Garamond, 1990), 51–78.

30   Christine James, "The Great Divide," *Boxoffice*, May 1999, 43.

31   Martin Peers, "Exhibs Vexed by Wall St. Hex on Plex," 83.

32   Similar tendencies toward oligopoly have been evident in other aspects of the audiovisual business. In 1993 *Variety* noted that Canadian video retail was only 20 percent chain controlled but that many were about to expand dramatically. Brendan Kelly, "Major Video Chains Prepare for a Boom," *Variety*, November 22, 1993, 54. Two video distributors, Astral and Video One, accounted for almost 80 percent of the market. Carolyn Leitch, "Astral Considering Acquisitions: Company May Buy Small Video Distributors to Consolidate Market," *Globe and Mail*, January 31, 1997, B8.

33   Karen Mazurkewich, "Film Grosses Far Below Target," *Playback*, August 19, 1991, 16.

34   Shlomo Schwartzberg, "Major Players," 34.

35   These smaller chains, especially when operating in close markets to Famous Players and

Cineplex Odeon, have complained about limited access to the most lucrative films. Quebec's Guzzo, for example, has brought a lawsuit against the two, claiming it was actively denied access to first-run films. Shlomo Schwartzberg, "Guzzo's Gusto," *Boxoffice*, May 1999, 28, 30, 31.

36 Martin Peers, "Cinemark, Cineplex Merge Ops," *Variety*, March 6–12, 1995, 22.

37 Harvey Enchin, "Deal Creates Box Office Giant," *Globe and Mail*, October 1, 1997, B1, B14.

38 Shawn McCarthy, "Ottawa Eyes Cineplex Merger," *Globe and Mail*, October 2, 1997, A14, A15.

39 Shawn McCarthy, "Cineplex Deal May Hinge on Sale of Unit," *Globe and Mail*, October 3, 1997, B1, B20.

40 Andy Hoffman, "Cineplex Deal Raises Multiplex of Scenarios," *Playback*, January 12, 1998, 1, 26.

41 Bruce Orwall, "Theatre Closings Possible in Cineplex-Sony Merger: Draft Document Filed with SEC Also Foresees Expansion," *Globe and Mail*, February 4, 1998, B12.

42 Loews Cineplex Entertainment, "News Release—10/8/1998—Announces Financial Results for Second Quarter," *Canadian NewsWire*, http://www.newswire.ca/release/October1998/08/c2008.html, 1998, last accessed May 8, 2000.

43 Harvey Enchin, "Theatre Deal Highlights Market Fragmentation," *Globe and Mail*, October 3, 1997, B20.

44 Gayle MacDonald and John Partridge, "Cineplex Executives Let Go: Loews Merger Pushes Managers Out Door," *Globe and Mail*, May 2, 1998, B1, B5.

45 Three of the partners involved have ties to other distribution and exhibition companies. Ellis Jacob is an executive at Cineplex Odeon, Robert Lantos was chair of Alliance Communication, and Victor Loewy is head of Alliance Atlantis Motion Picture Group, which has started its own chain, Alliance Atlantis Cinemas, with Famous Players. Gayle MacDonald, "Onex Partners Launch Cinema Chain to Show Flicks to the Sticks," *Globe and Mail*, September 15, 1999, B1, B4.

46 Leo Rice-Barker, "Industry Banks on New Technology, Expanded Slates," 19; Brendan Kelly, "Bigger, Better Plexes: With Eight Decades in Business, Circuit is on Expansion Course," *Variety*, November 29–December 5, 1999, 35.

47 Rice-Barker, "Industry Banks on New Technology, Expanded Slates," 19; "Canadian Giants of Exhibition," *Boxoffice*, May 1999, 42.

48 "Famous Players Sets $C 50-Million Toronto Expansion," *Variety*, May 18, 1988, 39.

49 "Summer BO Surge Posted in Canada by Famous Players," *Variety*, October 15, 1986, 34.

50 "Cinemas Need a Personal Touch," *Playback*, November 10, 1986, 1.

51 Sid Adilman, "Cineplex Odeon Circuit to Add 200 Canadian Screens thru '88," *Variety*, July 2, 1986, 6, 27. Other activity included Cineplex Odeon buying RKO Century Warner Theaters' 97 screens and 152 screens at 55 sites in Western Canada. Jim Robbins, "Drabinsky Confirms Cineplex' Buy of RKO Century Warner; To Add 38 N.Y.-Area Screens," *Variety*, August 6, 1986, 3, 21; "CO Completes Buy of 152 Screens in Western Canada," *Variety*, February 7, 1990, 24.

52 Morry Roth, "Cineplex Boss Details Chi Plans; Aims for 400 New U.S. Screens," *Variety*, April 2, 1986, 27.

53 Douglas Gomery, "Building a Movie Theater Giant: The Rise of Cineplex Odeon," 377.

54 "Cineplex Readies Montreal Fourplex," *Variety*, November 26, 1986, 7.

55 Jen Mitchell, "Cineplex Making a Comeback," *Playback,* December 5, 1994, 27.

56 Christopher Harris, "Faith in Popcorn," C3.

57 These included the introduction of 6,000-foot reels, replacing the standard 2,500-foot reels, expected to reduce the labor needed for projection. Mary Ellen Armstrong, "Expansion and Change," *Playback,* May 19, 1997, 8, 14. Another was the recent switch from acetate-based film to polyester, which had the advantage of durability but had caused projection problems. Pamela Swedko, "Theatre Executives Gather for ShowCanada Confab," 26.

58 Mary Ellen Armstrong, "Service, Disney Style," *Playback,* May 19, 1997, 8.

59 Allison Vale, "Boffo Screen Build," 1.

60 Leonard Klady, "BO Tastes Yank-Flavored," *Variety,* September 2–8, 1996, 42.

61 Ibid.

62 Vale, "Boffo Screen Build," 28.

63 Will Tusher, "Cineplex Odeon Agrees to Sell 57 Canadian Multiplexes in Fall," *Variety,* August 17, 1988, 6. In 1990 Cineplex sold screens in U.S. smaller markets, with a number going to Carmike and Plitt. Brian Milner, "Cineplex to Stick to Film Exhibiting: Karp Says Sell-Offs Exceed $100-Million," *Globe and Mail,* June 16, 1990, B5.

64 From Patricia Thompson, ed., *Film Canada Yearbook* (Toronto: Cine-Communications, 1994); Statistics Canada, "Film and Video, 1992–93, Culture Statistics" (Ottawa: Ministry of Industry, Science, and Technology, 1995); Motion Picture Theatres Association of Canada, "Canadian Statistics," http://www.mptac.ca/stats.html, 2001, last accessed June 23, 2002; and Statistics Canada, "Movie Theatres and Drive-ins, 1997–98, Culture Statistics" (Ottawa: Culture, Tourism, and the Centre for Education Statistics, 1999).

65 "Screaming into Iqaluit," *Globe and Mail,* December 9, 1997, A15.

66 Ted Magder, *Canada's Hollywood: The Canadian State and Feature Films* (Toronto: University of Toronto Press, 1993), 217.

67 Ibid., 220.

68 Ibid., 222.

69 Karen Mazurkewich, "Many Reasons Why Cdn. Box Office Bad," *Playback,* June 8, 1992, 4.

70 Quoted in Karen Mazurkewich, "Film Grosses Far Below Target," *Playback,* August 19, 1991, 19.

71 Suzan Ayscough, "Local Distribs Grabbing More BO," *Variety,* November 16, 1992, 42 (both quotations).

72 In his detailed discussion, Pendakur places the introduction of the Film Products Importation Bill in the context of other policy and industry developments including the Federal Task Force on Film and Paramount's severing off from Canadian distributor Norstar, which had relied on Paramount, as a major source for films. Pendakur, *Canadian Dreams and American Control,* 264–265.

73 "Canada Limits U.S. Majors Unless They Hold World Rights," *Variety,* February 18, 1987, 1, 128.

74 "Canada Vows to Pass Legislation Curbing Power of U.S. Distribs Despite Bilateral Free Trade Pact," *Variety,* November 25, 1987, 43, 60, 62.

75 Earl Green, "Canada Reinforcing Distrib Borders; Hefty Fines Face Import Violators," *Variety,* June 22, 1988, 5.

76 Ian Mccallum, "Government's Role May Be Ending: Can the Industry Carry the Ball?," *Playback,* April 6, 1987, 12.

77 Ibid.

78 Marlene Orfton, "Reagan Questions Licensing," *Playback,* April 20, 1987, 1, 6.

79 Colin Wright, " 'We Won't Give Up'—Distribs," *Playback,* August 24, 1987, 4.

80 Sid Adilman, "Canadian Distribs Shut Out of Pics: Sellers Fear Upsetting U.S.," *Variety,* May 20, 1987, 3.

81 "Distribs Go Crazy for New Canadian Fund; But that Pot's Not All Honey," *Variety,* November 23, 1988, 37; "Alberta Gets International Distributor," *Playback,* June 27, 1988, 3; "Year at a Glance," *Playback,* October 16, 1989, 32.

82 Cineplex Odeon Films had deals to handle Columbia, TriStar, Savoy, and Gramercy films for Canada. Karen Murray, "Cineplex Films Finds Canuck Screens for Pix," *Variety,* July 25–31, 1994, 42. They also signed a four-year deal with October Films, a division of MCA/Universal. Andy Hoffman, "Cineplex Gets October Deal; Ownership Still in Question," *Playback,* March 23, 1998, 9, 24.

83 Famous Players and Cinepix jointly owned C/FP Distribution from 1989 until 1994, when the former bought the latter's 49 percent stake. Pamela Cuthbert, "Cinepix Takes Over," *Playback,* August 29, 1994, 1. C/FP distributed Miramax from 1991 to 1994. Karen Mazurkewich, "C/FP Inks Distrib Deal with Miramax," *Playback,* September 2, 1991, 1, 4.

84 Suzan Ayscough, "Recession Divides the Distrib Waters," *Variety,* November 16, 1992, 46; Ayscough, "Local Distribs Grabbing More BO," 42; Brendan Kelly, "Biz Maps New Routes North," *Variety,* November 21–27, 1994, 53, 62. Another distributor, the Montreal-based Malofilm, to be renamed Behaviour, handled Samuel Goldwyn films. Pamela Cuthbert, "Distributors Post Record Results," P-6. In an illustration of the utter unpredictability of international audiovisual financing, Behaviour was in turn renamed MDP Worldwide Entertainment and subsequently formed the division Neverland Pictures after Michael Jackson's Neverland Entertainment became the second largest shareholder. Keith Damsell, "Michael Jackson Invests in Montreal Film Company," *Globe and Mail,* February 26, 2002, B2.

85 "Astral Bellevue and G&W Talking Joint Distribbery," *Variety,* November 19, 1986, 5.

86 "Buena Vista Opens Disney Distrib Subsidiary in Toronto," *Playback,* November 28, 1988, 40. Pendakur notes that this was prompted by changes in Disney's ownership as well as new marketing and production plans, and that it was a typical branch plant tactic. Pendakur, *Canadian Dreams and American Control,* 267–269.

87 Val Ross, "U.S. Doesn't Get the Picture," *Globe and Mail,* December 8, 1993, B1, B4.

88 Ray Conlogue, "Taking a Stand for the Cinematic National Soul," *Globe and Mail,* December 21, 1993, C2.

89 For a full account of the similarities between the Quebec Cinema Act and Bill C-134, see Michael I. Prupas, "The Control of Film and Video Distribution in Canada and Quebec," *Entertainment Law Reporter,* 10, no. 9 (February 1989): 8–17.

90 Magder, *Canada's Hollywood,* 219–220.

91 This was to affect approximately 150 English-language films, which would potentially be

distributed by Quebec firms. Sid Adilman, "MPAA Pact with Quebec Govt. Lets Locals Handle More Pics," *Variety*, October 29, 1986, 7, 45.

92 Sid Adilman, "Valenti Says Agreement with Quebec Government Suits Singular Situation," *Variety*, October 29, 1986, 7. In 1992 the MPEAA extended its agreement to comply with the Quebec Cinema Act until 2000. Leo Rice-Barker, "Quebec, US Ink New Distrib Deal," *Playback*, February 3, 1992, 1, 9.

93 Suzan Ayscough, "Stronghold for Non-U.S. Fare Weakens," *Variety*, December 2, 1991, 74, 86.

94 Brendan Kelly, "Distribs Fight Dominance of Big-Ticket U.S. Pix," *Variety*, November 22, 1993, 52.

95 Pendakur, *Canadian Dreams and American Control*, 263.

96 Sid Adilman, "Quebec Opening Door to Yank Majors, Toronto Distribs Will Be Shut Out," *Variety*, February 3, 1988, 5, 31.

97 Suzan Ayscough, "All Canada to Play by Quebec's Rules; U.S. Bigs Exempt from Distrib Law," *Variety*, September 28, 1988, 3.

98 Christopher Harris, "Quebec Law Has Distribs Angered," *Playback*, October 3, 1988, 1, 5. In 1997 Quebec invoked this law to prohibit Alliance Releasing from operating in that province. Alliance then quickly negotiated a distribution deal with Cineplex Odeon Films for Quebec, itself in an uncertain position with the merger of Cineplex Odeon and Loews then under review. Brendan Kelly, "Quebec Law Trips Up Alliance Releasing," *Variety*, December 22, 1997–January 4, 1998, 7.

99 Karen Mazurkewich, "Ontario Distributors Aim to Mirror Quebec Legislation," *Playback*, October 1, 1990, 3.

100 Prupas, "The Control of Film and Video Distribution in Canada and Quebec," 8–17.

101 Pamela Cuthbert, "PolyGram Controversy Escalates," *Playback*, September 23, 1996, 1.

102 Hugh Winsor, "Film Law Sparks Cabinet Clash," *Globe and Mail*, October 16, 1996, A1, A5; Harvey Enchin, "PolyGram to Proceed with Film Company," *Globe and Mail*, March 14, 1997, B1, B6.

103 Leo Rice-Barker, "EC to Take Case to WTO," *Playback*, May 5, 1997, 1, 14.

104 Steven Globerman, "Foreign Ownership of Feature Film Distribution and the Canadian Film Industry," *Canadian Journal of Communication* 16 (1991): 191–206.

105 An example of this argument is Paul Attallah, "Narrowcasting: Home Video and DBS," in *The Cultural Industries in Canada: Problems, Policies, and Prospects*, ed. Michael Dorland (Toronto: Lorimer, 1996), 257–279.

106 Ted Madger, "Film and Video Production," in *The Cultural Industries in Canada: Problems, Policies, and Prospects*, ed. Michael Dorland (Toronto: Lorimer, 1996), 145–177.

107 Karen Mazurkewich, "Many Films Find Home on Video," *Playback*, September 16, 1991, 9.

108 Ellis, *Split Screen*, 101.

109 Several distributors went bankrupt, including Cinema Plus, Brightstar, Festival Films, and Nova Entertainment. Ayscough, "Local Distribs Grabbing More BO," 42.

110 Brendan Kelly, "Canadian Shakin'," *Variety*, February 23–March 1, 1998, 15, 52.

111 Christopher Harris, "Alliance Deal Opens Doors," *Playback*, April 18, 1988, 3. Alliance expanded its distribution operations by buying Electric Pictures PLC in 1997, a British film

distributor, and Canadian distributor Norstar, thus acquiring one of its key rivals. Alliance's genre film division, Le Monde Entertainment, based in Los Angeles, distributed internationally some of Alliance's made-for-TV movies. Harvey Enchin, "Alliance Extends International Reach in Film Distribution," *Globe and Mail*, September 24, 1997, B1, B8; Gayle MacDonald, "Alliance Buys Film Distributor Norstar," *Globe and Mail*, December 23, 1997, B3; Brendan Kelly, "Alliance Snaps Up Canuck Indie Norstar," *Variety*, January 5–11, 1989, 32; Brendan Kelly, "Alliance's Le Monde Ups Slate," *Variety*, January 19–25, 1998, 29.

112   Ayscough, "Recession Divides the Distrib Waters," 46.

113   Alliance Releasing agreed to distribute 50 of Miramax's films from 1994 to 1999 in Canada, with exclusive rights. In return, Miramax would distribute 5 of Alliance's productions in the United States. Alliance acquired Cineplex Odeon Films in 1998 adding 300 films to its library, including its deal to handle October Films product. Gayle MacDonald, "Alliance to Close Cineplex Odeon Films Deal," *Globe and Mail*, May 21, 1998, B4; Pamela Cuthbert, "Two-Way," *Playback*, March 28, 1994, 1.

114   Brendan Kelly, "TV's Global Reach," *Variety*, December 14–20, 1998, 113.

115   Alliance Atlantis Communications Inc., "1999 Annual Report," Toronto, 2, 25.

116   Demonstrating the presumed advantages of integration for this producer/distributor/exhibitor, Burger also described the joint venture as a way "to ensure the product supply." Quoted in Gayle MacDonald, "Partners Plan Art-House Cinema Chain: Alliance, Famous Players to Invest Up to $30-Million to Build, Lease Multiplexes," *Globe and Mail*, June 19, 1998, B1, B8.

117   Ibid.

118   Alliance Atlantis Communications Inc., "1999 Annual Report," 22.

119   Kevin Dowler, "The Cultural Industries Policy Apparatus," in *The Cultural Industries in Canada: Problems, Policies, and Prospects*, ed. Michael Dorland (Toronto: Lorimer, 1996), 328–346.

120   Sam Wendt, "Canadian Films and the American Market," in *Selling It: The Marketing of Canadian Feature Films*, ed. Joan Irving (Toronto: Doubleday Canada, 1995), 83.

121   Advertisement for *The Insider, The Montreal Gazette*, November 12, 1999, D8.

122   Christopher Harris, "Support Our Own, Says Cineplex Head," *Playback*, May 14, 1990, 3.

123   Mary Ellen Armstrong, "Are Exhibitors Doing Their Share?" *Playback*, May 6, 1996, 22.

124   The first work, for the Beverly Center in LA, appeared in 1982. In 1989 thirty-one theaters in Canada and twenty-one in the United States had one of these art works. Sid Adilman, "Thou 'Art' the Only Cinema Chain in U.S. Canada to Seek Original Pieces." *Variety Cannes '89: special issue*, May 3–9, 1989, 463, 499.

125   Seth Feldman, ed., *Take Two: A Tribute to Film in Canada* (Toronto: Irwin, 1984), ix.

126   Peter Harcourt, *A Canadian Journey: Conversations with Time* (Ottawa: Oberon, 1994), 100.

127   Bronwyn Drainie, "Finally, a Canadian Movie That Ranks at the Top," *Globe and Mail*, February 22, 1996, A14.

128   Blockbuster Video argues that they receive the classification for their videos from the head office in the United States, hence the penchant for categorizing Canadian film as foreign.

129   O'Regan, *Australian National Cinema*, 47.

130   John Caughie, "Playing at Being American," 54.

131   Linda Hutcheon, *Splitting Images: Contemporary Canadian Ironies* (Toronto: Oxford University Press, 1991); and Kieran Keohane, *Symptoms of Canada: An Essay on Canadian Identity* (Toronto: University of Toronto Press, 1997).

132   Richard Collins, "National Culture: A Contradiction in Terms?," *Canadian Journal of Communication* 16 (1991): 225–238. He puts forward a claim that horizontal allegiances to other communities resist vertical hierarchies at home. With this focus, however, he neglects to consider the formation of international hierarchies, which may be just as "vertical" as domestic ones.

133   For more detailed treatment of this history, see Charles R. Acland, "National Dreams, International Encounters: The Formation of Canadian Film Culture in the 1930s," *Canadian Journal of Film Studies* 3, no. 1 (1994): 3–26; Charles R. Acland, "Patterns of Cultural Authority: The National Film Society of Canada and the Institutionalization of Film Education, 1938–1941, *Canadian Journal of Film Studies* 10, no. 1 (2001): 2–27; Charles R. Acland, "Mapping the Serious and the Dangerous: Film and the National Council of Education, 1920–1939," *Cinéma* 6, no. 1 (fall 1995): 101–118; Paul Litt, *The Muses, the Masses, and the Massey Commission* (Toronto: University of Toronto Press, 1992); and Mary Vipond, "The Nationalist Network: English Canada's Intellectuals and Artists in the 1920s," *Canadian Review of Studies in Nationalism* 5 (spring 1980), 32–52.

134   An exceptional rendering of the discourses of industry, culture, and nation related to these issues is found in Michael Dorland, *So Close to the State/s: The Emergence of Canadian Feature Film Policy* (Toronto: University of Toronto Press, 1998).

135   See Charles R. Acland, "IMAX in Canadian Cinema: Geographic Transformation and Discourses of Nationhood," *Studies in Cultures, Organizations, and Societies* 3 (1997): 289–305.

136   O'Regan, *Australian National Cinema*, and Thomas Elsaesser, *New German Cinema: A History* (New Brunswick: Rutgers University Press, 1989), comment on the importance of international festivals for definitions of national cinemas. My argument is that Canadian national cinema relies on a highly evolved circuit of domestic festivals as well. An incomplete list includes the Montreal World Film Festival, the Toronto International Film Festival, Local Heroes International Screen Festival in Edmonton, Hot Docs documentary film festival in Toronto, the Banff Television Festival, the Ottawa Animation Festival, Vancouver International Film Festival, Festival du cinéma francophone international en Acadie, the Yorkton Short Film and Video Festival (started in 1947, which makes it the oldest film festival in Canada), Rendez-vous de cinéma québécois, Dreamspeakers Film Forum, and Halifax's Atlantic Film Festival.

137   Pierre Bourdieu, *Distinction*.

138   Ibid.

139   Pierre Bourdieu, *In Other Words: Essays Towards a Reflexive Sociology,* trans. Matthew Adamson (Stanford: Stanford University Press, 1990), 9.

1 Gayle MacDonald, "Red Sky Reels in High-brow Flicks for Mainstream Venues," *Globe and Mail,* February 23, 1998, B1.

2 Ibid.

3 Holly Willis, "Beyond the Theater: Tactical Approaches to Independent Exhibition and Distribution," *Spectator* 18, no. 2 (spring/summer 1998): 84–90.

4 Dade Hayes, "Pix Take Slow Road to BO Success 'Tenenbaums,' 'Gosford' Hold a Platform Party," *Variety,* January 28–February 3, 2002, 12, 14.

5 Peter Bart, *The Gross,* 311.

6 Greg Evans, "Sony's NY 'Theme-Plex' Stirs Exhibs' Interest," *Variety,* December 12–18, 1994, 9.

7 Chris Petrikin, "AMC Bows Centertainment Plexes," *Variety,* December 18–31, 1995, 25.

8 Ian Mohr, "FunScapes Marry Movies, Entertainment Options," *Variety,* March 8–14, 1999, 34, 46.

9 Geoffrey Rowan, "Playdium to Build Toronto Complex," *Globe and Mail,* August 28, 1997, B7; Ann Kerr, "High-Tech Centre Hopes to Be Fun City," *Globe and Mail,* July 23, 1996, C2.

10 Tom Gunning, "An Aesthetic of Astonishment: Early Film and the (In)Credulous Spectator," 115.

11 Ibid., 129.

12 This argument is developed in Charles R. Acland, "IMAX Technology and the Tourist Gaze," *Cultural Studies* 12, no. 3 (1998): 429–445.

13 Advertisement for *Twister, Globe and Mail,* May 24, 1996, C4.

14 Susan G. Davis, "The Theme Park: Global Industry and Cultural Form," 407.

15 Greg Evans, "Showbiz Is Psyched for Cybermalls," *Variety,* March 27–April 2, 1995, 1.

16 Ibid.

17 Ibid., 90.

18 Ibid.

19 See John Hannigan, *Fantasy City: Pleasure and Profit in the Post Modern Metropolis* (New York: Routledge, 1998) for a full study of the city as a "themed" entertainment environment.

20 Andrew Hindes, "The New Plex-Busters? Location-Based Diversions Vie for Moviegoers' Dollars," *Variety,* May 10–16, 1999, 9.

21 Ibid.

22 Ibid.

23 Ibid.

24 Kathleen O'Steen, "Exhibs Ride Hi-Tech Edge," *Variety,* October 24–30, 1994, 13.

25 Ibid.

26 Jim Slotek, "Moviegoing in the Millennium," 34.

27 "Distribs Exhort Exhibs To Try To Increase Viewer Satisfaction," *Variety,* February 19, 1986, 11.

28 Todd McCarthy, "MCA, Cineplex Odeon Teaming on Fla. Studio-Tourist Facility," *Variety,* December 17, 1986, 3, 104.

29 Jean Baudrillard, *Simulations,* trans. Paul Foss, Paul Patton, and Philip Beitchman (New York: Semiotext(e), 1983), 25–26.

30 Walter Benjamin, "The Work of Art in the Age of Mechanical Reproduction."

31 Davis, "The Theme Park: Global Industry and Cultural Form," 399.

32 Ibid., 415.

33 Ibid.

34 Ibid., 416.

35 Edward Soja, "Inside Exopolis: Scenes from Orange County," in *Variations on a Theme Park: The New American City and the End of Public Space,* ed. Michael Sorkin (New York: Hill and Wang, 1992), 121.

36 For an examination of the economic and significatory context of this restaurant chain, see Josh Stenger, "Consuming the Planet: Planet Hollywood, Stars, and the Global Consumer Culture," *The Velvet Light Trap,* 40 (fall 1997): 42–55.

37 Margaret Crawford, "The World in a Shopping Mall," in *Variations on a Theme Park: The New American City and the End of Public Space,* ed. Michael Sorkin (New York: Hill and Wang, 1992), 30.

38 Will Straw, " 'Organized Disorder': The Changing Space of the Record Shop," in *The Club-cultures Reader: Readings in Popular Cultural Studies,* ed. Steve Redhead (Oxford: Blackwell, 1997), 59.

39 Ibid., 63.

40 For a study of connotative dimensions of themed spaces, see Mark Gottdiener, *The Theming of America: Dreams, Visions, and Commercial Spaces* (Boulder: Westview, 1997).

41 Ibid., 29.

42 Ibid., 31.

43 Davis, "The Theme Park: Global Industry and Cultural Form," 403.

44 Susan Willis, *A Primer for Daily Life* (New York: Routledge, 1991), 13.

45 Ibid., 58.

46 Constance Balides, "Jurassic Post-Fordism: Tall Tales of Economics in the Theme Park," *Screen* 41, no. 2 (summer 2000): 141.

47 Ibid., 147.

48 Ibid., 148.

49 Pat Kramer, "Bold Design Drives Expansion," 40.

50 Ibid.

51 Michael Sorkin, "Introduction," in *Variations on a Theme Park,* xiii.

52 Ibid., xii.

53 Lawrence Grossberg, "The Space of Culture, the Power of Space," 187.

54 Alexander Kluge, "On Film and the Public Sphere," *New German Critique* 24/25 (fall/winter 1981/82): 214.

55 Janet Staiger, "Individualism versus Collectivism," *Screen* 24, nos. 4/5 (July–October 1983): 79.

56 Leonard Klady, "Exhibs Trip on Glitz," 9.

57 Martin Peers, "Megaplex Strength Lifts AMC Earnings," Variety.com, October 23, 1997, last accessed June 25, 2002.

58 Martin Peers and Andrew Hindes, "AMC Scales Back Plexes in Reversal," *Variety*, May 24–30, 1999, 10.

59 Don Groves, "BO World Is Flat; Local Pix, Strong Dollar Hurt Yanks O'seas," Variety.com, June 11, 2002, last accessed June 25, 2002.

60 Carl Diorio, "Distrib Jury Still Out on Day-&-date Releases; Tactic Best for Event Pix; Others need U.S. Buzz," Variety.com, June 25, 2002, last accessed June 26, 2002.

61 Henri-Pierre Penel, "Deux innovations pour une révolution," *Science et Vie* (April 2000): 128; Michel Marriott, "Digital Projectors Use Flashes of Light to Paint a Movie," *New York Times*, May 27, 1999, G7.

62 "Major Studios Agree to Set Digital Standards," *Globe and Mail*, April 4, 2002, R2.

63 William Boddy, *Fifties Television*.

64 Anna McCarthy, *Ambient Television: Visual Culture and Public Space*.

65 For a discussion of some of these developments in the late 1980s and early 1990s, see Janet Wasko, *Hollywood in the Information Age*, 183–184.

66 "NATO's Warner Foresees Global Film Industry," *Boxoffice*, October 1991, 96.

67 Matt Rothman, "Digital Tech Points to Pix' Future," *Daily Variety*, May 12, 1992, 1.

68 "Satellite, PPV News," *Boxoffice*, August/September 1992, 105.

69 Terry Yushchyshyn, "The Digital Future of Film," *Boxoffice*, April 1994, SW-12.

70 Andrew Hindes, "When Prints Will No Longer Be King," *Variety*, January 25–31, 1999, 9, 16.

71 Christine James, "Island Getaway," *Boxoffice*, May 1999, 38.

72 Tim Avis, "Digital Revolution?," *Variety*, June 21–27, 1999, 45.

73 Ibid., 46.

74 Jill Goldsmith, "ShowEast: Who Picks Up the Digital Check?," *Variety*, October 25–31, 1999, 9, 16.

75 Simon Tuck, "Projections of the Future," *Globe and Mail*, October 28, 1999, T3. Others place the cost closer to $125,000, saying it is five times that of a conventional projector. Rob Sabin, "The End/Restart: The Movies' Digital Future Is in Sight and It Works," *New York Times*, November 26, 2000, section 2, 22.

76 Dade Hayes and Jill Goldsmith, "Exhibs' New Tech-ing Order," *Variety*, March 13–19, 2000, 9.

77 Ibid., 11, 12.

78 Tuck, "Projections of the Future," T3. The first feature digitally projected in commercial cinemas was *The Last Broadcast* (Lance Weiler and Stefan Avalos 1998) a year earlier. Continuing the experiment in e-cinema, the same film was distributed via satellite in October 1998. Stephen R. Bissette, "Letter: 'The Last Broadcast,'" *New York Times*, December 10, 2000, AR4.

79 Sabin, "The End/Restart," 22.

80 Melissa Morrison, "New Cinema Design," *Boxoffice*, March 2000, 24, 25, 26, 27, 28, 29.

81 Motion Picture Association of America, "Motion Picture Association Goals for Digital Cinema," http://www.mpaa.org/dcinema/dCinemaGoals.htm, 2000, last accessed May 1, 2002.

82 Ibid.

83 Clyde McKinney, "Poised for Takeoff: Boeing to Unveil Business Plan in Las Vegas," *Film Journal International*, March 2001, 82, 84.

84 One manager claimed that exhibitors expect distributors' representatives to be checking their films every weekend.

85 I do not have any evidence of exhibitors having considered this loss of control over textual flow; however, some already have their advertisements and announcements on video and slide projection apart from that of the feature presentation, effectively separating exhibitors' textual flow from that received from distributors. Additionally, I would not discount the possibility that the use of video projection for advertisements, infrequent as it may still be, is a way to gradually acclimatize audiences to a different visual standard for theatrical projections.

86 On this last point, some have begun to question the very idea of projection. For example, "Lasse Svanberg, Swedish Film Institute, asked 'Why do we even need projection? Is it just to mimic celluloid?', and suggested that new screen technologies using LCD and LED based solutions are likely to bring large screens at a fraction of the cost of digital projectors . . . and might actually eliminate the need for projectors altogether." "Digital 'Screen of the Future?' Used for Robbie Williams TV Spectacular," *Cinema Technology,* March 2002, 17.

87 "D-Cinema Yet to Take Over," *Playback,* January 21, 2002, 25, 26.

88 Peter Vamos, "Famous Goes Digital," *Playback,* January 10, 2000, 2. Signaling the slowdown in conversion, two years later Famous Players still had only these two original projectors installed. Reportedly, the first purchase of a digital projector was by Madstone Films, who installed it at Loews E-Walk in New York. "Madstone Becomes First Exhibitor to Purchase a DLP Cinema Projector," *Cinema Technology,* September 2001, 4. The first fully digital theater was TJOY Cinema in Hiroshima. " 'World's First' Digital Theater Is a Success 'Without Reels'," *Cinema Technology,* December 2001, 28.

89 "D-cinema Yet to Take Over," 25, 26.

90 As a sign of the kind of legal worries the film industry has about the possible pirating of digital film, WWE has been involved in litigation against unauthorized presentation of its PPV events for public consumption. Jason S. T. Kotler, "Direct to Supreme Court: Unscrambling Satellite Wars," *Playback,* August 6, 2001, 29.

91 "Electronic Cinema—One Year On," *Cinema Technology,* December 2000, 22, 23.

92 Mike Boone, "Wrestling Fans Thrown by Porn-Movie Scene," *Montreal Gazette,* February 29, 2000, A1, A2. Interestingly, the unintended pornographic broadcast appears to have an almost folkloric status as a tale of the fallibility of new technology and the deterioration of distinctions between the world of adults and that of children. McCarthy, *Ambient Television,* 12, for instance, refers to a similar incident when an angry employee replaced a soccer match with a pornographic film for twenty seconds on the TV system at an airport in Bangkok.

93 Nicolas Tittley, "Notes Musique," *Voir,* February 21, 2002, 30. Author's translation.

94 Martin-Pierre Duguay, "Technologies moderne," *Voir,* February 28, 2002, 5. This lackluster assessment might not have been the fault of the theatrecast itself, as reports circulated of extreme disappointment at the original event, which, as one reviewer put it, could have been easily reproduced at home with a videotape and some shadow puppets. Ben Rayner, " 'Virtual Band' an Interesting Failure," *Toronto Star,* February 25, 2002, 3; Joshua Ostroff, "Pop Go the Shadow Puppets," *Globe and Mail,* February 25, 2002, R5.

95 Canadian Corporate Newswire, "Famous Players: Gorillaz Larger than Live Series . . . First

Ever Theatre-Cast," Teledata Group, February 11, 2002. Famous Players is one of the few exhibitors testing such presentations, but it is not the only one. In fall 2000 a joint venture between Odeon and Quantum in the UK offered a digital projection of the Broadway musical *Putting It Together* at the Odeon Leicester Square. Its success led them to continue planning for further special-event presentations ranging from concerts to sporting events. "Odeon Digital Cinema—the Dawn of a New Era," *Cinema Technology,* March 2002, 4.

96   Toby Miller, Nitin Govil, John McMurria, and Richard Maxwell, *Global Hollywood,* 193.

97   John Belton, "Digital Cinema: A False Revolution," *October,* no. 100 (spring 2002): 99–114.

98   Godfrey Cheshire, "Letter: Expect a Shift to TV," *New York Times,* December 10, 2000, AR4.

99   Godfrey Cheshire, "The Death of Film and the Decay of Cinema," "The Death of Film?—A Millennial Symposium," Museum of Modern Art, Department of Film and Video, January 11, 2000.

100 Stanley Kauffmann, "Fade-Out?," *New Republic,* September 6, 1999, 28, 30.

101 Walter Murch, "A Digital Cinema of the Mind? Could Be," *New York Times,* May 2, 1999, section 2A, 1.

102 Doug Saunders, "Is Film Dead?," *Globe and Mail,* January 31, 2002, R1, R3.

103 Sabin, "The End/Restart," 1.

104 Ibid., 22.

105 Ibid.

106 Mark MacKinnon, "Imax Buys High-Tech Projector Maker," *Globe and Mail,* September 8, 1999, B5.

107 Annlee Ellingson, "Surf's Up: Exhibition Comes to the World Wide Web," *Boxoffice,* September 1999, http://www.boxoffice.com/issues/sept99/sept99story2.html, last accessed November 22, 2000.

108 Marc Graser and Paul Sweeting, "Get Ready for Piracy.com," *Variety,* November 1–7, 1999, 1, 107.

109 Annlee Ellingson, "New Technologies: Digital Cinema: Titan DC," *Boxoffice,* October 2000, 58.

110 Paul Sweeting, "Top Vid Chains Nurture 'Net Eggs,'" *Variety,* November 8–14, 1999, 17, 26.

111 Monte Williams, "The Art of the Grand Old Cinemas, the Science of the New," *New York Times,* August 13, 2000, WK 3.

112 Jill Goldsmith, "Exhibs Fishin' for Intermission," *Variety,* August 28–September 3, 2000, 9, 123; Keith Damsell, "Darkened Screens Loom for Cineplex Odeon," *Globe and Mail,* August 29, 2000, B1, B4; Loews Cineplex Entertainment, "News Release—12/8/2000—Announces Extension of Waiver under its Credit Facility to January 26, 2001," *Canadian News-Wire,* 2000, http://www.newswire.ca/releases/December2000, last accessed January 24, 2001.

113 "IMAX says Cinema Sector Turmoil Will Stunt Growth," *Globe and Mail,* January 13, 2001, B9.

114 Daniela Deane, "Multiplexes Glut the American Marketplace," *Montreal Gazette,* September 30, 2000, D3.

115 Editorial, "Theatre of the Overextended," *Globe and Mail,* August 30, 2000, A12.

116 Daniela Deane, "Multiplexes Glut the American Marketplace," D3.

117 "EDI Box Office News: Inventory Falls for Bigscreens," *Variety,* January 15–21, 2001, 34; "EDI Box Office News: Theaters Downsize in 2001," 22.

118 Loews Cineplex Entertainment, "News Release—1/22/2001—Announces Financial Results for Third Quarter," *Canadian NewsWire,* 2001, http://www.newswire.ca/releases/January 2001, last accessed January 24, 2001.

119 Keith Damsell, "Cineplex Closings Seen as Rebirth," *Globe and Mail,* February 19, 2001, B1, B5.

120 Andy Hoffman, "Quebec Indie Takes on Majors, *Playback,* July 13, 1998, 1.

121 Ibid., 22.

122 Ibid.

123 Michael Posner, "Cineplex CEO Blasts Collusion Charges," *Globe and Mail,* December 20, 2000, B7.

124 Randy Cohen, "Throwing a Curve," *New York Times Magazine,* December 24, 2000, 18.

125 Quoted in Miriam Hansen, "Early Cinema, Late Cinema," 202.

NINE. CINEMAGOING AS "FELT INTERNATIONALISM"

1 Roland Barthes, "Upon Leaving a Movie Theatre," in *Apparatus,* ed. Theresa Hak Kyung Cha (New York: Tanam, 1979:1981), 1–4.

2 Oskar Negt and Alexander Kluge, "The Public Sphere and Experience: Selections," trans. Peter Labanyi, *October* 46 (fall 1988 [1972]): 65.

3 Miriam Hansen, "Early Cinema, Late Cinema."

4 Ien Ang, "In the Realm of Uncertainty: The Global Village and Capitalist Postmodernity," in *Living Room Wars: Rethinking Media Audiences for a Postmodern World* (New York: Routledge, 1996), 162–80.

5 Cees J. Hamelink, *Cultural Autonomy in Global Communications* (New York: Longman, 1983).

6 Benedict Anderson, *Imagined Communities: Reflections on the Origin and Spread of Nationalism* (New York: Verso, 1991), 22–36.

7 Peter DeCherney, "Cult of Attention: An Introduction to Seymour Stern and Harry Allan Potamkin (Contra Kracauer) on the Ideal Movie Theater," *Spectator* 18, no. 2 (spring/summer, 1998): 23.

8 Ibid., 24; Siegfried Kracauer, "Cult of Distraction," in *The Mass Ornament,* ed. and trans. Thomas Y. Levin (Cambridge: Harvard University Press, 1995 [1927]), 325.

9 Kracauer, "Cult of Distraction," 326.

10 Ibid.

11 Ulf Hannerz, "Cosmopolitans and Locals in World Culture," in *Global Culture: Nationalism, Globalization, and Modernity,* ed. Mike Featherstone (Newbury Park: Sage, 1990), 239.

12 John Hartley, *The Politics of Pictures: The Creation of the Public in the Age of Popular Media* (New York: Routledge, 1992); Arjun Appadurai, *Modernity at Large.*

13 Timothy Brennan, *At Home in the World: Cosmopolitanism Now* (Cambridge: Harvard University Press, 1994).

14 Bruce Robbins, *Feeling Global: Internationalism in Distress* (New York: New York University Press, 1999), 5.

15 Ibid., 6.

16 Ibid., 45.

17 Ibid., 154.

18 Marcia Landy, *Film, Politics, and Gramsci,* 28.

19 Saskia Sassen, "Whose City Is It? Globalization and the Formation of New Claims," *Public Culture* 8, no. 2 (winter 1996): 221.

20 Ibid., 210.

21 See David B. Clarke, ed., *The Cinematic City* (New York: Routledge, 1997), and Tony Fitzmaurice and Mark Shiel, eds. *Cinema and the City: Film and Urban Societies in a Global Context* (Oxford: Blackwell, 2000).

22 Ulf Hannerz, "Cosmopolitans and Locals in World Culture."

23 Ibid., 238.

24 Ibid., 239.

25 Lawrence Grossberg, "Wandering Audiences, Nomadic Critics," in *Bringing It All Back Home: Essays on Cultural Studies* (Durham: Duke University Press, 1997 [1988]), 313. See also Meaghan Morris, "At Henry Parkes Motel," *Cultural Studies* 2, no. 1(1988): 1–47.

26 Grossberg, "Wandering Audiences, Nomadic Critics," 313.

27 Cf. Raymond Williams, *Marxism and Literature* (New York: Oxford University Press, 1977).

28 Laila Fulton, "10-Screen Complex for Calgary," *Calgary Herald,* February 26, 1997, C7.

29 Susan Bourette and Michael Grange, "Mega-Complex Coming to a Theatre Near You," B1.

"1985 Chronology of Major Industry Events." *Boxoffice*, April 1986, 14, 15.

"1986 Chronology of Major Industry Events." *Boxoffice*, April 1987, 13, 14.

"1987 Chronology of Major Industry Events." *Boxoffice*, May 1988, 22, 24.

AC Nielsen EDI. "School Holiday Calendar." www.entdata.com. Last accessed June 23, 2002.

Acland, Charles R. "IMAX in Canadian Cinema: Geographic Transformation and Discourses of Nationhood." *Studies in Cultures, Organizations, and Societies* 3 (1997): 289–305.

——. "IMAX Technology and the Tourist Gaze." *Cultural Studies* 12, no. 3 (1998): 429–445.

——. "Mapping the Serious and the Dangerous: Film and the National Council of Education, 1920–1939." *Cinéma* 6, no. 1 (1995): 101–118.

——. "National Dreams, International Encounters: The Formation of Canadian Film Culture in the 1930s." *Canadian Journal of Film Studies* 3, no. 1 (1994): 3–26.

——. "Patterns of Cultural Authority: The National Film Society of Canada and the Institutionalization of Film Education, 1938–1941." *Canadian Journal of Film Studies* 10, no. 1 (2001): 2–27.

Adilman, Sid. "Canada Can't Get Enough Camcorders." *Variety*, April 8, 1991, 46.

——. "Canadian Distrib Fund Proves Success; Helps Int'l Pick-Ups." *Variety Cannes '89*. Special issue. May 3–9, 1989, 461, 495.

——. "Canadian Distribs Shut Out of Pics: Sellers Fear Upsetting U.S." *Variety*, May 20, 1987, 3, 39.

——. "Cineplex Odeon Circuit to Add 200 Canadian Screens thru '88." *Variety*, July 2, 1986, 6, 27.

——. "The Man Behind the Multiplex, and Cineplex." *Variety*, April 26–May 2, 1989, 50, 84, 86.

——. "MPAA Pact with Quebec Govt. Lets Locals Handle More Pics." *Variety*, October 29, 1986, 7, 45.

——. "Quebec Opening Door to Yank Majors, Toronto Distribs Will Be Shut Out." *Variety*, February 3, 1988, 5, 31.

——. "Thou 'Art' the Only Cinema Chain in U.S., Canada to Seek Original Pieces." *Variety Cannes '89: Special Issue*, May 3–9, 1989, 463, 499.

——. "Valenti Says Agreement with Quebec Government Suits Singular Situation." *Variety*, October 29, 1986, 7.

Advertisement for *The Insider. Montreal Gazette,* November 12, 1999, D8.

Advertisement for *Twister. Globe and Mail,* May 24, 1996, C4.

Aksoy, Asu, and Kevin Robins. "Hollywood for the 21st Century: Global Competition for Critical Mass in Image Markets." *Cambridge Journal of Economics* 16 (1992): 1–22.

Albanese, Alex. "The Shape of Things to Come?" *Boxoffice,* March 1995, SW-16, SW-17, SW-18.

"Alberta Gets International Distributor." *Playback,* June 27, 1988, 3.

Allen, Jeanne. "The Film Viewer as Consumer." *Quarterly Review of Film Studies,* 5, no. 4 (1980): 481–499.

Allen, Robert C. "From Exhibition to Reception: Reflections on the Audience in Film History." *Screen* 31, no. 4 (1990): 347–356.

Alliance Atlantis Communications Inc. 1999 Annual Report. Toronto, 1999.

Allor, Martin. "Relocating the Site of the Audience." *Critical Studies in Mass Communication* 5 (1988): 217–233.

"AMC Goes Global." *Boxoffice,* January 1993, 40.

"AMC Skein to Add Sites in Inner Cities and Globally." *Variety,* September 21, 1992, 15.

" 'American' Violence." *Boxoffice,* March 1992.

Anderson, Benedict. *Imagined Communities: Reflections on the Origin and Spread of Nationalism,* revised edition. New York: Verso, 1991.

Anderson, Christopher. *Hollywood TV: The Studio System in the Fifties.* Austin: University of Texas Press, 1994.

Ang, Ien. "Cultural Studies, Media Reception, and the Transnational Media System." In *Living Room Wars: Rethinking Media Audiences for a Postmodern World,* 133–149. New York: Routledge, 1996.

——. *Desperately Seeking the Audience.* New York: Routledge, 1991.

——. "In the Realm of Uncertainty: The Global Village and Capitalist Postmodernity." In *Living Room Wars: Rethinking Media Audiences for a Postmodern World,* 162–180. New York: Routledge, 1996.

Appadurai, Arjun. *Modernity at Large: Cultural Dimensions of Globalization.* Minneapolis: University of Minnesota Press, 1996.

Arched, Army, and Suzan Ayscough. " 'Poetic' Violence Surfaces." *Variety,* August 9, 1993, 11, 14.

Argy, Stephanie. "Changes in Tech Toys Help Pix Look, Sound their Best." *Variety,* December 22–January 4, 1997/8, 42, 50.

——. "High-Tech Add-Ons Usher in 'New Wave' of Filmgoing." *Variety,* March 16–22, 1998, 50.

"Arizona Exhib in Midst of Two Major Antitrust Offensives." *Variety,* December 10, 1986, 40.

Armstrong, Mary Ellen. "Are Exhibitors Doing Their Share?" *Playback,* May 6, 1996, 22.

——. "Expansion and Change." *Playback,* May 19, 1997, 8, 14.

——. "Service, Disney Style." *Playback,* May 19, 1997, 8.

Arnold, Robert F. "Film Space/Audience Space: Notes Toward a Theory of Spectatorship." *Velvet Light Trap* 25 (spring 1990): 44–52.

"Astral Bellevue and G&W Talking Joint Distribbery." *Variety,* November 19, 1986, 5.

Attallah, Paul. "Narrowcasting: Home Video and DBS." In *The Cultural Industries in Canada: Problems, Policies, and Prospects,* ed. Michael Dorland, 257–279. Toronto: Lorimer, 1996.

Austin, Bruce A. "Home Video: The Second-Run 'Theater' of the 1990s." In *Hollywood in the Age of Television,* ed. Tino Balio, 319–349. Boston: Unwin Hyman, 1990.

——. *Immediate Seating: A Look at Movie Audiences.* Belmont, California: Wadsworth, 1989.

"Automated Ticket Vendor, 1st in U.S. Bows on Coast." *Variety,* April 11, 1990, 13.

"Average Cinema Admissions per Head." *Screen Digest,* September 1998, 205.

Avis, Tim. "Digital Revolution?" *Variety,* June 21–27, 1999, 45.

Ayscough, Suzan. "All Canada to Play by Quebec's Rules; U.S. Bigs Exempt from Distrib Law." *Variety,* September 28, 1988, 3.

——. "Canada Wants Euro Status for Distribbing." *Variety,* April 15, 1991, 51.

——. "Local Distribs Grabbing More BO." *Variety,* November 16, 1992, 42.

——. "Recession Divides the Distrib Waters." *Variety,* November 16, 1992, 46.

——. "Stronghold for Non-U.S. Fare Weakens." *Variety,* December 2, 1991, 74, 86.

Ayscough, Suzan, and Judy Brennan. "Will Movie Meccas Do the Right Thing?" *Variety,* July 12, 1993, 1, 69.

Baker, Laura. "Screening Race: Responses to Theater Violence at *New Jack City* and *Boyz N the Hood.*" *Velvet Light Trap* 44, no. 3 (1999): 4–19.

Balides, Constance. "Jurassic Post-Fordism: Tall Tales of Economics in the Theme Park." *Screen* 41, no. 2 (summer 2000): 139–160.

Balio, Tino. " 'A Major Presence in All of the World's Important Markets': The Globalization of Hollywood in the 1990s." In *Contemporary Hollywood Cinema,* ed. Steve Neale and Murray Smith, 58–73. New York: Routledge, 1998.

——. *United Artists: The Company that Changed the Film Industry.* Madison: University of Wisconsin Press, 1987.

——, ed. *Hollywood in the Age of Television.* Boston: Unwin Hyman, 1990.

"Barometer '92: 1991 Year in Review." *Boxoffice,* March 1992, 12, 13.

"Barometer '94: 1993 Year in Review." *Boxoffice,* March 1994, 18, 19, 22.

"Barometer '95: 1994 in Review: National Headlines." *Boxoffice,* March 1995, 18, 19.

"Barometer '96: 1995 in Review: National Headlines." *Boxoffice,* March 1996, 28, 29, 30.

Bart, Peter. "Bite-Sized Reality." *Variety,* July 12, 1993, 3, 5.

——. *The Gross: The Hits, the Flops—the Summer that Ate Hollywood.* New York: St. Martin's Press, 1999.

——. "View from the War Room." *Variety,* May 27, 1991, 3, 102.

Barthes, Roland. "Upon Leaving a Movie Theatre." In *Apparatus,* ed. Theresz Hak and Kyung Cha, 1–4. New York: Tanam, 1981 (1979).

Baudrillard, Jean. *Simulations.* Trans. Paul Foss, Paul Patton, and Philip Beitchman. New York: Semiotext(e), 1983.

Beaupré, Lee. "How to Distribute a Film." In *The Hollywood Film Industry,* ed. Paul Kerr, 185–203. New York: Routledge and Kegan Paul, 1986 (1977).

Becker, Mark. "Stepping Up Cinema Security." *Variety,* July 22, 1991, 13.

Belton, John. "Digital Cinema: A False Revolution." *October,* no. 100 (spring 2002): 99–114.

——. *Widescreen Cinema.* Cambridge: Harvard University Press, 1992.

Benjamin, Walter. "The Work of Art in the Age of Mechanical Reproduction." In *Illuminations,* ed. Hannah Arendt and trans. Harry Zohn, 217–251. New York: Schocken, 1968 (1936).

Berland, Jody. "Space at the Margins: Critical Theory and Colonial Space after Innis." In *Harold Innis in the New Century: Reflections and Refractions,* ed. Charles R. Acland and William J. Buxton, 281–308. Montreal: McGill-Queen's University Press, 1999.

Birchenough, Tom. "Slow Progress for Soviets." *Variety,* June 15–21, 1998, 82.

Bird, S. Elizabeth. "Travels in Nowhere Land: Ethnography and the 'Impossible' Audience." *Critical Studies in Mass Communication* 9, no. 3 (1992): 250–260.

Bissette, Stephen R. "Letter: 'The Last Broadcast'." *New York Times,* December 10, 2000, AR 4.

Blanchard, Simon. "Cinema-Going, Going, Gone?" *Screen* 24, no. 4/5 (1983): 108–113.

Blickstein, Jay. "Small-Town Dixie Chain on Exhib Fast Track." *Variety,* March 30, 1992, 51, 64, 66.

Blumenthal, Sidney. *The Permanent Campaign: Inside the World of Elite Political Operatives.* Boston: Beacon, 1980.

Boddy, William. *Fifties Television: The Industry and Its Critics.* Champaign: University of Illinois Press, 1990.

Boone, Mike. "Wrestling Fans Thrown by Porn-Movie Scene." *Montreal Gazette,* February 29, 2000, A1, A2.

Bourdieu, Pierre. *Distinction: A Social Critique of the Judgment of Taste.* Trans. Richard Nice. Cambridge: Harvard University Press, 1984.

——. *In Other Words: Essays Towards a Reflexive Sociology.* Trans. Matthew Adamson. Stanford: Stanford University Press, 1990.

Bourette, Susan, and Michael Grange. "Mega-Complex Coming to a Theatre Near You: Famous Players to Unveil 'A New Level of Movie-Going Experience'." *Globe and Mail,* August 28, 1995, B1, B2.

Brehl, Robert. "Famous Players Signs Up for 10 Imax 3-D Theatres." *Globe and Mail,* February 5, 1998, B8.

Brennan, Timothy. *At Home in the World: Cosmopolitanism Now.* Cambridge: Harvard University Press, 1997.

Brent, Willie. "China Opens but Film Supply Still Closed." *Variety,* November 30–December 6, 1998, 34.

Brill, Louis M. "Megaplex Rising." *Boxoffice,* November 1994, 44, 46, 48, 50.

Brodie, John. "Coming Soon to a Theater Near You: TV Trailers." *Variety,* August 31, 1992, 20.

Brookman, Faye. "Trailers: The Big Business of Drawing Crowds." *Variety,* June 13, 1990, 48.

"Buena Vista Opens Disney Distrib Subsidiary in Toronto." *Playback,* November 28, 1988, 40.

Busch, Anita. "ShoWest's Growing Pains." *Variety,* March 13–19, 1995, 7, 14.

Cajuiero, Marcelo. "Cinemark Targets Brazil with 6 Plexes." *Variety,* April 6–12, 1998, 17.

Cameron, James. "The Role of Exhibition in the Information Age." *Boxoffice,* October 1995, 11.

"Canada Limits U.S. Majors Unless They Hold World Rights." *Variety,* February 18, 1987, 1, 128.

"Canada Vows to Pass Legislation Curbing Power of U.S. Distribs Despite Bilateral Free Trade Pact." *Variety,* November 25, 1987, 43, 60, 62.

Canadian Corporate Newswire. "Famous Players: Gorillaz Larger than Live Series . . . First ever Theatre-cast." Teledata Group, February 11, 2002.

"Canadian Giants of Exhibition." *Boxoffice,* May 1999, 42.

"Canadian Giants of Exhibition." *Boxoffice,* July 2000, 34, 35.

Carmike Cinemas. "Carmike Corporate History," www.carmike.com, 2002. Last accessed July 10, 2002.

Carter, Nancy. "Tom Moyer's Luxury Theatres Opens Dazzling Ten-Plex." *Boxoffice*, March 1987, 88, 89.

Carveth, Rod. "The Reconstruction of the Global Media Marketplace." *Communication Research* 19, no. 6 (December 1992): 705–723.

Caughie, John. "Playing at Being American: Games and Tactics." In *Logics of Television: Essays in Cultural Criticism*, ed. Patricia Mellencamp, 44–58. Bloomington: Indiana University Press, 1990.

Cernetig, Miro. "Hooray for Brollywood." *Globe and Mail*, May 13, 1995, D1, D3.

Certeau, Michel de. *The Practice of Everyday Life*. Trans. Steve Rendall. Berkeley: University of California Press, 1984.

Chaivoraporn, Anchalee. "Thai Film Prod'n Suffers." *Variety*, November 30–December 6, 1998, 42.

Charney, Leo, and Vanessa R. Schwartz, eds. *Cinema and the Invention of Modern Life*. Berkeley: University of California Press, 1995.

Cheshire, Godfrey. "The Death of Film and the Decay of Cinema." *The Death of Film? A Millenial Symposium*. Museum of Modern Art, Department of Film and Video, January 11, 2000.

——. "Letter: Expect a Shift to TV." *New York Times*, December 10, 2000, AR 4.

Christian, Jacqueline. "Modernization Means Money." *Variety*, June 15–21, 1998, 56.

Chronis, George T. " 'Eau' Canada!" *Boxoffice*, April 1994, 24, 26, 28.

Cieply, Michael, and Leonard Zehr. "MCA Agrees to Buy 33% of Cineplex for $106.7 Million." *Wall Street Journal*, January 16, 1986, 8.

"Cinemas Need a Personal Touch." *Playback*, November 10, 1986, 1.

"Cineplex Readies Montreal Fourplex." *Variety*, November 26, 1986, 7.

Clark, Jennifer. "Italy: Setting Houses in Order after Decades of Neglect." *Variety*, June 29, 1992, 62.

Clarke, David B., ed. *The Cinematic City*. New York: Routledge, 1997.

Clarke, John. *New Times and Old Enemies: Essays on Cultural Studies and America*. London: HarperCollins, 1991.

"CO Completes Buy of 152 Screens in Western Canada." *Variety*, February 7, 1990, 24.

Cohen, Randy. "Throwing a Curve." *New York Times Magazine*. December 24, 2000, 18.

Cohen, Lawrence. "Big-Buck Scorecard, 1986–1988." *Variety*, January 11–17, 1989, 30.

——. "Fast-Lane Releases Are Short on Legs." *Variety*, July 12, 1993, 3, 5.

——. "Fewer Plexes but More Multi, Sites Down, Screens Up as Boom Fades." *Variety*, October 29, 1990, 1, 76.

——. "It's Still Paying to Play the Movies: Majors Recouped Costs on '87 Pix." *Variety*, March 2, 1988, 3, 115.

——. "New Economy of Scale in Hollywood: Majors' Buys Wide-Reaching." *Variety*, January 14, 1987, 7, 44.

——. "Overproduction Hurts Distribs: But Theatrical Playoff a Must for Credibility." *Variety*, February 25, 1987, 1, 86, 98.

——. "Overseas Pics Grow at L.A. Mart: 25% of Films from Outside U.S." *Variety*, February 19, 1986, 3, 340.

Collins, Richard. *Culture, Communication, and National Identity: The Case of Canadian Television.* Toronto: University of Toronto Press, 1990.

——. "National Culture: A Contradiction in Terms?" *Canadian Journal of Communication* 16 (1991): 225–238.

Conlogue, Ray. "Taking a Stand for the Cinematic National Soul." *Globe and Mail,* December 21, 1993, C1, C2.

Corbett, Kevin J. "The Big Picture: Theatrical Moviegoing, Digital Television, and Beyond the Substitution Effect." *Cinema Journal* 40, no. 2 (2001): 17–34.

Cox, Dan. "H'wood Hunts 'the Great Idea'." *Variety,* February 2–8, 1998, 1, 52, 53, 54.

Crary, Jonathan. *Techniques of the Observer: On Vision and Modernity in the Nineteenth Century.* Cambridge: MIT Press, 1990.

Crawford, Margaret. "The World in a Shopping Mall." In *Variations on a Theme Park: The New American City and the End of Public Space,* ed. Michael Sorkin, 3–30. New York: Hill and Wang, 1992.

Cunha, Uma da. "WB Scraps Multiplex Project." *Variety,* September 11–17, 1995, 41.

Cunningham, Stuart. *Featuring Australia: The Cinema of Charles Chauvel.* Sydney: Allen and Unwin, 1991.

Cuthbert, Pamela. "Cinepix Takes Over." *Playback,* August 29, 1994, 1, 17.

——. "Distributors Post Record Results." *Playback,* February 13, 1995, P-6.

——. "PolyGram Controversy Escalates." *Playback,* September 23, 1996, 1.

——. "Two-way." *Playback,* March 28, 1994, 1.

"Daily Variety Editor Predicts Exhib Crisis." *Variety,* March 2, 1988, 8, 114.

Damsell, Keith. "Cineplex Closings Seen as Rebirth." *Globe and Mail,* February 19, 2001, B1, B5.

——. "Darkened Screens Loom for Cineplex Odeon." *Globe and Mail,* August 29, 2000, B1, B4.

——. "Michael Jackson Invests in Montreal Film Company." *Globe and Mail,* February 26, 2002, B2.

"Databox." *Screen Digest,* September 1999, 19.

"Dateline 1997: Charting Our Year's Hottest News and Quotes." *Boxoffice,* March 1998, 36, 37, 38, 39.

"Dateline 1998: Charting Our Year's Hottest News and Quotes." *Boxoffice,* March 1999, 21–25.

Davis, Susan G. "The Theme Park: Global Industry and Cultural Form." *Media, Culture and Society* 18, no. 3 (1996): 399–422.

Dawes, Amy. "Global Batmania Lifts Warners to Foreign Mark; Success Mirrors 1989 U.S. Results; Firm Cites Euro Screen Proliferation." *Variety,* February 28, 1990, 7, 16.

Dawtrey, Adam. "Euros Go on Screen-Building Spree." *Variety,* February 6–12, 1995, 1, 15.

——. "Is Planetary Pic Peddling Passe?" *Variety,* October 30–November 5, 1995, 1, 182.

Dayan, Daniel, and Elihu Katz. *Media Events: The Live Broadcasting of History.* Cambridge: Harvard University Press, 1992.

"D-cinema Yet to Take Over." *Playback,* January 21, 2002, 25, 26.

Deane, Daniela. "Multiplexes Glut the American Marketplace." *Montreal Gazette,* September 30, 2000, D3.

DeCherney, Peter. "Cult of Attention: An Introduction to Seymour Stern and Harry Allan Potamkin (Contra Kracauer) on the Ideal Movie Theater." *Spectator* 18, no. 2 (spring/summer 1998): 18–25.

Derfel, Aaron. "U.S. Movie Chain for Forum." *Montreal Gazette,* August 13, 1996, A1, A9.

Dempsey, John. "Theatricals Rate Second Look." *Variety,* September 20–26, 1999, 33, 39.

"Digital Movies Released for DLP Projectors." *Film Journal International,* March 2001, 88.

"Digital 'Screen of the Future?' Used for Robbie Williams TV Spectacular." *Cinema Technology,* March 2002, 17.

Diorio, Carl. "Distrib Jury Still Out on Day-&-Date Releases; Tactic Best for Event Pix; Others need U.S. Buzz." Variety.com, June 25, 2002. Last accessed June 26, 2002.

"Distribs Exhort Exhibs to Try to Increase Viewer Satisfaction." *Variety,* February 19, 1986, 11.

"Distribs Go Crazy for New Canadian Fund; But That Pot's Not All Honey." *Variety,* November 23, 1988, 37.

"Distribution Revenue Rising." *Screen Digest,* June 1998, 134.

Dorland, Michael. *So Close to the State/s: The Emergence of Canadian Feature Film Policy.* Toronto: University of Toronto Press, 1998.

——. "Theses on Canadian Nationalism: In Memoriam George P. Grant." *Cineaction* 16 (1988): 3–5.

"Doubt Clouds Canada's Film Future." *Calgary Herald,* September 9, 1997, C3.

Dowler, Kevin. "The Cultural Industries Policy Apparatus." In *The Cultural Industries in Canada: Problems, Policies, and Prospects,* ed. Michael Dorland, 328–346. Toronto: Lorimer, 1996.

Drabinsky, Garth. "New Strategies for the Future: Two Challenges Facing Exhibition, Part 1." *Boxoffice,* February 1988, 10, 11.

——. "New Strategies for the Future: Two Challenges Facing Exhibition, Part 2." *Boxoffice,* March 1988, 81, 82.

Drainie, Bronwyn. "Finally, a Canadian Movie that Ranks at the Top." *Globe and Mail,* February 22, 1996, A14.

Duguay, Martin-Pierre. "Technologies moderne." *Voir,* February 28, 2002, 5.

During, Simon. "Popular Culture on a Global Scale: A Challenge for Cultural Studies?" *Critical Inquiry,* no. 23 (1997): 808–833.

Eckler, Rebecca. "Curtain Set to Rise: Theatre Complex Hopes to Entice the Entire Family." *Calgary Herald,* July 17, 1996, C7.

Edgerton, Gary R. *American Film Exhibition and an Analysis of the Motion Picture Industry's Market Structure, 1963–1980.* London: Garland, 1983.

"EDI Box Office News: A Decade of Limited Releases." *Variety,* February 23–March 1, 1998, 42.

"EDI Box Office News: Inventory Falls for Big Screens." *Variety,* January 15–21, 2001, 34.

"EDI Box Office News: More New Screens in 1997." *Variety,* January 19–23, 1998.

"EDI Box Office News: More Shelf Space for Films." *Variety,* January 5–11, 1998, 30.

"EDI Box Office News: Wide, Wider, Widest." *Variety,* January 26–February 1, 1998.

"EDI Box Office News: Theaters Downsize in 2001." *Variety,* January 7–13, 2002, 22.

Edmunds, Marlene. "Competitors Ramp Up to Greet 'Superbrand'." *Variety,* June 15–21, 1998, 62, 66.

——. "Kinepolis Keeps the Plexes Coming." *Variety,* June 15–21, 1998, 74.

——. "Moviegoing Hits New High." *Variety,* June 15–21, 1998, 74.

——. "No Plex Unturned in Nordic Hardtop Frenzy." *Variety,* February 9–15, 1998, 66.

Edmunds, Marlene, and Adam Dawtrey. "Cinema Expo Stirs Exhib-Distrib Debate." *Variety,* July 1–14, 1996, 7, 17.

"Edwards Gargantuplex." *Boxoffice,* April 1995, 124.

"Electronic Cinema—One Year On." *Cinema Technology,* December 2000, 22, 23.

Eller, Claudia. "Theater Giant Warms Up to Disney's Big Ad Chill." *Variety,* March 28, 1990, 7.

Ellingson, Annlee. "New Technologies: Digital Cinema; Titan DC." *Boxoffice,* October 2000, 58, 59.

——. "Surf's Up: Exhibition Comes to the World Wide Web." *Boxoffice,* September 1999. http://www.boxoffice.com/issues/sept99/sept99story2.html. Last accessed November 22, 2000.

Ellis, David. *Split Screen: Home Entertainment and New Technologies.* Toronto: Friends of Canadian Broadcasting, 1992.

Ellis, John. *Visible Fictions: Cinema, Television, Video.* Boston: Routledge and Kegan Paul, 1982.

Elsaesser, Thomas. *New German Cinema: A History.* New Brunswick: Rutgers University Press, 1989.

Enchin, Harvey. "Alliance Extends International Reach in Film Distribution." *Globe and Mail,* September 24, 1997, B1, B8.

——. "Canadians Going Back to the Movies." *Globe and Mail,* July 11, 1996, B1, B4.

——. "Chain Reaction: Exhibitor Is Ready for Coming Attractions." *Variety,* December 9–15, 1996, 55, 56.

——. "Coliseum: Theater in the Round." *Variety,* December 9–15, 1996, 56.

——. "Deal Creates Box Office Giant." *Globe and Mail,* October 1, 1997, B1, B14.

——. "Famous Players Striving to Get More People Out More Often." *Globe and Mail,* May 15, 1997, B7.

——. "The Lobby Is the Main Attraction." *Variety,* December 9–15, 1996, 58.

——. "PolyGram to Proceed with Film Company." *Globe and Mail,* March 14, 1997, B1, B6.

——. "Theatre Deal Highlights Market Fragmentation." *Globe and Mail,* October 3, 1997, B20.

"Euro Screen Growth: Multiplex Boom Continues." *Variety,* June 23–29, 1997, 53.

Evans, Greg. "Manhattan MovieFone Mania." *Variety,* January 24–30, 1994, 7, 19, 21.

——. "Showbiz Is Psyched for Cybermalls." *Variety,* March 27–April 2, 1995, 1, 90.

——. "Sony's NY 'Theme-plex' Stirs Exhibs' Interest." *Variety,* December 12–18, 1994, 9, 26.

Everett-Green, Robert. "Not Coming Soon to a Theatre Near You." *Globe and Mail,* January 18, 1997, C2.

"Exhibition Explodes in Asia." *Variety,* May 3, 1993, 37.

"Exhibition Looks to the Future." *Boxoffice,* December 1987, 33, 34, 35, 36, 37.

"Exhibs Gear for Multiplex Era." *Variety,* August 22–28, 1994, 41.

Eyles, Allen. "The Last Remaining Sites for UK Plexes." *Variety,* June 15–21, 1998, 49, 50.

——. "Megaplexing Comes to Great Britain." *Variety,* June 15–21, 1998, 50.

"Fabulous Fifty." *Boxoffice,* January 1999, 24.

"Fabulous Fifty." *Boxoffice,* January 2001, 40.

Famous Players Corporation. "Infokit, Historical Facts." www.famousplayers.com/fp_infokits.asp, 2000. Last accessed November 22, 2000.

"Famous Players Locks Out Staff." *Winnipeg Free Press*, February 13, 1995, B2.

"Famous Players Sets $C 50-Million Toronto Expansion." *Variety*, May 18, 1988, 39.

Featherstone, Mike. "Lifestyle and Consumer Culture." *Theory, Culture, and Society* 4 (1987): 55–70.

Feldman, Seth, ed. *Take Two: A Tribute to Film in Canada*. Toronto: Irwin, 1984.

Felski, Rita. "The Invention of Everyday Life." *New Formations* 39 (1999): 15–31.

Fitzmaurice, Tony, and Mark Shiel, eds. *Cinema and the City: Film and Urban Societies in a Global Context*. Oxford: Blackwell, 2000.

Fleming, Charles. "Snackbar Slowdown Bitter Pill for Exhibs." *Variety*, January 21, 1991, 3, 93.

Friedberg, Anne. *Window Shopping: Cinema and the Postmodern*. Berkeley: University of California Press, 1993.

Foucault, Michel. "Questions of Geography." In *Power/Knowledge*, ed. Colin Gordon, 63–77. New York: Pantheon, 1980 (1976).

——. "Two Lectures." In *Power/Knowledge*, ed. Colin Gordon, 77–108. New York: Pantheon, 1980 (1977).

Frook, John Evan. "Advance-Ticket Test Underway in Texas." *Variety*, May 11, 1992, 30.

——. "Chain Tests Distrib Waters." *Variety*, March 8, 1993, 50, 56.

——. "Exhib Bigs on PPV Pix: Not in My Theater." *Variety*, May 10, 1993, 26.

Fuller, Kathryn H. *At the Picture Show: Small-Town Audiences and the Creation of Movie Fan Culture*. Washington: Smithsonian Institution Press, 1996.

Fulton, Laila. "10-Screen Complex for Calgary." *Calgary Herald*, February 26, 1997, C7.

Gasher, Mike. "The Audiovisual Locations Industry in Canada: Considering British Columbia as Hollywood North." *Canadian Journal of Communication* 20 (1995): 231–254.

"Gen. Cinema Says VCRs Are a Help to Exhibition Biz." *Variety*, January 14, 1987, 7, 48.

Gilroy, Dan. "Harlem Unveils New Multiplex; First Theaters in Two Decades." *Variety*, December 10, 1986, 28.

Globerman, Steven. "Foreign Ownership of Feature Film Distribution and the Canadian Film Industry." *Canadian Journal of Communication* 16 (1991): 191–206.

Gold, Richard. "Globalization: Gospel for the '90s." *Variety*, May 2, 1990, S-1, S-104.

——. "No Exit? Studios Itch to Ditch Exhib Biz." *Variety*, October 8, 1990, 3, 84.

——. "U.S. Overscreened? Not for Mega-Hits." *Variety*, January 28, 1991, 60.

——. "U.S. Pix Tighten Global Grip: Major Studios Speed Up Their Foreign Openings to Synch with U.S. Push." *Variety*, August 22, 1990, 1, 96.

Goldsmith, Jill. "Exhibs Fishin' for Intermission." *Variety*, August 28–September 3, 2000, 9, 123.

——. "ShowEast: Who Picks Up the Digital Check?" *Variety*, October 25–31, 1999, 9, 16.

Gomery, Douglas. "Building a Movie Theatre Giant: The Rise of Cineplex Odeon." In *Hollywood in the Age of Television*, ed. Tino Balio, 377–391. Boston: Unwin Hyman, 1990.

——. "Hollywood Corporate Business Practice and Periodizing Contemporary Film History." In *Contemporary Hollywood Cinema*, ed. Steve Neale and Murray Smith, 47–57. New York: Routledge, 1998.

——. *The Hollywood Studio System*. New York: St. Martin's Press, 1986.

——. *Shared Pleasures: A History of Movie Presentation in the United States*. Madison: University of Wisconsin Press, 1992.

——. "U.S. Film Exhibition: The Formation of a Big Business." In *The American Film Industry*, ed. Tino Balio, 218–228. Madison: University of Wisconsin Press, 1985.

Gottdiener, Mark. *The Theming of America: Dreams, Visions, and Commercial Spaces*. Boulder: Westview, 1997.

Goyoaga, Beatriz. "Aussie Distrib Hoyts Enters Argentina." *Variety*, March 16–22, 1998, 19.

Gramsci, Antonio. *An Antonio Gramsci Reader: Selected Writings, 1916–1935*. Ed. and trans. David Forgacs. New York: Schocken, 1988.

——. *Selections from the Prison Notebooks of Antonio Gramsci*. Ed. and trans. Quintin Hoare and Geoffrey Nowell Smith. London: Lawrence and Wishart, 1971.

Graser, Marc, and Paul Sweeting. "Get Ready for Piracy.com." *Variety*, November 1–7, 1999, 1, 107.

Gray, Ann. *Video Playtime: The Gendering of a Leisure Technology*. London: Routledge, 1992.

Gray, Katti. "Screening Starts Before the Movie." *Newsday*, March 31, 1991. www.newsday.com. Last accessed August 20, 1998.

Green, Earl. "Canada Reinforcing Distrib Borders; Hefty Fines Face Import Violators." *Variety*, June 22, 1988, 5.

Greene, David A. "The Movie Mall: Selling Cinema at the New Megaplex." *Spin*. January 1998, 38, 39.

Griffin, Nancy, and Kim Masters. *Hit and Run: How Jon Peters and Peter Guber Took Sony for a Ride in Hollywood*. New York: Simon and Schuster, 1996.

Grossberg, Lawrence. "The Space of Culture, the Power of Space." In *The Post-Colonial Question: Common Skies, Divided Horizons*, ed. Iain Chambers and Lidia Curti, 169–188. New York: Routledge, 1996.

——. "Wandering Audiences, Nomadic Critics." In *Bringing It All Back Home: Essays on Cultural Studies*. Durham: Duke University Press, 1997 (1988).

Grove, Christopher. "Programming Screens is Multi-Complex Task for Theater Managers." *Variety*, March 16–22, 1998, 46.

Groves, Don. "Art Pix Plex Plan: Village Roadshow Establishing a Global Brand." *Variety*, October 19–25, 1998, 26.

——. "Aussie Exhibs Stretch Abroad." *Variety*, June 15–21, 1998, 78, 84.

——. "BO World Is Flat; Local Pix, Strong Dollar Hurt Yanks O'seas." Variety.com, June 11, 2002. Last accessed June 25, 2002.

——. "Boffo Year for Aussie Box Office." *Variety*, January 19–25, 1998, 21.

——. "Boffo Year for O'seas Markets." *Variety*, April 21–27, 1997, 9, 16.

——. "Boom Resounds Worldwide." *Variety*, June 29, 1992, 61.

——. "Exhib Battle Goes Global." *Variety*, July 26, 1993, 23, 32.

——. "Hoyts, GCC Merge Latin America Ops." *Variety*, August 3–9, 1998, 22.

——. "Hoyts Trims Expansion." *Variety*, November 23–29, 1998, 14.

——. "Megahits Push Global BO to Record High." *Variety*, December 16–22, 1996, 9, 14.

——. "Mergers Boost Hot Hoyts." *Variety*, February 23–March 1, 1998, 34.

——. "Multiplying Multiplexes." *Variety*, June 12–18, 1995, 42.

——. "New Multiplex Building Boom May Reshape Euro Film Biz." *Variety*, June 13, 1990, 1, 20, 21.

——. "Oz, Distribs, Exhibs Extract Peace Pact." *Variety*, August 3–9, 1998, 14.

———. "Pix Flash but Sides Clash at Oz Confab." *Variety,* August 24–30, 1998, 12.

———. "Plex Push Piques Overseas Exhib Ire." *Variety,* September 23–29, 1996, 17, 23.

———. "Prexy Predicts Global Golden Age." *Variety,* September 11–17, 1995, 56, 98.

———. "Reading Battles Aussie Biz in Multiplex Offerings." *Variety,* August 17–23, 1998, 16.

———. "TW Announces Co-Ventures for European Hardtops." *Variety,* May 27, 1991, 35, 39.

Guback, Thomas. "The Evolution of the Motion Picture Theatre Business in the 1980s." *Journal of Communication* 37, no. 2 (1987): 60–77.

———. *The International Film Industry.* Bloomington: Indiana University Press, 1969.

Gunning, Tom. "An Aesthetic of Astonishment: Early Film and the (In)Credulous Spectator." In *Viewing Positions: Ways of Seeing Film,* ed. Linda Williams, 114–133. New Brunswick: Rutgers University Press, 1997 (1989).

Hall, Stuart. "The 'Rediscovery' of Ideology: Return of the Repressed in Media Studies." In *Culture, Society, and the Media,* ed. Michael Gurevitch, Tony Bennett, James Curran, and Janet Woollacott, 56–90. London: Sage, 1982.

———. "Signification, Representation, Ideology: Althusser and the Post-Structuralist Debates." *Critical Studies in Mass Communication* 2, no. 2 (1985): 91–114.

Hamelink, Cees J. *Cultural Autonomy in Global Communications.* New York: Longman, 1983.

Handel, Leo A. *Hollywood Looks at Its Audience: A Report on Film Audience Research.* Urbana: University of Illinois Press, 1950.

Hannerz, Ulf. "Cosmopolitans and Locals in World Culture." In *Global Culture: Nationalism, Globalization, and Modernity,* ed. Mike Featherstone, 237–251. Newbury Park, California: Sage, 1990.

Hannigan, John. *Fantasy City: Pleasure and Profit in the Post Modern Metropolis.* New York: Routledge, 1998.

Hansen, Miriam. *Babel and Babylon: Spectatorship in American Silent Film.* Cambridge: Harvard University Press, 1991.

———. "Early Cinema, Late Cinema: Permutations of the Public Sphere." *Screen* 34, no. 3 (autumn 1993): 197–210.

Hanson, Stuart. "Spoilt for Choice? Multiplexes in the 90's." In *British Cinema of the 90's,* ed. R. Murphy, 48–59, London: Routledge, 2000.

Harcourt, Peter. *A Canadian Journey: Conversations with Time.* Ottawa: Oberon, 1994.

———. "The Invisible Cinema." *CineTracts* 1, no. 4 (1978): 48–49.

Harris, Christopher. "Alliance Deal Opens Doors." *Playback,* April 18, 1988, 3.

———. "Faith in Popcorn." *Globe and Mail,* May 10, 1997, C3.

———. "Quebec Law Has Distribs Angered." *Playback,* October 3, 1988, 1, 5.

———. "Support Our Own, Says Cineplex Head." *Playback,* May 14, 1990, 3.

Harris, Paul. "MPAA Puts '88 BO at Peak of $4.46-Bil; Aud Gets Older." *Variety,* February 15–21, 1989, 1, 4.

Hartley, John. *The Politics of Pictures: The Creation of the Public in the Age of Popular Media.* New York: Routledge, 1992.

Hay, James. "Piecing Together What Remains of the Cinematic City." In *The Cinematic City,* ed. David B. Clarke, 209–229. New York: Routledge, 1997.

Hayes, Dade. "Grant vs. Goliath in Summer Gamble." *Variety,* March 10, 2002, 16.

———. "Pix Take Slow Road to BO Success 'Tenenbaums,' 'Gosford' Hold a Platform Party." *Variety,* January 29, 2002, 12, 14.

Hayes, Dade, and Jill Goldsmith. "Exhibs' New Tech-ing Order." *Variety,* March 13–19, 2000, 9, 11, 12.

Hayward, Susan. "Framing National Cinemas." In *Cinema and Nation,* ed. Mette Hjort and Scott MacKenzie, 88–102. New York: Routledge, 2000.

Hebdige, Dick. "Towards a Cartography of Taste, 1935–1962." In *Hiding in the Light: On Images and Things,* 45–76. New York: Routledge, 1988.

"Here Come the Global Moguls; Newest H'wood Invaders are Building, Not Buying." *Variety,* October 21, 1991, 1, 94.

Herskovitz, Jon. "Japanese Biz Thriving in Face of Economic Troubles." *Variety,* November 30– December 6, 1998, 32.

———. "Virgin Bows 14-Screen Megaplex in Japan; Move Puts Exhib on Map." Variety.com, April 26, 1999. Last accessed June 26, 2002.

Higson, Andrew. "The Concept of National Cinema." *Screen* 30, no. 4 (1989): 345–347.

———. "The Limiting Imagination of National Cinema." In *Cinema and Nation,* ed. Mette Hjort and Scott MacKenzie, 63–74. New York: Routledge, 2000.

Hils, Miriam. "Busy BO Propels Building." *Variety,* June 15–21, 1998, 52.

———. "Plex Mentality Causes Concern." *Variety: Global Media Report,* June 8–14, 1998, 10.

Hindes, Andrew. "Megaplex Dominance Intact: Chain Fends off Rivals as Company Pushes for Bigger and Smarter." *Variety,* March 16–22, 1998, 39, 48.

———. "Megaplex to Power Up London." *Variety,* June 23–29, 1997, 20.

———. "New Plex-Busters? Location-Based Diversions Vie for Moviegoers' Dollars." *Variety,* May 10–16, 1999, 9, 40.

———. "Prints and the Paupers: Multiplex Mania Spurs Big Ad Buys, Wide Bows." *Variety,* April 8– 14, 1996, 1, 74, 75.

———. "ShoWest Boasts New Event Hosts." *Variety,* February 23–March 1, 1998, 30.

———. "Study Marks Global Shift." *Variety,* October 30–November 5, 1995, M44, M46.

———. "When Prints Will No Longer Be King." *Variety,* January 25–31, 1999, 9, 16.

Hindes, Andrew, and Monica Roman. "Video Titles Do Pitstops on Screens." *Variety,* September 16–22, 1996, 11, 16.

Hirsch, Paul. "Globalization of Mass Media Ownership: Implications and Effects." *Communication Research* 19, no. 6 (December 1992): 677–681.

Hoffman, Andy. "Cineplex Deal Raises Multiplex of Scenarios." *Playback,* January 12, 1998, 1, 26.

———. "Cineplex Gets October Deal; Ownership Still in Question." *Playback,* March 23, 1998, 9, 24.

———. "Quebec Indie Takes on Majors." *Playback,* July 13, 1998, 1, 14, 22.

Hollinger, Hy. "Merger Mania Facing Congress: Democrats May Pressure Justice Dept. Sec." *Variety,* January 14, 1987, 1, 50.

Holston, James, and Arjun Appadurai. "Cities and Citizenship." *Public Culture* 8, no. 2 (winter 1996): 187–204.

Hopewell, John. "Multiplex Boom: Spain Exhibs Post Robust Figures." *Variety,* June 26–July 9, 1995, 56, 58.

——. "Portugal Ripe for Growth." *Variety*, June 26–July 9, 1995, 56.

Hoskins, Colin, and Rolf Mirus. "Reasons for the U.S. Domination of the International Trade in Television Programs." *Media, Culture, and Society* 10, no. 4 (1988): 499–516.

Hoskins, Colin, Stuart McFadyen, and Adam Finn. "The Environment in Which Cultural Industries Operate and Some Implications." *Canadian Journal of Communication* 19, nos. 3/4 (1994): 353–376.

Hume, Christopher. "All Roads Lead to FunCity." *Toronto Star*, November 1, 1997, M1, M16.

Hutcheon, Linda. *Splitting Images: Contemporary Canadian Ironies*. Toronto: Oxford University Press, 1991.

Hyde, John. "How Foreign Distribution Works." *Variety*, February 19, 1986, 18, 336.

Ilott, Terry. "Multiplexing Still Perplexing." *Variety*, January 4, 1993, 52.

"IMAX Says Cinema Sector Turmoil Will Stunt Growth." *Globe and Mail*, January 13, 2001, B9.

"Interactive Service Moviefone, Now On Line in LA, Coming to Gotham; Offers Info on Screen Locales, Times." *Variety*, November 8, 1989, 30.

"International Movie Marketplace: Mother Lode, or Just Fool's Gold?" *Variety*, February 22–28, 1989, 35, 47.

"Intl. Exhibition Roundup." *Variety*, May 11, 1988, 84, 85, 88, 90, 91, 92.

Ivany, Peter A. "The Development of the International Market." *Boxoffice*, February 1992, SW-17, SW-19.

Izod, John. *Hollywood and the Box Office, 1895–1986*. New York: Columbia University Press, 1988.

Jackman, Philip. "Movie Marketing Hits $25-Million per Picture." *Globe and Mail*, March 11, 1999, A22.

James, Christine. "Island Getaway." *Boxoffice*, May 1999, 38.

——. "The Great Divide." *Boxoffice*, May 1999, 43.

Jarvie, Ian. *Hollywood's Overseas Campaign: The North Atlantic Movie Trade, 1920–1950*. New York: Cambridge University Press, 1992.

Jaremko, Gordon. "Chain Wants Picketing Limited." *Calgary Herald*, February 7, 1995, A13.

"Justice Dept. Memo Gives Insight into Agency's Distrib-Exhib Ideas." *Variety*, June 17, 1987, 3, 34.

Kauffmann, Stanley. "Fade-out?" *New Republic*, September 6, 1999, 28, 30.

Kelly, Brendan. "Alliance's Le Monde Ups Slate." *Variety*, January 19–25, 1998, 29.

——. "Alliance Snaps Up Canuck Indie Norstar." *Variety*, January 5–11, 1998, 32.

——. "Bigger, Better Plexes: With Eight Decades in Business, Circuit is on Expansion Course." *Variety*, November 29–December 5, 1999, 35, 44.

——. "Biz Maps New Routes North." *Variety*, November 21–27, 1994, 53, 62.

——. "Canada Sets New Pic Policy." *Variety*, February 9–15, 1998, 26.

——. "Canadians Finding Global Sales Respect." *Variety*, October 21–27, 1996, M20.

——. "Canadian Shakin'." *Variety*, February 23–March 1, 1998, 15, 52.

——. "Distribs Fight Dominance of Big-Ticket U.S. Pix." *Variety*, November 22, 1993, 52.

——. "Loop Hums with High-Tech Sounds." *Variety*, December 9–15, 1996, 60.

——. "Major Video Chains Prepare for a Boom." *Variety*, November 22, 1993, 54.

——. "Marketers Make Most of Moviegoing Experience." *Variety*, December 9–15, 1996, 81.

——. "More Cinemas! Beaming Down to a Suburb Near You!" *Montreal Gazette*, December 4, 1999, D1, D2.

——. "Quebec Law Trips Up Alliance Releasing." *Variety,* December 22–January 4, 1998, 7.

——. "TV's Global Reach." *Variety,* December 14–20, 1998, 113, 120.

Keohane, Kieran. *Symptoms of Canada: An Essay on Canadian Identity.* Toronto: University of Toronto Press, 1997.

Kerr, Ann. "High-Tech Centre Hopes to Be Fun City." *Globe and Mail,* July 23, 1996, C2.

Klady, Leonard. "Blockbusters Trigger Box Office Record O'seas." *Variety,* January 25–31, 1999, 9, 18.

——. "BO Tastes Yank-Flavored." *Variety,* September 2–8, 1996, 42, 62.

——. "BO with a Vengeance: $9.1 Billion Worldwide." *Variety,* February 19–25, 1996, 1, 26.

——. "Discount Houses Feel Freeze in Exhib Squeeze." *Variety,* November 4–10, 1996, 7, 14.

——. "Exhibs' Expansion Buoys Distribs." *Variety,* March 20–26, 1995, 7, 16.

——. "Exhibs Fight Screen Demons." *Variety,* July 31–August 6, 1995, 7, 16.

——. "Exhibs Trip on Glitz: Serious Issues May Get Lost in ShoWest Blitz." *Variety,* March 9–15, 1998, 9, 16.

——. "Foreign BO Beckons: Comedies, Dramas Get More of the Action." *Variety,* August 28–September 3, 1995, 1, 79.

——. "Hitting and Missing the Market: Studios Show Savvy—or Just Luck—With Pic Release Strategies." *Variety,* January 19–25, 1998, 18.

——. "Holiday Hits Ignite Fights for More Sites." *Variety,* December 9–15, 1996, 11, 12, 119.

——. "H'wood: Land of the Rising Sum." *Variety,* March 13–19, 1995, 14.

——. "H'wood's BO Blast: '97 Admissions Highest in Three Decades." *Variety,* January 5–11, 1998, 1, 96.

——. "Locals Boost BO: Plexes, Homegrown Heroes Pump Global 100." *Variety,* February 9–15, 1998, 9, 30.

——. "More BO Oracles Take up Trackin'." *Variety,* October 19–25, 1998, 9.

——. "MPAA Trumpets Pains, Gains; BO Take of $5.91 Bil Hurt by Cost Rise." Variety.com, March 5, 1997. Last accessed June 26, 2002.

——. "Screen Squeeze Sows Exhib-Distrib Discord." *Variety,* October 3–9, 1994, 13, 16.

——. "Top 250 of 1997." *Variety,* January 26–February 1, 1998, 17, 18.

——. "Tracking a Lost Generation: Stunted Growth of Core Audience Frustrates Filmers." *Variety,* November 29, 1993, 1, 74.

——. "U.S. Exhibs Discover the Joy of Plex O'seas." *Variety,* April 8–14, 1996, 9, 14.

Klinger, Barbara. "The New Media Aristocrats: Home Theater and the Domestic Film Experience." *Velvet Light Trap* 42 (1998): 4–19.

Kluge, Alexander. "On Film and the Public Sphere." *New German Critique* 24/ 25 (fall/winter 1981/82): 206–220.

Kotler, Jason S. T. "Direct to Supreme Court: Unscrambling Satellite Wars." *Playback,* August 6, 2001, 29.

Kracauer, Siegfried. "Cult of Distraction." In *The Mass Ornament: Weimar Essays,* ed. and trans. Thomas Y. Levin, 323–328. Cambridge: Harvard University Press, 1995 (1927).

Kramer, Pat. "A Busy Day in the Life of Exhibition." *Variety,* December 22–January 4 1997/8, 44, 46.

——. "Bold Design Drives Expansion." *Variety,* March 16–22, 1998, 40, 48.

——. "Cinescape Artists." *Boxoffice*, September 1996, 28, 29, 30.

——. "FunScape: Exhibition's New Landscape?" *Boxoffice*, September 1995, 16, 17, 18.

Landy, Marcia. *Film, Politics, and Gramsci*. Minneapolis: University of Minnesota Press, 1994.

Latif, Bahrudin. "Chan, Godzilla Battle It Out on Malaysian Screens." *Variety*, November 30–December 6, 1998, 36.

Lefebvre, Henri. *The Production of Space*. Trans. Donald Nicholson-Smith. Oxford: Blackwell, 1991.

Leitch, Carolyn. "Astral Considering Acquisitions: Company May Buy Small Video Distributors to Consolidate Market." *Globe and Mail*, Friday, January 31, 1997, B8.

Leventhal, Larry. "Cinema Trade Show Makes Euro Debut." *Variety*, June 29, 1992, 61, 62.

Levy, Harold. "Projectionists Locked Out by Cineplex." *Toronto Star*, October 27, 1996, A4.

Levy, Shawn. "Exhibition Wars: Per-Capitas Battle Fought at ShoWest." *Boxoffice*, April 1990, 20, 22.

Lewis, Jon. "Money Matters: Hollywood in the Corporate Era." In *The New American Cinema*, ed. Jon Lewis, 87–121. Durham: Duke University Press, 1998.

Lichtman, Howard, with Harriet Bernstein. "Marketing Canadian Feature Films: A Perspective." In *Selling It: The Marketing of Canadian Feature Films*, ed. Joan Irving, 1–17. Toronto: Doubleday Canada, 1995.

Litman, Barry. *The Motion Picture Mega-Industry*. Toronto: Allyn and Bacon, 1998.

Litman, Barry, and Anne M. Hoag. "Merger Madness." In Barry Litman, *The Motion Picture Mega-Industry*, 97–121. Toronto: Allyn and Bacon, 1998.

Litt, Paul. *The Muses, the Masses, and the Massey Commission*. Toronto: University of Toronto Press, 1992.

"Locked Out Projectionists Picketing Vancouver Film Fest." *Globe and Mail*, September 25, 1999, C6.

Loews Cineplex Entertainment. "News Release—10/8/1998—Announces Financial Results for Second Quarter." *Canadian NewsWire*, http://www.newswire.ca/releases/October1998/, 1998. Last accessed May 8, 2000.

——. "News Release—12/8/2000—Announces Extension of Waiver Under its Credit Facility to January 26, 2001." *Canadian NewsWire*, http://www.newswire.ca/releases/December2000/, 2000. Last accessed January 24, 2001.

——. "News Release—1/22/2001—Announces Financial Results for Third Quarter." *Canadian NewsWire*, http://www.newswire.ca/releases/January2001/, 2001. Last accessed January 24, 2001.

Lull, James. "Critical Response: The Audience as Nuisance." *Critical Studies in Mass Communication* 5 (1988): 239–242.

Lury, Karen, and Doreen Massey. "Making Connections." *Screen* 40, no. 3 (1999): 229–238.

MacDonald, Gayle. "Alliance Buys Film Distributor Norstar." *Globe and Mail*, December 23, 1997, B3.

——. "Alliance to Close Cineplex Odeon Films Deal." *Globe and Mail*, May 21, 1998, B4.

——. "Onex Partners Launch Cinema Chain to Show Flicks to the Sticks." *Globe and Mail*, September 15, 1999, B1, B4.

——. "Partners Plan Art-house Cinema Chain: Alliance, Famous Players to Invest Up to $30-million to Build, Lease Multiplexes." *Globe and Mail,* June 19, 1998, B1, B8.

——. "Red Sky Reels in High-Brow Flicks for Mainstream Venues." *Globe and Mail,* February 23, 1998, B1, B5.

——. "The Vast Picture Show." *Globe and Mail,* January 17, 1998, B1, B5.

MacDonald, Gayle, and John Partridge. "Cineplex Executives Let Go: Loews Merger Pushes Managers Out Door." *Globe and Mail,* May 2, 1998, B1, B5.

MacKinnon, Mark. "IMAX Buys High-Tech Projector Maker." *Globe and Mail,* September 8, 1999, B5.

Mackey, Stephen. "Foreign Exhibs Fuel Boom." *Variety,* June 15–21, 1998, 71.

——. "Madrid's Megaplex Mania." *Variety,* April 20–26, 1998, 33.

Maddever, Mary. "Kingdom Targeted the Rep Circuit." *Playback,* June 17, 1996, 11.

Madigan, Nick. "Runaways Inspire Taxing Questions." *Variety,* August 23–29, 1999, 7, 9.

"Madstone Becomes First Exhibitor to Purchase a DLP Cinema Projector." *Cinema Technology,* September 2001, 4.

Magder, Ted. *Canada's Hollywood: The Canadian State and Feature Films.* Toronto: University of Toronto Press, 1993.

——. "Film and Video Production." In *The Cultural Industries in Canada: Problems, Policies, and Prospects,* ed. Michael Dorland, 145–177. Toronto: Lorimer, 1996.

Maglera, Marcy. "Advertisers Crowd onto Big Screen." *Advertising Age,* September 18, 1989, 14, 15.

"Major Cineplex Acquisitions from 1985." *Variety,* April 26–May 2, 1989, 47.

"Major Studios Agree to Set Digital Standards." *Globe and Mail,* April 4, 2002, R2.

Maltby, Richard. " 'Nobody Knows Everything': Post-Classical Historiographies and Consolidated Entertainment." In *Contemporary Hollywood Cinema,* ed. Steve Neale and Murray Smith, 21–44. New York: Routledge, 1998.

"Man Killed During 'Raw' Fracas; Film is Pulled from One Theater." *Variety,* December 23, 1987, 7.

Mario, Toneguzzi. "Famous Players Dispute Locks Out Projectionists." *Calgary Herald,* January 16, 1995, A1.

Marriot, Michel. "Digital Projectors Use Flashes of Light to Paint a Movie." *New York Times,* May 27, 1999, G7.

Massey, Doreen. "The Political Place of Locality Studies." *Environment and Planning* A 23, no. 2 (1991): 267–281.

Matthews, Tom. "Jack Loeks' Studio 28." *Boxoffice,* August 1988, 18, 20, 24.

——. "Playing the Numbers." *Boxoffice,* September 1989, 12.

——. "The Free Film Phone." *Boxoffice,* April 1990, 20.

Mayne, Judith. *Cinema and Spectatorship.* New York: Routledge, 1993.

Mazurkewich, Karen. "C/FP Inks Distrib Deal with Miramax." *Playback,* September 2, 1991, 1, 4.

——. "Film Grosses Far Below Target." *Playback,* August 19, 1991, 16, 19.

——. "Many Films Find Home on Video." *Playback,* September 16, 1991, 9, 18.

——. "Many Reasons Why Cdn. Box Office Bad." *Playback,* June 8, 1992, 4, 33.

——. "Ontario Distributors Aim to Mirror Quebec Legislation." *Playback,* October 1, 1990, 3.

Mccallum, Ian. "Government's Role May be Ending: Can the Industry Carry the Ball?" *Playback,* April 6, 1987, 12.

McCarthy, Anna. *Ambient Television: Visual Culture and Public Space.* Durham: Duke University Press, 2001.

McCarthy, Shawn. "Cineplex Deal May Hinge on Sale of Unit." *Globe and Mail,* October 3, 1997, B1, B20.

——. "Ottawa Eyes Cineplex Merger." *Globe and Mail,* October 2, 1997, A14, A15.

McCarthy, Todd. "MCA, Cineplex Odeon Teaming on Fla. Studio-Tourist Facility." *Variety,* December 17, 1986, 3, 104.

McKie, Paul. "Coming Soon! More Theatres, Screens!" *Winnipeg Free Press,* January 13, 1998, A1, A2.

McKinney, Clyde. "Poised for Takeoff: Boeing to Unveil Business Plan in Las Vegas." *Film Journal International,* March 2001, 82, 84.

"Mega-Multiplex for St. Petersburg." *Variety,* May 17, 1993, 34.

Meils, Cathy. "Arthouses Hopping in Prague." *Variety,* June 15–21, 1998, 82.

——. "Austria's Plexes Target Small-town Expansion." *Variety,* January 5–11, 1998, 26.

——. "Politics Plays Havoc with Plexes." *Variety,* June 15–21, 1998, 86.

Michaan, Allen. "Recapturing the Movie Palace Magic." *Boxoffice,* March 1989, SW-6, SW-8.

Miller, Toby. "The Crime of Monsieur Lang: GATT, the Screen, and the New International Division of Cultural Labor." In *Film Policy: International, National and Regional Perspectives,* ed. Albert Moran, 72–84. New York: Routledge, 1996.

Miller, Toby, Nitin Govil, John McMurria, and Richard Maxwell. *Global Hollywood.* London: British Film Institute, 2001.

Milner, Brian. "Cineplex to Stick to Film Exhibiting: Karp Says Sell-Offs Exceed $100-Million." *Globe and Mail,* June 16, 1990, B5.

Mitchell, Jen. "Cineplex Making a Comeback." *Playback,* December 5, 1994, 27.

Mofina, Rick. "Unionists Videotaped at Rally for Locked-out Projectionists." *Calgary Herald,* April 8, 1995, G8.

Mohr, Ian. "FunScapes Marry Movies, Entertainment Options." *Variety,* March 8–14, 1999, 34, 46.

"More New Screens in 1997." *Variety,* January 19–25, 1998, 38.

"More Shelf Space for Films." *Variety,* January 5–11, 1998, 30.

Morley, David. *Television, Audiences, and Cultural Studies.* New York: Routledge, 1992.

Moore, Linda. "Spain: The Multiplex Pick-Me-Up Arrives Late but Strong." *Variety,* June 29, 1992, 62.

Morris, Meaghan. "At Henry Parkes Motel." *Cultural Studies* 2, no. 1 (1988): 1–47.

Morrison, Melissa. "New Cinema Design." *Boxoffice,* March 2000, 24, 25, 26, 27, 28, 29.

Motion Picture Association of America. "2001 U.S. Economic Review." http://www.mpaa.org/useconomicreview/2001Economic, 2001. Last accessed June 23, 2002.

——. "Motion Picture Association Goals for Digital Cinema." http://www.mpaa.org/dcinema/dCinemaGoals.htm, 2000. Last accessed May 1, 2002.

——. "Worldwide Location of Digital Cinema Theatres," http://www.mpaa.org/dcinema/, 2000. Last accessed April 30, 2003.

Motion Picture Theatres Association of Canada. "Canadian Statistics." http://www.mptac.ca/stats.html, 2001. Last accessed June 23, 2002.

"Movies Keep Rolling as Projectionists Accept Pay Cut." *Vancouver Sun,* June 17, 1995, A5.

"MPAA Gives Pix Clean Bill of Health: Graying Audience Won't Crimp BO." *Variety*, November 25, 1987, 3, 33.

"MPAA Reports First-Half BO at Lowest Point in Four Years; Videocassette Penetration Balloons." *Variety*, August 13, 1986, 3.

"MPEA, Studios Promote Big-Screen Film-Watching." *Variety*, February 15–21, 1989, 48.

"Multiplexes Recharge BO." *Variety*, April 27, 1992, 64, 66.

"The Multiplexing of Latin America." *Variety*, March 23–29, 1998, 68.

"Multiplex Mania Hits Exhibitors." *Variety*, September 26–October 2, 1994, 55.

Murch, Walter. "A Digital Cinema of the Mind? Could Be." *New York Times*, May 2, 1999, section 2A, 1, 35.

Murdoch, Blake. "Multiplexes, Weak TV Scene Change the Distribution Map." *Variety*, April 29, 1991, 66, 74.

Murphy, A. D. "Globe Gobbling Up U.S. Pix in Record Doses; Worldwide Rentals to Yank Distribs Shattered Marks in '89; Japan Key." *Variety*, June 13, 1990, 7, 10.

——. "Majors' Global Rentals Boffo: Soft Dollar Boosts 87 to a Record." *Variety*, May 18, 1988, 1, 30.

——. "Recap of Top Foreign Markets: Japan Nudged Canada from 1st." *Variety*, October 22, 1986, 52, 154.

Murray, Karen. "Cineplex Films Finds Canuck Screens for Pix." *Variety*, July 25–31, 1994, 42.

——. "Designing Theaters Around Environment." *Variety*, July 25–32, 1994, 40.

Nadler, John. "Cineplex Enters Turkey." *Variety*, April 27–May 3, 1998, 16.

——. "More Multis Mean More Magyar Moviegoers." *Variety*, June 15–21, 1998, 82.

——. "Multiplex Mania Strikes Exhib Biz." *Variety*, May 18–24, 1998, 64.

Nasaw, David. *Going Out: The Rise and Fall of Public Amusements*. New York: Basic Books, 1993.

Natale, Richard. "Hollywood's Got the Billion-Ticket Blahs." *Variety*, March 30, 1992, 5, 10.

Natale, Richard, and Charles Fleming. "Distribs Say 'Open Wide!' " *Variety*, June 24, 1991, 1, 69.

National Amusements, Inc. "An Open Letter to the Patrons of Sunrise Multiplex Cinemas." *Newsday*, March 28, 1991, www.newsday.com. Last accessed August 20, 1998.

"NATO Changes Stance on Theatre Ownership." *Boxoffice*, October 1986, 21.

"NATO Pushes for Print Changes." *Variety*, November 25, 1987, 7.

"NATO Puts U.S. Screen Tally at 22,721, Highest on Record." *Variety*, November 25, 1987, 6, 33.

"NATO's Warner Foresees Global Film Industry." *Boxoffice*, October 1991, 96.

Neale, Steve. *Cinema Technology: Image, Sound, Color*. Bloomington: Indiana University Press, 1985.

Negt, Oskar, and Alexander Kluge. "The Public Sphere and Experience: Selections." Trans. Peter Labanyi. *October* 46 (fall 1988 [1972]): 60–82.

Nielsen EDI Box Office News. "Late-Year Flurry from Exhibs." *Variety*, January 13–19, 2003, 26.

Noglows, Paul. "Here Come the Megaplexes: Exhibs Usher in 24-Screen 'Destinations'." *Variety*, August 22–28, 1994, 1, 65.

——. "Studios Stuck in Screen Jam." *Variety*, March 9, 1992, 1, 73.

Ochs, Millard L. "Cost Considerations in Developing the International Market." *Boxoffice*, February 1992, SW-16, SW-18.

"Odeon Digital Cinema—the Dawn of a New Era." *Cinema Technology*, March 2002, 4.

Olson, Scott Robert. *Hollywood Planet: Global Media and the Competitive Advantage of Narrative Transparency.* Mahwah, N.J.: Lawrence Erlbaum, 1999.

O'Regan, Tom. *Australian National Cinema.* New York: Routledge, 1996.

Orfton, Marlene. "Reagan Questions Licensing." *Playback,* April 20, 1987, 1, 6.

Orwall, Bruce. "Theatre Closings Possible in Cineplex-Sony Merger: Draft Document Filled with SEC also Foresees Expansion." *Globe and Mail,* February 4, 1998, B12.

O'Steen, Kathleen. "Exhibs Ride Hi-Tech Edge." *Variety,* October 24–30, 1994, 13, 16.

Ostroff, Joshua. "Pop Go the Shadow Puppets." *Globe and Mail,* February 25, 2002, R5.

Paul, William. "The K-Mart Audience at the Mall Movies." *Film History* 6 (1994): 487–501.

Paxman, Andrew. "Latin BO Surges 13%: Regional Revs Up but Stock Market Blasts Brazil." *Variety,* January 19–25, 1998, 21.

———. "Southern Renaissance: Corporate Ventures Multiply Region's Booming Multiplexes." *Variety,* March 23–29, 1998, 42, 43, 68.

Pearson, Bryan. "South African Exhib Builds on Euro Stake." *Variety,* August 30–September 5, 1999, 45.

Peers, Martin. ". . . And Threatens to Short-circuit Exhibs." *Variety,* April 8–14, 1996, 1, 74, 75.

———. "Cinemark, Cineplex Merge Ops." *Variety,* March 6–12, 1995, 22.

———. "Consolidation Alters Face of Exhibition." *Variety,* December 22–January 4, 1997/98, 37, 52.

———. "Exhibs Vexed by Wall St. Hex on Plex." *Variety,* January 26–February 1, 1998, 1, 83.

———. "Hicks Nixes High-Priced UA Theaters Acquisition." *Variety,* February 23–March 1, 1998, 4.

———. "Loews Lines Up World: Shugrue Tapped to Lead Exhib in Global Moves." *Variety,* June 15–21, 1998, 12.

———. "Mega Building Punctures Profits." *Variety,* June 8–14, 1998, 8.

———. "Megaplex Strength Lifts AMC Earnings." Variety.com, October 23, 1997. Last accessed June 25, 2002.

Peers, Martin, and Andrew Hindes. "AMC Scales Back Plexes in Reversal." *Variety,* May 24–30, 1999, 10.

Peiss, Kathy. *Cheap Amusements: Working Women and Leisure in Turn-of-the-Century New York.* Philadelphia: Temple University Press, 1986.

Pendakur, Manjunath. *Canadian Dreams and American Control: The Political Economy of the Canadian Film Industry.* Toronto: Garamond, 1990.

Pendleton, Jennifer. "Chain Sees Possibilities in Midst of Recession." *Variety,* March 30, 1992, 51, 60.

Penel, Henri-Pierre. "Deux innovations pour une révolution." *Science et Vie,* April 2000, 126–131.

Pener, Degen. "Tyrannosauras Plex." *Entertainment Weekly,* June 6, 1997, 32, 33, 35.

Petrikin, Chris. "AMC Bows Centertainment Plexes." *Variety,* December 18–25, 1997, 25.

Phillips, Braden. "Chain Plans 1,000 New Screens in '99." *Variety,* March 8–14, 1999, 31, 32.

Pierson, John. *Spike, Mike, Slackers, and Dykes.* New York: Hyperion, 1995.

"Pix-Video Wedding Closer." *Variety,* December 31, 1952, 19.

Pommer, Dave. "Picketing Limit Denied." *Calgary Herald,* April 21, 1995, D6.

Posner, Michael. "Cineplex CEO Blasts Collusion Charges." *Globe and Mail,* December 20, 2000, B7.

———. "A Really Big Show." *Maclean's,* August 11, 1997, 38, 39.

Prince, Stephen. *A New Pot of Gold: Hollywood under the Electronic Rainbow, 1980–1989*. Berkeley: University of California Press, 2000.

Prupas, Michael I. "The Control of Film and Video Distribution in Canada and Quebec." *Entertainment Law Reporter,* 10, no. 9 (February 1989): 8–17.

Pruzin, Daniel R. "The Americanization of Europe, Part I: How Hollywood Dominates the European Film Market." *Boxoffice,* February 1991, SW-56, SW-57.

———. "The Americanization of Europe, Part II: The Old World Fights Back." *Boxoffice,* February 1991, SW-58. SW-59, SW-60, SW-61.

Pryor, Thomas M. "The New Exhibition Mania." *Variety,* August 6, 1986, 5, 31.

Pursell, Chris. "Auds Lured by Virtual Arcades." *Variety,* December 22–January 4, 1998, 49.

Quick Canadian Facts, 1966–1967. 22d edition. Toronto: Thorn Press, 1966.

Quinn, John. "AMC's Plastic Plan Gaining after Slow Start in Kansas." *Variety,* April 5–11, 1989, 12, 16.

———. "Exhibs Bellied Up to Candy/Popcorn Bar at ShoWest's Trade Fair." *Variety,* February 25, 1987, 9.

———. "Movies Make a Town Square." *Variety,* March 16–22, 1998, 58.

Ramirez, Anthony. "At Theaters Near You: Reserved Seating Comes to Manhattan Movies." *New York Times,* November 16, 1997, 41, 47.

Ramirez, Marc. "Crying Time Again? Moviegoing Parents Will Have a Refuge." *Wall Street Journal,* June 23, 1989, B4.

Rayner, Ben. " 'Virtual Band' an Interesting Failure." *Toronto Star,* February 25, 2002, 3.

"Redstone Decries 'Complacency' of Exhibs in Couch-Potato World." *Variety,* November 25, 1987, 7, 32.

Rice-Barker, Leo. "EC to Take Case to WTO." *Playback,* May 5, 1997, 1, 14.

———. "Industry Banks on New Technology, Expanded Slates." *Playback,* May 6, 1996, 19, 20.

———. "Quebec, U.S. Ink New Distrib Deal." *Playback,* February 3, 1992, 1, 9.

Richardson, Rick. "Underscreened Market Soldiers On." *Variety,* June 15–21, 1998, 78.

The Road to Success: Report of the Feature Film Advisory Committee. Ottawa: Canadian Heritage, 1999.

Robbins, Bruce. *Feeling Global: Internationalism in Distress.* New York: New York University Press, 1999.

Robbins, Jim. "Drabinsky Confirms Cineplex' Buy of RKO Century Warner; To Add 38 NY-Area Screens. "*Variety,* August 6, 1986, 3, 21.

———. "Euphoria Over, But Not New Builds." *Variety,* May 11–17, 1988, 83, 92.

———. "Exhibition's Future: Too Many Theaters, Little to Put in Them, Predict Tradesters at Cinetex." *Variety,* September 27–October 3, 1989, 3.

———. "Exhibitor Sees Falling Prices for Theaters." *Variety,* January 28, 1987, 1, 76.

———. "Exhibs Are in Expansion Frenzy; Busy Month for Theater Acquisitions." *Variety,* July 1, 1987, 1, 31.

———. "A $400-Million Strategy for Success: Cineplex Odeon Builds and Rebuilds." *Variety,* April 26–May 2, 1989, 70.

———. "High Spirits Usher in NATO Gathering; Strong Lineup of Execs to Speak." *Variety,* November 18, 1987, 7, 11.

——. "NATO Marched Quietly into Atlanta; Leaders Promise to Improve Assn." *Variety,* November 25, 1987, 7, 34.

Robins, Kevin. *Into the Image: Culture and Politics in the Field of Vision.* New York: Routledge, 1996.

Robinson, Gwen. " 'Plexes Proliferate amid Downward Box Office Trend." *Variety,* March 6–12, 1995, 49.

Roman, Monica. "Exhibs Adding Fuel to Urban Renewal." *Variety,* April 21–27, 1997, 9, 16.

Rooney, David. "Mega Opposition: Italian Filmmakers Blast Studio-Lot Plex." Variety.com, April 6, 1999. Last accessed June 26, 2002.

——. "Plexing of Rome May Feel Sting of Regs." *Variety,* November 30–December 6, 1998, 15.

Rosenzweig, Roy. *Eight Hours for What We Will.* Cambridge: Cambridge University Press, 1984.

Ross, Andrew. *No Respect: Intellectuals and Popular Culture.* New York: Routledge, 1989.

Ross, Val. "U.S. Doesn't get the Picture." *Globe and Mail,* December 8, 1993, B1, B4.

Roth, Morry. "Cineplex Boss Details Chi Plans; Aims for 400 New U.S. Screens." *Variety,* April 2, 1986, 7, 37.

Rothman, Matt. "Digital Tech Points to Pix' Future." *Daily Variety,* May 12, 1992, 1.

Rotzoll, Kim B. "The Captive Audience: The Troubled Odyssey of Cinema Advertising." In *Current Research in Film: Audience, Economics, and Law,* ed. Bruce Austin, 72–87. Norwood, N.J.: Ablex, 1987.

"Roundtable: Distribution and Exhibition, the Ties that Bind." *Boxoffice,* March 1998, SW-28.

Rowan, Geoffrey. "Playdium to Build Toronto Complex." *Globe and Mail,* August 28, 1997, B7.

Rubin, Sandra. "Coming Soon—New, Mega Movie Experience." *Calgary Herald,* August 29, 1995, D7.

Sabin, Rob. "The End/Restart: The Movies' Digital Future Is in Sight and It Works." *New York Times,* November 26, 2000, sec. 2, 1, 22.

Sandler, Adam. "Milestone in Mexican Video Biz." *Variety,* October 3–9, 1994, 16.

——. "Sound Systems Spar over Theater Sign-Ups." *Variety,* August 22–28, 1994, 4.

"Satellite, PPV News." *Boxoffice,* August/September 1992, 105.

Sassen, Saskia. "Whose City Is It? Globalization and the Formation of New Claims." *Public Culture* 8, no. 2 (winter 1996): 205–223.

Saunders, Doug. "Is Film Dead?" *Globe and Mail,* January 31, 2001, R1, R3.

——. "Maple Leaf No Hit at Hollywood Bowl." *Globe and Mail,* December 3, 2001, A10.

——. "Trouble in Hollywood North: Controversy Is Rising over Canada's Subsidies to U.S. Movie Moguls." *Globe and Mail,* May 13, 2000, A1, A3.

——. "We Want Flubber?" *Globe and Mail,* February 14, 1998, C1, C3.

Scannell, Paddy. *Radio, Television, and Modern Life.* Oxford: Blackwell, 1996.

Schatz, Thomas. "The New Hollywood." In *Film Theory Goes to the Movies,* ed. Jim Collins, Hilary Radner, and Ava Preacher Collins, 8–36. New York: Routledge, 1993.

Scheller, Johanna. "Focus on This: The Projector's On but Nobody's Home." *Globe and Mail,* January 15, 1999, A14.

Schlesinger, Philip. "The Sociological Scope of 'National Cinema'. " In *Cinema and Nation,* ed. Mette Hjort and Scott MacKenzie, 19–31. New York: Routledge, 2000.

Schmidt, Sarah. "Hold the Popcorn, Pass the Plate." *Globe and Mail,* February 14, 2000, R10.

Schwager, Jeff. "A Celebration of Our Industry: NATO/ShoWest '92 Generates Excitement." *Box-office*, April 1992, 14, 15.

Schwartzberg, Shlomo. "Guzzo's Gusto." *Boxoffice*, May 1999, 28, 30, 31.

——. "Major Players." *Boxoffice*, May 1999, 34–37.

——. "War of the Gargantuans." *Boxoffice*, February 1990, 105, 106.

"Screaming into Iqaluit." *Globe and Mail*, December 9, 1997, A15.

Secor Group. "Canadian Government Intervention in the Film and Video Industry." October 19, 1994.

"Shocked to Silence: Exhibitors React to Drabinsky's Move." *Variety*, November 25, 1987, 7, 32.

"ShoWest Keynoter to Settle Exhib Worries re: Distrib Acquisitions." *Variety*, February 4, 1987, 5, 8.

Silverman, M. "Distribs Exhort Exhibs to Try to Increase Viewer Satisfaction." *Variety*, February 19, 1986, 11.

Silverstone, Roger, and Eric Hirsch, eds. *Consuming Technologies: Media and Information in Domestic Spaces*. New York: Routledge, 1992.

Slack, Jennifer. "Contextualizing Technology." In *Rethinking Communication, Volume 2: Paradigm Exemplars*, ed. Brenda Dervin, Lawrence Grossberg, Barbara J. O'Keefe, and Ellen Wartella, 329–345. London: Sage, 1989.

Slotek, Jim. "Moviegoing in the Millennium." *Tribute*, June 1997, 34, 36.

Soja, Edward. "Inside Exopolis: Scenes from Orange County." In *Variations on a Theme Park: The New American City and the End of Public Space*, ed. Michael Sorkin, 94–122. New York: Hill and Wang, 1992.

Sorkin, Michael. "Introduction." In *Variations on a Theme Park: The New American City and the End of Public Space*, ed. Michael Sorkin, xi–xv. New York: Hill and Wang, 1992.

——. ed. *Variations on a Theme Park: The New American City and the End of Public Space*. New York: Hill and Wang, 1992.

Spigel, Lynn. *Make Room for TV: Television and the Family Ideal in Postwar America*. Chicago: University of Chicago Press, 1992.

Spigel, Lynn, and Denise Mann, eds. *Private Screening: Television and the Female Consumer*. Minneapolis: University of Minnesota Press, 1992.

Stacey, Jackie. "Textual Obsessions: Methodology, History, and Researching Female Spectatorship." *Screen* 34, no. 3 (1993): 260–274.

Staiger, Janet. "Individualism versus Collectivism." *Screen* 24, no. 4/5 (July–October 1983): 68–79.

——. *Interpreting Films: Studies in the Historical Reception of American Cinema*. Princeton: Princeton University Press, 1992.

Statistics Canada. *Film and Video, 1992–93, Culture Statistics*. Ottawa: Ministry of Industry, Science, and Technology, 1995.

——. *Motion Picture Theatres Survey*. Ottawa: Culture, Tourism, and the Centre for Education Statistics, 1999.

——. *Movie Theatres and Drive-ins, 1997–98, Culture Statistics*. Ottawa: Culture, Tourism, and the Centre for Education Statistics, 1999.

Stenger, Josh. "Consuming the Planet: Planet Hollywood, Stars, and the Global Consumer Culture." *Velvet Light Trap* 40 (1997): 42–55.

Stephenson, Wendy. "Theatres Getting Facelift." *Winnipeg Sun,* August 30, 1995, 21.

Stewart, Monte. "Cinescape Ushers in New Era in Movies." *Calgary Herald,* August 22, 1996, C3.

Stokes, Melvyn, and Richard Maltby, eds. *American Movie Audiences: From the Turn of the Century to the Early Sound Era.* London: British Film Institute, 1999.

Stone, Jay. "Movie Madness." *Ottawa Citizen,* January 9, 1998, E1, E2.

"Strategic Trends in Theatrical Exhibition: The Independent Exhibitor's Survival Guide." *Boxoffice,* July 1989, 14–22.

Straw, Will. " 'Organized Disorder': The Changing Space of the Record Shop." In *The Clubcultures Reader: Readings in Popular Cultural Studies,* ed. Steve Redhead, 57–65. Oxford: Blackwell, 1997.

Sullivan, Maureen. "Hong Kong Adds Screens." *Variety,* November 30–December 6, 1998, 38.

"Summer BO Surge Posted in Canada by Famous Players." *Variety,* October 15, 1986, 34.

Summers, Jimmy. "Cineplex Odeon Launches a Dazzling New Flagship." *Boxoffice,* September 1987, 8, 10, 16.

Swedko, Pamela. "Theatre Executives Gather for ShowCanada Confab." *Playback,* May 5, 1997, 26.

Sweeting, Paul. "Top Vid Chains Nurture 'Net Eggs." *Variety,* November 8–14, 1999, 17, 26.

Tartaglione, Nancy. "Arthouse Exhibs Fight Back." *Variety,* June 15–21, 1998, 49.

Tasker, Yvonne. "Dumb Movies for Dumb People: Masculinity, the Body, and the Voice in Contemporary Action Cinema." In *Screening the Male: Exploring Masculinities in Hollywood Cinema,* ed. Steven Cohan and Ina Rae Hark, 230–244. New York: Routledge, 1993.

"The Teachings of Chairman Jeff." *Variety,* February 4, 1991, 24.

"Theatre of the Overextended." *Globe and Mail,* August 30, 2000, A12.

"Theater Owners Win Antitrust Round: Justice Dept. Suit Dismissed." *Variety,* December 17, 1986, 3, 104.

Thompson, Kristin. *Exporting Entertainment: America in the World Film Market, 1907–1934.* London: British Film Institute, 1985.

Thompson, Patricia, ed. *Film Canada Yearbook.* Toronto: Cine-Communications, 1994.

"Three Indie Exhibits Register Scorn for Demise of Consent." *Variety,* May 27, 1987, 5, 36.

Tittley, Nicolas. "Notes Musique." *Voir,* February 21, 2002, 30.

Toneguzzi, Mario. "Famous Players Dispute Locks Out Projectionists." *Calgary Herald,* January 16, 1995, A1.

"Top 250 of 1999." *Variety,* January 10–16, 2000, 20, 22.

"Top 20 North American Exhibitors of 1990." *Boxoffice,* December 1990, 18.

"Tri-Star & Loews Seek Relief from Consent Decrees." *Variety,* April 8, 1987, 4, 24.

"Tri-Star Gets Nod from NATO in its Bid to Book Loews." *Variety,* May 6, 1987, 8, 579.

Tuck, Simon. "Projections of the Future." *Globe and Mail,* October 28, 1999, T1, T3.

Turnquist, Kris. "NATO '86: Exhibitors Come to Grips with Their New Partners—Distributors." *Boxoffice,* February 1987, 12.

Turow, Joseph. "The Organizational Underpinnings of Contemporary Media Conglomerates." *Communication Research* 19, no. 6 (December 1992): 682–704.

Tusher, Will. "Cineplex Odeon Agrees to Sell 57 Canadian Multiplexes in Fall." *Variety,* August 17, 1988, 6.

——. "Cineplex Odeon Declares Support for Distribs in Policy Statement." *Variety*, April 9, 1986, 7.

——. "Distribution's Theater Buys Near Peak, '86 a Watershed in Acquisitions." *Variety*, January 7, 1987, 3, 24.

——. "Exhibs Follow their Manifest Destiny: Not Dissuaded by Rise of Video Biz." *Variety*, May 13, 1987, 3, 54.

——. "GCC Prez Is Not Concerned over Distributors' Return to Exhibition." *Variety*, June 18, 1986, 7, 26.

——. "Indie Exhib to Have its Day in Court: Harkins Circuit Is Suing Majors." *Variety*, April 13, 1988, 3, 34.

——. "Justice Dept. Says Customer Selection Okay for Distribs." *Variety*, December 21–27, 1988, 10, 26.

——. "Nation's Screen Tally Reached a New High in '90." *Variety*, January 28, 1991, 3.

——. "NATO Hears Indie Exhibs' Cries for Earlier Access to New Pics." *Variety*, November 23, 1988, 7.

——. "Small Theaters Blast Circuits." *Variety*, March 2, 1988, 1, 9.

——. "Theater Owners Assn.'s Plan Suggests Practices to Help Better Moviegoing Experience." *Variety*, May 10–16, 1989, 34.

——. "Warners Mulls Franchise Option in Theater Deals." *Variety*, December 17, 1986, 1, 106.

"Union and Exhibs Traded Praise at ShoWest Opening." *Variety*, February 18, 1987, 7, 42.

"U Pix on 6,792 Screens, a Record." *Variety*, January 24, 1990, 12.

Urry, John. *The Tourist Gaze: Leisure and Travel in Contemporary Societies*. Newbury Park, California: Sage, 1990.

"USA Cinemas Confirms Cinema National Merger." *Variety*, August 13, 1986, 3.

"USA Snapshots." *USA Today*, May 26, 1998, D1.

"U.S. Folks Are Big Spenders on Entertainment." *Variety*, October 8, 1986, 1, 160.

"U.S. Symposium Nixed." *Playback*, May 2, 1988, 3.

Vale, Allison. "Boffo Screen Build." *Playback*, May 5, 1997, 1, 22, 28, 29.

"Valenti to Take on Exhib-Distrib Tensions as ShoWest Keynoter." *Variety*, February 5, 1986, 7.

Vamos, Peter. "Famous Goes Digital." *Playback*, January 10, 2000, 2.

Veronis, Suhler, and Associates, Inc. "Filmed Entertainment Growth: A Five-Year Forecast." *Boxoffice*, October 1990, 53, 54, 56, 58, 60, 62, 63.

——. "Filmed Entertainment Growth: A Five-Year Forecast." *Boxoffice*, October 1991, 34, 36, 38, 40, 42, 44.

——. "Filmed Entertainment Growth: A Five-Year Forecast." *Boxoffice*, October 1992, 30, 32, 34, 38, 40, 42.

——. "Filmed Entertainment Growth: A Five-Year Forecast." *Boxoffice*, November 1993, 52, 54, 56, 60, 62.

"Violence Mars 'Juice' Opening." *Boxoffice*, March 1992, 24.

"Violence 'N the Hood'." *Boxoffice*, September 1991, 17.

Vipond, Mary. "The Nationalist Network: English Canada's Intellectuals and Artists in the 1920s." *Canadian Review of Studies in Nationalism* 5 (spring 1980): 32–52.

Wakefield, Phil. "Cinema Pins Hopes on Multiplex Solution." *Variety,* September 30, 1991, 59, 60.

Waller, Gregory A. *Main Street Amusements: Movies and Commercial Entertainment in a Southern City, 1896–1930.* Washington: Smithsonian Institution Press, 1995.

Wasko, Janet. *Hollywood in the Information Age.* Austin: University of Texas Press, 1994.

Wasser, Frederick. "Four Walling Exhibition: Regional Resistance to the Hollywood Film Industry." *Cinema Journal* 34, no. 2 (winter 1995): 51–65.

——. "Is Hollywood America? The Trans-Nationalization of the American Film Industry." *Critical Studies in Mass Communication* 12, no. 4 (1995): 423–437.

——. *Veni, Vidi, Video: The Hollywood Empire and the VCR.* Austin: University of Texas Press, 2001.

Weder, Adele. "Architecture? Or Abomination." *National Post,* December 26, 1998, 4, 5.

Weiner, Rex. "Bumpy Interactive Ride." *Variety,* May 22–28, 1995, 7, 14.

Wendel, Sam. "Canadian Films and the American Market." In *Selling It: The Marketing of Canadian Feature Films,* ed. Joan Irving, 81–93. Toronto: Doubleday Canada, 1995.

Whittington, William. "Home Theater: Mastering the Exhibition Experience." *Spectator* 18, no. 2 (1998): 76–83.

"Wide, Wider, Widest." *Variety,* January 26–February 1, 1998, 21.

Wilinsky, Barbara. *Sure Seaters: The Emergence of Art House Cinema.* Minneapolis: University of Minnesota Press, 2001.

Willcocks, Paul. "Size Does Matter in the Future of Movie Theatres." *Globe and Mail,* May 15, 1998, D2.

Williams, Michael. "Gauls to AMC: Yankee Go Home!" *Variety,* April 20–26, 1998, 14.

Williams, Monte. "The Art of the Grand Old Cinemas, the Science of the New." *New York Times,* August 13, 2000, WK 3.

Williams, Raymond. "Culture Is Ordinary." In *Studying Culture: An Introductory Reader,* 2d edition, ed. Ann Gray and Jim McGuigan, 5–14. New York: Arnold, 1997 (1958).

——. *The Long Revolution.* New York: Columbia University Press, 1961.

——. *Marxism and Literature.* New York: Oxford University Press, 1977.

——. *Television: Technology and Cultural Form.* New York: Schocken, 1975.

Williamson, Kim. "A Small World After All." *Boxoffice,* July 1994, 26, 28, 30, 32.

Willis, Holly. "Beyond the Theater: Tactical Approaches to Independent Exhibition and Distribution." *Spectator* 18, no. 2. (1998): 84–90.

Willis, Susan. *A Primer for Daily Life.* New York: Routledge, 1991.

Winsor, Hugh. "Film Law Sparks Cabinet Clash." *Globe and Mail,* October 16, 1996, A1, A5

Woods, Mark, " 'Con Air' Flies to O'seas BO Highs." *Variety,* June 16–22, 1997, 14, 54.

——. "Aussie GU Pacts with Dutch Exhib." *Variety,* March 23–29, 1998, 20.

"World Cinema Fails to Keep Up with USA; Global Spending Now Close to $17 Billion." *Screen Digest,* September 1999, 21–28.

" 'World's First' Digital Theater is a Success 'Without Reels.' " *Cinema Technology,* December 2001, 28.

Wright, Colin. " 'We Won't Give Up'—Distribs." *Playback,* August 24, 1987, 3, 4.

Wyatt, Justin. "From Roadshowing to Saturation Release: Majors, Independents, and Marketing/

Distribution Innovations." In *The New American Cinema,* ed. Jon Lewis, 64–86. Durham: Duke University Press, 1998.

——. *High Concept: Movies and Marketing in Hollywood.* Austin: University of Texas Press, 1994.

Yakabuski, Konrad. "AMC Targets Forum for 'Megaplex'." *Globe and Mail,* August 15, 1996, B1, B4.

"Year at a Glance." *Playback,* October 16, 1989, 29, 30, 32, 34, 35, 36.

Yushchyshyn, Terry. "The Digital Future of Film." *Boxoffice,* April 1994, SW-12.

tion, 178–79. *See also* Exhibitors; United States exhibitors

Canadian Federal Competition Bureau, 225

Canadian film industry, 163; concerns about maturity, 178; feature film policy, 177; Telefilm recommendations for, 168

Canadian Motion Picture Distributors Association, 178

Canadian Project Pictures, 188

Canadian talent, 6, 7, 22; in U.S., 190–91

Canal Plus, 132

Cannes Film Festival, 178

Capitalism: and difference, 211

Carmike Theaters, 87, 104, 128, 287 n.63

Carolco, 153

Carrey, Jim, 3–4, 6–7, 21

Caughie, John, 61, 191

Centertainment, 197

C/FP Distribution, 288 n.83

Chelsea Piers project, 200

Chicago, Illinois, 89

Chicken Run, 197

China, 137, 141

Christopher, William, 45

Cianciotta, Tony, 196

Cinecitta Studios, 139

Cinema: in commodity cycle, 146; and community, 52, 172; as controlled public sphere, 120, 231; as cultural text, 150–51; culture and everyday life, 55; death of, 71, 222–23, 267 n.3; European construction of, 136; and modernity, 50; and popular experience, 18; and public spectatorship, 71; racialization of security in, 149; relations of local and global, 239; security in, 148; as site of struggle over globalization, 32; space of, 59; vectors of temporality, 62–67

Cinema Avant-Garde, 117

Cinema complex, 239, 241, 245–46; cross-promotion, 199–200; and public life, 244–45; signification of, 243

Cinema Expo International, 138, 215

Cinemagoer: global, 11. *See also* Audience

Cinemagoing, 20, 43–44, 59; in Canada, 187, 195; in Canada and popular cosmopolitanism, 237; Canadianizing, 188; and community, 242; concept of, 58; as event, 145; changing practice of, 242; as cultural practice, 119; decreasing sites of, 176; discourses about, 113, 119, 212; early shifts, 19–20; as educational, 193; extra-filmic reasons for, 193; experience of, 229; forces behind change, 18–19; geographic elements, 240; global concept, 134; institutional formation, 227; as minivacation, 102; and popular taste, 189; practice of, 57–58, 71, 81; reconfiguration, 129, 226, 244; regulation of behavior, 232, 234; renewed interest in, 172; and scholarship, 59; sites, 92; strength of, 145–46; upscaling, 99–100; vectors of temporality, 221

CinemaNow, 223

Cinema of attractions, 36, 198

Cinemascope, 89, 122

Cinema space: assessments of reconfiguration, 174–75

Cinema technology, 219

Cinepix, 288 n.83

Cineplex Odeon, 64, 89, 92, 97, 99, 103, 105, 115–16, 121, 123, 125, 149, 170–72, 174, 188, 204, 225, 266 n.1, 286 nn.35, 45, and 51, 287 n.63; closings, 175; international consolidation, 171; ownership of, 170. *See also* MCA/Universal

Cineplex Odeon Films, 282 n.113, 289 n.98; exhibition deals, 288 n.82

Cinerama, 89

Cinescape, 115–16; and interactive games, 115–16

Citywalk. *See* Universal CityWalk complex

Clarke, John, 16–17, 39, 212

Clear Channel Entertainment, 220–21

Clearances, 88, 124–25, 158

Clockwork Orange, A, 57

Coca-Cola, 97

Cohen, Randy, 227

Cohn, Lawrence, 103, 133–35, 158

Columbia, 97, 147, 272 n.43

Columbus, Georgia, 104

Common sense, 14. *See also* Industry common sense

Con Air: international release of, 160

Concession sales, 99, 125

Conjuncturalism, 15

Consolidated Theaters, 104

Consumption: location of, 24–26; private and public, spatial and temporal aspects of, 123, 155

Cook, Richard, 92

Copps, Sheila, 177

Coproduction, 164

Copyright: international, 134

Corbett, Kevin, 57

Corporate mergers: intermedia, 93

Cosmopolitanism, 236–37; concept of, 240; popular, 237–38. *See also* Cinemagoing; Nationhood; Structure of feeling; Transnational public

Counter-programming, 161

Cross-media integration, 93, 95

Cry rooms, 144

Cultural commodities: consumption, 192; ephemerality of, 80

Cultural currency, 194–95

Cultural discount, 33–34, 38–39, 131

Cultural labor: and ownership structure, 132

Cultural protectionism, 179, 181–82

Cultural studies, 17; and film departments, 47

Cultural synchronization, 234–35

Cultural texts: aging of, 152

Culture: definitions, 41; global, 37; global, analysis of, 39–40; mobility in locations of, 241; national, 238; and national cinema, 166

Current cinema, 22, 67, 77–78, 161–62; avid filmgoers' knowledge of, 78; and Canadian cinema culture, 194; sources of knowledge about, 76–77

Data tracking: companies, 134; methods, 4–6

Davis, Susan, 199, 205, 207

de Certeau, Michel, 56–57; representation and behavior, 59

Dedifferentiation, 119

Del Rossi, Paul, 105–6

Demolition Man, 205

Dench, Judy, 191

DeNiro, Robert, 222

Detroit: Southfield Cinemas, 147

Die Hard, 205

Digital distribution, 214, 217, 218, 222

Digital film. *See* Digital projection; New screen technologies

Digital Light Processor (DLP), 213–14, 223

Digital projection, 213, 215, 221, 294 n.78, 295 n.88; barriers to introduction, 216; benefits, 223; conversion financing, 216; new delivery systems, 214; projectionist duties, 217; temporal aspects, 221. *See also* MPAA; Television

Digital Projection International, 223

Digital sound technology, 277 n.58

Digital Theater System, 115, 275 n.5

Diller, Barry, 159

Discourse, 14; audience and entertainment, 17–18; concept of, 9; global audience, 17; themespace, 207. *See also* Cinemagoing; Exhibition

Disney, 64, 155, 200, 204, 216, 245, 288 n.86; diversity of operations, 204; as model, 92, 175, 203

Disneyfication, 203

Disney University, 175

Distribution: in Canada, 169; evolution, 24; new channels, 10; and public policy, 182. *See also* Alliance Atlantis

Distributors, 101, 102, 213, 217–18; advantages of consolidation, 93; alignment with exhibitors, 92–94, 97–98; bankruptcy, 289 n.109; conflicts with exhibitors, 86, 87, 90, 91, 125; deals with exhibitors, 170; demands, 92; expanding market, 124; grievances, 100; independent film, 196; and international box office, 133; move into exhibition, 159; negotiation with exhibitors, 88; strategies, 87–88; view of theatrical release, 155. *See also* Canadian distributors; Exhibitors; United States distributors

Dogma '95, 227

Dolby Stereo SR-D, 115

Dowler, Kevin, 186

Drabinsky, Garth, 99–100, 70, 172

Drainie, Bronwyn, 189

DreamWorks, 181

Due South, 190

Dunkirk, France, 139, 209

During, Simon, 36–38

Durwood, Stan, 103

Eau Claire Market, 116

Economic Resources Group, 89

Eddie Murphy Raw, 146

Edge, The, 67

EDI, 6. *See also* AC Nielsen EDI

Egyptien Cinema, 173–74

Electric Pictures, 289 n.111

Elgin Theatre, 103, 144–45, 154

"Elsewhen," 155

Elvis Gratton II, 164

Emerging Cinemas, 223

Empire Theatres, 171, 172

English-language films, 288 n.91

Entertainment: as event, 101; location based, 200–201

Entertainment Tonight, 5, 187

Entertainment Weekly, 5

Essantee, 104

Ethiopia, 141

Europe, 85, 135, 180; Central, 141–42; Eastern, 137, 141–42; Western, 135–37, 141

European Film Distribution Office, 12

Eutelsat, 214

Event: location of, 154

Everyday life, 54–55; and popular film culture, 17. *See also* Cinema; Film; Television

Excellence Theaters, 104

Exhibition, 52–53; analysis of, 53; chains, 128; culture of, 52; discourses about, 109; future of, 143; reconfiguration of, 126; shifting sites of, 89; trends in, 100

Exhibitors, 86, 91, 93, 97, 99, 106, 125, 217, 295 n.85; Canada and U.S., 170; and Canadian film, 187; Canadian regional chains, 171; changing influence of, 124; code of conduct, 140; concentration of ownership, 98; expectations, 295 n.84; first look arrangements, 88; global coordination, 138; and global markets, 135; grievances, 100; house nut, 271 n.1; independent, 225–26; international chains, 135; international consolidation, 171; internationally owned, 138; labor, 45, 270 n.77; megaplex construction, 174; move into distribution, 104; rating system, 102; response to distributors, 94; security, 148–49; short runs, 158; smaller chains, 285 n.35; strategies, 88; view of theatrical release, 155. *See also* Canadian exhibitors; Distributors; Megaplex; Multiplex; United States exhibitors

Expo '67, 193

Expo-mentality, 193–94

Extra filmic activities, 197

Family Channel, 245

Famous Players, 45, 109, 115–16, 123, 170–72, 175, 184, 188, 202, 218–20, 225, 232, 245, 266 n.1, 285 nn.29, 35, 286 n.45, 288 n.83, 295 n.88, 296 n.95; in Canada and U.S., 113; Coliseum, 116; Colossus, 119; megaplex branding, 115; rally, 45; trailer for, 120–21; unions, 45; Western operations, 118

Featherstone, Mike, 78–79

Federal Task Force on Film (Canada), 287 n.72

Felski, Rita, 54

Felt internationalism, 239

Film festivals, 291 n.136

Filming: audience and location, 131–32; in Can-

Hollywood, 131, 223; global influence of, 139; as a theme, 210; transnational, 9. *See also* Globalization; National culture

Hollywood films, 26; in Canadian theaters, 167–68

Hollywood majors: expansion into distribution, 93; independent arms of, 185; international ownership, 9; policy exemption, 180, 181

Hollywood Video, 223

Home theatres, 122–23

How the West Was Fun, 190

Hoyts Cinema, 99, 135; international expansion, 138

Hunt for Red October, The, 160

Ifilm, 223

IMAX, 193, 198, 223; in Canada, 115

Independent films: and Alliance Atlantis, 184–85

Independent theaters, 96; concerns, 100

Indiana Jones and the Last Crusade, 158

Indiana Jones and the Temple of Doom, 158

Industry common sense: formation, 11, 18, 21–22, 216, 224; inconsistencies, 218; U.S., 26

In Living Color, 4

Inner City Cinemas Corporation, 89

Insider, The, 187

Intercontextual relations, 43

International coproduction treaties, 130

Intertextual relations, 43

Investment Canada, 171, 181

Iqaluit, Nunavut, 176

Ireland, 6

Ironic knowingness, 191–92

Italy, 139; and U.S. culture, 16

Izod, John, 88, 89, 90, 122

Jacob, Ellis, 286 n.45

Japan, 105, 209

Jaws, 160

Jesus of Montreal, 166

Joan of Arc, 190

Johnston, Eric, 26

Juice, 147

Jurassic Park, 208

Justice Department (U.S.), 95–97, 272 n.43

Kansas City, 103; Power and Light District, 128

Karp, Allen, 149, 187

Kartozian, William, 102

Katzenberg, Jeffrey, 65

Kerkorian, Kirk, 272 n.43

Kingdom, The, 65

Klady, Leonard, 26, 35, 67, 124, 158

Kluge, Alexander, 49, 230

Kracauer, Siegfried, 235–36

Korff, Ira, 139

Kuhn, Michael, 181

Laguna Niguel, California, 144

Landy, Marcia, 17, 20

Langley, British Columbia, 119

Lantos, Robert, 177, 179, 286 n.45

Last Broadcast, The, 294 n.78

Latin America, 139

Le Monde Entertainment, 290 n.111

Lee, Spike, 89

Les Boys II, 164

Lewis, Jon, 272 n.43

Liar Liar, 3–4, 6, 67

Lichtman, Howard, 108

Lieberman Research, 5

Lifestyle, 78–80; of audiences, 78; new conception of, 79

Lincoln Square, 197

Litman, Barry, 98

Location. *See* Filming

Loews Cineplex Entertainment, 170–71, 225, 270 n.77

Loews E-Walk, 295 n.88

Loews Theater, 89, 96, 159

Loewy, Victor, 178, 286 n.45

London, England, 136, 166

Motion picture commodities: intermedia dimension of, 25; intermedia migration, 24; life cycle, 152–53, 156; metamorphosis, 23–24; migration, 23

Motion picture industry, 87; ancillary markets, 151, 153, 156; assumptions in, 60; consolidation, 96; expansion, 77, reinvention, 212. *See also* Canadian film industry; Globalization; Industry common sense

Motion Picture Theatre Association of Canada, 188

MovieFone, 106

Movie palace, 19, 100, 172, 235–36

Movie theaters: advertisements in, 269 n.54; changes to, 85; expansion and closure of, 142, 175; fluctuation in number, 72; and the global, 42; ideal, 235; international underdevelopment, 137; national standards, 102; security, 147; universality and placelessness, 90; violence, 146–48; as a work place, 45–46

Moyer, Thomas, 99

MPAA, 12, 63, 73, 92, 145, 157; digital guidelines, 216

MPEAA, 134

Mulroney, Brian, 178

Multiplex, 94–95, 102–3; Australia, 140; critique of, 138–39; in Eastern Europe, 137; environment, 64; European boom, 137; export, 135; international growth, 136; and labor rights, 104; origins of, 103; Southeast Asia, 138

Mulvey, Laura, 48

Music retail superstores, 206

NAFTA, 179

Nakama megaplex, 209

Nation: concept of, 167

National Amusements, 89, 94, 139, 146, 170; Sunrise Valley Stream, 147

National Association of Theater Owners (NATO), 91, 92, 94, 96, 99, 100–102, 135, 146, 148, 215, 224

National Cinema Network, 64

National cinema, 32–33, 35, 164, 166, 168, 169; and cinemagoing practices, 193; and foreignness, 189; and taste, 190

National culture: hierarchies, 291 n.132; and Hollywood, 167; and transnational distribution, 180

National Film Board of Canada, 192–93

National-popular, 15–16, 238, 245

National Research Group, 4

Nationhood: and popular cosmopolitanism, 237; and simultaneity, 235

Negt, Oskar, 230

Netherlands, the, 134

Neverland Entertainment, 288 n.84

New Amsterdam theatre, 200

New International Division of Cultural Labour (NICL), 10

New Jack City, 147

New media: expansion of, 24

New screen technologies, 295 n.87; fallibility, 295 n.92; legal worries, 295 n.90

New York City, 89, 197, 200, 216, 245

New Zealand, 139

Nickelodeons, 19

Norstar, 287 n.72, 290 n.111

Nova Scotia, 191

Nuremberg, 190

October Films, 290 n.113

Odeon Leicester Square, 296 n.95

Olson, Scott, 33

Olsen twins, 190

Ontario, California, 116–17

Ontario, Canada, 131

O'Regan, Tom, 164, 166

Orion Pictures, 99

Ottawa, Ontario, 103, 175

Overscreening, 224

Ownership structure: international, 132; vertical integration, 92

Rome, 139

Rooney, Mickey, 245

Roots, 269 n.54

Rosenzweig, Roy, 20

Ross, Andrew, 15–16

Runaway productions, 9–10, 131; rally against, 132–33

Satellite distribution, 216; experiment, 219; technical weakness, 219

Schatz, Thomas, 152

Schlesinger, Philip, 166

Schwarzenegger, Arnold, 36–37

Scream 2, 176, 243

Screen Gems Studio, 132

Screens: Australia, 140; blindspots in tally of, 141; Canada, 90, 105, 125, 172, 224; closing, 225; European trends, 136; expansion, 87; fluctuation in number of, 72; inadequate number of, 90; international shortage of, 137; international trends in tally of, 141; Japan, 105; number, 157; size, 172; U.S., 90, 98–99, 104–5, 125, 172, 224; value of multiple, 103–4

Screenvision Cinema Network, 64

Sega, 116

Sega Game Works, 198

Seinfeld, 243

Semiotic analysis, 206–7

Sheinberg, Sidney, 105

She's Gotta Have It, 89

Shipping News, The, 191

Short, Martin, 30

ShowCanada: *1997,* 175; *1998,* 121; *1999,* 215

ShowEast 1999, 216

ShoWest, 92, 100, 125; *1965,* 103; *1986,* 90–91, 100; *1987,* 99; *1988,* 100, 124; *1991,* 102, 105; *1992,* 135, 148; *1995,* 143; *1998,* 213; *2000,* 216

Shrine Auditorium, 4

SilverCity Riverport Theater, 218

Silverman, Alan, 101

Simmel, Georg, 79

Simulacrum, 204

Simultaneity, 194–95

Singleton, John, 146–47

Slack, Jennifer, 39

Slan, John, 166

Sony, 139, 155, 159; combination complex, 200; Digital Dynamic Sound, 275 n.5

Sony Picture Studios, 214

Sorkin, Michael, 210

Soul Food, 67

Sound systems, 115, 275 n.5

South Africa, 141

Southside Community Church, 119

Space: as practiced place, 56

Spacey, Kevin, 191

Special-event presentations, 296 n.95

Spectator, 20; active/passive binary, 19, 198; discursive construction of, 48–50; phases of, 49; prehistory, 267 n.14. *See also* Audience; Reception

Spectatorship, 57; concept of, 48, 51; conditions of, 51–52; and film business, 156; formation of, 234; implications of megaplex, 119; private vs. public, 144

Spin magazine, 116

Spy Who Shagged Me, The, 179

Stacey, Jackie, 53

Stadium seating, 123

Staiger, Janet, 50–51, 212

Star Wars: Episode I—The Phantom Menace, 216

Star Wars: Episode II—Attack of the Clones, 161

Stern, Seymour, 235

Straw, Will, 206

Structure of feeling, 40, 44; and cosmopolitanism, 236

Subject: addressed at entertainment complex, 202; and internationalism, 243

Super Video, 155

Supreme Court, 96

Sydney, 140

Syufy Enterprises, 97

Taste formation, 193

Taylor, Nat, 103

Technology: assumptions about new, 221

TechTown, 116, 198

Telefilm Canada, 168, 178; distribution fund,
178. *See also* Canadian film industry

Television: 145, 154; constructing audiences in,
60; digital technology, 214, 222; and everyday
life, 54; and film, 122; history related to film,
122; and megaplexes, 121–22; spatial and
temporal aspects of, 61; and theming, 210

Tentpole movie, 161

Terminator 2, 205

Texas Instruments, 214, 218

Textual migration, 25

Textual transparency, 33–34

The Reel Journal, 8

Theater Alignment Program, 102–3

Theater Association of California, 104

Theater ownership: Canadian concentration
of, 171

Theatrecast, 219–20

Theatrical run, 64–66, 151, 157

Theme, 203; and cross-promotion, 205; as
incoherent spaces, 208–9; location, 206; and
postmodern public, 208; and public space,
210. *See also* Discourse; Hollywood; Megaplex; Television

Theme parks: and U.S. cultural hegemony, 205

Theming, 197, 206; as a process, 210; producing
difference, 211

This Hour Has 22 Minutes, 191

This Is Cinerama, 198

Ticketmaster, 105

Time Code, 218

Times Square, 245

Titan AE, 223

Titanic, 33, 35, 67; release pattern of, 160–61

TNT, 63

Tomorrow Never Dies, 67

Toronto Eaton Centre, 170

Toronto Film Festival, 168

Toronto, Ontario, 123, 171, 178, 181, 185, 189, 198,
219, 245

Total Recall, 36

Toulouse, 139

Toy Story 2, 218

Trade agreements, 131

Trade publications, 76–77

Transnational cinema, 167, 191

Transnational film culture, 167

Transnational public: and cosmopolitanism,
236

Tremors, 160

Trial of Billy Jack, The, 160

Trigger Effect, The, 243

Trimark, 223

Tri-Star Pictures, 96, 159

Tulsa, Oklahoma, 216

Tumbleweeds, 161

Twentieth Century-Fox, 223

Twister, 199

Unions. *See* B.C. Projectionists Union; Famous
Players; Projectionists

United Artists, 104, 125, 126

United Cinemas International, 135, 140

United Kingdom, 6, 136, 156

United States, 3, 10, 11, 26, 66, 94, 141, 157, 160,
179, 194; cultural imperialism, 168; global
image empire, 131; as ideological isolationists, 30–31; and motion picture commodities, 130. *See also* Screens

United States culture: Canadian participation
in, 8; dominance, 182; international domination, 16. *See also* Canada

United States distributors, 179; and black markets, 134; largest export markets, 30. *See also*
Distributors

United States exhibitors: international operations of, 140–41; move to Canada by, 175. *See
also* Exhibitors

United States film, 10, 187; in Canada, 176, 190,
191; in global popular, 33

United States film industry, 26; and Canada, 8; internationalization, 13

United States popular culture: Canadian connection, 190; response to, 192

United States Securities and Exchange Commission, 171

United States Supreme Court: 1948 Paramount case, 86

Universal CityWalk complex, 108, 119, 148–49, 200

Universal Pictures, 97, 160

Universal Studios Florida, 204

University of Southern California, 146

Urban Entertainment Destination Project (UEDP), 200

Valenti, Jack, 90–91, 180

Vancouver, British Columbia, 218

Variety, 21

Varsity Cinemas VIP rooms, 123

VCR, 145, 155

Viacom, 45, 170

Video games: in megaplexes, 116

Video One, 285 n.32

Video stores, 189; Canada, 285 n.32

Videotape market, 65

Violence, 148

Vivafilm, 184

Vivendi Universal, 170

VSU, 134

Waller, Gregory A., 52–53

Walters, Barbara, 187

Warner Brothers, 134, 139, 156, 223

Warner, Timothy, 214

Wasser, Frederick, 93, 96

Watching: actions involved in, 57

Web-based cinema, 223

Wendt, Sam, 187

Williams, Raymond, 16–17, 40, 69, 212, 241; concept of flow, 64

Williams-Jones, Michael, 140

Willis, Susan, 207–8

Wilmington, N.C., 132

Windows of exhibition, 66; expansion of, 24; evolution of, 24

Winnipeg, Manitoba, 266 n.1

World Is Not Enough, The, 161

World Trade Organization, 181

World Wrestling Entertainment (WWE), 219, 221, 295 n.90

X-Files, 131

York University, 189

Yushchyshyn, Terry, 214

Charles R. Acland is associate professor of
communication studies at Concordia University
in Montreal. He is the author of *Youth, Murder,
Spectacle: The Cultural Politics of "Youth in Crisis"*
(1995) and editor, with William J. Buxton, of
*Harold Innis in the New Century: Reflections
and Refractions* (1999).

Library of Congress Cataloging-in-Publication Data
Acland, Charles R.   Screen traffic : movies, multiplexes,
and global culture / Charles R. Acland.
p. cm.   Includes bibliographical references and index.
ISBN 0-8223-3175-6 (cloth : alk. paper)
ISBN 0-8223-3163-2 (pbk. : alk. paper)
1. Motion picture audiences. 2. Motion pictures—
Distribution. I. Title.
PN1995.9.A8A28 2003   302.23′43—dc21   2003005050